The French Workers' Movement:
Economic Crisis and Political Change

The French Workers' Movement: Economic Crisis and Political Change

Edited by
Mark Kesselman

with the assistance of
Guy Groux

Translated by
Edouardo Diaz, Arthur Goldhammer, and Richard Shryock

London
GEORGE ALLEN & UNWIN
Boston   Sydney

© Mark Kesselman, 1984.

George Allen & Unwin (Publishers) Ltd,
40 Museum Street, London WC1A 1LU, UK

George Allen & Unwin (Publishers) Ltd,
Park Lane, Hemel Hempstead, Herts HP2 4TE, UK

Allen & Unwin, Inc.,
9 Winchester Terrace, Winchester, Mass. 01890, USA

George Allen & Unwin Australia Pty Ltd,
8 Napier Street, North Sydney, NSW 2060, Australia

First published in 1984.

British Library Cataloguing in Publication Data

Kesselman, Mark
 The French workers' movement.
1. Labor and laboring classes—France—Political activity—
History—20th century
I. Title II. Groux, Guy
335'2'0944   HD8435
ISBN 0-043-31095-8

Library of Congress Cataloging in Publication Data

Main entry under title:
 The French workers' movement.
Bibliography: p.
Includes index.
1. Trade-unions—France—Addresses, essays, lectures.
2. France—Economic conditions—1945— —Addresses, essays, lectures.
I. Kesselman, Mark. II. Groux, Guy.
HD6684.F74 1984   331.88'0944   84-9238
ISBN 0-04-331095-8 (alk. paper)

Set in 10 on 11 point Times by
Mathematical Composition Setters Ltd, Salisbury, UK
and printed in Great Britain by Butler & Tanner Ltd, Frome and London

Contents

Preface *page* vii

Introduction: The French Workers' Movement at the
Crossroads   *by Mark Kesselman*   1

Part One   The Crisis of Capitalist Regulation and the
Crisis of the Workers' Movement   15
1 Wage Labor, Capital Accumulation, and the Crisis,
1968–82   *by Robert Boyer*   17
2 Labor and Capital in the Crisis: France, 1966–82   *by
Benjamin Coriat*   39

Part Two   The Evolution of French Trade Unions   49
3 The CGT, Economic Crisis, and Political Change
by George Ross   51
4 The CFDT: From the Union of Popular Forces to the
Success of Social Change   *by René Mouriaux*   75
5 The Trade Union Strategy of the CGT–FO   *by Alain
Bergounioux*   93
6 The CGC and the Ambiguous Position of the Middle
Strata   *by Georges Benguigui and Dominique
Montjardet*   104

Part Three   "New Problems"   117
7 The Decomposition and Recomposition of the Working
Class   *by Jean Lojkine*   119
8 Trade Unionism and Technology   *by Guy Groux*   132
9 Trade Union Positions on the Organization of
Production   *by Anni Borzeix*   146
10 The "Problem" of Women   *by Jane Jenson*   159
11 Trade Unions, the Environment, and the Quality of
Life   *by Michelle Durand and Yvette Harff*   177

Part Four   Forms of Mobilization   197
12 Collective Action and Union Behavior
by Denis Segrestin   199
13 The Strike in France   *by Pierre Dubois*   210

14   The Industrial Counterproposal as an Element of Trade
     Union Strategy   *by Jean-Pierre Huiban*   224
15   Ideology and Industrial Practice: CGT, FO, CFDT
     by Bernard H. Moss   238

Part Five   The Trade Union Movement, Politics, and
                the State   255
16   Relations between the CGT and the CFDT: Politics and
     Mass Mobilization   *by Martin A. Schain*   257
17   From Economic Crisis to Victory of the Left: Workers'
     Reactions and Union Policies   *by Jacques Kergoat*   277
18   Trade Unions, Employers, and the State: Toward a New
     Relationship?   *by Sabine Erbès-Seguin*   297

     Conclusion   *by Mark Kesselman*   311

     Bibliography   323

     List of Contributors   340

     Index   343

Preface

This volume aims to describe and analyze the French labor movement during the critically important period of the past decade. During this conjuncture French trade unions were confronted by unusually serious challenges and unusually attractive opportunities. Have trade unions succeeded in developing new organizational capacity and vision adequate to this situation? To what extent have they represented the new segments of the working class and the new demands and issues emerging at this time?

North American and British scholars have closely scrutinized French political parties and elections, as evidenced by the numerous books and articles available on the topic in English. They have paid far less attention to the French labor movement. For example, the last comprehensive surveys in English of French trade unions (Ehrmann, 1947; Lorwin, 1954) were published thirty years ago! While French scholars—many of whom are among the contributors to the present work—have studied the labor movement, their research is not generally available in English.

This volume seeks to analyze the background and complexities of the situation created by the left's victory in 1981. Although the contributors diverge on many points, most agree that the gap has increased between the labor movement's innovations in the realm of ideology and practice. While unions have forged daring new programmatic approaches, they have been less successful in developing appropriate new forms of struggle which adequately reflect their ideological adaptations. Furthermore, labor's strength remains sapped by severe conflicts among rival trade unions.

This volume indirectly suggests why the left government elected in 1981 was unable to develop a cohesive, secure social base. As many of the essays which follow indicate, however, the economic and political situation in France is too complex to permit definitive judgment, either about the significance of the left government or the impact or future evolution of the labor movement. How difficult prediction is can be seen from the fact that planning for this volume began in 1980, when the prospects seemed dim for political change in France. And yet the election of a left government in a period of international economic recession has not proved an unmixed blessing for French labor.

We have incurred many debts in preparing this work. Bernard Moss and René Mouriaux were helpful at the early stages in clarifying the overall organization of the volume. Richard Shryock provided invaluable editorial assistance, in addition to helping translate French texts. He also compiled the Bibliography. We are grateful for secretarial help from Aurelia Enache and the Institute on Western Europe, Columbia University; and the Laboratoire de Sociologie du Travail et des Relations Professionnelles, Conservatoire National des Arts et Métiers. Mark Kesselman wishes to acknowledge financial support provided by a Rockefeller Foundation Humanities Fellowship, which enabled him to organize the volume while in France.

December 1983   MARK KESSELMAN
                                                          GUY GROUX

The French Workers' Movement:
Economic Crisis and Political Change

Introduction: The French Workers' Movement at the Crossroads

MARK KESSELMAN

Does the relatively more radical ideological stance of large segments of the French labor movement, compared to labor movements in other advanced capitalist nations, reflect French workers' militancy and strength or rather their weakness? Evidence to support the former interpretation is that the two largest French trade unions (the CGT and CFDT, who obtain about three-fifths of workers' votes in elections to works councils and labor arbitration boards) have officially adopted socialist positions going substantially beyond northern European social democracy. Further, during much of the twentieth century, French workers have displayed an especially great propensity to strike. The French working class may thus continue to embody a radical stance linked to its revolutionary past.

Yet the militancy of French unions and workers may be more apparent than real—a product of weakness, not strength. Among the evidence cited to support this interpretation is the low density of French unionism (less than one-quarter of French workers are enrolled in unions, among the lowest rate of any advanced capitalist nation), debilitating divisions within the labor movement, and unions' inability to extract benefits peacefully from French employers and the state. From this perspective it is understandable why Korpi and Shalev argue that a high strike rate is an admission of working-class impotence:

> In our view ... strikes must be regarded primarily as defensive actions by workers, actions which they are more or less forced to take because of the lack of better alternatives. We do not share the view that strikes must generally be seen as expressions of radicalism and class consciousness.
> (Korpi and Shalev, 1980, p. 327)

French industrial relations are characterized by a relative absence of formalized mechanisms that Pizzorno has called political exchange (Pizzorno, 1978). Political exchange requires the development of a unified, centralized union movement willing and able to exchange labor discipline or peace for a secure position within the dominant political and economic system. Central to understanding contemporary France is that, despite the lack of institutionalized political exchange, a mode of economic regulation developed that produced broadly similar results (see Boyer, Coriat and Erbès-Seguin in this volume). Although the two major unions, the CGT and CFDT, displayed a radical ideological stance for most of the period studied here—since the early 1960s—during much of the time they focussed mobilizing efforts on maintaining a kind of tradeoff or exchange reminiscent of what Pizzorno describes, in which private wages and social transfers (the social wage) increased commensurately with economic growth and productivity gains. Thus the French labor movement's radical rhetoric was usually translated into a quite reformist practice not very different from unions elsewhere.

However, the form that class compromise took in France differed from most other nations. Although, as Erbès-Seguin describes below, there was a sharp increase in peak-level collective bargaining agreements in the late 1960s, France still exhibited a relatively less institutionalized form of class conflict and compromise. This confrontational approach appears to reflect the strength and militancy of the French labor movement. After all, despite the lack of extensive mechanisms of economic and political mediation, French workers have achieved a standard of living roughly comparable to workers in other capitalist nations. Yet the French working class has not paid the characteristic cost involved in political exchange: integration within dominant institutions and the renunciation of radical goals (see Offe and Wiesenthal, 1980).

However, the failure to achieve a situation of political exchange can be interpreted as reflecting the weakness of French labor. First, the fact is that French workers have *not* achieved comparable benefits to workers elsewhere. Until 1982 unions and their members had fewer organizational protections; further, French workers possessed fewer legal safeguards with respect to technological innovations, plant shutdowns, and occupational health and safety. French unions have been unable to compel employers to bargain collectively over wages, hours, and working conditions. In the 1970s and early 1980s unions unsuccessfully demanded what had long been achieved already in many other nations. Thus French workers exerted greater efforts than workers elsewhere to achieve relatively fewer results.

Secondly, under the guise of refusing class collaboration, French unions have usually confined mobilizing efforts (in contrast to ideological pronouncements) to the traditional economistic goal of pressing workers' wage claims, thereby accepting capitalist domination of the workplace (see Moynot, 1979a, 1979b); partial exceptions were the 1968–73 period, when as the result of grassroots militancy the CFDT articulated new qualitative demands and forms of mobilization, and the late 1970s, in the abortive attempt at industrial counterproposals (described below by Huiban). By postponing to an ever-receding revolutionary future the attempt to organize production and politics, and/or delegating this task to left parties, French unions acted in quite similar ways to reformist unions elsewhere. Nor was this result much altered by union slogans identifying this very problem (for example, the CFDT's call for "living, working, and deciding in one's locality" or its advocacy of "experiencing the future society in the struggles of today").

As chapters in Part Three of this volume document, French unions have lagged by other progressive measures as well: they have been slow to represent female and immigrant workers, hesitant to mobilize around environmental protection, organization of work, and technological change, and ineffective in preventing the state and capital from restructuring industry in ways devastating to workers. In brief, the book presents abundant evidence of the present crisis of the French labor movement. (The decline in the membership of most unions—the CGT, in particular—is the most obvious sign of union difficulties.)

Before concluding, however, that the much-vaunted radicalism of French unions is largely rhetorical, consider the crucial role that unions and workers played in the left's electoral success in 1981. The Socialist–Communist government elected in 1981 is among the most progressive in any advanced capitalist nation, and workers' votes and trade union support were essential ingredients in the left's success. Trade union unity in the mid-1960s fostered socialist consciousness among workers and presaged left political unity. The trade union movement vigorously supported the Union of the Left in the 1970s (although the two major unions were sharply divided during the early 1980s, when the left finally achieved power).

And yet a further irony is that the left arrived in power in good measure because the French workers' movement had been unable to install a left government during the previous decades of economic expansion. During an era when the political balance throughout advanced capitalism leaned toward the center-left, with social democratic governments ruling most of northern Europe and the Democratic Party controlling American politics, France was governed by conservative governments. While the left was reaping political credit elsewhere for the unprecedented period of economic expansion, the Gaullist regime was in this fortunate situation in France.

As Boyer, Coriat and Erbès-Seguin analyze below, the political situation did not prevent French workers from sharing the fruits of economic expansion. But working-class gains were achieved by active mobilization, most dramatically symbolized by May 1968 (at one stroke, the minimum wage was raised 33 percent), not institutionalized bargaining (Feenberg, 1978).

On occasion conservative governments did attempt to involve the working class and its representatives in processes of organized class collaboration. (Examples include the Toutée-Grégoire procedures for determining wage levels in the public sector and the Chaban-Delmas/Delors *contrats de progrès*.) But active opposition by major segments of the trade union movement (the CGT, in particular), as well as resistance by private employers, doomed such efforts. And yet political exclusion in the 1960s and 1970s meant that, when the economic expansion of the 1950s and 1960s slowed down and stagflation set in beginning in the mid-1970s, the French left was in a position to benefit from the revolt against incumbent governments that elsewhere helped elect conservative parties.

Although the causes of the crisis are complex, it is probable that the pattern of class relationships forged in the earlier period played an important role. As described by Arrighi (1978), Bowles and Gintis (1982), and Boyer (in this volume), the key mechanism was a tradeoff between wage gains and political stability.

Initially generalized wage increases proved highly beneficial for capital, paving the way to an era of mass consumption (facilitated by welfare-statist countercyclical measures). Since working-class demands mostly concerned wage levels, capital had a relatively free hand to rationalize production, using Fordist and Taylorist methods.

However, what was beneficial to capital and labor in one era became devastating in the next. The long wave of expansion slowed, provoked in part by a profits squeeze linked to a wage push. Further, whereas state welfare policies proved effective in stimulating demand during a period of incipient recession, benefits had a secular tendency to increase—the "ratchet effect"—which produced inflationary pressures (O'Connor, 1973). Meanwhile labor rebelled as rationalization accelerated.

In brief, the same regulatory mechanisms that facilitated expansion in one era provoked stagflation in the next. This situation provided the context for the Barre policies of the late 1970s, modeled on the Japanese approach of expanding exports and improving the nation's position in the international division of labor. Among Barre's central aims were to reverse working-class gains, dampen public sector wages, and increase the latitude of private capital.

However, although the Barre policies maintained the strong standing of the French franc and boosted profits, they failed to improve France's international economic position or stimulate investments. The industrial "redeployment" policies of the late 1970s led to soaring unemployment; at the same time manufactured imports increased from 25 to 40 percent. Barre's failure helped the left achieve its 1981 electoral sweep.

What do events of the past two decades suggest about French working-class radicalism? To what extent is it born of confidence and strength, to what extent from weakness, desperation, and the inability to extract gains by institutionalized means? Indeed, how genuine is French working-class radicalism? As the chapter by Bergounioux describes, one of the three major French unions (Force Ouvrière) does not even make such a claim; the other two (the CGT and CFDT) proclaim radical pretensions but the situation is more mixed in practice (as the chapters by Ross, Mouriaux, and many other contributors describe). While the Conclusion will analyze this issue in greater detail, a provisional suggestion at this point is that the French workers' movement reflects divergent possibilities for effecting radical change. French workers achieved fewer concrete benefits than workers in comparable nations but the radical ideology of the workers' movement is more than merely rhetoric and has the potential for impelling France in a radically progressive direction. However, the returns are not yet in on this issue; much depends on the outcome of the current period, with a left government in power.

An Overview of this Volume

This book analyzes the political–economic framework of the labor movement and the contradictory tendencies of the past two decades: a period of enormous change and turmoil within France. Although all the authors are committed to a left perspective, they differ substantially in their assessment of the union movement. This diversity is testimony to the complexity of the issues analyzed.

The book's major focus is organized labor: the confederal unions, and their strategies, interrelations, and relationship with the state. Although unions represent less than one-quarter of the workforce, their power is quite out of proportion to this figure. Unions occupy an important legal position, especially after the passage of the Auroux laws in 1982 (analyzed in the Conclusion). Unions command the respect of most workers, as evidenced by elections to works councils and other representative mechanisms, where union candidates obtain an overwhelming majority of votes.

Part One of the book provides a framework to study the labor movement. Boyer's chapter (from which the preceding analysis has been borrowed), provides a theoretical and historical overview. As Coriat describes, there is more continuity than one might expect between the left government elected in 1981 and its predecessor. The Barre government was less neo-liberal than its rhetoric; in part for electoral reasons the Socialist government adopted a Keynesian countercyclical stance to achieve macroeconomic regulation. Like its predecessors, the Socialist government has come to accept the need for austerity to stimulate economic growth. Yet it has innovated by attempting to "contractualize" class relations and seeks union support for its policies (using, in return, the Auroux reforms to strengthen unions' organizational capacity and provide other incentives for union cooperation). The result, as Borzeix points out, may strengthen integrative tendencies. At a fundamental level, as Coriat suggests and the Conclusion analyzes, the Socialist government has limited the scope of economic reforms by failing to democratize relations of production.

Part Two describes the major unions. Ross analyzes important shifts in the CGT, contrary to misconceptions which see the CGT as a monolithic, unchanging, transmission belt of the PCF. Ross stresses that the CGT's strategy has been closely geared to the left's political fortunes. The left's defeat in the 1978 legislative elections forced the CGT to redefine its strategy, since it had placed its major priority in the preceding period on defending workers' immediate interests and seeking to install a left government in power that could legislate CGT demands for overall change. The CGT considered two options after the 1978 setback. One tendency, described in detail by Huiban, coincided with the PCF's

Eurocommunist face; it consisted in developing counterproposals for specific industries (notably steel, automobiles, and textiles). The counterproposal strategy asserted that the workers' movement should seize the initiative for reorganizing production within the crisis, rather than allowing capital and the state to dominate the process. In the past, the workers' movement had avoided "middle-range" proposals, dividing its energies between militant defense of workers' immediate, material interests and advocacy of the distant goal of socialist transformation. The counterproposition strategy sought to provide a missing link between the two levels and attempted to enlarge the space for workers' intervention.

However, internal changes within the CGT and PCF, as well as the futility of the counterproposition strategy given an intransigent, rightist government and private management, soon brought the experiment to an end. It was replaced by a close alliance between the CGT and PCF, aimed at denouncing what both organizations charged was a betrayal of French national interests by all other political parties and labor unions. During this period the CGT ended its unity of action pact with the CFDT, and the PCF denounced the "consensus à trois" of the other major political parties in France (including the PS). Consistent with this approach, CGT leaders (ostensibly in their capacity as individuals) supported the PCF's 1981 presidential candidate. Ironically the strategy was predicated upon the defeat of the left in 1981 and a subsequent restoration of PCF dominance on the left. The CGT was thus totally unprepared for François Mitterrand's victory in the 1981 presidential elections.

If Ross, contrary to established preconceptions, emphasizes extensive shifts in CGT strategy during this period, Mouriaux stresses continuities in the evolution of the CFDT—a union often interpreted as volatile and eratic. Mouriaux suggests that, from its origins in the CFTC and Catholic progressivism, the CFDT has displayed an anti-statist, anti-productivist approach. It has continually rejected the Leninist distinction between trade union activity and politics, in favor of an attempt to develop a global social project. The CFDT supported the Union of the Left political alliance in the 1970s with many expressed reservations; the CFDT's *recentrage* after 1978—a renewed emphasis on union struggles at the base to achieve short-term reforms as opposed to the unsuccessful political strategy symbolized by the Union of the Left—was therefore less substantial a shift than might appear (see Shryock, 1983).

These analyses suggest that both the CGT and the CFDT can be viewed in two quite divergent ways. The CGT may embody a revolutionary commitment, linking militant defense of workers' immediate material interests with struggles for a fundamental transformation of society carried out by political means (hence the CGT's informal alliance with the PCF). However, the CGT's stance may entail in practice a truncated role for workers' mass organization and a tendency to subordinate workers' interests to the PCF's long-term strategy—a tendency toward substitutionism (Geras, 1981) which does not bode well for the construction of socialism.

The CFDT's behavior can also be interpreted in opposite ways. On the one hand, the CFDT may represent a progressive vanguard which, rather than concentrating on traditional bread-and-butter issues, champions qualitative demands, such as ending inequalities of income, gender, and power; and contesting productivism, statism, and environmental spoliation. However, the CFDT's audacious ideology may remain at the level of rhetoric, while its practice may involve an acceptance of dominant capitalist imperatives in the name of producing "realistic" gains and seeking institutionalized, contractual relations with management. Thus the audacious rhetoric may culminate in the American model of unionism.

The division of labor between the two unions could be considered fruitful, as when the CFDT articulated qualitative demands that the CGT later accepted (for instance, autogestion, environmental issues, reducing wage differentials) while the CGT maintained a militant anti-capitalist stance that drew the CFDT leftward in the 1960s (along with the PCF, the CGT was first to stress France's industrial decline). However, divisions between the unions are also among the most important sources of worker demobilization, as analyzed below by Dubois, Kergoat, and Schain. Thus plural unions may result in creative ideology but practical stalemate (cf. Schain).

The remaining chapters in Part Two provide a useful reminder that the two major union confederations do not represent all organized labor. Bergounioux suggests that the CGT–FO has displayed a constant fidelity to certain key principles: the value of voluntarism, involving collective bargaining agreements reached without state interference, opposition to state regulation, opposition to politicizing unions by support or alliance with political parties, and priority on the realistic defense of workers' immediate interests. Force Ouvrière is usually ignored by scholars of organized labor, an unfortunate omission since it has nearly as many members as CFDT (about 1 million) and obtains close to one-fifth of workers' votes in elections for workers' delegates. (For example, FO received 17 percent of the vote in the December 1982 elections to the labor conciliation boards—*conseils des prud'hommes.*) (See Table I.1 for the vote distribution in these elections, which provide a comprehensive test of the various unions' relative standing.)

In addition, FO has a commanding influence in administering social insurance programs. Force Ouvrière represents a quite distinctive approach within France to defending French workers' interests, reminiscent of the American trade union movement. It has steadfastly eschewed partisan involvement and political projects for global transformation. That this approach responds to an important working-class current is reflected in the fact that FO has gained ground since the mid-1970s, when the two largest unions were declining. However, that FO, no less than the CGT and CFDT, was disoriented by the left victory in 1981 further suggests how the present period is one of self-examination for organized labor.

The CGC, described in the chapter by Benguigui and Montjardet, has constantly defended measures legitimating the privileged position of

Table I.1   *Voting Distribution, 1982 Elections to Labor Conciliation*
Boards

	Workers (in thousands)	(%)	Managers, superiors, technicians (in thousands)	(%)
Number enrolled	12,003		1,543	
Number voting	6,751	56·2	891	57·7
CGT	2,698	40·0	116	13·0
CFDT	1,645	24·3	156	17·5
FO	1,255	18·6	104	11·7
CFTC	566	8·4	81	9·1
CGC	368	5·4	369	41·5
Other	225	3·3	65	7·2

Source: Le Monde, 10 December 1982.

managers and supervisors, including differential compensation, retirement benefits, and tax reductions for cadres. Strategic continuity has not precluded tactical shifts. For example, under the presidency of Jean Menu, the CGC defined itself quite explicitly as a trade union rather than professional association and sought a reformist alliance with the CFTC and FO against the 'revolutionary' CGT and CFDT. Such a stance implies a center–left commitment for cadres. However, the CGC has refused to articulate a medium- or long-range vision, accepting the status quo and seeking to defend its members' interests within the existing order. (It might be noted that space precludes analyzing the unions of managers and technicians associated with the largest unions, as well as other unions, notably the CFTC and FEN.)

Part Two suggests that the trade union movement cannot easily be characterized along an axis of revolution and reformism. Part Three strengthens this impression by analyzing the labor movement's stance toward "new problems." The phrase is put in quotation marks since these problems are hardly new—except to the trade union movement. Indeed, organized labor's failure until recently to concern itself with the issues examined in Part Three suggests the extent of the labor movement's resistance to change. Lojkine challenges the idea that recent developments within capitalism inevitably fracture and disarm the working class. He suggests that recent tendencies toward working-class division are unprecedented only for certain scholars of the labor movement (those sympathetic to the CFDT). Further, this approach neglects tendencies toward reunification within the working class rooted in production. (Lojkine opposes those wishing to reconstitute working-class unity around bases outside production.) Take technology which, Lojkine asserts, is often regarded as deskilling and emasculating the working class. He suggests that, on the contrary, technological change and automation have a revolutionary potential, for these require new skills for those workers who are to operate and maintain the modernized productive apparatus, and the new technology increases the possibility for decentralizing production.

Groux's study of unions' response to technological change finds that the labor movement has been slow to grasp the primordial importance of this issue. The labor movement began to express concern about technology only in the 1970s. Further, save for the unions of managers and technicians affiliated with the CFDT and CGT (which are small and marginal within the two major union confederations), organized labor has generally been less concerned with the content of technology than with its impact on other areas, such as employment. And the unions have failed to devise ways to incorporate a concern with technological change in their mobilizing strategy. Groux suggests that this situation may change as a result of the left's victory. The Auroux laws provide works councils (*comités d'entreprise*) with a consultative voice concerning the introduction of new technology at the plant level and works councils are henceforth entitled to obtain additional information about the firm's operations and to hire outside experts.

Borzeix traces a shift in unions' attitude toward the organization of work and production that parallels changes occurring in other areas. Organized labor was surprisingly supportive of Taylorism until the 1960s. Unions began to challenge capitalist domination of the workplace only after militant strikes by assembly-line workers in the 1968–75 period. The unions remain confused about the appropriate stance toward the organization of work. Management often retains the initiative for introducing innovations in the labor process, many of which weaken unions but are accepted and even supported by workers (for instance, flexible hours, the compressed workweek, and so on). Further, as unions become more concerned with the organization of production, the chances of their becoming more integrated within the firm are increased.

Jenson suggests that partisan factors were the key ones in the CGT approach to the issue of women. The PCF's and CGT's Eurocommunist shift led the CGT toward a greater flexibility and acceptance of the partial autonomy of women's issues. The CFDT was more sensitive in its rhetoric to the specificity of women's demands—but as with other issues analyzed above it failed to incorporate these demands in its mobilizing strategy. The CGT retreated from the attempt to reconcile women's specific demands with the CGT's anti-capitalist emphasis once the Union of the Left foundered in 1977–8. It disciplined the editorial board of *Antoinette*, the CGT's publication for female members, which had led the way in dramatizing women's demands. The CGT placed renewed emphasis on a workerist (*ouvrièriste*) appeal. The CFDT remained more responsive to women's issues—as illustrated by its 1982 decision, providing for a quota of women within CFDT leadership ranks. But the CFDT has not yet devised effective means of acting on behalf of its principles.

Durand and Harff describe how, beginning in the 1960s and 1970s, the union movement began to embrace concerns going beyond economistic, workplace-based demands. The CFDT was first, probably because it sought to distinguish itself from the CGT and because it aimed to develop a global project bridging the Leninist division between trade union and political activity. In the 1960s the CFDT became involved with such issues as urbanism and democratic planning, whose scope entailed challenging the very logic of industrialization.

The CFDT's position quickly encountered fierce opposition from the CGT which, while pointing to the pernicious effects of industrialization as organized by capitalism, stressed its potentially progressive implications. The CGT–CFDT conflicts in this sphere were crystallized in their opposing positions on nuclear energy and the automobile industry, which the CFDT regarded as embodying mindless growth, hierarchy, and environmental dangers and the CGT regarded as facilitating jobs. The election of a left government has done little to alleviate this split. Indeed the fact that, after reaching power, the PS shifted toward the CGT and PCF positions provoked bitter CFDT criticism.

Part Four studies how unions mobilize around traditional and newly emergent issues. Segrestin suggests that, at the level of collective identity formation and mobilization, there is far more continuity through time and among unions than is generally recognized—and union ideological pronouncements might suggest. The unions have generally organized on the basis of crafts skills, albeit within an industrial setting. Class identification and activity build on occupational communities—which runs counter to the idea that class-wide identification develops directly. However, mobilization on the basis of craft identity has been challenged recently by struggles among younger workers, women, and immigrants, based on what Segrestin considers a more diffuse base than skill.

Dubois assesses the causes of the substantial variations in the strike rate during the past two decades, which he considers a key indication of working-class militancy. He suggests that political factors play more of a role than purely economic factors in explaining such changes. Thus the breakup of the Union of the Left among left parties and the unity of action pact between the CGT and CFDT outweigh the economic crisis in accounting for the dramatic decline in strike rates beginning in the late 1970s.

Huiban studies the union movement's attempt to sponsor industrial counterpropositions. The initiative represented an attempt to forge a new role for the union movement as the crisis jeopardized unions' traditional defense of wages linked to economic growth, productivity increases, and high employment levels. Huiban stresses the failure of this short-lived attempt. The unions failed to involve rank-and-file workers in developing counterproposals, which may help to account for the lack of active worker support for the counterproposals and the unions' inability to devise imaginative forms of action to press its new strategy. The counterproposal strategy was largely moribund by 1981 and has been only partially resuscitated after the left's victory.

Moss stresses the importance of ideology in shaping union actions. In contrast to Segrestin, he suggests that the unions differ sharply in their stance depending on their ideological vision. For Moss, the CGT has been the only union to adopt a revolutionary stance and to develop a militant practice. One way to reconcile these two analyses is that Segrestin focusses on the process of identity formation and mobilization at the base, whereas Moss analyzes the behavior of union leaders; as Schain points out, union leaders need to maximize the distinctiveness of their organizations even when in practice such distinctiveness is clouded.

The volume opens with an examination of the social, economic, and political context; Part Two studies the union organizations; the next two parts examine organized labor's orientation toward social issues. Part Five returns to the relationship between unions and the wider system. Schain challenges a commonly held view that relations between the two major unions are determined by relations between the two major leftist political parties. He suggests that trade union relations follow a partially autonomous logic. For example, the CGT and CFDT cooperated closely in the 1966–8 period, when the PCF and PS were at loggerheads, whereas the PCF and PS drew together in 1972–7—a period of strife between the unions (especially the early 1970s). Schain stresses the importance of structural constraints: since the unions must compete for the same potential members—and the overlap between their members is greater than often realized—they are forced to assess organizational self-interest when calculating the benefits of unity. Although unity promotes mobilization, it also blurs the unions' distinctive organizational identities in the eyes of rank-and-file workers, which complicates the militants' task of defending the separate interests of each union.

Kergoat analyzes the relationships between union strategy socio-economic conditions, and the changing balance of power among classes. He argues that labor unions are neither perfectly representative of their members nor completely unresponsive to rank-and-file demands. For example, rising militancy in the early 1970s provided pressure to promote the left political parties' electoral agreement yet made party leaders fearful of renewing the agreement because of the risk of local militancy. Contrary to an economically determinist argument that explains the shift toward demobilization of the late 1970s solely by reference to the effects of the crisis, Kergoat argues that divisions between left political parties and trade unions were an important factor in demobilizing workers.

Nevertheless, Kergoat suggests, the left's victory was a result of increased class consciousness among the working class. Unable to achieve their demands by economistic struggles or support for the Communist Party, workers promoted the only unity that was feasible by backing the Socialist Party. What, then, was the effect of the 1981 electoral shift? Kergoat believes that it increased grassroots militancy, although not on the scale of earlier periods of left victories. Furthermore, given their high degree of class consciousness, workers will not be placated by the Socialist government's mildly reformist policies. The result may be further radicalization which, in the short run, might benefit the major left parties—but which will take other forms if the left parties prove unresponsive.

Erbès-Seguin studies the relationship among business, unions, and the state. She argues that French labor has been more excluded from access to the state than comparable labor movements but, through direct action, labor has achieved roughly comparable benefits. However, the crisis has shifted the balance of class conflict from positive to zero-sum; whereas in the earlier period management and unions could agree on labor receiving a proportionate share of an expanding surplus, in a period of crisis the aims of the two forces diverge. Management seeks to diminish labor's share of what is a stagnant national product and wants a freer hand in rationalizing production and laying-off workers. This tendency has been inhibited by the fact that, in the previous era of economic growth and a tight labor market, organized labor succeeded in gaining management agreement for employment protections. However, in face of increased employee protections, management has been less likely to hire new workers—even in face of the new demand stimulated by the left government's initial policies. Labor alternatively seeks to maintain past achievements and to protect employment.

Given the stalemate between social forces in the late 1970s, both capital and labor shifted toward seeking to use the state to defend their interests. State policies became openly supportive of large-scale capital once the right surmounted the 1978 electoral challenge; and the process would doubtless have accelerated had the right won the 1981 elections.

The crisis also impelled the union movement to seek greater recourse to the state, as evidenced by its support for the Union of the Left. Unions placed high priority on nationalization, inspired by past precedents. Thus the crisis forced a questioning of the prevalent mode of economic regulation, which crystallized struggles around wage levels. Creating and protecting employment has now become the major stake in the present period.

While the left government elected in 1981 made nationalization its first major legislative priority, it is unclear how this will resolve the problem of employment and growth: it may only further fragment the working class by creating a privileged sector of protected employment. (The state has acted in other ways to redefine class relations, as described in the Conclusion, but the overall coherence of the left's "grand design" is unclear, as well as its chances of success.)

Although the former mode of regulation that shaped class relations around wage struggles has become untenable in an era of economic stagnation, high unemployment, and capitalist restructuring, a new pattern has not emerged. The Socialist government's attempt to develop such a project is examined in the Conclusion.

A constant theme in the book is that the workers' movement has been in a state of flux and crisis during an epoch when capitalism has experienced important changes and, in the last decade, deepening crisis. The contributors to this volume agree that there has been substantial continuity and change within organized labor. But disagreements occur concerning their character and significance. Are divisions among French unions as great as they themselves assert? If so, which of the major unions presents the best analysis and means of mobilizing to defend workers' interests? Is it the CGT's global condemnation of capitalism, translated in practice into day-to-day defense of workers' immediate material interests along with support for the PCF as the political party best qualified to sponsor global political change? Or the CFDT, which analyzes multiple sources of domination, often arising outside the sphere of production and reflected in a hierarchical, productivist, statist society, and which devises autonomous actions to confront this situation? Or Force Ouvrière, which stresses the need for unions to confine attention to the essentials: the realistic defense of workers' interests, and leave to others the issue of the global organization of society?

Conversely, do unions exhibit greater convergence in day-to-day practice than in the ideological realm? How aggressively have unions adapted to changes in French and international capitalism? To what extent do unions shape the French working class, as opposed to reflecting currents and divisions with roots elsewhere? A key issue, examined in the Conclusion, is the extent to which the election of a left government will reshape the character of the French workers' movement and the terms of class relations.

Socialist structural reforms, in particular the Auroux reforms and nationalization, promise to strengthen the tendency that emerged in the 1960s and 1970s for the union movement to seek wider responsibilities than merely defense of wage claims. The picture is mixed. We have seen how unions became concerned with issues involving the environment, women, and the like. Yet the unions were slow to embrace these demands, they remained marginal within overall union strategy and severely divided the union movement. Further, these issues reflect contradictory possibilities: they may involve a more global challenge to capitalist development, or they may create the basis for partial struggles that ignore the global character of capitalist domination.

The Conclusion argues that the policies and reforms sponsored by the Socialist–Communist coalition contain multiple possibilities for new terms of class compromise and socioeconomic regulation. While the government seeks to mobilize unions for a unified national effort at economic rationalization that would not fundamentally democratize relations of production, leftist reforms erode the division between capitalist production and democratic policies. The result is to enlarge the possibilities for struggles to organize production and politics on a democratic socialist basis. But whether such struggles will actually occur and what their outcome might be are not yet clear. Furthermore, the left government's actions have not only created the basis for progressive struggles but for demobilization and division within the ranks of the workers' movement. Thus, organized labor is at a crossroads, forced to confront capitalist crisis, a declining mode of regulation, and new historic possibilities. At the same time organized labor must confront its own divisions, which have persisted in face of a left electoral victory. The next years will provide a critical test of organized labor's strength and radical commitment.

PART ONE

The Crisis of Capitalist Regulation and the Crisis of the Workers' Movement

1

Wage Labor, Capital Accumulation, and the Crisis, 1968–82

ROBERT BOYER

The deepening of the economic crisis in recent years has not failed to arouse lively discussion of the origins of the problem and the stakes involved. Against this background many analyses have been proposed of the labor movement, union strategies, and industrial relations. This is hardly surprising, given the fact that the effects of the crisis have been felt in almost every sphere of society.

For many liberal economists, the economy's present troubles are due in large part to unacceptable "rigidities" introduced into the system as a direct result of the labor movement's principal triumphs. Accordingly, and as they see it quite logically, these economists propose returning to some mythical form of the "free market economy" as a way of overcoming the crisis. In the present chapter I shall develop another line of argument: namely, that industrial relations are not established in some deterministic fashion by the "labor market" but are rather the result of a compromise, temporarily embodying the balance of power that exists between labor and management. The institutionalization of this relationship shapes the general orientation of the process of capital accumulation; the contradictions and disequilibria of capital accumulation find their resolution, needless to say only temporarily, in a specific form of regulation.

An analysis along these lines of the main trends in the area of labor relations in France since World War II quickly leads to three conclusions. First, what used to be called the "French miracle" was made possible by a unique system of labor relations, without historical precedent. As a result workers' struggles themselves were shaped by the logic of the postwar pattern of development. Secondly, since the early 1970s it has been clear that there is a close link between the economic crisis and the crisis in labor–management relations. There is good reason to argue that there are in fact two crises: on the one hand, a crisis of accumulation, a crisis in the forms of domination; and on the other hand, a crisis in the labor movement, in the strategies of the unions themselves. It is therefore hard to imagine a way out of the crisis based on the present practices of employers, unions, and government. Thirdly, it may well be, in consequence, that a crucial role in overcoming the current crisis will be played by the kind of issues that workers choose to emphasize and the kinds of tactics unions choose to adopt.

These are the themes that I shall develop in this chapter. I shall begin by making a few basic points, which I use to analyze the period 1945–70, and then go on to ask what is unique to France in the area of labor relations and trade union practice. I shall then focus on the years 1968–81 and try to explain the sequence of events leading up to the collapse of the old system of labor relations and the simultaneous halting of the process of capital accumulation. Finally, I shall sketch a few possibilities opened up by the political change that occurred in May 1981.

The Postwar Wage Compromise and the Growth of the French Economy

A great deal of economic research has been devoted to the question of why the depression of the 1930s was not repeated in the 1950s and 1960s. Recent work on the "regulation" of the capitalist system (Aglietta, 1979; CEPREMAP, 1977; GRESP, 1981a, 1981b) suggests that the answer is closely linked to changes in the organization of work and the way workers live. Many historians now agree that the crisis of 1929 was the result of an incompatibility between assembly-line production à la Ford and a way of life that remained traditional. During the 1920s Taylorian "scientific management" increased productivity to unprecedented levels without any equivalent change in real wages. Initially this created a situation conducive to increased profits and hence favorable to capital accumulation, but eventually the accumulation process was impeded by the inadequate level of total effective demand, itself related to the fact that workers were included to only a limited extent in the economic circuit. To put it another way the problem was a growing divergence between the productive capacity that workers were helping to create and the rate of increase of workers' consumption. Thus it was the inadequacy of worker income and expenditure that brought about a structural crisis in the economy, leading to the depression of 1930–2. This crisis was not really overcome until World War II (Sauvy, 1967–72). Thus the economic and social position of workers turns out to play a crucial role in determining the long-term viability of a particular mode of accumulation.

To restate all of this in more technical language let us use the term "wage labor relation" to denote all social aspects of the productive process under capitalism. The direct producers can be dominated by the owners of the means of production in a variety of ways. By "form of the wage labor relation" I shall mean, in this chapter, the set of conditions governing the use and reproduction of the workforce (for further discussion of this terminology, see Boyer, 1980, 1981; an application of these ideas to changes in the nominal wage level may be found in Boyer, 1978). Under this head are subsumed the organization of the labor process, the stratification of skills, the degree of job mobility, and finally the factors that determine the level and use not only of wages but also of fringe benefits and other indirect forms of worker income.

Another notion that figures in the works cited above is that of a "regime of accumulation." By this I mean any pattern of capital allocation capable of bringing about a fairly long-term accommodation between the rate of change in the means of production and the rate of change in the means of consumption. Since wage labor is the dominant form of activity in our society, it is intuitively clear that there is a close link between the wage labor relation and the regime of accumulation.

Finally, the term "regulation" refers to the dynamic pattern of economic change determined not only by the strategies adopted by individuals in the context of a given wage labor relation but also by economic competition, government intervention, and the country's position in the world economy. In what follows the term "mode of regulation" refers to a particular pattern of causal factors and mechanisms which together ensure the overall reproduction of the system with its implicit configuration of economic structures and social forms.

Using these three notions I shall next attempt to interpret the growth of the French economy in the postwar period and then go on to give a somewhat more detailed account of why that growth came to a halt.

Productivity vs Wages

The years immediately following World War II saw a complete breakdown in the social compromise that had prevailed in the previous period. The bankruptcy of the political elites that had held power between the two world wars and through the Vichy regime permitted the emergence of a new, modernist bourgeoisie eager to undertake the rebuilding of France's industrial base. Intense political and labor struggles forced this bourgeoisie to carry out certain economic and social changes laid down by the Conseil National de la Résistance. There were also fundamental changes in the government's way of thinking about, as well as its methods of intervening in, the economy. Meanwhile the United States was laying the groundwork for a new international economic system, as a foundation on which to base its own hegemony.

In this context perhaps one of the most fundamental changes has been in the relationship between top union and business leaders. The mandate to reconstruct the country in the wake of World War II gave the workers' movement leeway to accommodate itself to the logic of modernization while leaving the initiative almost completely in the hands of management (in this connection it is significant, for example, that in 1945 it was the CGT that took the lead in the "battle for production" as *quid pro quo* for the wage increase embodied in the Parodi-Croizat wage schedules. After all, it was none other than Gaston Monmousseau who uttered the celebrated dictum that "strikes are a weapon of the trusts": see Mouriaux, 1982, pp. 89–90). This accommodation removed one of the obstacles that had prevented the introduction of the new methods recommended by scientific management.

Yet this change alone was not sufficient to eliminate contradictions of the sort responsible for the crisis of the 1930s. The "new deal" in labor—management relations in fact brought about five key changes, closely related to one another. First, rank-and-file workers as well as union leaders assented to the reconstruction and modernization of the system of production without questioning its underlying logic, even though the "struggle against capitalism" still figured prominently in union rhetoric. Some automation was introduced into the production process, with expanded use of assembly-line production in some branches of industry. Accordingly it is hardly surprising that the 1950s and 1960s saw a sharp rise in productivity, which climbed at a rate equaled during the past century only by one decade of the interwar period, 1920—30.

Secondly, worker demands in this period focussed on the nominal wage level. Explicitly or not, wage negotiations dealt with the apportionment of productivity gains between workers and firms. Broadly speaking, what emerged gradually over the years was a typical form of labor contract allowing for some rise in nominal wages in keeping with rises in the cost of living and anticipated increases in productivity. This led to a sort of built-in increase in real wages without necessitating, as in the past, periodic crises involving a decline in the overall price level. Productivity and real wages moved together, in contrast to the disequilibrium that was such a prominent feature of the interwar period.

Thirdly, "indirect wages" (that is, fringe benefits, social programs, and so on), whose guiding principles had been laid down following World War I, assumed genuine economic importance after World War II. Whereas total indirect wages represented only 1 percent of disposable household income in 1913, that percentage has increased steadily from 1950 to the present, so that indirect wages now account for nearly one-third of workers' income. The system now has a new logic and runs on principles different from those that governed its operation in the past, when income was associated with actually holding a job. As a result worker income has become increasingly independent of the situation in the "job market."

Fourthly, wage labor has become the dominant form of productive activity. When we consider this in the light of the other changes listed above, there is no escaping the conclusion that the position of the wage-earner in French society has changed. In the nineteenth century wage-earners, primarily industrial workers, played only a small part in the overall reproduction of the system, whereas today wage-earners play a major role as both producers and consumers. We can even say that wage-earners today are almost completely integrated in the economic system on a lifetime basis (Meillassoux, 1975).

Fifthly, the early 1960s marked a profound change in the lifestyle of industrial workers and wage-earners generally: mass production expanded as rapidly as workers could afford to purchase the goods that formed the basis of the new industrialized urban lifestyle (automobiles, appliances, housing). Sweeping changes in agriculture and food processing enabled even the least-skilled workers to acquire these key commodities. It is worth noting, for example, that from 1950 to the present the number of appliances per household has been higher for industrial workers than for office workers, higher even than for the population as a whole.

Thus in the 1950s and 1960s, against the background of widening and deepening capitalist industry, we see unprecedented changes in the wage labor relation (as defined above), changes that were not without influence on the orientation of economic growth, the structure of society, trade union activities, and more generally on the major economic policy issues.

Accumulation and the New Wage Labor Relation

Taken together, all these changes altered the manner in which productive capacity dynamically adjusts to total effective demand: the fact that workers now play a fundamental part both in the production of goods and in the purchase of the products of industry has radically altered the way in which supply and demand are brought into equilibrium.

The fact that labor struggles came to focus on increasing wages helped to stimulate growth in the real wage, and this made intensive modernization of the productive apparatus possible, particularly in the consumer goods industries. In these industries greatly increased productive capacity was more or less matched by greatly expanded markets. This growth in turn led to the purchase of capital goods, leading to increased division of labor and major gains in productivity. Thus the capital goods industries also experienced the beneficial effects of rising consumption, so that the aggregate rate of profit and capital accumulation increased apace (for a rigorous analysis of this process see Bertrand, 1983; Bertrand *et al.*, 1982). The general upswing led firms to anticipate still further growth, thus stimulating additional capital accumulation; when the whole economy is growing, firms find it easy to invest in such a way as to take advantage of the existing pattern of growth, which influences their anticipations of the future and guides their investment behavior.

This pattern of capital accumulation is in fact without historical precedent (at any rate in France). In the 1920s the postwar boom quickly ran out of steam owing to the deficiency of effective demand relative to productive capacity, which led to the depression and the ensuing stagnation (Morsel, 1979; Boyer, 1979, 1982; Bertrand, 1983; Bertrand *et al.*, 1982; GRESP, 1981a, 1981b). Nor has this change been without effect on macroeconomic phenomena.

Indeed the increase in nominal wages resulting from workers' demands has proved beneficial to both workers and their employers. At times when productive capacity is not fully utilized and there is little foreign competition, wage increases yield a rise in worker income and hence, with a slight lag, a rise in the production of consumer goods, which in turn gives rise to a new round of investment. Provided that the initial wage increase can be compensated for by accelerating productivity increases over the short and medium term, consumption and investment will increase together, accompanied by equivalent changes in income from wages and profits. Although these adjustments are frequently accompanied by creeping but moderate inflation, total employment increases. It is easy to understand why this virtuous circle of growth should have led many observers to believe that the "golden age" of capitalism had arrived: the endless series of crises and depressions seemed finally to have been overcome and replaced by mere recessions. Thus much praise was heaped on macroeconomic stabilization policies of Keynesian inspiration, and theories of crisis came to be seen as outmoded. The logic of trade union strategy and tactics, always closely related to the dynamics of accumulation, was also forced to change in significant ways.

Trade Union Action and the Logic of Capitalism

At first sight it might seem that the structure of the French labor movement would not easily lend itself to such changes, which ideally involve collective bargaining between labor and management directed almost exclusively to questions of the nominal wage. In every respect French labor would appear to be unsuited to the purpose: French unions are highly politicized (and the largest of them are committed to the overthrow of capitalism), compete with one another, claim only a small percentage of the workforce as members, and are relatively weakly represented within the firm.

Nevertheless, French unions have, in their own way, helped first to establish and then to expand the influence of the postwar growth model. During the 1960s worker demands often originated in a particular firm and later spread to the entire branch of the industry, or originated in a particular branch and later spread to the economy as a whole. In other periods negotiation concentrated on establishing minimum wage levels for a branch of industry; individual firms were then allowed to vary these minima, usually by raising them, depending on special circumstances pertaining to each firm. In this connection it is worth pausing a moment to point out one of the peculiarities of the French case which explains why wages generally increased, even though the unions are weak or even nonexistent in a great many small- and medium-sized firms. The 1950 Law on Collective Bargaining Agreements gives the Ministry of Labor the power to enforce the terms of collective bargaining agreements signed by a sufficient number of firms in any given branch of industry. This explains why wages were generally increased and why wage increases were largely independent of skills, regions, and even branches of industry. The weakness of the unions at the local level was offset by industry-wide negotiations "at the summit" (involving top union, industry, and government officials). In consequence the wage labor relation in France is highly homogeneous despite major differences in the economic condition of various firms, the power of unions, and other factors affecting the balance of power between labor and management at the local level.

In the area of labor relations, then, the state has played a central role in assuring that real wages rise steadily and that these increases are smoothly distributed among different occupational groups. Mention should also be made of the state's policy in regard to the minimum wage, which in 1968 was indexed to the growth of the economy as a whole, reflecting the state's concern to ensure that even the least-skilled workers would help to sustain the rising level of mass consumption. Finally, a variety of tripartite agreements have steadily extended such social benefits as health insurance, retirement benefits, unemployment compensation, job-training, and so on. All of these have helped to consolidate the position of workers as consumers by making worker consumption relatively independent of difficulties affecting workers as individuals or as a collectivity. These benefits are generally won by the workers after fierce struggle, given the fact that French employers have on the whole shown themselves relatively unwilling to innovate in the area of labor and social welfare legislation.

Except for periods of rapid political change, labor conflicts in industry have mainly concentrated on wage issues. Demands for higher wages can of course mask other issues, such as the pace of work, the organization of production, and hierarchical relations in the workplace. As Erbès-Seguin (in the present volume) has perceptively noted, however, throughout the period that concerns us here wages served as a sort of general substitute for all other worker demands. To take one example the change to night-shift work was in many cases accepted by labor in exchange for wage concessions by employers. During the 1960s almost all labor conflicts, no matter how intense or what other issues may have been involved, were settled primarily by the granting of wage increases. These only accelerated the pace of accumulation, as we have seen. Various authors have accordingly written about a supposed integration of workers into the system, which Edelman (1978) refers to as "the legalization of the working class." It is tempting to argue that union struggles played a relatively functional role with respect to the imperatives of economic reproduction, but this would doubtless be an oversimplification.

In fact the Fordist wage labor relation described above could not be totally or permanently stabilized. Long-term historical studies have shown that every regime of accumulation is subject to cyclical crises that ultimately lead to complete stagnation. By "major crisis" I mean an episode in which social forms and institutional modalities enter into contradiction with the prevailing mode of regulation, thus signifying that a crisis of the regime of accumulation is under way. The period 1968–81 is a typical case, representing the ultimate limit of development of the Fordist wage labor relation together with its associated modes of intercapitalist competition, state intervention, and insertion in the international economy.

1968–81: A Period of Crises

It is instructive to distinguish three distinct periods in the years 1968–81. The outburst of social and political conflict that occurred in May 1968 resulted in a period of accelerated growth (1968–73). The paradox is more apparent than real, since the resolution of the crisis in fact reactivated the cycle of growth associated with the prevailing regime of accumulation. But increasing international tensions and imbalances, capped by a rise in the price of petroleum, provoked a recession in France and elsewhere, quickly followed by a brief period of recovery which suggested that the "troubles" had been only temporary (1974–6). Unfortunately from 1976 on, and even more after 1978, it became clear that a period of crisis had begun, casting doubt on the viability of the entire regime of accumulation, the existing wage labor relation, and prevailing trade union strategies (1976–81).

From Political Crisis to the Accumulation Boom: 1968–73

The stabilization plan first put into effect in 1963 by Valéry Giscard d'Estaing, then Minister of Finance, was designed to reduce inflationary pressures in the economy and, more fundamentally, to encourage the formation of industrial conglomerates sufficiently large to compete in the European and indeed the international marketplace. In 1967, however, the unemployment rate began a steady rise, albeit at a moderate rate. In one sense the social explosion of May 1968 resulted, by way of complex mediations, from tensions introduced into French society by these economic changes and difficulties, in such diverse realms as education, industry, and the role of the state in managing the economy. Students were the first to strike in 1968, but the movement quickly spread until it engulfed most industrial plants. The mobilization was so vast that it nearly toppled not only the government then in power but the very institutions of the Fifth Republic.

As is well known, the acute political crisis was resolved by negotiation, under pressure from the government, of a compromise between labor unions and employers. The Grenelle accords in fact codified a New Deal in the social realm, or at any rate reinvigorated the previously existing compromise. They provided for a substantial increase in the minimum wage (33 percent, part of which represents compensation for stagnation in earlier years), more modest increases in higher wages, and above all new rights for union locals (*sections d'entreprises*) and national trade union confederations (with the spread of industry-wide, multi-occupational agreements). Notwithstanding early fears on the part of employers, the accords turned out to be quite favorable to accumulation. The increase in both the lowest wages and the overall average wage helped to revive consumption, particularly in the branches that had suffered most under the stabilization plan. Improved efficiency in the utilization of productive plant increased productivity, so that production costs rose only slightly despite the increase in wages. A very slight increase in the rate of inflation went hand in hand with a renewal of economic growth and employment, an increase in real wages, and a restoration of the rate of profit and hence investment. Although it proved necessary to devalue the franc in 1969, the devaluation encouraged exports and, more generally, helped to make export industries more competitive. Until 1973, then, conditions were eminently favorable to an "intensive" regime of accumulation resting primarily on mass consumption.

Nevertheless, it would be an error to conclude that trade union struggles in this period served an entirely "functional" purpose. The strengthening of the workers' position actually made it possible for new demands to emerge, demands that no longer involved wage issues alone but extended to such other issues as the organization of work (for example, in strikes of semiskilled automobile assembly-line workers), challenges to the authority hierarchy in the plant, and protests against the forced geographical redistribution of employment opportunities associated with the restructuring of industry ("defending jobs" became the order of the day and the slogan "live and work in the region" was heard for the first time). It is of course difficult to give an explicit account of the impact of these new forms of labor protest on the economy in general and productivity in particular, but it seems likely that the impact was profound, especially after 1973 when the crisis of accumulation became obvious. It is not impossible, moreover, that the rapid rise in real wages hastened the substitution of capital goods for direct labor—a substitution which, if it occurred, would have made it difficult to maintain the high rates of profit attained earlier (Bertrand, 1983).

From the end of the 1960s, moreover, capital accumulation in France was based to an ever-greater degree on a turning-outward of the French economy: exports grew far more rapidly than internal demand. The change had qualitative as well as quantitative aspects; while some industries (such as automobiles) were highly competitive internationally, many traditional industries (such as textiles, wearing apparel, and so on) were not and suffered a sharp decline. Whereas the growth of the 1950s rested largely on a rapid increase in the output of producers' goods, growth after 1968 depended to a considerable extent on rising production for export. This structural change played a crucial role in gradually whittling away the remaining autonomy of the French economy, a development not without consequences for subsequent battles to maintain employment.

Finally, from the late 1960s on, management attempted to get around progressive social legislation in a variety of ways which, while not as extensively developed as the strategies of Italian business in this regard, can nevertheless be read as signs that the existing wage labor relation might be in danger of breaking down. Increasingly harried by intense international competition, major French firms relied more and more on temporary labor and subcontracting. At the same time they transferred some operations to areas benefiting from government subsidies (available for assembly plants in the west of France, for instance) as well as to regions where wages and social benefits were relatively low (including moves to newly industrialized countries or to "duty-free zones" of the sort that proliferated in the early 1970s).

While the macroeconomic indicators were still pointing to a healthy economy, then, we can already detect signs of instability in the existing wage labor relation, which had played a crucial part in the postwar growth of the French economy. In the following period these signs of stagnation and instability became increasingly apparent.

Uncertainties and Illusions: 1974–6
Starting in the late 1960s the international economy suffered from a number of imbalances, first evident in the areas of credit and currency rates. The accumulation boom of the late 1960s had led to rising prices for raw materials, a trend that culminated in OPEC's spectacular decision to quadruple the price of oil. The effects of this decision were compounded by the fact that it diminished the total volume of profit in the leading capitalist countries without generating a foreign demand equivalent to the reduction of domestic demand (Boyer, 1979; Boyer and Mistral, 1982a). This eventually led (in mid-1974) to a recession deeper than any France had seen for a quarter of a century.

The government then in power (led by Prime Minister Jacques Chirac) took the view that the economic difficulties attendant upon the increase in the price of oil were purely transitory. Accordingly it attempted to stimulate the economy in the standard ways by increasing government expenditures and tolerating a large budget deficit. Against this background the unions negotiated improved unemployment benefits and expanded aid for worker training from business and government.

Table 1.1   *Rate of Strikes in France, 1959–81*

	Number of strikes	Number of workers on strike (in thousands)	Number of days lost from strikes (in thousands)
Average: 1959–67	2,005	1,282	2,963
1968	—	—	150,000
1969	2,207	1,444	2,223
1970	2,942	1,080	1,742
1971	4,318	1,080	4,388
1972	3,464	2,721	3,755
1973	3,731	2,246	3,915
Average: 1968–73	3,332	1,873	3,027
1974	3,381	1,563	3,380
1975	3,888	1,827	3,869
1976	4,348	2,022	5,011
1977	3,302	1,919	3,666
1978	3,206	705	2,200
Average: 1973–8	3,625	1,607	3,625
1979	3,104	967	3,656
1980	3,542	501	1,674
1981	3,048	416	1,442
Average: 1978–81	3,231	628	2,257

Source: Ministry of Labor, 1982.

Continuing the trend of the 1960s, the number of labor disputes remained high, reaching a peak in 1976 (Table 1.1). The one new element was the large number of disputes in which defense of jobs was an issue. The government itself looked with favor upon the demand to save jobs, and to that end offered various subsidies and loans to industry.

The extension of existing wage agreements, together with these new demands and forms of labor struggle, explains much of what happened in the economy in the period 1974–6. Real wages continued to rise, in keeping with wage agreements then in force. Nominal wages reflected the rising cost of energy, with the result that real wages rose sharply while productivity growth slowed. At the same time strikes to save jobs coupled with the relative rigidity of the production process limited shrinkage in employment. Hence, even if we leave aside the effects of the expansionist economic policy adopted in the middle of 1975, the effect of the existing "Fordist" wage labor relation was to allow continued growth in consumption. A comparison of the years 1929–32 and 1974–6 suggests that the current wage labor relation helped to restore economic equilibrium by maintaining growth of aggregate demand and preventing a progressive collapse of accumulation (Boyer, 1982; Boyer and Mistral, 1982a). (It is particularly noteworthy that economic policy orientation is not a decisive factor.)

Despite the brisk recovery that came in the middle of 1975, the economy never regained the growth rate it had achieved in the 1960s. At one level of analysis this can be explained as the result of a redistribution of income in favor of wage-earners, resulting in higher consumption but lower rates of profit, thus slowing the rate of capital accumulation. In the early years of the crisis increased oil payments seem to have come almost entirely out of profits. At the same time productivity declined, as it had not done in the 1960s, thus further exacerbating tensions over the distribution of income and heightening inflation, which the monetary authorities were willing to accept as the price of short-term stabilization. The balance-of-payments deficit worsened as did the national debt without stemming a sharp drop in employment in 1975. Unemployment, which had been slowly but steadily on the rise since 1967, increased to a degree unprecedented since the end of World War II. Thus the reflation policy did not produce the desired reequilibrating effects.

By mid-1976 the government, along with most of the other major players, had realized that the 1974–5 recession and the subsequent recovery were atypical: Keynesian demand-stimulus policies coupled with extended unemployment benefits and increased job-training programs proved insufficient to restore economic growth on a lasting basis. It was at this point that people in official circles began circulating the idea that the Western economies had entered upon a period of "fundamental change," owing to major developments in the technological, economic, and geopolitical realms.

At the same time the academic literature and conservative politicians began emphasizing the perturbations and imbalances associated with supposed "rigidities" introduced by labor legislation. "Back to the free market economy" gained in popularity and in some countries was used to justify a new tack in economic policy, opposite to the one followed previously. Supported initially only by a minority, the new policies garnered additional backing as traditional stabilization policies proved incapable of restoring intensive accumulation based on an economy of mass consumption. France was no exception to this general rule.

The Crisis of Accumulation: 1976–81

The nomination of Raymond Barre as Prime Minister marked the advent of a new economic diagnosis and a new direction in economic policy. The problem, it was now asserted, was no longer the inadequacy of internal demand but rather the inability of French firms to compete in international markets. The battle against inflation therefore became the number-one priority. Hiring was made dependent on internal financing by firms in order to encourage renewed capital formation. Government intervention was now directed toward the restoration of profit, to be accomplished by reducing taxes on production, establishing stringent controls over spending for social programs, encouraging workers to accept greater job flexibility and mobility, and making the French economy more competitive.

Although the policies actually carried out by the Barre government served purposes that varied sharply from their declared intentions, there is little doubt that the year 1976 marked the beginning of a shift to a radically new orientation. Major efforts to restructure industry, a rapid rise in unemployment, and government intervention in the sphere of labor relations combined to weaken the position of workers and labor unions. Budgetary controls and monetary policies were tightened, moreover, stiffening management's resolve to resist wage demands. The defeat of the left in the 1978 legislative elections enabled the government to accelerate changes begun in 1976. The rate of growth of real wages declined sharply, and in 1980 real disposable income fell slightly for the first time. While nominal wage increases were slowed, the rate of inflation did not decline as much as the government had predicted.

What is more, contrary to the initial diagnosis, the curtailment of wage increases proved insufficient to encourage new investment, because profits were subject to the contradictory effects of two additional factors. Initially a rate of growth of real wages less than the rate of growth of productivity helped increase the share of profit in the national income. But subsequently the slowing of wage growth led to a decline in consumption. As a result investment, much of which had gone to modernization of plants producing consumer goods, dropped (over the medium term, in fact, investment remained stagnant). Despite considerable secondary effects from investments made by large firms in the public sector (in telecommunications, nuclear power plants, and so on), growth came to a halt, leading to further increases in unemployment. If we allow for the underutilization of productive capacity, it is clear that the attempt to restore profit rates failed, particularly after a "second oil crisis" led to further deterioration in the French economy. Thus began a vicious circle, leading from increased payments for oil to wage austerity to slowed growth, in turn requiring austerity on the part of the government and cutbacks in social welfare programs.

The approach taken here suggests that the end of the intensive accumulation cycle is not merely the result of conservative government policies but is also a sign that the "regime of accumulation" itself has run out of steam. At a more fundamental level it is no longer possible to maintain the high rate of growth of productivity that was the driving force behind the economic growth of the 1960s. For one thing, "Fordist" forms of labor organization have been pushed to the limit in certain key industries (such as automobiles), while process industries have taken a beating from the extended slowdown in the economy. If the rising social costs associated with this mode of growth are taken into account, it is clear that the persistent slowing in the rate of productivity growth is a logical consequence of earlier developments. Then, too, the stabilization of workers' purchasing power has put an end to the dialectic which in the 1960s created a link between rapid changes in the conditions of production and alterations in the lifestyle of workers. The fact that economic growth has not resumed is therefore no accident, nor is it merely the result of government policies designed to destabilize the "Fordist" wage labor relation. The wage labor relation itself is in crisis, and along with it an economic system based on intensive accumulation and government regulation—a system established at the end of World War II.

On the eve of the April–May 1981 elections there was little doubt about the magnitude of the economic crisis. Industrial modernization and expansion had proceeded at a rapid pace between 1967 and 1973, but after that the loss of jobs in industry completely nullified the progress that had been made in the late 1960s. The period 1974–80 saw major changes in all sectors of the economy. The increase in aggregate employment was made possible only by expansion of the commercial and non-commercial service sectors. Under the combined effects of higher oil prices, a rising dollar, and internal difficulties, the size of the French workforce diminished in 1981, in itself a sign that the end of the crisis was not yet in sight. Rising unemployment had little effect on the demographics of the active population, however, in contrast to what we observe in the recessions of the 1960s. The average rate of activity remained remarkably constant, with persistent employment of women compensating for a slight drop in employment of men. The reason for the unprecedented persistence of female employment rates is undoubtedly related to changes in the cultural values of workers' households, necessitating a second income.

Demographic and employment trends thus pulled in opposite directions until, by the end of 1981, the number of unemployed workers stood at 2 million, a figure long thought to be of ominous significance. It has been impossible to reverse this trend either by imposing a virtual halt on worker immigration or by reducing the length of the workweek. The latter dropped rapidly between 1970 and 1975 but until recently seemed frozen owing in part to the 40-hour legal barrier, in part to the management strategy of relying on overtime rather than hiring additional workers.

The crisis of accumulation has also accentuated challenges to the prevailing wage labor relation. Business has exploited various forms of temporary employment with which it first began experimenting in the late 1960s. While temporary employment and employment under fixed-term contracts still affect only a small fraction of all workers, their impact on the "core" of the industrial workforce has not been negligible. Extrapolating from this, some liberal theorists (such as Christian Stoffaes in debates over the Eighth Plan) have called for the institution of a "dual society" as a way of dealing with the expected reduction in the number of "permanent" jobs. The same theorists even refer to some of the aspirations expressed in May 1968 as justification for expanding various forms of marginal employment as a safety valve to relieve the pressures caused by the decrease in the number of stable jobs at decent pay. The government has responded to these developments by adopting a policy of high exchange rates and tight credit, which has encouraged firms to resist union demands in regard to wages and jobs. Official thinking has been concerned with ways of limiting wage growth and stabilizing social expenditures by "rationalizing" the present system. The worsening of international financial imbalances and the stiffening of international competition have added still more to the pressures to redefine the wage labor relation in such a way as to encourage greater flexibility in the labor process, greater mobility of workers, and greater adaptation of wages to economic circumstances, together with some revision of social benefits (Dourdan Conference, 1982).

In face of united opposition of business and government the labor movement steadily lost ground throughout the period 1976–81. Labor disputes were less frequent than before, and their scope was more limited (Table 1.1). What disputes there were tended to be increasingly defensive (whether directed against layoffs in the industries most affected by the crisis or toward the defense of concessions won previously) and were intended primarily to slow changes over which the workers' movement had little or no control. What is more, management capitalized on worker desires that the unions had been unwilling or unable to incorporate into their programs (such as flexible hours and part-time work). Finally, since there are so many unions in France, there was a wide range of labor analyses of the crisis as well as strategies for coping with it. In particular, the split between the CGT and the CFDT was not without influence throughout the period in question, during which the unions lost a significant fraction of their members.

Despite the relative weakness of the workers' movement, Raymond Barre's strategy was still far from achieving its goals on the eve of the 1981 presidential elections. From a strictly economic standpoint, the conservative strategy had accentuated the breakdown of the old regime of accumulation without finding a substitute for it, so that, despite the sacrifices asked of the workers, the conditions for a restoration of growth and hence employment were not yet in sight. The breakdown increased the need to develop a two-tiered workforce, in which only a fraction of the workers could hope for a decent and reasonably permanent job. But to move in this direction was extremely risky, for it implied repudiating the traditional aspiration of the trade union movement in France for greater equality within the workforce; the long-term implications for labor's power were immense. A further effect of Giscard's policies was to undermine the position of a significant portion of the "new middle class", particularly that part of it with ties to the state apparatus or the "modern" service sector.

Thus Giscard's defeat at the polls was not really surprising. Even if there was no major swing to the left, the defeat does indicate that the majority of voters rejected the conservative strategy for overcoming (or, rather, for not overcoming) the crisis (Jaffré, 1982).

Après-Mai 1981

Underlying the new government's actions since May–June 1981 is a two-part diagnosis of the crisis, which differs in many respects from the diagnosis offered by the previous government. The deterioration of the economic and social situation in the years 1976–81 is blamed by the left government on Giscard's austerity policies and attempts to dismantle social programs, as well as on limits inherent in the postwar mode of economic development (Parti Socialiste, 1980, pp. 35–43, 86–95). Reference is frequently made to the need to devise and apply new ways of producing goods, ways that require democratization of the workplace. While it is relatively easy to reverse short-term economic policies, making profound changes in the system of industrial relations and the production process will inevitably inaugurate a lengthy period of conflict and experimentation before a mode of development can be found that is compatible with both the aspirations of the workers and the economic imperatives of the world market, itself in crisis. It was not long before the new economic and social policies introduced by the left ran into difficulty.

Summer 1981: Demand Stimulus and New Workers' Rights

In June and July of 1981 the government decided to authorize a modest increase in the minimum wage as well as some social benefits. Though industrial modernization was not altogether neglected, the 1982 budget can be read as a document inspired essentially by a policy of Keynesian demand stimulus. The assumption was that by increasing wage income and thereby stimulating consumer demand, industry would gear up for increased production, leading after a few months to renewed capital formation, which had not increased in aggregate since 1974.

It is worth noting that a key assumption in the 1982 strategy was that productivity would increase at a particularly rapid rate: this assumption made it possible to envision a simultaneous increase in social benefits and direct wages, a simultaneous reduction in the length of the workweek and in taxes, and an improvement in the financial position of industrial firms. In effect, the miraculous properties of the system of regulation that prevailed in the 1960s had made it possible to satisfy the demands of business, labor, and government simultaneously. In many respects the government's 1982 strategy is comparable to the reflationary policies implicit in the Grenelle accords of 1968.

But the economic situation in 1982 was quite different from that of 1968 both nationally and internationally, and the government's 1982 strategy differed in many ways from previous demand-stimulus policies. Official forecasts were preoccupied with the effects of the worldwide crisis. The upturn in domestic demand was in fact supposed to precede international recovery—and to be initiated by a cyclical upturn in the United States—by six months. (Of course, this was premissed on the assumption that the Reagan policies, whose methods and objectives were radically different from those of the French government, would work. We may well ask if this was a reasonable assumption—or do we have to admit that French calculations should have made allowance for the errors of the Americans?)

The nationalization of major industrial groups and holding companies in France, along with nearly all banks, need not detain us here. The essential purpose of the nationalizations was to give the initiative to the state along with the means of carrying out an industrial policy unfettered by short-term financial constraints. (In previous years such constraints had led to overcautious decisions harmful to employment and to French autonomy.) With the nationalizations, the "reconquest of the domestic market," in which the newly nationalized companies were to play a key role, became the order of the day. But in fact, given the legal battle over the constitutionality of the nationalizations, their effect was minimal in the first eighteen months of the new government.

By contrast, the importance of reforms whose purpose has been to redefine the wage labor relation cannot be overemphasized. Prominent among these are the laws sponsored by Labor Minister Jean Auroux strengthening the rights of workers. The Auroux laws require management to inform workers about firms' operations as well as to discuss firms' economic and technological plans with workers' committees. Regular negotiations between labor and management are also compulsory. In one sense the Auroux laws merely provide French workers with rights long ago granted their West German and Scandinavian counterparts. In another sense the laws strengthen the hand of the unions within the firm rather than give rank-and-file workers a real voice. Nevertheless, the CNPF (the employers' organization), true to its traditions, has been quick to paint these changes in labor law as a dangerous and irredeemable attack on the authority and responsibility of employers. As for the nationalized firms, democratization has been slowed by legal delays in the courts as well as by problems the government has encountered in defining the overall shape of its policy with regard to the public sector.

Finally, the primary objective of economic policy in 1981 switched from curbing inflation or restoring competitiveness to promoting employment. Accordingly, the government created more than 200,000 new civil service jobs, stepped up job-training programs for young workers just entering the labor market, and through "solidarity contracts" with businesses encouraged early retirement and shortened hours provided these led to hiring new workers. Taking note of the divergence between demographic and employment trends the government concluded that the best way to reduce unemployment was to speed up the process of reducing the length of the workweek. To that end the 40-hour week was reduced to 39 hours in 1982 with the objective of achieving a 35-hour week by 1985. Along with this went the right to a fifth week of paid vacation.

Incontestably no such sweeping institutional and legal changes had been seen in France for many years. But these changes came at a time when the prevailing attitude among employers was "wait and see," if not downright hostility, and the government's feverish activity contrasts sharply with the fact that little pressure was exerted by the workers on their employers. History shows, moreover, that there is always a considerable lapse of time between the inauguration of an institutional reform and any real change in social behavior or in the structural determinants of economic development. By early 1982 the government's policy had run up against this kind of resistance.

The Limits of Consensus and Crisis Management "in One Country": 1982

By the end of 1981 the sharp rise in transfer payments and public expenditure had in fact stimulated increased household demand (which had grown slowly in 1979 and 1980 and somewhat more rapidly in the first quarter of 1981). But the increased domestic demand did not lead to an increase in production, since more than half of it went to the purchase of imports; penetration of the home market, the Achilles' heel of the French economy since 1975, began to increase at the end of 1981. Here we see the effects of the internationalization of production and trade, which limit the freedom of any one government to adopt policies at variance with the conservative majority. The French left has suffered, in its choices of political and economic strategies, from the absence of debate as to the desirable degree of involvement of the French economy in a crisis-ridden international system.

To make matters worse, the international recovery expected at the end of 1981 or beginning of 1982 failed to materialize. In the United States President Reagan's economic program remained largely unchanged, aggravating business's financial difficulties, increasing the public deficit, and precipitating a rise in interest rates to levels unprecedented (in real terms) since the 1930s. A spate of bankruptcies and rising unemployment were the predictable consequences of this policy, with the paradoxical result that the dollar became stronger despite the seriousness of the American economic crisis. The situation in Europe was scarcely better, and for the first time in a quarter-century French exports fell between May 1981 and May 1982 while imports continued to rise as rapidly as before. The balance-of-payments deficit, which had already entailed one devaluation in October 1981, worsened in the first half of 1982. Notwithstanding forecasts to the contrary from the international banking community, the French inflation rate remained at the same level as before, but the speedy deflation achieved in the United States, Britain and West Germany led to an exchange crisis and, in June 1982, to a second devaluation of the franc.

Once the government decided to abide by the international rules requiring an open economy, it was inevitable that its emphasis on combating unemployment would come into conflict with the emphasis of most of its major trading partners on combating inflation. Doubtless this contradiction explains the reorientation of economic and social policy that occurred in the summer of 1982. Prices and incomes were frozen across the board until 31 October 1982, it was announced that worker purchasing power would be maintained but only in late 1983, an "austerity" budget was adopted, plans for trimming social security were announced, and the terms for receiving unemployment compensation were tightened.

The international crisis by itself is not sufficient to explain why the left-wing government's hopes for the economy met with disappointment, however. The abortive recovery heightened demands from various social groups, so that starting in the fall of 1981 the government was forced to make one concession after another to farmers, small businesses, large businesses, civil servants, and the middle classes, thereby exacerbating tensions around issues of income distribution and perpetuating inflation as a temporary solution to renewed social conflict. The exhaustion of the postwar mode of development made it difficult if not impossible to achieve a broad consensus concerning the proper strategy for overcoming the crisis.

The move to a 39-hour week is illustrative of this kind of contradiction. Whereas official studies had reached the conclusion that simultaneous sharing of work and income was required (Commissariat Général du Plan, 1981), management in many firms decided to take advantage of the workers' weakness by cutting nominal wages in proportion to the reduction in working hours. This resulted in a spate of labor disputes, in which workers sought to maintain their standard of living. In response to the threat of labor unrest the government decreed that full wages must be paid to all workers, regardless of their income level—the thrust of this decree running precisely counter to the medium-range government objective, which is to reduce income inequalities. The temporarily higher rate of wage increases that resulted from this decision led to further tension over the issue of income distribution and drove prices up, even where firms sought to compensate for the concession on wages by achieving higher levels of productivity. At the same time the argument has been made, just as it was when the 40-hour week was introduced in 1936, that the reduced workweek is impairing the capacity of French firms to compete abroad, aggravating the crisis, and thus adding to unemployment (cf. Sauvy, 1967–72).

Beyond this, many firms adopted a "wait-and-see" attitude and investment did not pick up. Most new demand-pull felt by French firms quickly evaporated, while the failure of profits to rise, coupled with high rates of interest (which had to be kept high to defend the franc), made businesses highly reluctant to invest, so that aggregate investment fell in 1982. So much for the economic side of the picture.

As for the political side, French business organizations were far from willing to enter into any lasting compromise with the new government: business–government disputes were resolved either by granting new financial benefits to the private sector without any firm commitments in return or by dropping (ostensibly on a temporary basis only) certain social programs and tax reforms. (Further reductions in the workweek are to come as a result of agreement between labor and management rather than by new laws or government fiats and there was a moratorium on new social taxes on businesses until July 1983.) The newly nationalized firms have not been able to play an energizing role, as had been hoped, owing to the fact that major investments undertaken in the 1970s are just now coming to fruition and losses incurred by most of these firms in 1981–2 have slowed the development of new industrial strategies.

When all is said and done, the reflation of 1981 differs, then, from that of 1968 in nearly every respect, despite the fact that a left-wing government has equipped itself with the means to carry out a much more ambitious policy than Chaban-Delmas's "new society" program. The course of events has pointed up very clearly that the two elements in the left's diagnosis of the crisis were not of equal importance. The contradictions that have been encountered up to the present cannot be blamed on conservative hostility to the workers' movement but must be laid to the fact that France has exhausted the possibilities offered by the prevailing regime of accumulation. The major revision of the government's program in the summer of 1982 reflects the conclusions drawn from this fact. Against this background it should come as no surprise that the trade unions' strategies and organizational structures must be reexamined in response to the worsening crisis.

The Crisis of Accumulation and the Crisis of Labor: A Hidden Dialectic

The events of 1976–81 repeatedly pointed up the inadequacy of existing labor organizations and tactics (developed in a period of relative stability) for coping with the crisis. The unions responded to this situation in one of two rather different ways, depending on their traditions and their general outlook.

On the one hand, holding on to previously acquired concessions and if possible extending them remained, for some, a primary imperative of trade union strategy. In consequence those who felt this way pressed for higher real wages and social benefits and at the same time opposed any layoffs for economic reasons. The CGT, for example, argued that this strategy would help to end the crisis and that the only opposition came from the political forces of the right and the power of the business community. Other unions, such as the CFDT, held that strict adherence to the strategy inherited from the 1960s would ultimately produce results opposite to those desired: layoffs might be delayed but not prevented in the absence of an alternative industrial strategy (as in the case of the steel industry), the polarization between the "core" of the workforce and young workers just entering the job market would be exacerbated, raises for the worst-paid workers would be diffused through the entire wage hierarchy, inaugurating a wage–price spiral that would ultimately wipe out any gains won initially by the worst off, and so on. Accordingly, some previously acquired benefits would have to be trimmed in exchange for new rights and a strengthening of worker solidarity.

Both strategies encountered important obstacles. In a time of major crisis nothing guarantees that the best option for the workers' movement is to stick with demands that have worked before. For example, labor's refusal to take part in choosing technologies or setting industrial policy can be justified as a way of maintaining the autonomy of the labor movement *vis-à-vis* the imperatives of capitalist management. Yet the effect of such a refusal is to commit labor to waging a preeminently defensive battle, the outcome of which is not necessarily favorable to the working class. Even more it freezes the hierarchies that have resulted from past struggles, which may run counter not only to new worker aspirations but also to the harsh logic of resuming capital accumulation, the need for which labor may in some respects be willing to admit.

The possibility that such a strategy is merely a left-wing version of corporatism cannot be ruled out either; the history of the French workers' movement provides numerous previous examples of such corporatism, not all of which resulted in reduced inequality and increased solidarity among workers. There is every reason to believe that social corporatism (to borrow Pierre Rosanvallon's term) will present a real danger in coming years, even though political scientists and economists can easily show, reasoning in the abstract, that corporatism is no answer to the crisis but quite the opposite. Finally, certain experiences of labor movements in other countries show that, when labor defends only narrow interests and particular occupational groups, the result may be lasting division of the working class, in the end sapping its power (trade unionism in the United States provides a good example of how the short-term interests of unionized workers may conflict with the long-term cohesiveness of the workers' movement as a whole).

As for the second or "modernist" strategy discussed above, it too faces dangers. To be sure, it does allow for the raising of new demands and is much more effective in protecting employment in the medium and long run. It can also help workers begin to gain control over certain aspects of work organization and the overall orientation of production (Zarifian,

1981; Beaujolin, 1982; Moynot, 1982a). If, however, such a strategy is pushed to an extreme and labor relaxes its guard, it may weaken the "safety net" that prevented the recessions of 1974–5 and 1979–80 from developing into full-blown depressions. Accepting significant reductions in real wages over a period of several years would indeed reduce inflationary pressures and enhance the competitiveness of French industry. But the resulting decline in demand for consumer goods would affect the intermediate and producers' goods sectors of the economy. This in turn would slow the rate of productivity growth despite efforts by industry to restructure production with the consent of labor. The French productive system is characterized, over the long term, by a close relationship between major gains in productivity and rapid increases in aggregate demand.

As a result production costs might well not fall as rapidly as expected, and in any case less rapidly than in other industrialized countries where industry and labor relations are structured in different ways. Hence there would be no improvement in the foreign trade position of France to compensate for the shrinkage of the domestic market with the result that, despite austerity measures, there would be no improvement in the financial position of industry or employment, much less in workers' standard of living. If such an eventuality were coupled with a decrease in the amount of transfer payments (for the moment unlikely), there would be a great risk that a recession initially brought on by some new aggravation of the international crisis would induce a major, cumulative decline in output, employment, and investment. We can gain some idea of the catastrophic sequence by looking at what happened in 1929–32. If one has a taste for paradox, it might be argued that a weak labor movement increases the danger of disaster in time of crisis, whereas by way of contrast the case of Britain today shows that strong unions are not enough to bring about an outcome that is both progressive and favorable to workers.

As trade unionists themselves have noted, the current economic crisis has brought about a crisis in the unions as well, bearing on their organization, their strategies, and even their relations with the workers (Moynot, 1982a, 1982b). This offers both a risk and an opportunity: there is every reason to believe that we are entering upon a period in which the confrontation between union strategies and business strategies can have a significant impact on the development of a new form of wage labor relation and hence on a new mode of development whereby some of the perverse effects of the last decade might be overcome.

A New Wage Labor Relation?

I hope to have shown that the current crisis is structural and not merely temporary. It is generally acknowledged that a Fordist wage labor relation has played a central role in the intensive regime of accumulation, based on mass consumption, that underlies the exceptional growth of the postwar period. It is therefore logical to expect that redefinition of the wage labor relation will prove to be a necessary prerequisite to any attenuation of the contradictions that have grown ever more glaring in the period 1974–82.

If in periods of more or less stable growth workers' struggles have at best a limited influence on the overall dynamics of the economy, by contrast in periods of major crisis the orientation of such struggles can play a decisive role in determining the way in which the crisis is resolved. The present crisis is doubtless no exception to this rule.

This suggests that the very seriousness of the crisis of trade unionism opens the way to possible renewal, in keeping with the magnitude of the hopes that have traditionally been invested in the labor movement. Although corporatism is not a viable solution for labor, or for that matter for management, it is not clear that the economic and social problems that France faces today can be resolved by unconditionally accepting economic modernization. The danger for the labor movement is clearly that it will waver between these two extremes until the outlines of some new form of wage labor relation become clear. This is just another way of saying that the 1980s are a time of fundamental uncertainty, made all the more uncertain by an international situation that threatens to aggravate not only conflicts between nations but domestic social conflicts as well.

2

Labor and Capital in the Crisis: France, 1966–82

BENJAMIN CORIAT

Introduction

Along with a number of other authors (Aglietta, 1979; and especially Boyer, 1979, 1981), I subscribe to the thesis that the crisis now afflicting the capitalist world is a long-term crisis of capital accumulation, which requires, and is bringing about, a complete reworking of the capital accumulation "model," the core of which consists of the various aspects of the wage labor relation and its associated institutional arrangements. By "wage labor relation" I mean, to borrow Boyer's words (1979), "the whole range of conditions that govern the use and reproduction of the work force: the organization of the labor process, the mobilization of labor, and the factors that determine the level and distribution of wages." In other words, both the conditions under which the workforce is used for productive purposes in the labor process and the reproduction of the workforce via the distribution of direct and indirect wages are involved.

De facto confirmation of this argument is provided by examining trends in social policy and labor policy in the major capitalist countries. Prior to 10 May, and even more obviously since that time, the economic policies of Raymond Barre and later of Pierre Mauroy have sponsored a whole range of changes including certain key aspects of the wage labor relation.

The present chapter has two main purposes: first, to evaluate the scope and effect of measures taken by the government since 10 May 1981; and secondly, to relate that evaluation to a description of the underlying tendencies of the French economy over the past fifteen years.

In other words, the policies of the new government are described and evaluated in conjunction with a description of the neo-liberal "legacy" of the period prior to the elections. I shall deliberately limit my remarks, moreover, to the workplace and to labor relations in and around the workplace.

Two Intertwined Cycles of Workers' Struggle

To explain the current situation we must begin not with the movement of capital and the period after 1974–5 (during which mass unemployment took hold in the capitalist countries) but rather with resistance and struggle by the workers in the preceding period (1966–74).

This choice deserves a word of explanation. In proposing that we begin with 1966 rather than 1974 I do not mean to suggest that the date 1974, which marks the abrupt beginning of the recession, is insignificant. I simply want to indicate that understanding the measures taken since then—and recall that in France the policy change really began in 1976 when Raymond Barre replaced Jacques Chirac as Prime Minister—requires analyzing the major changes affecting labor relations in France between 1966 and 1974 (including of course 1968).

Furthermore, my reason for focussing initially on resistance and struggle (rather than the movement of capital) is that, in my view, the initiative rested with the workers in the period 1966–74. The essential steps in the management of the wage labor relation were taken in response to strikes, protests, and other worker actions.

Looked at from this angle the central feature of the period 1966–74 is the relative instability of capitalist industry based on repetitive, Taylorized labor, an instability brought about by frequent and forceful struggle by workers in the workplace, especially struggles involving the most exploited and vulnerable of workers, including immigrants, semiskilled laborers, young workers, women, and workers in plants situated in rural areas.

Worker resistance took many forms. In addition to such manifest forms of resistance as strikes, there was an increase in the number of undeclared, "latent" labor problems such as absenteeism, job turnover, and poor-quality work. Taken together, these various kinds of resistance resulted in marked destabilization of large-scale, Taylorized industry. Worker resistance, whether open or covert, signified a number of different things. To begin with, it showed that workers were no longer willing to perform repetitious, assembly-line tasks and, more generally, that they rejected the "rationalized" work processes stemming from scientific management techniques. Broadly speaking, there was a shift from traditional demands, which revolved around wages, to demands more clearly focussed on working conditions, amounting to a sweeping assault on Taylorist and Fordist principles of industrial organization (see Borzeix, below).

With respect to capital accumulation, these struggles raised doubts about the viability of the type of labor process on which capitalist production had been based since at least World War II. Mass production itself was under attack in these assaults on the labor process (for a discussion see Aglietta, 1979; Coriat, 1979a; Boyer, 1979, 1981; Lipietz, 1979).

A spate of new demands claimed increasing attention. Among these were demands for equal rights for immigrant workers, elimination of the lowest-graded job categories, automatic entry into the skilled occupational ranks, establishment of regular promotion procedures for industrial workers, incorporation of bonuses into the basic wage, and elimination of piecework. Taken together, these demands constituted something close to a program for revision of workplace relations, a program for which the working class actively fought and struggled (Coriat, 1979a).

Against this background the recession of 1974–5 suddenly plunged the developed capitalist countries into a situation of mass unemployment. These circumstances favored an attempt by business and government to regain the initiative. What followed was a period of intensive industrial restructuring, marked by worker opposition to layoffs, particularly in hard-hit industries such as steel, ship construction and repair, newspapers, and publishing. These struggles by skilled workers added to and in some cases overshadowed struggles by so-called "unskilled" workers.

What we see, then, is in a sense an overlapping of two phases of working-class struggle: one under the leadership of "unskilled" workers and aimed primarily at Taylorized assembly-line work and the institutional arrangements that make it possible, the other under the leadership of skilled workers and aimed primarily at preventing plant closures and the elimination of jobs as well as defending the traditional skilled trades against threats contained in plans for modernizing plants or restructuring whole sectors of the economy.

The celebrated occupation of the LIP watch factory is the point at which these two phases meet and indeed almost coincide. This happened because the LIP affair symbolized a struggle not only to prevent a plant closing and accompanying layoffs but also to reorganize production under "worker management." The slogan used at the beginning of the LIP affair ("It can be done: produce, sell, and pay ourselves") clearly embodies, in a symbolic sense at any rate, the synthesis that was sought (and in part achieved) between the refusal to allow the plant to close and the assertion that workers were capable of managing its operations in a new way.

If, with this as a background, we attempt to interpret the "neo-liberal" counteroffensive launched in France in 1976, after the reality of the crisis became manifest, it becomes clear that the counteroffensive had several objectives, including the workplace, wages, and social welfare policy.

Transformation of the Labor and Production Process

Three points are worthy of note. First, an effort was made to "redesign jobs." Secondly, robotics and microelectronics made a dramatic entry into the workplace. And thirdly, efforts were made to decentralize industry and promote a more uniform geographical distribution of production.

The job-redesign process began in the 1960s, in the euphoric climate of stable economic growth, and was not interrupted by the crisis, which in some respects it helped to shape. At the origin of job redesign was a long series of labor disputes involving semiskilled workers. In response to their demands management attempted, by redesigning jobs, to introduce some measure of flexibility into the rigid organization of the assembly line. At the time people spoke of "enriching" or "humanizing" the job. When the economic crisis hit, the job-redesign movement did not disappear. Reports published recently by the European Foundation for the Improvement of Living and Working Conditions, in Dublin, show that in fact it continued to thrive.

There were two reasons for this. First, job redesign continued to be attractive to employers because it led to substantial increases not only in the productivity but even more in the intensity of labor. Part of the waste involved in the strict application of Taylorist principles (one worker one job, one work station) was eliminated by these new techniques. By according "autonomy" to a group of workers, employers obtained greater efficiency and/or a higher-quality product. Further study has shown, moreover, that the creation of "enriched" jobs—often bringing higher wages—fostered competition within the plant between different groups of workers: young and old, men and women, immigrants and French nationals. Thus job redesign helped employers to refurbish their techniques for controlling the workforce, a task made urgently necessary by the previous period of strikes. Frequent predictions to the contrary notwithstanding, it should therefore come as no surprise that the job-redesign movement continued to flourish. It was nothing less than a key element in a broad strategy to reorganize the factory and control the working class—a strategy necessitated by the crisis.

Robotics and Microelectronics in the Workplace

Another important innovation whose development was encouraged by the crisis is automation and, more generally, what is known as "industrial microelectronics." In batch-production industries the number of robots currently in operation is still relatively small (some 20,000 throughout the world, of which 8,000 are in Japan and 3,000 in Europe: see ADEFI, 1981; and the special issue on automation of *Industrie et technique*, no. 441, 31 December 1980). The importance of the phenomenon cannot be measured by numbers alone, however. The ever more sophisticated equipment being marketed daily is leading to qualitative changes in the nature of work.

The important change is not really the substitution of machines for individual workers. The major innovation lies elsewhere, namely, in the fact that with the aid of microelectronics information about the production process can be gathered, stored, and processed while the work is going on, thus making possible new forms of time management and flow control on the shopfloor. The purpose of these innovations, which we shall refer to as "integrated automation," is to speed up the production rate (Coriat, 1981b). It can result in considerable time-savings in production as well as increased efficiency in the utilization of machines and tools. Reductions in energy consumption and wastage can also be achieved. Used in other ways, microprocessors can become a tool for surveillance of the workforce. Microprocessors attached to each machine can send real-time information on a worker's deviation from prescribed standards, with respect to output, work rate, time out, and rate of material consumption to a central control room monitored by a foreman.

Like job redesign, industrial microelectronics is making possible a new economy in production time management. Microelectronics often complements job redesign: at Renault and Fiat, for example, newly automated assembly lines are frequently staffed by "autonomous workgroups." The logic and objectives of both methods are the same: namely, to increase the productivity and intensity of labor, and to do so by eliminating dead time, "holes" in the working day, and converting wasted minutes into real productive time, while simultaneously tightening control over each worker's job performance.

Decentralization of Production

Just as the heart of the factory is changing to allow greater flexibility and efficiency in production, so too sweeping changes are concerned in the geographical distribution of productive capacity. Subcontracting has become a widely used means of reducing the size of large factories in metropolitan areas, with the result that the workforce is dispersed among a large number of smaller (and, in the jargon of business, more "manageable") firms. These are located in areas where there is less labor unrest, workers are less demanding, and the danger of a labor dispute spreading from one plant to neighboring companies is diminished. While this has happened to some extent in France, Italy presents an even more striking example of the phenomenon. There the small firm has been revived by the crisis and dwells on the borderline between legal and clandestine activity. Small companies are now commonly seen as the cornerstone of the "second Italian miracle." In France a recent study by the Institut national des statistiques et des études économiques (INSEE, 1982a) shows that, for the first time since World War II, the crisis has brought about a situation in which small firms are growing faster than large ones. The long-term trend of the past several decades toward greater monopoly seems to have been temporarily halted and perhaps even reversed.

Crisis thus has other effects than merely giving impetus to innovation. It can also lead to a revival of old ways of doing things. Putting out, subcontracting, and "sweated labor," once thought to have all but vanished from most Western countries, are making a comeback under big business control. Dispersed production (or the "diffused factory," as the Italians say) using varying levels of technological sophistication depending on the nature of the work and the location of the plant is a prominent feature of the new geographical distribution of production brought on by the crisis. In France entire industries (such as ready-to-wear apparel) are operating in semiclandestine conditions. These developments have been reinforced by parallel changes in the labor market, where temporary labor has been flourishing in a myriad of forms since the late 1970s. Thus the contours of the dual economy held out as a model by some Western political economists—and in France by some within the governing Socialist Party—are beginning to take shape.

Labor Markets: Wages and Social Benefits

A central element in employer strategies, associated with the developments described in the previous section, has been an attack on what had been considered to be well-established labor regulations. This has happened in all Western countries, but in different contexts the attack has taken different forms. In France there has been a proliferation of temporary labor contracts (Caire, 1982), in Italy and the United States a rise in "moonlighting" (*Intersocial*, 1980). These facts are well known and need not detain us here. It should be noted, however, that the number of people voluntarily taking second jobs has been on the rise (Piore, 1978).

New methods for dealing with immigration have reinforced identifiable trends in the labor market. Immigration restrictions, deportations, and inspections, coupled with a revival of racist propaganda (and practice), have produced new profits for business both economically (by forcing immigrants to accept clandestine work) and politically (by accentuating divisions within the working class). At the policy level there have been attempts to regulate immigration so as to secure the advantages of a renewable source of cheap, disposable labor (Cordeiro, 1981; Quiminal, 1982).

An additional effort under way seeks to establish a new policy in regard to wages. In essence the aim is to change the formula that has ensured a relatively stable rate of growth of real wages since the end of World War II and to shift to a zero or negative growth rate of wages (see Piore, 1982; Coriat, 1982; and, more generally, in regard to the institution of wage policies compatible with the development of mass production, Boyer, 1979, 1981). Broadly speaking, one can discern a reduction in real wages for occupational groups not covered by agreements ensuring that wages keep up with inflation. At the same time some wage-earners are suffering significant setbacks in their purchasing power as formulas guaranteeing a link between productivity increases and wage increases are abandoned.

Social programs generally have suffered from a shortfall in revenues due to the crisis, leading to major changes in the social security system. It is useful to distinguish three broad trends (paralleling changes in the labor market). First, there has been a tendency to emphasize the insurance aspects of the system over the welfare aspects, though both of course continue to coexist. "Insurance" is based on the idea that workers pay a tax in proportion to their income, in exchange for benefits. By contrast, "welfare" is based on the notion that everyone is entitled to certain basic guarantees and protections, a notion that has faded somewhat in recent years. The trend is illustrated by recent reforms in the eligibility requirements for unemployment assistance, which are intended to individualize benefits and shift the burden of financing them to the private sector, thus abandoning the idea of collective guarantees on behalf of the worst-off members of society (Greffe, 1980).

The second major trend has been the increased targeting of social benefits for specific, politically sensitive groups such as youth. The third trend attempts to eliminate certain benefits, such as payments for drugs or for specialized kinds of medical treatment. The overall aim is to reduce the cost of reproducing the workforce.

A General Description of the Neo-liberal Strategy

When we attempt to gain a comprehensive idea of the measures discussed above, it becomes clear that they aim to change two things: first, the conditions under which labor is used in the productive process; and secondly, the conditions affecting the reproduction of the workforce (namely, wages and fringe benefits). What we are witnessing, then, is an attempt to make sweeping changes in what Marx called "factory legislation," an expression he used in discussing changes in the wage labor relation that accompanied a major technological and economic change.

The new policy is best explained by contrasting it with Keynesian methods of regulating the wage labor relation. Two remarks are in order. First, although the new policy is often described in terms of *laissez-faire* rhetoric, what is really happening is not a reduction but rather an increase in the level of government involvement in the economy, particularly with respect to the elimination of existing contractual procedures and their replacement by new regulations. Secondly, the purpose of the policy is to promote capital accumulation. Instead of attempting to do this by stimulating demand (in which contracts linking productivity and wages played a central role), the new policy is aimed at the "supply side." In plain English this means that labor, previously regarded as a constituent of demand and a stimulus to growth, is now viewed as a cost, an obstacle to the accumulation of capital, as in the Barre–Schmidt theorem (Barre, 1978). This new policy orientation might be termed "neo-liberal" to distinguish it from both Keynesian (or monopolistic) and "competitive" policies of regulation. The main object is to combat labor in order to open new avenues of capital accumulation (Boyer, 1979; Coriat, 1982).

This type of policy, employed in France in a less spectacular manner than in Britain or the United States but with greater persistence and tenacity, ultimately met with rejection by the voters on 10 May 1981.

After 10 May: Projects and Processes

In the attempt initiated by the government to redefine and shape the wage labor relation there are two new elements. Both are countervailing tendencies to the underlying trends of the preceding period, tendencies that the economic and social policies of the left government are designed to foster. Before attempting to analyze the new elements, we must first distinguish two phases in the new government's policy-making, one stretching from June 1981 to June 1982 and the other beginning with the wage and price freeze of June 1982.

The first notable change in policy since 10 May has to do with the implicit as well as explicit points of reference adopted by the government. First, there has been a return to Keynesian demand-stimulus policies (aimed at increasing demand both by households and by industrial firms). The social security system has in part gone back to playing the role it played in an earlier period, that of compensating for short-term fluctuations in demand. At the same time social policy again emphasized "transfer payments" to low-income groups. The new wage policy also sought to ensure that the lowest workers (those receiving the minimum wage) receive a higher rate of wage increase than other workers. Family benefits and old-age insurance payments were increased. Instead of a "supply side" policy aimed at reducing labor costs, the government moved (via nationalization) to create a vast public sector in industry and finance, which it intends to use to sponsor a policy of technological development (in the areas of nuclear power, electronics, computers, and genetic engineering) tailored to serve its new industrial policy (which save for plans for the electronics industry are rather vague as of this writing).

Secondly, one can discern three innovations in the government's methods, which all aim to reactivate and encourage wage setting through contract negotiations. First, the Auroux laws would increase the power of the unions (in terms of both representation within the firm and negotiation with employers). This would be coupled with other measures designed to give workers an "increased voice" in the workplace. Secondly, the government has proposed that regular increases in nominal wages be set by contract talks. These talks would take account of anti-inflation measures proposed by Finance Minister Jacques Delors and already partially put into effect. Thirdly, contracts would be signed with industrial firms to encourage them to create new jobs (so-called "employment/solidarity contracts"). For the time being this is merely a declaration of intention; the effect of this move on the overall wage policy cannot yet be judged.

As for the content of the new government's policies, it should be noted that while they run counter in some respects to certain of the major policy objectives of the previous period, those objectives have not been entirely rejected. Rather the left government's policies introduce new objectives and combine new aims with old ones. In major respects the new policy incorporates some of the main options of the old policy, even though it attempts to reorient the thrust of that policy. Thus, for example, the new policy still seeks to reduce the length of the workweek and make work scheduling more flexible, but this goal is now incorporated in the larger one of preserving old jobs and creating new ones. Without modifying the objectives of the overall policy, it is clear that the readjustment instituted in June 1982 (with devaluation, wage and price freezes, increases in social security payments, and so on) is in line with the objectives that the previous government sought, not always successfully, to achieve. (That such a continuity exists can hardly be disputed, even if one wants to argue that it is justified by a "deepening" of the crisis or external constraints.)

If we look at the new policy from the standpoint of the organized social forces in France, in relation to the cycles of struggle that began under the previous government and continue today, two remarks are called for. The first has to do with the decision to base the new contractual policies on a strengthening of the unions at a time when the unions themselves must cope with fundamental changes in the composition of the working class—changes that have apparently reduced their capacity to mobilize support and act as intermediaries. The danger here is that the institutional position of unions will be strengthened just when they are becoming less able to represent workers' demands. The second point has to do with the disparity or if preferred lack of coordination between the proposed new wage settlement and the aspirations and demands actually voiced by workers. For example, what will become of an immigration policy that imposes stringent conditions on undocumented workers who wish to regularize their status at a time when it is also being asserted that immigrant workers enjoy the same rights as French workers and important groups within the labor movement are calling for a regularization of the status of all foreign workers present in France (Quiminal, 1982)?

To date there has been virtually no thought given to, and little desire expressed for, changes in labor–management relations at the shopfloor level. Will the means adopted for bringing about such changes prove compatible with the desires of workers, manifested as recently as the fall of 1981 at Renault's Billancourt and Sandouville plants and Peugeot's Sochaux plant, where semiskilled workers forcefully expressed their traditional set of demands? And in the spring of 1982, in what has been called the "May of the immigrant automobile workers," workers mounted a frontal assault on a labor discipline system imposed by company unions (CFT and CSL), clearly demonstrating their demand for substantial changes in working conditions.

As for the impact of the new policy on labor, we see that the chances of success are impaired, on the one hand, by the growing divergence between the composition of the unions and the composition of the working class and, on the other hand, by the disparity between the kinds of compromise proposed and the phase of labor struggle we are now in. The plan to deal with labor relations problems in a new way, by making a more forthright attempt to hammer out negotiated contracts, may well be defeated by long-term trends. There is no assurance that the government's policies will be able to alter this situation.

PART TWO

The Evolution of French Trade Unions

3

The CGT, Economic Crisis, and Political Change

GEORGE ROSS

Introduction

The Confédération Générale du Travail approached the economic crisis of the 1970s initially with a strategic package—composed of different sets of goals for the labor market, for relationships with other unions in France, and for effectiveness in the political sphere—which had been shaped in the 1960s. The growing inappropriateness of this package in the context of economic difficulties and the defeat of the political left in 1977–8 led the confederation to a moment of self-examination and reevaluation. Ultimately the CGT forged a new strategic posture in 1979, only to see this new posture collapse in the face of the Mitterrand victory of 1981. This chapter will outline the dimensions of CGT strategy prior to the critical juncture of 1977–8 and discuss its changing fortunes. The second part will review the post-1978 strategic debate and describe the ill-fated resolution of this debate. The chapter concludes with a brief survey of CGT reactions to the victory of the left in May–June 1981, up to and including the Forty-first Congress of the confederation in June 1982.

Political Hopes and Economic Crisis: The CGT to 1978

Pre-Crisis Origins of CGT Strategy

By the 1960s the CGT had settled into a characteristic mode of action in the labor market which, stated as simply as possible, might be labeled "defensive unionism." The confederation, together with its federations and their local components, deployed their labor market resources through agitation and striking (when possible) to generate bread-and-butter material gains for the CGT's base, mainly the higher-paid workers. In this defensive unionist mode the CGT—rather belligerently—assumed no responsibility whatever for the broader economic implications of its actions. The *patronat* and the manager state were left to cope with the results of union activity. Union activity and the tight labor market of the 1960s thus might prod productivity-enhancing investment, or wage drift, or difficulty for marginal firms, depending upon what responsive initiatives employers and policy-makers decided to undertake (Moynot, 1982a, recognizes this clearly, pp. 55–8).

Those who know the recent general history of unionism will recognize that such a union market posture was not uncommon in these postwar boom years. Relatively constant economic expansion and tight labor markets made concessions on wages and living standards the common currency of union–employer relations. The French industrial relations system, plus CGT ties to the French Communist Party, did make CGT defensive unionism none the less rather unique, in comparative terms. The low level of institutionalized collective bargaining in France, the anti-labor hostility of French employers, and the "class" orientations of French unions made French industrial relations less a "web of rules" in Clark Kerr's optimistic sense than a battlefield. Agreements between social partners, rare in any case, were perceived on both sides as but brief truces to be renounced whenever a new balance of power seemed to have emerged. The CGT was a major player in this conflictual status quo. It systematically rejected "class collaborationism" in any identifiable form. Not only did it shy away from open productivity bargaining but it also had a history of going to war against any efforts at broader "corporatism" (incomes policy, for example). There was a pedagogical goal in this. By defensive unionism, and by radical rejection of "class collaborationism," the CGT helped to impart to the working-class rank-and-file the lesson that little of significance could really be won by making short-run deals with capital and the capitalist state. Real change, change that would genuinely modify the position of workers, could come only from transcending capitalism and moving toward socialism, a task which could be undertaken only by left political parties.

The CGT's defensive "popular Keynesian" market posture was of course generally similar to the postures of many other national union movements most of which held very different political beliefs from the confederation's. None the less, the intimate connections which existed between the CGT and the French Communist Party did confer uniqueness not only on the CGT's specifically political activities but on the subtleties of its market behavior as well. The PCF, faced with rapidly changing political and social circumstances in the later 1960s and early 1970s, turned all of its resources toward promoting new United Frontism. Until 1972, when the PCF–PS–MRG Common Program was signed, the party's central task was to persuade the French Socialists to agree to a program which reflected the PCF's priorities. After 1972, until 1977, the party's job was to bring the new coalition to power in the circumstances desired by the PCF. These political objectives were very important to the CGT (Ross, 1982). Defensive, "popular Keynesian" unionism can be carried out in a number of different ways. In these years the CGT, when it chose its precise unionist tactics, made sure that they would be congruent with the political goals of the PCF.

We have already mentioned one important way in which the CGT's defensive unionism was tailored to fit general PCF politics—the confederation's consistent refusal of "class collaborationism." The CGT's job was to act to prevent French unions and workers from sharing any responsibility, actually or ideologically, for the fate of French capitalism. The CGT also had very strong opinions about how defensive union protest ought to be mobilized which were in part shaped by political reflection. It consistently desired to turn local union actions in more general directions, toward higher-level and publicly spectacular negotiations with peak sectoral employer associations, the CNPF and/or the state. The Matignon/Grenelle model of resolving industrial conflict exercised a powerful hold over the CGT. These concerns had important tactical manifestations. From the mid-1960s through 1977 the CGT's main mobilizing device, over and above local activity, was the *journée d'action*—day-long strikes/manifestations at branch, national/sectoral, or even national/general levels.

"Days of action" as a general tactic had a simultaneous trade unionist and political logic. In union terms "days" constantly incited local action, testing the waters without huge risks, while also counteracting the inevitable bias of defensive unionism toward localized particularistic arrangements with specific employers. The "days" approach also meant that general, "class and mass" demands were kept in front of the base's eyes, so that localism and parochialism, which undercut class identity, could be minimized. The political side was obvious. Localized, scatter-gun strike action tended to be perceived by media, other social actors, and workers themselves as, at best, *faits divers* carrying no general message. Large days of action on general demands, when they succeeded, were in contrast major events which advertized growing working-class opposition to economic conditions and often governmental economic policies as well. This kind of mass labor mobilization, the CGT reasoned, was also likely to enhance the case for left unity and success, especially if careful union work was devoted to communicating the message that real change, and a real response to the problems which elicited worker protest, could come only from a change in the political sphere.

In most national union situations it would be sufficient to stop describing a union's strategic package at this point. Given the pluralistic nature of organized labor in France, however, the CGT's strategy also had to have an interunion dimension. The cornerstone of this dimension until the later 1970s was unity-in-action with the CFDT. Treaties of unity with the CFDT after 1966 (when the first treaty was negotiated) were mainly prioritized lists of issues around which the two confederations agreed to struggle, without agreement on *how* to struggle for them. The logic of union (and working-class) pluralism in France dictated that the CGT and CFDT were not only allies but also rivals and competitors, to a degree, for rank-and-file support. For this reason—and for many others—each confederation had its own unique approach to the *hows* of union struggle, even if the priority goals of such struggle could be agreed upon mutually. Thus the CFDT, as it gathered steam in the later 1960s, developed a propensity for advocating "new demands" about working conditions and authority in the workplace more generally. Such new demands had obvious social roots, which the CGT given its long history and fixed outlook on defensive unionism had difficulty recognizing. The CFDT, a "newer" organization with a less settled base, could afford to risk welcoming these new conflicts.[1]

Such tactical divergences meant that the CGT's general interunion strategic goal of unity-in-action with the CFDT necessarily implied conflict. In particular, the CGT disliked the CFDT's interest in "new demands"—which the CFDT formalized in its reflections on *autogestion* after May–June 1968. In the CGT's eyes such a focus might easily lead the CFDT toward "class collaborationism." It was likely also to "mislead" workers to believe that significant change might occur without left political parties coming to power. Furthermore, to the CGT, the CFDT's focus on militant local struggles risked disaggregating the broad "mass and class" front of union protest which the CGT desired. The CFDT's impatience with *journées d'action* didn't help, either. Thus in its interunion strategic activities the CGT set out not only to create unity with the CFDT but also to dissuade the CFDT from these wayward tactical directions. Since the CFDT needed the CGT, and since the CGT was a much stronger organization (the ratio in terms of membership and support in professional elections was about 2·5 to 1 in the 1960s and early 1970s), the CGT did have the leverage to try a great deal of dissuading.

The CGT's immediate pre-crisis strategic package, with its heavy emphasis on bread-and-butter defensive concerns, did allow the confederation considerable autonomy from the PCF, even if important questions of union tactics were considered in the light of their political implications. But there were also ways in which ties between the PCF and CGT were open or quasi-open. The ways in which the CGT *theorized* the dynamics of the economic world, for example, were borrowed directly from the PCF. As the PCF shifted toward its new "state monopoly capitalist" views in the early 1970s the CGT followed closely behind.[2] At its regular Congresses the CGT solemnly approved general programs for social and political change in France, being reasonably careful to confront only issues which could be considered as falling within a trade union purview. None the less, with monotonous consistency, these programs were stripped-down versions of those advanced by the PCF at the same moment, a good example being the program of the Thirty-ninth Congress in 1969 which pushed forward the core proposals—nationalizations, *gestion démocratique*, planning, and the like (CGT, 1970, p. 473 ff.)—of the program which the PCF was urging on the Socialists.

Partial Success: 1968–74

The CGT lived with this general strategic package from the late 1960s until 1977–8, as we have noted. None the less, these years were divided into two distinct periods. From 1968 to 1974 the package worked reasonably well, marred in its implementation mainly by disagreements with the CFDT over tactics. "Simple defensive unionism" succeeded, in conjunction with a number of other important factors, in keeping the living standards of French workers rising. The CGT also went to war after 1969 to defeat what it perceived as "class collaborationist" initiatives coming from the Chaban-Delmas government (Jacques Delors's *Nouvelle Société* program and the *contrats du progrès* which involved both an incomes policy and governmental incitation toward American-style collective bargaining) (Delors, 1970). The CGT was quite successful in this, eventually persuading the CFDT to cooperate. The *Nouvelle Société* program was, in time, eviscerated (Ross, 1981).

Persuading the CFDT to abandon its *gauchiste* leanings was not quite so easy. The period 1968–74 was the high point in the CFDT's conversion to *autogestion*, its sensitivity to "new demands" and to the needs of new categories of workers (OS, women, immigrants), and its eagerness to promote hypermilitant local strikes (CFDT *Syndicalisme*, no. 1279, 1970; CFDT, 1973). The CGT's disapproval of such inclinations in these years meant that unity-in-action was unity-in-conflict. In the name of *autogestion* the CFDT resisted most CGT imprecations toward "more responsible" unionism—demonstrating a distinct lack of enthusiasm for *journées d'action*, persisting with extreme tactics in local strikes (sit-downs, imprisoning the boss, and the like), and taking *gauchiste* egalitarian positions on reducing the wage hierarchy between job categories (which the CGT, much later, was itself to adopt).[3] Indeed in this period the CFDT acquired a reputation (which was to be ephemeral) as the most militant wing of French labor. Squabbles over tactics were only one dimension of CGT–CFDT unity-in-conflict in these years, however. In the early 1970s the two confederations also pursued a high-level debate about the relationships between trade unionism and socialism which clarified the CGT's strategic trajectory and the CFDT's reasons for rejecting important parts of it (Krasucki, 1972; CFDT *Syndicalisme*, no. 1366, 1971). But both this general debate and more specific fights over labor market tactics were a standoff. The CGT could not badger, bully, or persuade the CFDT to conform.

The Strategy Collapses: 1974–8
The years 1974–8 brought unprecedented success for the CGT's inter-union strategic goals, but within an economic setting in which union action in the labor market generally became progressively more difficult to generate. In 1974–5, largely because of indirect impulsions from the PCF, the CGT moved to preempt the CFDT's "vanguard" role in the promotion of hypermilitant local struggles.[4] The confederation decided to try and turn to its own advantage the sharp local conflicts about layoffs, industrial relocation, and regional distress which the CFDT had used as its springboard to fame prior to 1974. From mid-1974 onwards the CGT therefore sought out such local actions and tried to shape them around nationally salient "mass" protest issues—"no to unemployment," "no to the dismantling of French industry," "no to redeployment." Success, albeit brief, was not long in coming. Numbers of sharp

CGT-directed actions in crisis-ridden industrial sectors occurred (ship-building, printing, the railroads, the Post Office).[5] This preemptive operation was of course directly aided by the ways in which the coming of crisis impinged on the labor market. The end of the boom era, inflation, and rising unemployment tended to shift rank-and-file perspectives away from the "qualitative new demand" approach of the CFDT toward more defensive, national policy-oriented issues such as employment security. In fact from 1974 onwards the CFDT's local hyper-militancy and advocacy of *autogestionnaire* unionism gradually disappeared.

A different logic was at work underneath the changing shape of labor market action, however. After the signature of the Left Common Program in 1972, generating labor mobilization which might be translated into electoral support for Union de la Gauche became a higher CGT priority. But before crisis began to affect the labor market severely, increased political emphasis in CGT action was relatively compatible with defensive union tactics.

Beginning in 1975–6, however, political mobilization began to *displace* trade union action, rather than supplementing it. This meant, in essence, that the CGT placed ever-greater stress on the "left electoral victory is the only solution" line, at the expense of more orthodox union concerns. Moreover, at the same time, and not accidentally, the CGT pressed more and more urgently toward high-level and publicly spectacular union activities of the *journée d'action* type. Such movements, designed to be symbolic and to raise high political issues, progressively left grassroots union issues behind in favor of electoral concerns. It was during this period that the CGT put forth the slogan "Union, Action, Programme Commun."

The development of the crisis, which intimidated workers away from risky industrial struggles, favored the CGT's progressively more elector-alist labor market tactics. *Journées d'action*, whose justification originally had been as a device to prod rank-and-file workers to act locally, more and more led simply to further *journées d'action* (as the CFDT, which none the less participated, was wont to point out). But beginning in 1975 such *journées* became more and more spectacularly successful in themselves, attracting ever-larger masses of participants, especially after the introduction of the Barre austerity policies in the fall of 1976. Workers were distressed by the incidence of crisis, and "days" offered them safe ways of demonstrating this distress. The *journées* of 7 October 1976 and 24 May 1977 were, each in its turn, the largest industrial protests to occur in France since May–June 1968.

Thus in the brief space of time between 1974 and 1977 the CGT won a nearly complete victory over the CFDT in the interunion sphere, while simultaneously the general balance between the two other major axes of CGT strategy, labor market action and partisan political mobilization, shifted noticeably. Defensive labor market activity at the base became ever more difficult to promote in ways which naturally pushed the entire labor movement toward the massive, symbolic public demonstrations around highly general demands which the CGT preferred. And the CGT's own analysis of the crisis, which held that no real solutions could come from labor market action, that workers' real salvation lay in a change in those holding political power, led the confederation to use these massive demonstrations as quasi-electoral rallies for Union de la Gauche (Lange *et al.*, 1982, ch. 1).

CGT politicization in favor of Union de la Gauche, however dangerous from the point of view of the confederation's capacities to defend the material interests of its rank-and-file, was at least not particularly *divisive*. Almost everyone in French labor and on the French left believed, in these years, that the 1978 legislative elections would be the moment of truth for Union de la Gauche. The left was in a good position to come to power and, after twenty years of right-wing government, few union supporters disagreed that unions should help it to do so. The CGT's next step toward politicization was cruder and more destructive, however. After the failure of negotiations to update the Common Program in September 1977, Union de la Gauche came to an untimely end. After *rupture*, the runup to the 1978 election was characterized mainly by poisonous acrimony between the PCF and the PS, each blaming the other for the split. Not surprisingly the CGT rushed to take the PCF's side. Politicization in favor of Union de la Gauche rapidly gave way, after September 1977, to politicization in favor of the PCF.[6]

By March 1978, then, the CGT's strategy was in complete disarray. The crisis had completely undermined the defensive unionist labor market tactics which had served the confederation reasonably well in the 1960s. The growing politicization of the CGT after 1974 in a new crisis labor market context had further accentuated the confederation's incapacity to generate mobilization which would defend the rank-and-file. Events after September 1977 simply made things worse, as the CGT slid rapidly backwards toward a classic "transmission belt" posture. All this occurred of course at a moment when dramatically changing economic circumstances—rising unemployment, deindustrialization, and changing economic structures—were creating rank-and-file insecurity, demoralization, and particularism (the desire to protect one's own situation, no matter what befell others). Overpoliticized and overgeneralized trade unionism of the kind which the CGT increasingly produced had the effect of diverting workers' attention away from shopfloor issues and toward politics as a solution to the problems of the crisis.

Strategic Review I: The Brief Flowering of Proposition Force Unionism

For a year after the 1978 elections the CGT seemed to be opening to changes generated, for once, not primarily by PCF "overdetermination" but from its own internal debates. An unusual degree of strategic pluralism and discussion emerged after the electoral disaster of March 1978. With a new, and seemingly long-term, lease on political power, the right would be free to pursue the Barre austerity policies with greater vigor, while capital itself would be certain to "redeploy" even more actively, at the expense of workers and unions. For these reasons alone, CGT strategy needed reconsideration. Political differences about the confederation's posture during the campaign provided one more source of debate: between Socialists and Communists about the CGT's political leanings.[7] On top of this the top leadership of the confederation—the Bureau Confédéral (BC)—began to depart from its usual unanimism on issues of general policy for the future. The BC included sixteen people—half PCF, half non-Communist. After March, four secretaries—two Communists (Christiane Gilles and Jean-Louis Moynot) and two non-Communists (René Buhl and Jacqueline Lambert)—began to speak out for new departures, each in his or her own way. Such pluralistic debate at the top—similar things emerged in the Commission Executive—encouraged imitation in federations and departmental unions.

More general political and institutional factors played facilitating roles. The PCF itself was in disarray, wracked by a huge explosion of rank-and-file discontent as well as disunity at leadership level about the course to follow. Since the party was in a difficult position to do much decisive "overdetermining" of CGT activity, the situation allowed greater CGT autonomy, even if only momentarily. Moreover, there were serious disagreements between the major Communist leaders within the CGT itself both about PCF policies and CGT strategy. Georges Séguy, the secretary-general (and PCF Bureau Politique member) had a history, like Benoît Frachon before him, of dragging his feet in party and union whenever the party turned in sectarian directions which could damage the CGT's ability to function as a truly mass labor organization.[8] Henri Krasucki (also on the BP) was known, justifiably, as a reliable *lignard*. For a brief period after March 1978 Séguy (opposed step-by-step by Krasucki) clearly attempted to use the new situation and the PCF's uncertainty to carve out greater strategic autonomy for the CGT. What Séguy had in mind—beyond giving the CGT greater strategic space from the party—we can only imagine. Perhaps he was attempting to deploy the CGT as a resource in strategic discussions inside the party leadership itself.[9] Whatever his motives, he was to pay dearly for them later. Then, institutionally the CGT was obligated to hold a Congress in rather close proximity to the complex events of the spring of 1978. The electoral disaster inevitably caused considerable effervescence inside the confederation, while the leadership simply did not have time to "take things in hand" before the late autumn Congress, even had it so desired.

Indications that the Fortieth Congress would be different came in the late spring of 1978 both from the confederal press and from the fact that the original Congress proposal (drafted largely by Krasucki in classic, orthodox ways) was modified because of opposition both in the Confederal Bureau and in the Commission Executive.[10] Actual Congress preparations, beginning in the early fall of 1978, were unique in CGT history. The Bureau Confédéral solicited full and open discussion throughout the CGT, and pledged that any and all written contributions to pre-Congress debates would be published—which they were. Nothing was taboo, as a reading of *Le Peuple, Antoinette, Options* and *La Vie Ouvrière* from these months demonstrates. Moreover, literally thousands of open meetings at every level of CGT organization across the country were held: CGT politics in 1977–8 was one issue. But the great bulk of the letters underlined the necessity for the union to get back in touch with rank-and-file concerns. The sense that the CGT had slipped away from the problems of ordinary workers was everywhere. Many writers and speakers also urged the CGT to reconsider its views on the crisis, to look for new ways to cope with changes in the work process at shopfloor level.

The Congress itself was in many ways unprecedented. The lead was taken by Séguy himself in his opening report. The secretary-general refused the usual self-congratulatory recounting of the past in favor of a series of "themes for reflection." His primary concern was putting the CGT back in touch with rank-and-file concerns. Reinforcing unity-in-action was essential—Séguy proposed new initiatives to the CFDT on this question. Séguy also roundly attacked what he called the "productivist" model of economic development—in ways which would have been quite at home at a CFDT Congress—which intensified and deskilled work. The CGT ought to give more attention to issues of workplace *aliénation*, said Séguy. The secretary-general also recognized the confederation's responsibilities in the overpoliticization of union action in the pre-electoral years. Then by suggesting that "trade union struggle for material gains is, by definition, struggle for reforms, small, middle-sized and large", Séguy was not only advocating increased CGT contractualism, but also implying that the confederation's older defensive unionism/political change dualism might be transcended, that certain structural reforms might be won by unions in labor market struggle itself (*Le Peuple*, 1978, Fortieth Congress, no. 2).

Following Séguy's lead were both Jean-Louis Moynot and René Buhl (who gave the closing address to the Congress). If the confederation ought to consider a specific program and strategy for social change based on its strictly trade union positions, then one example of the kind of issues which it might embrace under the new rubric of *autogestion*—which the CGT had adopted in the autumn of 1977, after years of excoriating the CFDT for its *autogestionnaire* pretensions—was struggle for *conseils d'atelier et de service*, an approach to direct democracy in the workplace elaborated by Moynot (*Le Peuple*, 1978, Fortieth Congress, no. 4). To Buhl the crisis called for an entirely new trade union strategy involving step-by-step union struggles for structural reforms. As he remarked,

For many years the CGT—justly—avoided mixing the economic realm and ... day-to-day demands. But today we face not only destructive political policies, but also an economic crisis whose roots are profound. Whole industries, whole areas of economic activity, social services and culture are menaced with pure and simple disappearance. We must therefore struggle ... against such policies and decisions while ourselves advancing solutions which will create a minimum number of durable economic guarantees. The only way to do this is for us to put forth our own industrial solutions by defining them in perspectives of democratic change, all the while realizing that we can obtain only partial results in this way. (*Le Peuple*, 1978, Fortieth Congress, no. 7, p. 2)

This notion that the CGT should be a "proposition force" for "industrial solutions" of a democratizing, *autogestionnaire* kind was at the core of proposals for strategic change at the Fortieth Congress. (See also Huiban, in this volume.) Observers at the Congress were readily able to see, however, that this spirit of innovation had not yet penetrated very far. Only a few front-line leaders, including of course the all-important secretary-general, articulated such suggestions convincingly. Speakers from the floor only rarely took up the leaders' ideas. In fact the Fortieth Congress faced in two directions at once; it had "two readings," to use the parlance of the confederation. The Congress Proposal itself, even though slightly different from earlier proposals, could be interpreted either as advocacy of continuity along old lines, with changes necessary to take account of changed circumstances, or as an opening to a much more decisive shift. And while numbers of front-line CGT leaders seemed—carefully—to be pushing for the second interpretation, other important leaders (Krasucki in the first instance, plus those known to be in his *mouvance*, Lomet, Warcholack, and others) spoke much more conventionally. Thus the Fortieth Congress indicated only that major change in CGT strategy was possible, not that it had already happened. As Edmond Maire of the CFDT commented cautiously afterwards, "there have been other brief springtimes, and this one is only in its very first days" (Ross, 1982, ch. 10).

The crisis in the iron and steel industry gave CGT "proposition-forcers" their most substantial opening. The steel situation needs no detailed review here—suffice it to say that the virtual bankruptcy of major steel companies in France in 1977–8 forced the government, in the context of the EEC's Davignon Plan for European steel, to move toward a reorganizing bailout. Tens of thousands of jobs in iron and steel were threatened, as were entire regions where steel had been a major source of livelihood for generations (Longwy, Denain). For a time "proposition-forcers" were in charge of formulating the CGT's response to this situation. Old CGT postures would have dictated simply resisting change outright, justifying this by the claim that French iron and steel was basically sound and could be salvaged by moving away from the anti-social strategies of *patronat* and government primarily by nationalization. In contrast to this "proposition-forcers" drew up a counterproposal to the government's crisis plan designed to promote a restructuring of the industry which would make it newly competitive and more socially responsible *without* major loss of jobs. The CGT Metalworkers' Memorandum which put forth the counterproposal did assert that France needed a strong basic iron and steel industry to protect the nation's economic integrity—a traditional CGT attitude. Beyond this, however, it proposed major changes to allow the industry to restore its strength, including extensive government investment programs in steel-consuming areas and new plans for diversification of the industry into metal-finishing and raw materials plus new high-technology steels. Along with such changes the Memorandum also proposed a series of measures to humanize work which would simultaneously preserve employment and make the steel industry a better place to work (CGT FTM, 1978).

The ultimate purpose of all this was to mobilize the steel rank-and-file to press for new negotiations over restructuring, while at the same time providing steelworkers with the level of knowledge about their industry which would allow them to demand industrial democracy in a plausible way. Mobilization around the Memorandum proposals was in fact quite impressive into 1979. Perhaps more important, the CGT initiative caught other actors off-balance. The CFDT, to begin with, felt obliged to develop its own counterplan, which was quite similar to that of the CGT, if less demanding (CFDT FGM, 1979). The Ministry of Industry itself, used to decreeing policy, was also caught short by the CGT's move and the skill with which it was executed, to the point where it felt obliged to consent to new negotiations with the unions, a step which it had not originally expected to take.

The advocates of "proposition force/industrial solutions" unionism were offering a reformulated general strategic package to the CGT. In the labor market defensive unionism, if it could obviously not be abandoned, was clearly insufficient. The basic structures of the French economy and workforce were being recast in crisis. Defensive unionism, whether successful or unsuccessful, left decision-making on such matters to employers and the state. In crisis this meant that such decisions would be made without, and to the detriment of, workers. Rather than awaiting the delivery of palatable economic change from the political left, "proposition-forcers" suggested that the CGT ought to become a conflictual actor in the making of day-to-day economic decisions through struggle in the labor market and elsewhere. If capital and the state were compelled to propose anti-working-class policies of structural change to regenerate profitability in crisis, then the CGT ought to use its own resources to promote economic solutions of a more just kind which would, moreover, point toward more profound social transformation (Moynot, 1979b, 1982a).

In labor market terms, then, the key innovation proposed by the "proposition-forcers" was embodied in the term "industrial solutions." The CGT should move away from its traditional strategic dualism between defensive unionism in the labor market and mobilization for longer-term political change toward specific sector-by-sector campaigns for union-imposed structural reforms. In order to make counter-proposals for "industrial solutions" the CGT itself had to acquire new knowledge and build up a realistic "countermap" of the development of French industry, case by case.[11] Perhaps more important, in order to mobilize workers for "industrial solutions" the union rank-and-file itself would have to acquire a newly sophisticated understanding of the dynamics of its own industry and the industry's place in the broader economic situation. In the process of acquiring such understanding ordinary workers would begin to accumulate the insight which would make real *autogestion* a possibility (Zarifian, 1979a, 1979b).

"Proposition force" unionism had profound implications for the CGT's political perspectives as well. Because of its focus on the development of autonomous union struggles for sectoral changes in economic life, it proposed a decentralization of social mobilization away from the CGT's traditional focus on national-level political action as the only source of significant change.[12] "Proposition-forcers" did not of course advocate that the CGT ought to take the place of political parties. Nationalizations and other major structural reforms could only come through politics. Indeed part of the motivation of the "proposition-forcers" came from a conviction that the confederation's old approach had failed to make new nationalizations plausible to ordinary workers in terms of the day-to-day logic of their work situation.[13] Thus the new approach would be designed to provide the connection, missing prior to 1978, between global, general political programs and the workplace needs of workers. None the less, the "proposition force" perspective foresaw a significant expansion in CGT activity of a "neo-syndicalist" kind. If the pre-1978 strategic package involved defensive unionism plus mobilization for global political change, then proposition force unionism proposed a new level of union activity situated between these two extremes, in which the CGT would seek to use its union resources to influence industrial redeployment and change, economic planning, and other basic structural decisions, as well as to work toward possible progressive changes for workers no matter what happened in the political sphere.

Strategic Review II: Toward New Transmission-Beltism?

"Proposition-forcers" were not alone in proposing a new strategic package to the CGT. Unionists closer to the PCF, and therefore much less concerned with using the post-1978 period to give the CGT greater union autonomy from politics, had their own solutions to propose. In the party itself a degree of internal order and strategic clarity was reestablished by mid-1979. The party's Twenty-third Congress essentially reaffirmed the *de facto* strategic shift which the party leadership had engineered in 1977 and which had caused the inner-party protest of 1978. The Congress asserted that Union de la Gauche had favored the development of Socialist strength at the expense of the PCF. What mattered, then, was to "reequilibrate" the left by cutting the PS down to size. This was to be done by relentless PCF attacks on the PS for "class collaborationism" (attacks designed to deny the PS the left-wing *cachet* which the Union had earlier conferred) plus lots of old-style PCF *ouvrièrisme*, all carried on with greater intensity than had been the case in 1977–8. In essence the party leadership had decided to run a Communist candidate in the 1981 presidential elections, which were seen as the critical point in "reequilibration." It is also worth noting that, for a number of reasons (most having to do with the internal play of factions inside the PCF), the Twenty-third Congress also brought a renaissance of PCF pro-Sovietism (*Cahiers du Communisme*, 1979).

Decisively turning toward a new sectarianism and with its eyes fixed upon 1981 the PCF thus wanted a very different CGT from that advocated by the "proposition force/industrial solutions" school. What mattered most was promoting a unionism which would help draw hard-and-fast ideological lines on the French left between "revolutionaries" and "reformists." Interposing a new layer of autonomous union structural reform activity to promote "industrial solutions" would not only be a diversion from these goals but also tend to inculcate "class collaborationism." What was needed instead was a new variant on traditional CGT defensive unionism, connected with more strident CGT support for the PCF in the political realm. At the core of this new pro-PCF strategic package was the notion of "struggle." The CGT's major labor market thrust should involve promoting hypermilitant defensive actions—strikes wherever possible—against manifestations of crisis (cutbacks, shutdowns, unemployment, declining living standards). Such struggles should inculcate the lesson that "the crisis was not inevitable," that crisis was occurring because of the "strategy of decline" of capital and the regime. The right and the monopolists were also in *de facto* alliance with "reformists" (the PS), in a campaign to create the "consensus" necessary to "manage the crisis." Such struggle, if conducted properly, would mobilize workers to understand which forces were on their side (the PCF and CGT) and which were not.

This new approach was not, strictly speaking, pure "transmission-beltism." The PCF and CGT set out to develop *parallel but different* formulations of sectarianism. The CGT, through "struggle," was to try to draw an absolutely clear line for workers between what was "reformist" and what was not in terms of working-class material interests—wages, hours, employment security, working conditions. The PCF was to draw a similar line, if possible, in the political sphere, which would pass between it and the PS. Ultimately, however, both lines were to push workers in the same political directions.

The defensive "struggle" approach to labor market action had an important corollary for the CGT along the interunion dimensions of its strategic package. If "proposition force/industrial solutions" advocates strongly favored continued unity-in-action with the CFDT, leaders of the pro-PCF "militant struggle" line were biassed against it. To the degree to which such unity-in-action blurred the basic distinctions which union action should draw between "strugglers" and "compromisers," it should be foregone. There was also considerable sentiment in the CGT that unity-in-action had worked to diminish the CGT's relative advantage over other unions in the same way that Union de la Gauche had undercut the PCF. There were abundant indices of CGT decline in membership and support in professional elections to support this view. Might not a reassertion of *ouvrièriste* sectarianism pay off for the CGT in the same way, it was hoped, that it was likely to pay off for the PCF? Too much *unitaire* concern had caused the CGT to dilute its identity, the argument ran. The time had come to reassert it and "reequilibrate" the union movement.

In 1978–9, then, two conflicting proposals for CGT strategic change did battle. Ironically the first clear sign that the "struggle-pro-PCF" side was winning came in iron and steel, where the "proposition-forcers" had made their greatest advances. As the steel mobilization proceeded the CGT metalworkers, still working within the guidelines of the "proposition force" memorandum, decided that a massive "March on Paris" on 23 March 1979 would be useful to dramatize the crisis. It was in the last stage of preparing this march that the balance of power within the Steelworkers' campaign changed. The major issue, to begin with, was unity-in-action with the CFDT for the march. With such unity virtually signed, sealed, and delivered (Jean-Claude Thénard, Alphonse Veronèse, both federal secretaries of the CGT FTM, and André Sainjon, the young secretary-general of the federation, were the leaders of the CGT negotiating team), Sainjon telephoned Krasucki, who was confederal secretary in charge of *revendications* and head of a special confederal committee to coordinate struggle action. As a result of this conversation Sainjon returned to break off the unity talks with the CFDT. From 23 March onwards the focus of the steel effort was now diverted and, under Krasucki's close supervision, rapidly shifted from proposing "industrial solutions" to attacking the EEC (via the Davignon Plan for steel) in ways which would be congruent with the PCF's campaign for the June 1979 elections to the European Assembly.

From this point it was simply a matter of time before the new "struggle-pro-PCF" package won out completely. It was international events, however, which underlined the end of the CGT's period of openness. After the PCF supported the Soviet intervention in Afghanistan, there was a strong push inside the CGT to do the same. Opposition inside the Bureau Confédéral prevented this, but pro-PCF elements in the leadership were none the less able to push through a resolution which refused to condemn the Soviet action. This was opposed by half of the BC (two Communists, Moynot and Gilles; one Socialist, Gaumé; an ex-Socialist, Mascarello; two Catholics, Galland and Deiss; and two "non-politicals," Buhl and Lambert). Opposition in the CGT Executive Committee was also strong and vocal. Strategic debate had given way to internal crisis in the confederation (*Le Peuple*, 1–15 February 1980). The advocates of the "struggle-pro-PCF" position, by this point in 1980, had decided to shut down the post-Fortieth Congress "springtime" and bring the CGT into line. Individual opposition on foreign policy issues coincided with strategic disagreement and both often correlated with political unorthodoxy. Thus as the CGT slid toward pro-PCF international positions and the "struggle-pro-PCF" strategic package, advocacy of "proposition force" strategy was amalgamated with other forms of dissidence. Dissidents, in turn, became "opponents" who were to be quarantined and isolated.

The "struggle-pro-PCF" strategy had its own proposals for the inter-union dimension of CGT activity, as we have already noted. With the CGT moving toward the "struggle-pro-PCF" position and the CFDT moving toward the moderation of *recentrage*, unity-in-action was contradictory until the fall of 1979, when it began to deteriorate completely. In the labor market the CGT began to propose ever more hypermilitant campaigns—such as the "week of action" prior to the *rentrée* in 1979—which the CFDT refused to support. This in turn allowed certain CGT leaders to castigate the CFDT as "reformist." Unity-in-action survived interconfederal discussions in September 1979, in only the most tenuous of ways. The CGT's position on Afghanistan further poisoned the atmosphere, prompting Edmond Maire to fulminate about the "subordination of the CGT to a restalinized PCF." Such rhetoric was responded to in kind, by regular editorials by Krasucki in *La Vie Ouvrière* (later collected and published as a book, *Syndicats et unité*) (Krasucki, 1980).

The spring of 1980 brought full rupture (Mouriaux, 1981b, 1982). The CGT resorted more persistently to "struggle" and the CFDT quite as persistently refused to cooperate. The CFDT labeled the CGT's 25 April *journée d'action* as a *"grande messe* with no future," 1 May occurred in a divided way, and the CFDT held back from a 13 May "day" on social security. Jean-Claude Laroze's report to the May CGT National Confederal Council left no doubt that things had passed the point of no return (*Le Peuple*, 1–15 June 1980) and in June a communiqué from the CGT made the split definitive (*Le Peuple*, 1–15 July 1980). The CGT's position saw the political and economic world divided into "two camps," the camp of "struggle" against capital, and those who desired to "manage the crisis." The CFDT, following its *recentrage*, had joined the latter camp. In the words of the CGT statement breaking off unity-in-action:

> it is indispensable to be clear about the non-inevitability of the crisis, about the necessity for action, the possibility of forcing the regime to retreat, even on advanced kinds of demands, and on the nature of the divergences which separate union organizations, particularly on the profound significance of the CFDT's new strategy.

Then, as Séguy announced more bluntly, "all unity-in-action at the top is impossible as long as the CFDT has not abandoned its policy of *recentrage*" (*Le Monde*, 17 July 1980).

By autumn 1980, then, the "struggle-pro-PCF" strategy was fully in place. In the labor market this strategy was characterized by CGT organizational efforts—alone—to produce sharp local struggles and national campaigns to say *non* to the symptoms of crisis. This strategic thrust had both virtues and faults. As a variant of traditional CGT defensive unionism it gained support by tapping old reflexes at the base and at middle levels of CGT organizations. In its anti-reformist sectarianism it was congruent with the PCF's mood, important given the predominance of Communists in the apparatus of the CGT. It could promote a degree of CGT cohesion, then. But it did so at the cost of greatly intensified internal intolerance in the confederation. Moreover, generating struggle was to prove very difficult in the absence of unity-in-action at a moment when the crisis was cutting deeply into rank-and-file mobilization. Here the strategy was contradictory. Even in normal circumstances unity-in-action was the *sine qua non* of any union success in France. In crisis unity became even more essential to generate action. Yet the CGT had decided that it was possible to promote action *and* decree an end to unity-in-action. Thus the confederation's efforts at creating "struggle" either failed altogether or, at best, led to voluntaristic, cadre-type actions (Moynot, 1982a, pp. 61–5). In fact the "struggle-pro-PCF" strategy led the CGT toward the kind of vanguardist/substitutionist activity which had characterized the confederation's behavior during the Cold War.

The third dimension of the new CGT strategy was political. The congruence of the CGT's labor market activity with the general goals of the PCF as it moved toward the 1981 presidential campaign escaped no one. After the *rentrée* of 1980, as the election came closer, the confederation and its leaders began to support Marchais in open ways. Great pains were taken, repeatedly, to point out that the Marchais program and the CGT program were in agreement about most important things, while the PS's program diverged from the CGT's on essential matters. Séguy and Krasucki both urged voting for Marchais, although as usual putting on their "political" as opposed to "trade union" hats when doing so. Then in March 1981 considerable effort was devoted to getting top CGT leaders to sign a petition in favor of Marchais, even if there were a large number of abstainers. In general, the CGT mobilized *politically* in much more active ways behind the Marchais candidacy than it had done even in 1977–8 for the PCF.

By early 1981 failure along most dimensions of this strategy was apparent. Vanguardism, the absence of unity-in-action, and the effects of crisis combined to produce mediocre results in the labor market which CGT leaders, Krasucki in particular, tried to mask by absurdly optimistic pronouncements. Moreover, strong evidence emerged that the new strategy was accelerating the CGT's organizational decline, rather than stopping it. The confederation admitted to a 15 percent membership loss from 1977 through 1980. Well-informed sources estimated that the real figure was 32–33 percent for these years, with a net loss of 20 percent in the 1979–80 period alone (Kergoat, 1982b). The CGT losses in professional elections, which had been steady since the later 1960s, also accelerated. Severe financial difficulties, leading to layoffs of CGT staff, bore further witness to such problems.

Such dramatic labor market problems were eclipsed by the political failures of 1981, however. The Marchais results were as much of a catastrophe for the CGT as for the PCF. The "struggle-pro-PCF" strategic package had been designed, in large part, to enlist the CGT in the task of defeating the Socialist candidate in 1981. Implied was that the confederation would function in a setting characterized by right-wing rule for an indeterminate future, during which sectarian approaches would be pursued continuously to reconstitute CGT and PCF strength. The collapse of the PCF vote, the PS electoral breakthrough, the Mitterrand victory, the Union de la Gauche accepted by the PCF with an electoral gun to its head, and left government, all added up to a complete lack of options for the CGT. Whatever else the confederation might do in the circumstances which emerged after May–June 1981, it could certainly not continue its "struggle-pro-PCF" stance.

One final result of the victory of "struggle-pro-PCF" strategy after 1979 was the beginning of sectarian "normalization" in the CGT. The opponents of the new strategy who, more often than not, had also been the proponents of "proposition force" options prior to 1979 were first ostracized, then forced out, one by one. René Buhl and Jacqueline Lambert retired from the Bureau Confédéral in1980, hounded by attacks based on their signature on the Union dans les Luttes petition. The 1981 elections brought more. A dossier of accusations had been prepared in the Bureau Confédéral against Jean-Louis Moynot in the period between the presidential and legislative elections. Moynot would undoubtedly have been fired or forced to resign in June 1981 had not a combination of his own brief hospitalization and the accession to power of Communist ministers given him a stay of execution. The exclusion of Moynot and Christiane Gilles from preparatory discussions for the Forty-first Congress led to their resignations in October 1981 (*Le Peuple*, 1–15 October 1981). *Antoinette*, the CGT magazine for women which Gilles had made into the most interesting and innovative of all CGT publications, was "normalized" in May 1982 (its editor Chantal Rogerat and her staff were fired), allegedly because it had allowed pro-Solidarity (Poland) letters to be published. The most extraordinary casualty of normalization, however, was Georges Séguy himself. Séguy was held responsible by the PCF leadership for the "crisis in the CGT" because of his encouragement of opening in 1978–9. This "crisis" in turn was cited as one of the more important reasons why the Marchais campaign had not been "heard" by workers. The decision that Séguy should "retire"—in fact, be fired—was made, in all likelihood, in the immediate aftermath of the Marchais results by top PCF leaders.

Conclusions: The CGT in the New Political Setting

The major result up to 1981 of the CGT's strategic response to crisis was failure. During these years the CGT deployed two different strategic packages, each of which was oriented ultimately toward political payoffs. Both collapsed in political disasters. The first package, which had been painstakingly prepared over the 1960s, self-destructed in the dissolution of Union de la Gauche in 1977–8. The second disintegrated in the Marchais campaign of 1980–1. The two packages each over-politicized the CGT in ways which undermined its capacities to function in the labor market. Thus as 1981 approached the CGT was well advanced in organizational decline, as membership figures, finances, and results in professional elections indicated clearly.

How did the CGT react to the new political setting? Past strategic failings ruled out certain things, *a priori*. The systematic eradication through "normalization" of "proposition force/industrial solutions" forces inside the confederation meant that the CGT had very little of a creative nature to contribute to the practical design of many of these reform proposals. The acrimony and disunity which prevailed between unions, in large part a product of CGT strategy, meant that large-scale union mobilizations of the *Front Populaire*/Matignon kind were unlikely in the extreme. For the same reasons of disunity, the labor movement would be quite unlikely to be able to create informed popular support for and/or provide the core of an intelligent, popularly based left wing for the new regime. The new regime, with its rather pronounced "new middle class," *Colbertiste* and technocratic leanings, could well have used any and all of these things.

The CGT's slogan during year one of the new regime—*réussir le changement*—covered the same kind of ambivalence toward the new regime as that of the PCF. With the PCF in the majority and Communist ministers in the government, the hard edge of the CGT's pre-1981 anti-"reformist" sectarianism disappeared of course. None the less, the confederation (whose secretary-general-designate, Henri Krasucki, was allegedly among those in the PCF Bureau Politique who opposed PCF ministers) did not move toward any new strategic reflection. Instead it maintained as much as possible of its pre-1981 posture under the rubric of "critical support" for the new regime (not unlike the PCF's "party of struggle, party of government" position). This was a policy combining both "wait and see" and *deux fers au feu*.

"Critical support" allowed the CGT to act as a pressure group on the government for those policies it desired without making any substantial commitment to support the government down the line. In the circum-stances this was a reasonably astute position. One of the unique features of the post-1981 situation, comparatively, was that the Socialists had no organic—and few informal—ties to organized labor. Therefore, they had to bargain hard for union support. This in turn allowed the CGT to choose between different ways of getting what it could—by industrial struggle, the threat of industrial struggle, or wheeling-and-dealing with the government. The CGT had already obtained some tangible returns to this attitude as of mid-1982. Its position prevailed in conflicts about remuneration for the 39-hour week (no reduction in pay). The Auroux reforms promised enhanced CGT power on the shopfloor and the same could also follow from new industrial relations arrangements in nation-alized industries. Finally, hard struggle in the spring of 1982 held out some promise that more egregious anti-union employers—Peugeot-

Citroën, in particular—might finally have to deal seriously with the CGT.

The negative side of the CGT's posture was not negligible, however. Continuing as much as possible from the pre-1981 years meant, among other things, pro-Sovietism in international affairs. This led the CGT to react to the emergence of Solidarity in Poland in only the most grudging and minimal ways (the CGT never published the Gdansk accords of the summer of 1980, for example). Later the CGT followed the PCF in approving the Jaruzelski repression, a position which caused renewed internal difficulty for the union and, undoubtedly, additional loss of support and credibility. Moreover, disunity and conflict with the CFDT persisted, in ways which led both confederations into a competitive bravado about defending the workers which did little to help the new government.

Despite the new political situation, the major thrust of the pivotal CGT Forty-first Congress in June 1982 was internal: the new CGT leadership under Henri Krasucki was determined to "take the confederation in hand." In doctrinal and strategic terms this meant lining up the CGT behind a rewritten version of the recent past which wiped the bitter conflicts and failures of 1979–81 off the record. The Congress' *document d'orientation* asserted, for example, that one major source of left success in 1981 had been "the tenacious resistance of the working class, in which the CGT played an essential role ... nourishing multiple struggles on all terrains," and this after the CGT leadership had done all in its power to *prevent* any Socialist success in these years (*Le Peuple*, 16–28 February 1982, p. 5)! The Krasucki reading of the Fortieth Congress and its aftermath was enforced to delineate appropriate and inappropriate behavior as well. The CGT was the only labor organization in France which had consistently resisted powerful efforts toward "consensus" on "managing the capitalist crisis" and its notions about how to organize such resistance had been impeccably correct. It followed from this that one was either in agreement with these notions or else had slipped into the "camp" of the "reformist" adversaries. In particular, anyone in the CGT who had strayed from this hard line in the direction of greater realism about economic crisis or in that of "proposition force" unionism risked being portrayed as an agent of the CFDT and *recentrage*. In other words, the Forty-first Congress was a referendum on the hard-line policies which had been put into place after the defeat of the movements toward "opening" seen in the Fortieth Congress. One was either *for* the Krasucki line or disloyal. "Oppositional" figures, including several former top leaders, were allowed to address the Congress—although their reception from congressists was glacial when not openly hostile— but were then read out of the organization at all levels for their disloyalty and "reformism."[14] Partly because of this major "reading out," there was a substantial renewal of national leadership personnel around Krasucki, who became the new secretary-general.[15]

The proposals and proceedings of the Forty-first Congress strongly restated the CGT's traditional "popular Keynesian" focus on working-class demand expansion, the need to "soak the rich" rather than impose austerity on popular social groups (evident in the Congress' rejection of the government's June 1982 income policies), and the confederation's post-1979 militant "struggle" rhetoric. In all this, as well as in the Congress' theorization of economic processes—which was if anything even closer to the PCF's than it had been—there was a great deal of continuity. At the same time, however, the leadership was eager to proffer "support," even if guarded "critical" support, to the new government. There was much talk about how the new situation, if far from what the CGT really desired in terms of social change, did make important reforms possible. The CGT would thus use its resources to move things forward. Evidence that this was more than Congress talk was abundant. In terms of union tactics in the labor market the confederation had begun to reverse some of its earlier priorities. Rather than searching to develop local actions into large, mass-based branch or national movements of the *journée d'action* type, the CGT had begun to stress decentralized, local movements which, while they might conceivably win local victories, would not create a difficult national industrial climate for the government. Moreover, there were at the Congress insistent rumors in the air that some new movement toward unity-in-action negotiations with the CFDT was imminent.

The Forty-first Congress, then, faced in several directions at once. What attracted most attention of course was its most obvious goal, reconsolidating the confederation around unquestioned support of the Krasucki leadership. CGT officials and *permanents* were to line up behind the secretary-general and his positions, or leave. On the other hand, in strategic terms the Congress consecrated a *deux fers au feu* posture which was not devoid of shrewdness. Perpetuating a basic "popular Keynesian" defensive approach to the labor market allowed the confederation to be reasonably sure of being in the right place to respond to the emergence of rank-and-file discontent. Given the extremely gloomy economic prospects of the moment—Pierre Joxe, the Socialist parliamentary leader, had announced that there would be "two terrible years" after the June 1982 devaluation—wage/price policies crisis—such a posture seemed wise. Moreover, in a situation in which the "recentered" CFDT had announced its willingness to accept austerity and had clearly demonstrated its lack of eagerness to promote local union action, the CGT might well profit along the important strategic dimension of interunion competition. On top of this, in a series of gestures for both intra- and extra-Confederal consumption, a number of CGT leaders began to resurrect some of the positions promoted earlier by "oppositional" elements—the need for "industrial solutions" to the crisis, the desirability of *conseils d'atelier et de service*. It is of course classic in the history of organizations like the CGT that a purge be followed by the official adoption of many of the positions advanced by those purged. None the less, the resumption of such themes by the CGT might well give the confederation a more plausible voice in national economic policy discussions in the near future.

The CGT's basic "popular Keynesianism" was also congruent with the PCF's ambiguous political position. Communist participation in government after 1981 had been a *faute de mieux* choice. After a disastrous period of strategic failures *seriatim*, the party could come up with nothing better, despite the bitter taste of serving as a *force d'appoint* for the PS. As things stood at the time of the CGT's Forty-first Congress the PCF also looked in several different directions. If the left coalition government succeeded in the medium term, then the PCF could hope to be able to claim part of the credit. However, were the government to falter or even fall, in ways which elicited popular and working-class impatience, then the CGT's insistence upon a posture which would allow it to capitalize on such feelings might indirectly give the party itself new opportunities to recoup its fortunes, probably by leaving the government and aligning itself on the side of popular discontent.

The CGT's Forty-first Congress posture of covering all bases through "critical support" of the left experiment in France did not lack astuteness, then. The CGT desired to maximize its returns from whatever change occurred, while minimizing its concessions to, and public affection for, the new government. In the circumstances this seemed a plausible way to reassert its identity and strengthen its position while awaiting the longer-run outcome of left rule. It should be said of course that the CGT was not alone in adopting such a posture. One of the most striking aspects of the first year of left power in France was the paucity of unambiguous goodwill and enthusiasm for the new regime emanating from any major left social actors. Strategic reserve made most sense for the CGT for deeper reasons, however. The new Socialist-led experiment in France took shape in contradictory and problematic ways.

In June 1981 the new government had placed its hopes in a dualistic scenario. In the short-to-medium run mildly expansive Keynesian macroeconomic policies would allow some growth, limit the further growth of unemployment, and produce at least moderate material rewards for the political constituencies of the left, thus consolidating electoral support. While such immediate policies were being pursued, the regime would progressively put into place the longer-run major structural changes which, it believed, would "reconquer the domestic market" and increase French international competitiveness, thereby guaranteeing future growth. Here of course we are referring to the package of changes involving massive nationalizations, increased research and development, new planning and industrial policies. The new government's short-to-medium-run optimistic Keynesianism had collapsed by the spring of 1982, however. In an international context dominated by austerity and retrenchment even the mild demand stimulation promoted in France led to inordinate inflation levels and acute international trade problems culminating in the devaluation of June 1982 and the new austerity measures which accompanied it. From this point onwards the economic and political future of the left in power was murky at best. By endowing itself with a strategy which would allow it to move in a number of different directions in such a future the CGT was simply demonstrating prudence. Such prudence, however, sharply diminished the resources upon which the left regime could count at a critical juncture.

Notes: Chapter 3

1   The CGT, as a well-established and somewhat routinized organization, had a settled base, mainly in mass-production industry, which had become accustomed in the years after World War II to defensive types of mobilization. Moreover, the CGT's organizational infrastructure at federation and departmental union levels, was well oiled to produce such mobilization.

   The CFDT, in contrast, was an organization in rapid transition in the 1960s much less attached than the CGT to any such traditional approaches. Thus it could be open to "new" demands which stemmed primarily from the shift in French industrial development from extensive capital investment to rationalization as a result of growing competitive pressure in the international market. Both the intensification of work and plant shutdowns became issues at this point, contributing to the new demands. The CFDT's competitive position in the interunion sphere with the CGT also led it to be sensitive to this series of real issues which the CGT seemed not to perceive. On the mobilization around new demands see Crouch and Pizzorno, 1978.

2   The PCF's theoretical change began in the late 1960s, in *Economie et Politique*, around Paul Boccara and was eventually codified in the 1972 *Traité ... le capitalisme monopoliste d'état* (PCF, 1972). The conceptual vocabulary of this theory began appearing in CGT discussions in 1969 and continued throughout the 1970s.

3   This was the period of high-visibility CFDT local strikes; for example, those of the OS at Renault-le Mans in 1972, Pennaroya, les Nouvelles Galeries de Thionville and le Joint Français in St Brieuc in 1972, and of course LIP in 1973. For the 1971 actions see Durand and Dubois, 1975; for others see Capdevielle *et al.*, 1975; Kergoat, 1975.

4   The PCF, reacting to the first major evidence in 1974 that Union de la Gauche was primarily benefiting the PS, shifted its line, beginning at its Congress in 1974—*Cahiers du Communisme*, 1974—in a way which stressed renewed *ouvrièrisme* and industrial militancy. One manifestation of this was the party's attempt, in 1974–5, to be present and active in industrial conflicts. This "sharp-struggle" lead by the party was rapidly taken to heart by the CGT.

5   These actions, coordinated by Henri Krasucki for the most part, were symbolized in the long Fédération du Livre strike against the "dismantling" of the *Parisien Libéré*. Beginning with a militant sitdown strike, the *Parisien Libéré* affair turned into a virtual war between the strikers and Baron Amaury, owner of the paper. The dispute was eventually settled by negotiation, but not without a sizable loss of jobs. This kind of settlement, in which immense and costly union efforts over months led to victories whose fruits were incommensurate with the price paid for them, was to be typical of many such CGT struggles into the 1980s (*Râteau, Chaix*, and the like).

6   The CGT first responded to *rupture* by asserting that the CGT program was similar, in terms of nationalizations, to the PCF's position: *Le Peuple*, 1–15 October 1977. This posture was continued throughout, in CGT announcements and in a later manifesto: *Il faut que vive le programme commun*, November 1977. The confederation more openly sided with the PCF on programmatic issues after a CGT delegation made the rounds of all left parties in December. By early 1978 major CGT leaders, including Georges Séguy, were urging votes for the PCF.

7   The CGT had a longstanding practice of avoiding political, monochromatic leadership bodies, such that there were always minorities of *Socialistes d'office*, Catholics and "non-political" non-Communists on the Bureau Confédéral and the Commission Executive, although there were fewer on the CCN, where federation and UD leaders met, since most such leaders were PCF. In the 1977–8 campaign many of the

Socialistes d'office turned into real Socialists in the heat of the electoral campaign. Their efforts to keep the CGT from going too far in support of the PCF were a source of embarrassment to top CGT leaders. Claude Germon, editor of *Le Peuple* and a Socialist candidate for Parliament, was an important figure in this, as were Pierre Carassus and Pierre Feuilly on the CE.

8   Séguy had a strong record for reformist initiatives in the CGT. The 1969 Congress, for example, was somewhat critical of certain CGT practices in the May–June 1968 period and proposed "democratization" of the confederation, under Séguy's prodding. The proposals were repeated at the 1971 Grenoble Congress of the CGT Metalworkers and the Ile de Ré CCN of the same year. Séguy also had a deserved reputation for being "à la chasse" when PCF pressure toward sectarianism on the CGT made the situation difficult for him.

9   Séguy was in contact during this period with Jean Kanapa, who was the *éminence grise* behind PCF Eurocommunization (also renowned inside the party as Georges Marchais's brain). Kanapa was an essential figure in PCF strategic infighting in the mid-1970s and he was known, up to his death in the summer of 1978, to be pushing hard against the party's conversion to sectarianism in the 1977–8 period.

10 The early project was straight state monopoly capitalism/PCF theory in inspiration, a posture which posited that the crisis was primarily national—due to the misdeeds of the monopoly caste and the right—and that crisis issues for workers were primarily material-defensive. The changes worked in the document moved toward recognizing the international character of the crisis and toward perceiving work process and work authority issues as central for workers.

11 Here the work of the CGT Center for Economic Research under Jean-Louis Moynot was important. The Center did a number of specific monographs on French multinationals in 1977–9 (Rhône-Poulenc, Suez-Pont-à-Mousson), together with a number of industry studies, and worked on energy questions extensively. (See, for example, CGT, 1978a.)

12 The changing strategy of the Italian CGIL from the "hot autumn" onwards was a clear inspiration to "proposition-forcers": see Couffignal, 1979.

13 During the 1977–8 election campaign, when the CGT attempted to mobilize its base to support the PCF on nationalizations, it became quite clear that the base, if it believed that nationalizations in principle were good things, had very little idea what they were supposed to be economically and industrially and, more specifically, how nationalizations would affect their own work situations.

14 The Congress' attitude toward the *oppositionnels* was symbolized by the initial refusal of the *service d'ordre* to allow René Buhl and Jacqueline Lambert into the Congress hall. This act of aggressive rudeness to two former members of the Bureau Confédéral was later rectified, but not before the press had publicized it throughout the country. Jean-Louis Moynot, another critic, was allowed to make a long speech to the Congress: *Le Peuple*, 13 June–18 July 1982, p. 75; and earned thereby a long and pointed response from Henri Krasucki accusing him of disloyalty, of misrepresenting the Fortieth Congress and of CFDT-style reformism—Moynot was allegedly an agent of *recentrage*: *Le Peuple*, 13 June–18 July 1982, p. 110.

None of the major critics were reelected to official positions at the Congress, including the national Bureau, but also to the Commission Executive (from which Pierre Feuilly, Yves Peyrichou, and Aimé Pastre were removed). Moreover, in pre-Congress days the national leadership moved, in quite unsubtle ways, to "normalize" the Fédération des Finances—which had been critical. We have already mentioned the "normalization" of *Antoinette* which had occurred in May.

15 As of the Fortieth Congress in 1978, the Bureau Confédéral had had sixteen members. At the Forty-first Congress it was enlarged to eighteen. Since seven members of the 1978 Bureau had left by the Forty-first Congress (the critics, Gilles, Buhl, Lambert, Moynot, plus Séguy, Livio Mascarello, and André Allamy who retired) this meant that nine members, half of the BC, were new. Some of the new confederal secretaries had been installed prior to the Congress, as substitutes for the resigned critics (Gérard Alézard, Alphonse Veronèse, Bernard Lacombe, and Jacqueline Léonard). In general tried and true methods were used to find these new leaders. A number of them were

virtual unknowns, recruited because of their ascriptive qualities—because they were women, Catholics, Socialists, or non-Communists either taken separately or combined (Lydia Brovelli and Bernard Lacombe fit here). Others brought such ascriptive titles plus proven CGT experience (Veronèse). Besides such concerns with maintaining a formal political balance between Communists and non-Communists at the top, a traditional CGT practice, there were a number of noteworthy aspects of this leadership renewal worth mentioning: because anti-Socialist sectarianism had reached a fever pitch by Congress preparing time, there had existed a very serious danger that there would be a wholesale purge of Socialists and any other unorthodox figures both in the election of delegates to the Congress and in the reconstruction of federation and departmental union leaderships. The risk was so obvious that Lionel Jospin, first-secretary of the PS, summoned Krasucki to warn him against allowing this to happen. In some cases, however, the damage had already been done, leading to caricatural incidents of organizational manipulation from the top—moving in to federation deliberations to force the reversal of decisions already taken, for example.

Krasucki, whose desire to bring order and predictability to the confederation was clear, made sure that certain problems would be unlikely to reproduce themselves. The confederal *service économique* had been the major locus of "proposition force" innovations, for example, under the leadership of Jean-Louis Moynot. Krasucki saw to it that the staff of the *service* was fired or otherwise dispersed (in the process dismantling one of the more creative centers for economic reflection and research in France) while appointing a hard-line Communist, Gérard Alézard, to shape things up. The replacement of Christiane Gilles and the firing of the *Antoinette* team, plus the appointment of Jacqueline Léonard, amounted to the same thing.

Prior to the Forty-first Congress of course, both Séguy and Krasucki had been members of the Bureau Politique of the PCF. In the CGT leadership there had existed a clear division of labor between them. Séguy was secretary-general, the organizer and coordinator of the confederation, while Krasucki had been the "party man" with a number of essential organizational levers at his fingertips (*La Vie Ouvrière*, in charge of the *revendications* sector, supervisor of Michel Warcholack who himself controlled the CGT's cadres throughout federations and departmental unions). At the PCF Twenty-fourth Congress in February 1982 of course Séguy had "retired" from the Bureau Politique, preparatory to his retirement from the CGT at the Forty-first Congress. At the same Twenty-fourth Congress of the party Louis Viannet, leader of the CGT PTT Federation, had been promoted to the Bureau Politique, and at the Forty-first Congress of the CGT he joined the CGT Bureau. Subsequently there was every indication that the division of labor between Krasucki and Séguy earlier was being reconstructed between Viannet and Krasucki, with Krasucki assuming the public roles earlier held by Séguy and Viannet accumulating most of the sources of organizational leverage which Krasucki had once held.

4

The CFDT: From the Union of Popular Forces to the Success of Social Change

RENÉ MOURIAUX

The French Democratic Confederation of Labor (CFDT) exerts a certain fascination as an "original phenomenon" (Andrieux and Lignon, 1981), or at any rate an organization that can present itself as such and thereby enlist genuine support. While the CFDT placed itself at the forefront of the May–June 1968 strike movement, the following year it endorsed centrist Alain Poher in the presidential elections. After having supported the contracts of progress (*contrats de progrès*) promoted in 1969 by the Chaban-Delmas government, the CFDT in 1970 would call for a negotiating procedure purposely designed to disrupt the socioeconomic system.[1] In 1978 the CFDT adopted its policy of "recentering" (*recentrage*), and the following year its leader predicted future defeats for the left (*Le Républicain Lorrain*, 6 December 1979; Maire, 1980a, pp. 181–8). Its vigorous support of the Mauroy government nearly brought it the label of "official union," yet in October 1981 it would criticize the regime for the sluggishness of change.[2] Quite frequently, therefore, the confederation astonishes with its rapid shifts in direction and its protean mobility.

Ideological Evolution and the Ideology of Evolution

The CFDT came into being as a result of a change in the ruling majority of the CFTC (French Confederation of Christian Workers) at a special convention held in Issy-les-Moulineaux on 6–7 November 1964. At this convention Eugène Descamps, speaking for the Bureau Confédéral, presented a report appropriately entitled "The Evolution and [Future] Perspectives of the CFTC" (*Formation*, no. 59 supplement, September–October 1964). As this document had a major impact on the future of the organization, it merits review here.

Descamps introduced his report with a brief history of the CFTC in which he made three main points (CFDT, 1971, pp. 19–55). Although it had its origins in social catholicism, outside the working-class movement, and its leadership had been white collar, the CFTC had gradually sunk roots in the world of labor. The confederation, too, had asserted its independence *vis-à-vis* the church and Christian Democracy. Rejecting both the subordination of the CGT to the PCF and the weakness of Force Ouvrière, the CFTC sought to promote a unionism founded upon a recognition of individual dignity. This could only reach its full development if the union was not shackled by statutory references to a Christian heritage.

The second part of this document analyzed changes in the contemporary world situation. Eugène Descamps, in his attempt to decipher the "signs of the times" (an expression taken from the Apocrypha), drew on work conducted by INSEE and INED as well as material to be published in the SEDEIS bulletin and made reference to the writings of such scholars as economists Jean Fourastié and Pierre Massé and sociologists Jacques Ellul, Raymond Aron, and Vance Packard. According to Descamps, underlying forces were inexorably transforming France into a society of abundance. Its way of life would undergo not just quantitative changes; economic growth would be accompanied by a spread and diversification of wage labor, increased urbanization, a longer life expectancy, and a rise in new technologies. The spread of mass man (*massification*) would generate conformism and depoliticization. Trade unionism would be confronted with a double challenge: to adapt to the changes taking place and to combat new forms of alienation.

The third section argued that the "other trade union forces in France" were incapable of responding to the problems of the future. The conclusion attempted to establish that the CFTC, by "deconfessionalizing" and deepening its humanist and democratic conception of trade unionism, would be able to tap new energies. The clearly stated objective of overcoming the traditional cleavage between Catholics and laïcs, of assuring "the convergence" of Christian personalism and democratic socialism, rested on a dual rejection of "materialist society" and "totalitarian communism."[3] This found expression in the fundamental strategic options adopted: trade union autonomy, democratic planning, democratization of the firm, contractual politics, European construction, and assistance to developing countries. Whatever precautions might have been taken in the phrasing or whatever concessions were made, notably in drawing up the new statutes, the new majority had forcefully articulated its aims.[4]

The CFDT (the name change adopted at the 1964 Convention) at first paid for deconfessionalization with a reduction in support. A minority, including such important figures as Joseph Sauty, Jacques Tessier, and Jean Bornard, quit and established the "maintained CFTC." The loss of members was officially estimated at around 60,000. The early efforts of the new leadership thus aimed at stemming defections and asserting the confederation's legitimacy. Necessary, if mundane, battles were waged to retain rights to the CFTC logo and property holdings. Gilbert Grandval, then Minister of Labor (May 1962 to January 1966), ruled against the minority in the suits. His successor, Jean-Marcel Jeanneney, would quickly move to give the CFTC recognition as a representative organization (31 March 1966).[5]

At the start, therefore, the momentum that deconfessionalization was expected to generate was undercut by the schism and the ensuing quarrels. In order to limit the openings for attack by its opponents, and in light of the failure of Gaston Defferre's political initiative in June 1965, the CFDT's new majority tempered its ambition.[6] This was reflected in the position adopted with regard to the 1965 presidential elections. The confederation issued no directives on how its sympathizers should vote but instead asked workers "to be cognizant of the consequences for them, as well as for the country, of a continuation [in power] of the current regime" and "to choose an opposition candidate likely to present a democratic alternative to the present situation." In fact the CFDT declined to choose between Jean Lecanuet and François Mitterrand, which the latter would long remember (Mitterrand, 1980, p. 126).

The Thirty-third Congress (11–14 November 1965) was marked by a concern not only to strengthen internal cohesion but also, in face of managerial intransigence, to impart a new impetus to trade union action in 1966. Taking responsibility for accelerating events, Eugène Descamps met with CGT leaders and on 10 January 1966 concluded an agreement on united action with the confederation headed by Benoît Frachon (Declercq, 1974, pp. 124–8). This interunion entente prompted a revival of industrial struggles at both the firm and national levels. Days of action (*journées d'action*) were launched to defend social security and employment (notably on 17 May 1966, 23 November 1966, 1 February 1967, and 15 May 1967). The CFDT took care to spell out its ideological differences with the CGT and the parameters of the accord. At the Thirty-fourth Congress (9–12 November 1964) Eugène Descamps stressed that "the entente with the CGT has remained, as we intended, at a tactical stage" (*Syndicalisme*, no. 1152A, 9 September 1967, p. 13). To illustrate his point he cited CFDT refusal to stage a common 1 May rally or to undertake joint demonstrations on fiscal policy, the problems facing women, or the Vietnam war. He asserted, however, that the confederation had reaped benefits from the initiative (*Syndicalisme*, no. 1152A, 9 September 1967, p. 14):

> [Unity of action with the CGT] has helped to promote the CFDT name and bring it to public attention. Our militants have been seasoned. Mass action has proved educational for many of them who have learned better methods for organizing strikes, marches, etc.

Reporting on the hundred-odd speeches given during the course of the debate on the activity report (*rapport d'activité*) at the Thirty-fourth Congress, the CFDT confederal journal *Syndicalisme* (no. 1162, 16 November 1967) remarked that "unity of action was the major theme in the speeches; among the speakers, there were no 'nays' [heard] but only 'yeas' and 'yes, but ...'." While not incorrect, this depiction of the discussions downplayed the intensity of the reserves expressed and ignored the frequent references to a deterioration of relations between CFDT and CGT organs at the base.[7] Unity with the CGT was so little evident that negotiations (initiated before the CGT–CFDT pact) with Force Ouvrière continued.[8] By late 1967 real strains had developed in CGT–CFDT relations.[9] It was in this same period that relations between the CFDT and the FGDS (Federation of the Democratic and Socialist Left) became close.

During the pre-May 1968 period, as the first tremors of the mass social movement appeared, especially at Caen (Berliet) and Rhodiaceta, the CFDT evidenced a desire to disengage from the CGT and challenge the latter in the course of these radical struggles (*Le Monde*, 22 March 1967, 7 February 1968: Lettieri and Santi, 1969). The CFDT's refusal to sign the agreement on compensation for partial unemployment, approved by all the other unions on 22 February 1968, demonstrated this new intransigence at the national level.

When the student uprising came, the CFDT immediately gave it the union's support. Although the CFDT had favored a one-hour stoppage on 13 May, it finally accepted the CGT proposal for a 24-hour strike. Thereafter the CFDT did its best to place itself in the vanguard of the worker revolt. On 16 May 1968 the Bureau Confédéral called for the setting up in factories of "democratic structures based on [the principle of] self-management (*autogestion*)." This directive on *autogestion*, which had never been debated at a national CFDT congress, would serve to identify the CFDT with the May movement.[10]

On the morrow of the Grenelle negotiations the CFDT agreed to be represented at the Charlety Stadium rally on the 27th by Julien and Fredo Krumnow. On the 29th Eugène Descamps made an appeal to Pierre Mendès-France, "the man capable of guaranteeing the workers' rights conquered in the firms in the course of recent days, to carry out the indispensable structural reforms, to lead a team likely to respond to the great desire for democratization expressed by students and workers, and, therefore, to assume, with the left parties and the new [social] forces, the responsibilities of power" (CFDT, 1968, pp. 128–9). After de Gaulle succeeded in turning the political situation around, the CFDT sought to occupy the union terrain, pushing conflicts as far as possible and putting up opposition to any repressive measures. When the strike wave finally receded, the CFDT found itself strengthened by 250,000 new members. Its tendency toward spontaneity was reinforced, and the confederation took considerable distance from the CGT, criticizing the latter's "quantitativism" and its allegiance to the PCF.

With the fading of the epic 1968 events, CFDT activity began to lose its coherence. At the national level moderation set in, as the confederation lent its support to Alain Poher in the second-ballot voting of the 1969 presidential election. It was also sympathetic to the tone of the new Chaban-Delmas government which, under the authority of Jacques Delors, the Prime Minister's "social" advisor and former CFDT activist, prepared "contracts of progress" for the "New Society." In contrast, at the local level, the CFDT was noteworthy for the tough fights waged in conjunction with leftists (*gauchistes*) at Ernault-Somua of Cholet, spray-painters in Sochaux, and convoy personnel at Usinor-Dunkerque. At its Thirty-fifth Congress (5–10 May 1970) as many as six different currents contended.[11] The Congress ended with the adoption of the Jeanson report on "Perspectives and Strategy" (*Syndicalisme*, no. 1279A, February 1970; CFDT, 1971, pp. 125–41), which officially committed the CFDT to socialism. Socialism, in the CFDT's view, rested on three pillars: social ownership of the means of production, self-management (*autogestion*), and democratic planning.

The CGT viewed the CFDT's Congress in a positive light, albeit with some reservations, and proposed a resumption of joint action, abandoned since 1968. In November the CFDT agreed to reopen talks, and a second interunion accord was eventually signed on 1 December 1970. The CFDT still made efforts to differentiate itself from the CGT by asserting its ideological autonomy and supporting spectacular strikes, such as those at Ferodo, Pennaroya, Girosteel, Joint Français, and Renault-Le-Mans (Capdevielle *et al.*, 1975, pp. 8–14). While the CGT sought to downplay differences and underscore common ground, the CFDT chose to act on unifying issues and publicly air disagreements. The two confederations spelled out their differing conceptions of socialism with the publication of a CGT text on 31 March 1971 and a CFDT "contribution" on 30 October 1971. The CFDT, now directed by Edmond Maire due to the severe illness of Eugène Descamps, seemed more than ever to draw its inspiration from an affirmation of its distinctiveness *vis-à-vis* its major union rival. Generally speaking from June 1968 to June 1972, as a result of the collapse of the FGDS and faltering of the PSU (United Socialist Party), "the CFDT came to play a role beyond that of a trade union" (Martinet, 1979, p. 149).

With the signature in June 1972 of the left's Common Program, the CFDT faced a major dilemma: how to maintain its independent stance without appearing to impede a process which carried so many hopes? The confederation adopted a position of "critical support" in an attempt to circumvent this problem. The CFDT issued a call for a "union of popular forces," which would be narrower than the anti-capitalist alliance envisioned by the left yet more anti-capitalist, in the CFDT's view, because both the PSU and the *autogestionnaire* extreme left were to be included (Maire, 1973, pp 17–19; CFDT, 1974a, p. 19). This line was bolstered by a radicalization of the confederation's actions (prompted and facilitated when Pierre Messmer replaced Jacques Chaban-Delmas as Prime Minister).

In essence the CFDT was in the heyday of the LIP watch factory strike. At the Thirty-sixth Congress (30 May–3 June 1973) opposition to the "critical support" line emerged in the course of debates on socialist transition. Roger Toutain, in the name of thirty-seven locals and federations (Textiles, Health Services, Banking, PTT, and the PTT-Rhône), proposed an amendment stating that "the conquest of political and economic power is a prerequisite to the establishment of a self-managed socialist society." This was an indirect plea for the CFDT to give more serious consideration to the Union of the Left.

In the wake of the 1974 presidential election, when François Mitterrand garnered 49.3 percent of the vote, only 300,000 votes short of a majority, the CFDT underwent a shift in attitude. On 25 May Mitterrand appealed for a regrouping of all those with socialist leanings; on the 27th the CFDT Bureau Confédéral declared that the PS leader's call was a "positive element." On 11 June several CFDT notables issued an appeal for the formation of the broad socialist force which the workers' movement needed; among the signatories were Albert Detraz, Pierre Héritier, Jacques Julliard, and Jacques Chérèque (*Le Monde*, 12 June 1974). Within the "third component" of the proposed regrouping two distinct positions soon emerged: one favoring Michel Rocard and his PSU supporters, the other leaning toward the Center for Socialist Education and Research (CERES), the PS left wing (*Témoignage Chrétien*, 28 November 1974). Gilbert Declercq, of the Loire-Atlantique federation, came out in opposition to the entire operation (*Nouvel Observateur*, October 1974), while the Hacuitex federation (textiles) expressed major reserves (*Hacuitex CFDT*, August–September 1974). Thus the operation launched on 11 June lost most of its clarity and force.[12]

Eager to bring about an *autogestionnaire* socialism and now oriented toward the Parti Socialiste (especially its Rocardian faction), the CFDT turned to reinforcing united action with the CGT so as to reap the benefits of the trend toward left unity and weaken the perceived excessive grip of the extreme left within the confederation.[13] The CFDT–CGT accord of 26 June 1974 covered not only common demands but also "methods of action." This platform, the most comprehensive ever signed between the two unions, did not put an end to expressions of difference nor to outbreaks of controversy. The CGT continued to stress the CFDT's ideological weakness, while the CFDT lamented the revival of a certain CGT rigidity.[14] Nevertheless, important common ventures were undertaken, in particular the workers' forum held on the Champ de Mars in Paris on 10 July 1975. This demonstration, which brought together representatives from firms experiencing difficulties, pointed to a developing economic crisis, which would become more pronounced by the end of 1975.

A controversy arose within the CFDT over how to interpret the new economic conjuncture. In March 1975 *Syndicalisme* (no. 1486, 7 March 1975) devoted an entire issue to the economic crisis, but some CFDT members felt that the theses put forth too closely paralleled those of the CGT; a follow-up brochure on the crisis would adopt an entirely different tone (CFDT, 1976). This debate, however, was to be overtaken by events.

In early December 1975 Prime Minister Jacques Chirac launched an operation against "anti-military intrigues." CFDT offices in Besançon and Bordeaux were searched. The ultimate objective of this offensive remains clouded in mystery. In the short run it hurt relations between Edmond Maire's organization which called for unqualified solidarity with the soldiers' committees, and Georges Séguy's union which was little inclined to rally to their defense or to bolster the current of sympathy for its union rival.[15] Moreover, the CFDT elite concluded that a purge had to be carried out on some local leadership, notably in the Gironde federation and locals at the Banque Nationale de Paris (Paris) and the Lyon railroad station. These purges were directed primarily against the Ligue Communiste and against "ploum-ploum" leftists (LCR, 1979, pp. 62–3).

The Thirty-seventh Congress held in Annecy (25–29 May 1976) was dominated by, on the one hand, a battle against the leftist "coucous," and, on the other, the emergence of a left current—reformed and united around a common "Contribution"—grouping together the Banking, Construction, Textiles, PTT, Health Services and Rhône-Alpes region federations (CFDT Fédération de la Banque *et al.*, 1976). The confederal majority came under severe attack during the Congress. At the outset the expulsion of the American Embassy counselor for social affairs (an invited observer) created a heated atmosphere. Nevertheless, Edmond Maire's line was upheld in the end, and the left minority was brought in on the expulsion of *gauchistes* and the relatively few communists from the CFDT apparatus.[16]

Raymond Barre's appointment to replace Jacques Chirac as Prime Minister served to strengthen CGT–CFDT united action, which was now necessitated by the struggle against the government's austerity plan. Edmond Maire's confederation, in order to pull back somewhat from a rapprochement process viewed as dangerous, incorporated anti-hierarchic and self-management positions in the demand platform adopted in June 1977 (CFDT, 1978a). This document called for a reduction of wage differentials to a ratio of six to one, a three-year moratorium on investments in nuclear power, retirement at 60 for both sexes, and the establishment of shopfloor councils (*conseils d'atelier*) in nationalized firms.

The CFDT not only radicalized its positions but tried to emphasize their originality. In January 1976 the Bureau National adopted a document detailing the confederation's evolution and its sources of inspiration. According to this text, the collective elaboration of the CFDT project derived from praxis and was not subordinated to any external doctrine, whether that of Proudhon, Marx, Marcuse, or Illich (press conference, 9 January 1976; CFDT, 1977, pp. 123–7). However, it became apparent that Marxism was the principal target when a forthcoming brochure was announced "to foster a critical understanding [of Marxism]" (CFDT BRAEC, 1980). Edmond Maire on several occasions, notably in an effort to combat a CERES-promoted course in dialectical materialism, would come out against "Marxist clericalism" (*Syndicalisme*, no. 1625, 4 November 1976).

In counterposition to dogmas considered mechanistic and outdated the CFDT proposed its own reading of the crisis. The CGT's positions were criticized for being economistic in inspiration. According to the CFDT, the crisis had various causes: the limits inherent in a certain type of growth when confronted by working-class reaction, the rise of anti-hierarchical sentiments, a challenge to American hegemony, and a fall in the rate of profit. Corresponding to this pluralist view of the phenomenon's origins was a plural view of the phenomenon itself: the crisis being simultaneously political, economic, social, and cultural. Since it was structural in nature, the crisis was not the result of any particular government's mismanagement nor could it be overcome by a quick fix. A positive outcome was possible but not inevitable:

> The capitalist system is profoundly shaken but not irreparably condemned. No one can say how the crisis will come out. There can be no determinism or self-correction (*automatisme*). Between authoritarianism and self-managed democratic socialism, as well as all the intermediate solutions, nothing has yet been decided. (CFDT, 1977, p. 15)

The general resolution passed at the Thirty-seventh Congress declared that "there can be no truce in the class struggle; the CFDT rejects any moderation of [its] demands, any idea of a social truce" (CFDT, 1977, p. 16). The deepening of the crisis and the quarrels between the left parties, which the CFDT sought to escape although blaming the PCF, led the central leadership to rethink its positions on the content of demands and choice of alliances. Negotiations continued with the CGT to agree on a joint document based on the demand platform of June 1977. On 11 January 1978 Edmond Maire made clear that he did not wish to "issue a joint text before the legislative elections."[17] At the National Council meeting of 26–28 January 1978 Jacques Moreau, secretary for political affairs and one of Maire's key advisors, called for a new realism in demands, a revival of professional negotiations, a rejection of national days of action, and a rapprochement with Force Ouvrière. This proposal was not approved, however, and the confederation's stance officially remained unchanged.[18]

The legislative elections of March 1978 took place shortly thereafter, with the left suffering its sixth defeat since the establishment of the Fifth Republic in 1958. Immediately after the second ballot, Edmond Maire requested a meeting with President Giscard, which was seen as a symbolic act in support of the line laid out in the Moreau report. This new line was later ratified at a National Council meeting (27–28 May) when it adopted a declaration on the "Re-centering (*recentrage*) of Our Action" (*Syndicalisme*, no. 1703, 4 May 1979).

The electoral defeat of March 1978 and continuing division within left ranks nourished the impression that the right would retain the presidency in the 1981 elections and thus gave Edmond Maire latitude to persevere in his plans. According to the new line, the CFDT had placed too much weight on a potential change in regime. The CFDT now had to return to the essence of trade union decentralized action at the base and negotiation. When the time came for a vote on the *motion d'orientation* at the May National Council, 87–93 percent voted in support and the rest abstained. Not having their own alternative to put forward, the "*gauche syndicale*" (union left) had to acquiesce to the line of the majority.[19] *Recentrage* thus was accompanied by an internal realignment.

The public authorities at this time were calling for "concertation," while the CNPF (National Council of French Employers) announced a return to contractual negotiations. The CFDT geared its actions to the possibilities that were opening up.[20] It viewed favorably the reform of the *prud'homme* (arbitration) structures and even hoped to reap some benefits from this. On 27 March 1979 the CFDT signed an agreement on unemployment compensation, which would be showcased at the Thirty-eighth Congress as one of the confederation's major achievements. Even though the CGT Grenoble Congress was seen in a positive light by the CFDT leadership, united action with the CGT fluctuated. "The small patch of blue sky" was soon covered in clouds, brought on by the crisis in steel. Edmond Maire's organization believed that the CGT strategy to defend French steel was both unrealistic and electoralist; the CFDT thus refused to participate in the 23 March march on Paris.

The CFDT Thirty-eighth Congress held in Brest (8–12 May 1979) upheld the line in favor of negotiation and realism in demands. A majority, however, did vote against the *motion d'orientation*, which had proposed a reduction in the workweek without a corresponding wage compensation. Nevertheless, the central leadership judged that *recentrage* had become an established fact, so that the term itself was "dépassé" (Maire, 1980a, p. 153). In fact, because of its significance in terms of the French political spectrum, *recentrage* had come to be replaced by *resyndicalisation* (reunionization).

The CFDT's desire for compromise was evidenced by the signature of a social pact in the steel industry, union participation in the Communication and Society Conference, and its moderate proposals in regard to a reduction in working hours (Armington *et al.*, 1981, p. 191).[21] With respect to the last item, CGT leader Krasucki would later write that in the 12 November 1979 meeting the CFDT was even more moderate than Force Ouvrière (Mouriaux, 1982, p. 142).

The policies pursued by the CFDT became ever more irreconcilable with any coordination with the CGT. Although the unity pact was renewed in an agreement signed on 17 September, it had become an anachronism, a legacy cherished by union activists but seriously questioned by the CFDT leadership, which began to reach out to the CGC and FO. Before the *prud'homme* elections of 12 December, the CGC, headed by Jean Menu, agreed to an entente with the CFDT. In contrast FO summarily dismissed the CFDT's offer of alliance.[22]

The real rupture between the CGT and CFDT came in 1980. Edmond Maire's organization vigorously protested the positions taken by its rival on the Soviet intervention in Afghanistan: "The shadow of Kaboul extends over the French working-class movement." Relations with the PCF became increasingly acrimonious; a communist leader in the Territory of Belfort went so far as to accuse Emond Maire of having pacified Algeria with flame-throwers.[23] The CFDT's differences with the CGT became pronounced, especially over the conduct of conflicts (such as those of subway-cleaning personnel and commercial fishermen) and over the orientation of negotiations. On the issue of reducing the workweek the CFDT's Albert Mercier expressed initial interest in a proposed accord with the CGT, but the CFDT leadership later rejected the idea. The CFDT secretary-general delivered a speech on 4 September 1980 in Nantes vehemently denouncing the CGT, which even certain CFDT notables, such as Gilbert Declercq, found excessive (*Témoignage Chrétien*, 15 September 1980).

The ideological struggle against the CGT and PCF came to occupy an important place in CFDT activity; the union criticized the ACO (Catholic Workers' Action) for its cryptocommunism, condemned the errors committed in Georges Marchais's electoral campaign over the affairs at Vitry and Montigny, and supported the pan-syndicalist positions of Poland's Solidarity. The confederation remained guarded with respect to François Mitterrand's bid for the presidency, as his proposals were perceived as too dependent on the 1972 Common Program. Some union activists demanded stronger CFDT participation in the electoral debate and a commitment to support the left candidate on the second ballot. The CFDT would make the latter move only on the night of 26 April.

The CFDT thus embarked on a sudden and decisive change in course, demonstrating its ability to adapt to changing events. In an interview granted to the newspaper *Le Républicain Lorrain*, on 6 December 1979, Edmond Maire confirmed the low regard which he felt for Mitterrand and his deep sympathy for party rival Michel Rocard.[24] Now overcoming this previous reticence, the CFDT leadership perceived the conjuncture in May 1981 as particularly propitious, given the PCF's electoral setback (only 15·3 percent of the vote) and the internal disarray of the CGT. The situation seemed to present an opportunity for promoting an aggressive reformism and supplanting the CGT as the country's leading trade union.[25]

The CFDT cheered Mitterrand's 10 May victory, and the National Council quickly put forward its demand priorities: sectoral negotiations on reducing working hours, a gradual increase in the SMIC (minimum wage), and new rights and collective guarantees for all workers (*Syndicalisme*, no. 1863, 28 May 1981). Several CFDT leaders joined ministerial staffs, and Hubert Prévost was named Planning Commissioner.[26] The CFDT "countered" the wage claims made by the CGT in conjunction with the SMIC and the proposed 38-hour workweek, fearing that exaggerated quantitative demands might destabilize the economic system (Gonin *et al.*, 1981, p. 797). The CFDT was so steadfast in its defense of the actions taken by the Mauroy government that it began to take on the look of an official union. This behavior encountered problems within confederation ranks, even if public expressions of discontent were rare. In October 1981 Edmond Maire expressed his disagreement with the Socialist government's energy policies and the slow pace of change.

Problems continued within the confederation over the moderation of the demands put forward by the leadership, especially on the subject of reducing the workweek. In a speech given to the Paris region federal congress Maire criticized neo-corporatism for being revolutionary in word and conservative in action. The establishment of martial law in Poland on 13 December 1981 gave the CFDT a chance to position itself at the forefront of the protest movement and at the center of interunion debates on the issue (the CGT, as in the Cold War period, was effectively isolated by a FO–CFDT–CFTC–CGC–FEN front). The campaign in support of Solidarity mobilized the CFDT yet led to a further neglect of concrete struggles.

The decree issued by the government on 16 January 1982 relative to the reduction of the workweek disappointed the workers concerned. The recourse to this rather undemocratic procedure had been taken to avoid outbidding between Socialist and Communist deputies. The maneuver backfired, and the CGT was able to reap the benefit of the strong dissatisfaction among wage-earners. On 10 February President Mitterrand pledged that wage-earners' purchasing power would be protected, and Prime Minister Pierre Mauroy seconded his position (*Le Monde*, 11 February 1982). The CFDT criticized this move as incompatible with the first priority of increasing employment.

The left's defeat in the March 1982 cantonal elections brought a change in the line of the CGT. The CGT came out in favor of a unified 1 May commemoration, which the CFDT rejected so as not to efface the Polish issue nor sanction a union demonstration with political overtones.

As a result the CFDT Thirty-ninth Congress held in Metz was marked by a debate on interunion relations as well as on questions relative to the confederation's internal functioning and attitude toward austerity policies. A timid attempt was made to unblock CFDT–CGT relations. The secretary-general proposed unity of action "at several speeds," which either indicated a slow rapprochement with the CGT or meant little concretely, given FO's known opposition to any, even limited, coordination of efforts with the CGT. The way in which Alexandre Bilous, the CFDT representative to the CGT Forty-first Congress, characterized the meeting confirmed the CFDT's prudence on renewed contacts: "the Lille Congress is [a reminder] of all the difficulties" (*Syndicalisme*, no. 1919, 1 July 1982).

Numerous speakers at the Metz Congress criticized the absence of internal union democracy. Trotskyists from the Ligue Communiste, the "unifiers" of the Loire-Atlantique, and the populists of Hacuitex (textiles) complained of a Parisian *dirigisme* but could not agree on appropriate countermeasures. Edmond Maire's ruling group never had to fear a serious challenge. The final report, voted by 59·25 percent of the delegates, demonstrated that internal protest was still strong if waning, but masked the fundamental problem: the lack of a credible and coherent alternative.

A rather diffuse dissatisfaction with the union's economic proposals was also evident. On this sensitive point Edmond Maire raged against the CGT's attempt to claim that only its positions could be characterized as "revolutionary." In the cause of social solidarity the Thirty-ninth Congress, overturning the decision taken at the Brest Congress, called for a reduction in the workweek without integral salary compensation for those workers making over twice the called-for minimum wage.

When the Delors Plan was announced by the government after the devaluation of the franc, the CFDT Bureau National meeting on 17 June recalled that "the CFDT for several months had been asking the government for a real operation-truth." The CFDT Commission Executive of 21 June 1982 expressed its disagreement with the announced wage freeze, estimating that this precluded a catching-up by low-paid workers. The CFDT's two major demands—work-sharing through a reduction in working hours without wage compensation, and reduction in the wage hierarchy by cuts in the purchasing power of privileged groups—were put forward in the cause of rigor and ambition. The confederation also insisted on new rights for workers. Denunciation of corporatism continued to dominate its public discourse. At this writing it remains to be seen whether the positions laid out at the Thirty-ninth Congress can be translated into day-to-day action by union locals.

The CFDT prides itself on its capacity for change, which ostensibly derives from the union's internal life. In reality things are more complicated. What we see is a dialectic between the project clearly formulated by Eugène Descamps in 1964 and the conjunctures within which the CFDT must act. The relationship with the CGT would appear to be determinant in this process.

The Social Bases of the CFDT

A retracing of the course followed by the CFDT from 1964 to 1982 provides some understanding of the tactical capacity which the leadership possesses to adapt the union's actions to the mood of the moment—whether that be the libertarian push of the early 1970s or the disillusioned realism of the 1980s. Notwithstanding the paucity of data, we also need to examine the character of the CFDT ruling elite and the general membership in order to situate the actions of the actors in a social context.

Two characteristics distinguish the universe of the CFDT. Both FO and the CGT are thoroughly laïc—the latter's extended hand to Catholics meeting with scant success (Mouriaux, 1982, pp. 137–8). In contrast the sociology of the CFDT is linked to the realities of French catholicism. This is not to question the sincerity of the confederation's choice in favor of laïc schools (made in 1937 by its teachers' federation, SGEN) nor deconfessionalization viewed in terms of an emancipation from church tutelage or the limitations of confessional ideology. Yet, even after undergoing a major evolution, CFDT unionism still rests primarily on a certain religious specificity. This is certainly the case with respect to the leadership: all forty members elected to the Commission Executive or Bureau Confédéral since 1964 come from a Christian background.[27] As Jean-Daniel Reynaud has observed (1980, p. 52),when one examines the map of professional elections, "what is striking in regional distribution is the fairly close correlation between [areas of significant] CFTC (later CFDT) presence and traditionally Catholic zones."[28] The West (Pays de la Loire, Brittany, and Normandy), East (Alsace-Lorraine), and to a lesser extent North and Southeast, are regions favorable to CFDT influence. In contrast the Center and Southwest have remained relatively closed. The points of strength of Edmond Maire's organization were evident in the *prud'homme* elections. While some gains have certainly been made at the expense of FO and the CGT (Lozier, 1980b, pp. 16—34), the process of "nationalization" of the CFDT vote has not yet effaced the original linkage between union penetration and religious practice. The intellectual output of the confederation provides additional evidence. The genesis of CFDT ideas cannot be understood without reference to debates in the pages of such journals as *Responsables*, *Esprit*, and *Projet*. Furthermore, diffusion of CFDT-related materials relies heavily on the Seuil publishing house (Tavares, 1980, 1981).

Whereas the weight of manual workers in the CGT or of civil servants in FO colors the entire organization, the CFDT is characterized by a fairly uniform distribution among the different categories. Although the civil service sector had been relatively closed to the CFTC, the CFDT has gained here to the point that it now outstrips FO, according to official statistics (*Le Monde*, 27 January 1982).[29] In the public sector, although the CFTC–CFDT split hurt the CFDT in the mines, the confederation has achieved good results in the SNCF (railroads), the EDF (gas and electric utility), and the PTT. The CFDT ranks first among agricultural workers and has a strong position in industry (metallurgy, chemicals) and the tertiary sector (banks, social services, health services). As far as can be determined with respect to occupational categories, the CFDT would appear to recruit from the two extremes of the working class, that is, the semiskilled, especially immigrants, and technicians (Lozier, 1980a, p. 24).

The role of SGEN (the teachers' federation) should also be emphasized. While teachers are more or less absent from the CGT and FO due to the FEN's choice in 1947 to remain autonomous of both, the CFDT benefits from the support of an important number of educators, who have helped instill a taste for analyses and studies. The role played by people like Paul Vignaux, Jacques Julliard, and Jacques Moreau far exceeds that of an *éminence grise*. Moreover, many locals are able to operate thanks to the free time that teachers, more than other wage-earners, can give to the union.

As with the other union confederations, CFDT membership growth slowed down in 1974 and began to stagnate in 1977. The drop-off in membership, due to the crisis and the difficulties of left unity, was not accompanied by a reversal during professional elections; the CFDT generally continued to gain. Setbacks occurred at La Hague where the CFDT dropped 14·19 points in the total vote, and at Renault-Sandouville where it lost 3·3 points in workers' votes (*Syndicalisme*, no.

1801, 10 December 1981). Nevertheless, despite a comeback by the CGT between May 1981 and the Polish events (in voting at thirty-one firms), the CFDT has not seen its *recentrage* repudiated by the electorate. Moreover, its support of Solidarity brought additional votes from wage-earners disgruntled with the position taken by the CGT.

The Constants of the Ruling Majority's Project

There would seem to be a discrepancy between the tactical variations traced earlier and the relative stability in implantation just outlined. The sociological continuity pointed out here should only surprise those who believe in sharp breaks or change without the stigma of the past.

We begin by examining the theme of *autogestion*, which would seem to have no link to the ideological legacy of the CFTC. According to *Croire*, the posthumous work by Fredo Krumnow (1974), the first CFDT delegation to Yugoslavia was sent in 1965. The motivation for this was tactical: to furnish another socialist model than the Soviet one and to demonstrate the rigidity of the CGT, which had not yet renewed activities with Yugoslav unions.[30] The Titoist experiment would not have taken on such major dimensions, however, if it had not corresponded to deeper concerns independently arrived at by the technician-dominated Chemicals federation and the populist Hacuitex. Self-management touched the heart and spirit of CFDT militants because Catholic culture in France is the bearer of a certain anti-statism. The social morality of the church preaches respect for communal structures at the base; the *Quadragesimo anno* encyclical (Pius XI, 1937, pp. 208–9) reaffirmed the autonomy of low-level groupings which the state should aid and not supplant.

All too readily CFDT activists believe that the confederation foresees and wants a withering away of the state when what really is at stake is limiting the state's role and rejecting both Soviet instrumentalism and social democratic interventionism (Maire, 1980b, pp. 61–70; Fejtö, 1980, pp. 274–87). Direct expression by workers is more important than conquest of the state apparatus, and contractual organization of civil society is seen as the principal road to democratization (in contrast a social blueprint with a gelatinous civil society is seen as engendering totalitarianism).

A second theme seems to break with the attachment to the value of work, which the CFTC originally nourished. The anti-productivism of the CFDT is often perceived as a major reversal of CFDT philosophy. Again we do not mean to question the changes in attitude that have taken place *vis-à-vis* wage labor nor the CFDT's capacity to express the revulsion (*ras-le-bol*) of the young (and sometimes not so young) with working conditions. Still, knowledge of the past makes this attitude seem less novel. The CFTC, too, rejected production for its own sake rather than for the satisfaction of real needs. The 1947 Congress was held under the banner "Let us liberate man from the machine and money." The controversial study by Emile Poulat (1977), *The Church against the*

Bourgeoisie, permits a better understanding of the CFDT's anti-capitalism and humanism. The theoretical foundation does not stem from a critique of the capitalist mode of production, although the CFDT borrowed liberally from the Marxist paradigm in the 1970s. At the base of the CFDT's rejection of capitalism is an ethical protest—against the reign of wealth, against the established order (or disorder)—in the name of human needs.

With the onset of the economic crisis, and especially after *recentrage*, the CFDT carried out a dual critique of both Keynesianism and Marxism. The union advocated another type of growth, in which sharing income and time-consuming tasks would occupy a strategic place. The CFDT was inspired by certain ideas of Italian unions (especially the metalworkers' FLM) on austerity politics (*Syndicalisme*, no. 1903, 4 March 1982), and Edmond Maire denounced the neo-corporatism as practiced by the CGT and Force Ouvrière (*Syndicalisme*, no. 1890, 3 December 1981).

A third theme that links the CFDT to the CFTC is the affirmation of trade union autonomy. This position was not adopted solely to break with the MRP (Popular Republican Movement) but also represented, and still represents, a fundamental rejection of CGT-style unionism. Georges Lavau (1981, p. 122) has rigorously analyzed this concern: joining the CFDT "is, more than anything else, a repudiation of communist domination of the CGT and, therefore, a repudiation of the PCF first and of the CGT second (in this sense, Krasucki is correct [in saying] that union organizations other than the CGT are fundamentally 'anti-communist')." The roots of this opposition in the CFDT's case are multiple, antipathy toward Marxism, disgust toward the socialist countries, and rejection of the idea of vanguard. After the Polish events, Maire asked in a 24 February 1982 press conference, "how can one dare identify as leftist an organization which supports an anti-worker putsch?"[31] Without doubt the traditional distrust of politics held by Catholics continues to be influential, although this has considerably diminished. Moreover, the CFDT no longer hesitates to act as a substitute for the ideal party that it always hoped would appear.[32]

The above analysis essentially applies to the confederation taken as a whole; minority currents would not see themselves in this light. Otherwise the confederation's turnabouts are not so easily explained: for example, a majority of the delegates at the 1979 Brest Congress came out against reducing the workweek without a compensation in salary. Cleavages evidently exist between the base and summit. The *recentrage* readily accepted by such federations as Metallurgy and Chemicals is still debated in federations like Banking, Textiles, Construction, and (in part) SGEN (*Syndicalisme*, no. 1868, 2 July 1981).[33] The CGT attacks foster internal cohesion in a defensive reflex and tend to curtail public expressions of discord. In spite of these caveats, the overwhelming majority of CFDT members can be said to adhere to the grand project of the confederation: to dampen the effects of the crisis by promoting an evolution of French society in a more decentralized and egalitarian direction and to reequilibrate the trade union left so as to end the domination of the CGT.

Notes: Chapter 4

1   The *document d'orientation* adopted at the CFDT Thirty-fifth Congress contained the following passage, "Rather than reinforcing the capitalist system, negotiation should contribute to disequilibrating the system and creating the possibility for a new advance toward a democratic and socialist society": CFDT, 1974b, p. 45.

2   Pierre Hureau issued the warning about appearing to be the "official union" in a report presented at the National Council meeting of 22–24 October 1981: *Notes de Conjoncture Sociale*, 26 October 1981.

3   Maurice Blondel, Jacques Maritain, Albert Lachièze-Rey, and Jean Lacroix were cited in reference to Christian personalism, but Emmanuel Mounier was not mentioned (though the founder of the review *Esprit* is usually considered one of the principal theoreticians—*translator*). Excerpts from Proudhon, Leon Blum, R. H. S. Crossman, and the Bad Godesberg program were given in reference to democratic socialism.

4   According to Eugène Descamps, "constantly, in [the elaboration of confederal] texts and documents, there is an effort to strike a balance between the direction we would like to see taken and what we know to be the thoughts of our members; there must be a gradual development of education": CFDT, 1971, p. 168.

5   Eugène Descamps at this time was a member of the Union Démocratique du Travail, an organization of left Gaullists which Gilbert Grandval had helped establish. Jacques Tessier would later suggest (in an interview on 28 November 1981) that it was Grandval's hostility toward the "maintained CFTC" which led to his removal as Minister of Labor.

6   *Translator*: In the late spring of 1965 Socialist Party notable Gaston Defferre, seeking to give organizational weight to his presidential campaign, attempted to bring together the non-Communist left in a "grand federation." This initiative, and with it Defferre's presidential candidacy, collapsed when the Socialist Party and the Popular Republican Movement (MRP) failed to reach an accord.

7   Reference to CFDT–CGT problems can be found in remarks made in particular by Emile le Beller (PTT), Dumouche (Air France), Korein (Communaux Alsace), Amiral (Métaux Lyon), Benasse (EDF–GDF Paris), and Fromager (Métaux R.P.).

8   In 1964–5 Eugène Descamps had envisioned an eventual merger of the CFDT and Force Ouvrière: Descamps, 1971, pp. 103–5, 242–3. By 1969 CFDT relations with FO had "stalled": *CFDT Aujourd'hui*, no. 17, January–February 1976, p. 78.

9   The most notable failure to agree on joint action came during a railroad strike. A *journée d'action* was organized on 13 December 1967, but the CGT call for the elaboration of a common program for the left parties and unions angered the CFDT.

10   *Autogestion* had been debated within the Construction, Chemicals, and Textiles federations. In this respect Edmond Maire could claim that "the directive was not the result of a hasty improvisation by a few leaders under the pressure of events": Maire and Julliard, 1975, p. 59.

11   Philippe Bauchard—in *L'Expansion*, May 1970—indicated that, in addition to a *gauchiste* current, there were currents grouped around Edmond Maire, Michel Rolant, Gilbert Declercq, and Eugène Descamps.

12   Edmond Maire claimed that internal problems resulting from this operation were minimal: *Le Monde*, 5 October 1974. The CFDT would later attempt to clarify its position in an article: "Party–union relations in action today and tomorrow," *Syndicalisme*, no. 1528, 26 December 1974. *Gauchistes* in the confederation had issued a manifesto hostile to the *Assises*: *Le Monde*, 23 October 1974.

13   The CFDT leadership looked askance at the potential candidacy in the 1974 presidential election of Charles Piaget, the CFDT militant who had led the LIP strike. In June and July 1976 the CFDT condemned efforts to coordinate the struggles taking place at Besançon (the site of the LIP watch factory) and Fougères.

14 As evidence of CFDT ideological inconsistency, the CGT pointed to Laurent Lucas's nomination as counselor for social affairs to the French Embassy in Madrid—*Le Monde*, 3 July 1974—Albert Detraz's participation in the Sudreau Commission—*Le Monde*, 23 July 1974—and Hubert Maigrat's appointment to the staff of the State Secretary on Working Conditions—*Le Monde*, 24 January 1976.

15 When Alain le Leap of the CGT was arrested on 10 October 1952, Gaston Tessier (CFTC) declared, "We would hope that this prosecution is not related to normal union activities and assume that charges would not have been filed without serious legal grounds": Lefranc, 1969, pp. 116–17).

16 In the course of its Twentieth Congress (1972) the PCF had launched an appeal for CFDT militants to join the party; this led to atypical instances of cross-membership: *Etudes sociales et syndicales*, no. 237, November 1975, pp. 7–13. In September 1976 two CFDT officials of the Loire federation resigned as a result of systematic opposition to their membership in the PCF: *Le Monde*, 5–6 September 1976. Other instances, in the SNCF for example, can be cited of purges of PCF members from the CFDT.

17 Georges Séguy reported Edmond Maire's remark several years later: *Le Monde*, 13 September 1980. Nevertheless, the CGT and CFDT did establish on 24 January 1978 seven working groups.

18 At a National Bureau meeting (9–10 February 1978) Jacques Moreau, while pledging that the CFDT's line had not changed, commented that "if it had not been for the press and the behavior of the CGT, the [outcome of] the National Council would have been entirely different": transcript of Bureau National meeting of 9–10 February 1978, p. 7.

19 The *gauche syndicale* had been without a national leader since the death of Fredo Krumnow on 19 May 1974. Furthermore, it had been weakened not only by the unfavorable economic conjuncture but also by defections of militants who were disappointed over the left's electoral defeat in March 1978.

20 An agreement on guaranteed annual wage payments in the metallurgy sector was signed on 19 July by all the union confederations. The CFDT hailed this event as the beginning of a generalized trend; in reality this would later stall, as even Edmond Maire was forced to admit during the CFDT's Thirty-eighth Congress: Maire, 1980a, pp. 46, 88.

21 Edmond Maire's comments at the Colloquium were later cited by President Giscard. Agence France Presse observed that "Valéry Giscard d'Estaing has taken a [major] step: [the government] has shifted from discreet appeals to a policy of an outstretched hand."

22 FO officials had not forgotten the numerous criticisms of their union emanating from the CFDT in the past nor the split engendered in the FO Chemicals federation when its leader, Maurice Labi, had quit to join the CFDT federation headed by Jacques Moreau. FO leaders also did not appreciate the fact that the CFDT's *recentrage* jeopardized FO's position as privileged interlocutor with the *patronat* and the public authorities.

23 It is difficult to appraise accurately CFTC actions relative to the Algerian question. A number of different sensibilities on the issue coexisted within the confederation. Furthermore, the gap between the advanced positions put forward by the minority and those held by the majority was ultimately resolved in the adoption of certain progressive actions. In our view three points need to be made in this debate. First, actions prompted by ethical considerations early on led CFTC activists to oppose this dirty war. Secondly, the confederation only officially came out in favor of a negotiated solution in 1958 and for independence in 1961. Thirdly, the majority of the CFTC Algerian regional federation eventually came out in support of a French Algeria, despite the support the confederation had expressed for the federation's liberal faction headed by François Fraudeau and Alexandre Chaulet: Noziere, 1979, pp. 247–84. The statement by the PCF official in Belfort is thus unjustified and represents a sectarian and petty-minded amalgam.

24 Relations between the PSU and a number of CFDT officials and militants have never been studied as such. In March 1980 Edmond Maire declined an invitation to attend a Conference on "Twenty Years of the PSU." Roland Cayrol read a letter at this

meeting from the CFDT leader (11 March 1980), which gave the following explanation for his absence: "I never participated in PSU decision-making. My relations with officials of this party took place essentially in the context of [official] CFTC, and later CFDT, meetings with the PSU ... If I had any influence on positions or decisions taken by the PSU, it was in my capacity as a trade-unionist and as a function of the weight of the union organization which I represent."

25   This hope of rivalling the CGT membership figures evolved over time. In 1978 Pierre Rosanvallon estimated the ratio of CFDT to CGT members at 1:1·8: Madelin *et al.*, 1978, p. 547. In 1981 Edmond Maire spoke of a 1:1·5 ratio: *Le Monde*, 22–23 February 1981. On the basis of analyses carried out by Hubert Landier, Jacques Julliard foresaw the possibility that the two unions would reach rough equity: *Nouvel Observateur*, no. 886, 31 October 1981.

26   Among the other CFDT officials appointed to governmental posts were: Jeanette Laot (chargé du mission, Elysée staff), Hubert Lésire-Ogrel (chargé du mission, Ministry of Solidarity), Bernard Guileri (advisor, Foreign Affairs Ministry), René Decaillon (technical advisor, Ministry of Labor), and Henri Fauque (technical advisor, Ministry of Energy).

27   A Catholic background does not signify a continuity of religious practice or even faith. Rather it assures a community of culture and has an influence on behavior.

28   This uneven distribution of CFTC union density brought about the adoption of statutes which sought to balance the different regions while recognizing their relative roles. These statutes in effect gave the confederation itself an important regulating role.

29   The obstacles to CFTC unionization of civil servants were not entirely external to the union. One should recall the analysis of Georges Renard, "If the [CFTC] took the path of [establishing] civil servant unions, it was for a lateral [*sic*] reason—and hence superior to any juridical, economic or professional preoccupation—an apostolic preoccupation: to turn civil servants away from other unions by offering them a substitute, without any risk to their religious life": Renard *et al*, 1937, p. 31.

30   The CFDT had envisioned a similar move with China, but the poor state of the economy which the CFDT delegation found there dissuaded the confederation from entering into any alliance: *L'Unité*, 3–9 January 1975.

31   This quote can be found in the press dossier "Relations between the CFDT and CGT," 24 February 1982, p. 6. The summary that *Syndicalisme* published does not contain this phrase: no. 1903, 4 March 1982.

32   At various times the PSU, FGDS, and even the PS (during the *Assises*) embodied this hope—soon disappointed in each case. The majority of the CFDT sympathizes with Michel Rocard and not with François Mitterrand.

33   The *front du refus* at the Brest Congress included the PTT, Health Services, and Finance Federations. "Grumblings" could be heard in such regional federations as the Auvergne, *Syndicalisme*, no. 1889, 26 November 1981—Paris, *Syndicalisme*, no. 1888, 19 November 1981—and Rhône-Alpes, *Syndicalisme*, no. 1897, 21 January 1982.

5

The Trade Union Strategy of the CGT–FO

ALAIN BERGOUNIOUX

In the course of the last decade, as French unionism confronted both the economic crisis and the alternating effects of the union and disunion of the left, Force Ouvrière (FO) appeared to be the only organization which did not encounter any major difficulties. FO's membership actually increased, and its performance in various professional elections consolidated its position. Avowed reformism, however, is not usually deemed legitimate within the French working-class movement, which emphasizes class struggle and does not enter into durable compromises. Can we conclude from this that Force Ouvrière dares to expose French unionism for what it really is: a somewhat embarrassed reformism?

This hypothesis merits consideration in light of the strategic difficulties encountered by other union confederations in this period and in the marked absence of any significant social movement following François Mitterrand's victory of 10 May 1981. Moreover, the very concept of reformism is ambiguous. In a certain sense all trade unions are reformist in that they must win concessions for the demands of their constituents. This is true for the CGT as well as for the CFDT.

The question is, then, what is distinctive about the type of reformism practiced by Force Ouvrière? Did the strategy elaborated by FO correspond to deep-rooted aspirations of French wage-earners or did it meet with a certain success only within a political context that is now being altered? This question is crucial because FO has long been regarded by specialists in the field as a rather fragile entity with an uncertain future. The events of recent years, however, oblige the careful observer to pose the question of FO's future in different terms and to ascertain to what tradition FO belongs.

The Origins of FO's Originality

When it came into existence with the CGT's 1947 schism, FO inherited several guiding principles from the pre-1936 CGT of Léon Jouhaux, which served it for almost twenty years. These were essentially three: (1) autonomy of trade union action, with a stress on collective agreements; (2) a policy of presence, which entails participation in the regulatory powers of the state; and (3) workers' control. In the first years of FO's existence no serious discussion took place as to whether these three functions were in fact compatible. Over time, however, FO's position as a minority union facing ideological criticism and competition from other confederations engendered certain strategic choices. Thus FO slowly constructed a doctrinal system built around the concept of trade union independence and elaborated *ex post facto* a theory of praxis. This almost imperceptible transformation, which took shape during the 1960s, both provided continuity with and simultaneously altered the traditions of the pre-1936 reformist CGT.

This doctrine was neatly laid out in a report on "The place of trade unionism in society," by G. Ventejol for the union's 1971 Convention (Force Ouvrière, 1971). In this report FO officially rejects a strictly apolitical stance by affirming its commitment to the defense of liberal democracy. The direct intervention of trade unions in the political process is condemned, FO insisting that the roles of unions and political parties should be kept distinct. The trade union's duty is to "defend the specific interests of the working class," whether under a capitalist or socialist regime. The union must guard strictly against any form of integration into the apparatus of the state or the firm. The union is the exclusive representative of the working class. Its role is thus incompatible with the exercise of any sort of managerial responsibility.

According to FO, the trade union's primary instrument is the collective bargaining agreement and its existence is therefore dependent on maintaining the freedom to negotiate. At this same Congress André Bergeron, FO's secretary-general since 1963, declared:

> Collective bargaining (*politique contractuelle*), which facilitates continual discussion between those called upon to dialogue, negotiate, often argue, and ultimately reach agreement, is a component of democracy ... Trade unionism, engaged in contractual activity to defend the permanent interests of workers, is a potent counterweight to the oppressive tendencies secreted by the modern state. It thus serves to equilibrate the concepts of efficacy and liberty.

Force Ouvrière does not propose a political model for society. It deliberately limits its role to that of a "counterweight." This conception presupposes a strict separation between the political and the socioeconomic spheres. Any action in the political sphere takes as its point of departure civil society, where contradictory interests confront one another. The collective agreement is the manifestation of compromises reached between such conflicting interests.

This trade union doctrine thus stems from a pluralist conception of democracy. This is not the appropriate forum to analyze the historical origins of this conception of trade unionism (Bergounioux, 1975, pp. 203–13). It should be pointed out, however, that it derives from a French reformist tradition that, having shed its managerial aspirations, progressively relegated to secondary importance the theme of a "policy of presence" and adopted a formula close to the American practice of bargaining, albeit one still grounded in a class analysis of society. Force Ouvrière thus has a certain originality not only *vis-à-vis* French unionism but also compared to European unionism, since FO's reformism differs from the social democratic model.

This somewhat composite doctrine is not merely the product of a gradual evolution. It stemmed both from the particular problems faced by FO in the 1960s as well as from those besetting trade unions in the following decade. Three influences can be distinguished: the post-1958 political developments, the competition with the CGT and CFDT, and the internal heterogeneity of FO itself.

The establishment of the Fifth Republic in 1958 forced FO to redefine its relationship with the state. Until that time, due to the strategic position occupied by the SFIO within the Parliament (then the center of decision-making), Force Ouvrière sought to exert direct influence on the political institutions. The need to choose between the regulatory and contractual paths was not evident. Force Ouvrière accepted the advent to power of de Gaulle in 1958 as the only alternative barring the path to fascism or communism. The installation of Gaullism, however, forced FO to curtail its political involvement and notably to refuse any responsibility for incomes policies. Moreover, FO—with strong socialist leanings among its base in the public sector—retained a sympathy for some political regrouping of centrist parties. As a result interest in forms of state planning waned, and collective bargaining was elevated in importance. The ensuing political evolution accentuated this trend toward withdrawal from state policies, especially after 1971 when the Socialist and Communist parties began to move toward a left alliance.

The competition with the CGT and CFDT worked in the same direction. With respect to the former, the schism and ensuing polemics led FO to hold up trade union political independence as its distinguishing characteristic. As regards the latter, the post-1964 evolution of the CFDT posed the question of power within the factory in a new way, as concretized in the May 1968 theme of self-management (*autogestion*). Force Ouvrière thus had to clarify its conception of trade unionism which, in contradistinction to that of the CFDT, stressed the strict separation between the trade union and all forms of political authority. This twofold opposition toward the CGT and CFDT was reinforced when the CGT and CFDT signed an accord on united action in January 1966 and effectively isolated FO.

There is one additional element in FO's elevation of contractual policy to the rank of strategic principle. In effect, contractual policy proved to be the principle which least divided a confederation riddled with diverse currents. The two largest minorities within FO—the revolutionary syndicalists and the Trotskyists—both found that this principle allowed them the greatest latitude in action and judgement. As both these minorities reject any form of integration or sharing of managerial responsibilities, they prefer a confederation dominated by a reformist majority to one that poses directly difficult questions of power. They are thus free to stress the relevance of class struggle and the armistice character of the collective agreement.

A certain equilibrium has thus been established. Force Ouvrière, in adapting to new conjunctural constraints that limited its freedom of action, was able to expand a narrow defense of economic interests into a broad-based strategy. The May 1968 movement, in which FO played a minor role, did not pose a fundamental challenge. On the contrary, the social crisis stimulated previously frozen negotiations on social issues and led to a generalization of contractual arrangements in both the public and private sectors.

The strategy of FO can thus be seen as one of continuity. Force Ouvrière has been a signatory since 1957 of the major accords in the realm of social protection. It has also supported all interprofessional accords and the "contracts of progress" launched in the public sector. Finally, FO has been the confederation that has signed the greatest number of collective agreements in the private sector. By 1973, at the onset of the economic crisis, FO had found a certain coherence around contractual policy—in defiance of both the Communist and Christian traditions and in the absence of a well-defined political program.

A Strategy for the Crisis

Force Ouvrière quickly recognized the long-term nature of the crisis, and its analyses have not varied since 1974. In FO's view the crisis, which the escalation of oil prices brought into the open, is structural in essence and stems from a disequilibrium on a world scale. Any return to stability on some new basis can only come through international cooperation. Conjunctural remedies would thus be insufficient.

Force Ouvrière rejects any tradeoff between inflation and unemployment. While viewing a purely national solution as unworkable, FO nevertheless advocates a growth strategy that gives priority to employment. While it hopes that the Western economies can return to growth rates of the past, FO accepts that the present crisis sets limits on trade union objectives. To use an image suggested by André Bergeron, what is needed is to "keep the engine running, perhaps on idle, but ready to accelerate."

A dual concern has dominated the policy of FO: the maintenance of purchasing power, and social protection measures. Contractual policy is the vehicle for pursuing these ends. In a crisis period collective agreements are well suited to a reformist strategy. Collective bargaining gives the union a visible role by allowing it to take credit for certain immediate results which, however limited, are not deferred until some political resolution in the future. In addition, negotiations in some sectors not only preserve past gains but also win new advantages through the impact of wage drift. Force Ouvrière thus made contractual strategy its principal thrust, whereas the CFDT and CGT, while not altogether neglecting to press concrete demands, tended to push political change as the only real solution to the crisis and consequently, at least until 1978, aligned their demands with the platforms of the left parties.

Force Ouvrière's strategy has four basic components. First, FO is committed to defending the utility of contractual arrangements. Thus FO explores all possibilities for negotiation before resorting to the strike, which is viewed as the union's "weapon of last resort." Force Ouvrière sees the strike as most effective in a dissuasive capacity, that is, successful when not put in use. Secondly, although FO federations are given great latitude in deciding what actions should be taken, as a general rule FO prefers to sign accords even when the payoffs are minimal. Thirdly, at the confederal level FO seeks to maintain maximum pressure on public authorities, usually through frequent visits to the Elysée and Matignon, in order to defend free collective bargaining or to open or revive discussion. Fourthly, due to its important responsibilities in the joint administration of social insurance funds, notably social security and UNEDIC, the unemployment insurance fund managed by representatives of labor and management, FO publicizes these programs' financial difficulties, proposes solutions, and claims major credit for the signature of inter-professional accords designed to provide resources for the unemployed.

A detailed account of FO's actions in these domains is beyond the scope of this chapter. Force Ouvrière itself is proud of its overall performance (*FO Hebdo*, 7 December 1977, pp. 31–47), especially its having signed the largest number of collective agreements. A compilation of accords in the private sector for 1979 and 1980, drawn up by the Ministry of Labor, speaks eloquently of FO. In both years FO was, by a wide margin, the union signing the greatest number of collective bargaining agreements. Whereas it signed over four-fifths of the agreements negotiated in these years, the CGT signed about three-fifths, and the CFDT about one-half of all agreements (Jèzequel, 1981).

Force Ouvrière's efforts have been principally directed at keeping collective bargaining alive. Until 1976 FO concentrated on maintaining benefits already won for wage-earners. In most sectors FO's tactic was to alternate verbal pressure and negotiations.

The stabilization policies of the Barre government inhibited FO activity. Since the Barre measures aimed at instituting some sort of incomes policy, they posed a threat to free collective bargaining. When the EDF–GDF accord came up for negotiation, the government repudiated the provision which previously had guaranteed a minimal rise in purchasing power for gas and electricity workers. In September 1976 FO formally put the government on warning (*FO Hebdo*, 25 September 1976).

By early 1977 the obstacles to free collective bargaining had further hardened the stance of FO affiliates. Several FO locals participated in the national "days of action" of 7 October 1976 and 28 April 1977 alongside the CGT and CFDT. This rank-and-file pressure coincided with the leadership's concern over keeping alive its principal thrust, free collective bargaining. Force Ouvrière thus called a national strike on 24 May 1977, which the CGT, CFDT and FEN decided to join. On the day following the protest FO's confederal bureau requested an audience with the President and Prime Minister.

The ensuing relaxation of the government's guidelines proved too limited to breathe new life into collective bargaining. The demand for a fifth week of paid vacation, launched in November 1977, was put forward in part to give a boost to negotiations. At the confederal committee meeting of 11–12 February 1977 André Bergeron clearly stated FO's aims:

> It is only repeating the obvious to explain [to FO-affiliated organizations] that trade union action must confront, according to circumstances, greater or lesser obstacles. It sometimes may happen, as at present, that such obstacles cannot be confronted directly but must be skirted. The wage problem being more difficult to resolve at present than normally, we must find other arenas of combat ... We must find another axe to grind!

The outcome of this period, which nevertheless resulted in an overall maintenance of working-class purchasing power, cannot of course be attributed to the strategy pursued by any single union. Rather one must take into account the interweaving of the actions of the other confederations with those of FO. The somewhat paradoxical picture that this period offers in fact represents the great unstated reality of trade union life. The CGT and CFDT by and large rejected collective bargaining and often refused to sign agreements. None the less, their actions helped establish a certain balance of forces, which the reformist organizations took advantage of to push through accords. Furthermore, the extension of these accords to all wage-earners, including those belonging to the CGT and CFDT, satisfied certain demands that CFDT and CGT members would have made of their leaderships. This tacit arrangement thus permitted the CGT and CFDT to maintain their critical stance while allowing others to boast of positive accomplishments.

Not everyone can be a winner at this game. Force Ouvrière's determination in pursuing contractual actions undoubtedly contributed to its success, however, as the 1970s brought a significant rise in its clientele. Several studies in 1970 had estimated FO's membership as 600,000–700,000. However, some uncertainty as to FO's exact membership still exists, in part because the union does not distinguish between active and retired workers. There is no doubt, though, that gains have been made over the last ten years. *Le Monde* (4 October 1980) has estimated FO's membership at around 1,080,000. Employing somewhat more precise methods, another study estimated that 900,667 membership-cards and 6,755,001 monthly-dues stamps were sold in 1975 (*Etudes sociales et syndicales*, no. 254, May 1977). In the same fashion it can be shown that 983,000 cards and 7,313,520 stamps were sold in 1978.

As regards professional elections to works committees, Force Ouvrière gained 2 percentage points (going from 8 to 10 percent of the votes of all employees), while the CFDT rose only 1·3 percentage points and the CGT lost 12·3 points. Force Ouvrière's major strength lies in the civil service, where the CGT obtained 36·4 percent of the votes in 1975, FO got 27·7 percent, and the CFDT 15·7 percent (Salon, 1977). Finally, in the 1962 elections to the administrative positions for social security funds, in which all wage-earners voted, FO obtained 14·7 percent of the votes. For the labor conciliation boards (*prud'hommes*), where civil servants, public service and health sector workers, and civilian defense agency employees do not vote, FO gained 17·5 percent of the votes in 1979 and 17·8 percent in 1982. André Bergeron could justifiably boast that "we [FO] are the only union to get through this difficult period without major problems" (*FO Hebdo*, 24 December 1980). Paradoxically the crisis consolidated FO's position, because the confederation was not forced to alter its strategy as defined several years previously. Force Ouvrière has forged an image of realism and common sense and has developed a moderate discourse well-suited to current public opinion, which is still strongly impregnated with the values of a growth economy. Force Ouvrière thus did not attempt to swim against the mainstream of French society. Its efforts were directed at stressing the professional nature of trade union activity, at promoting a realistic unionism attentive to the everyday concerns of its membership and capable of coming up with technical solutions to problems. Thus FO was able to take advantage of the trend now present among wage-earners to use their organizations for concrete benefits.

Given FO's mission of promoting the trade union's unique and preeminent role as agent of the workers, it condemns all forms of direct expression for workers, whether such schemes are proposed by management or other union confederations. A resolution issued by the National Confederal Committee in December 1979 was explicit on this point:

The CCN [National Confederal Committee] opposes shopfloor office councils which, under the guise of addressing workers' concerns, in practice lead to increasing production and establishing new work norms and speedups ... This condemnation is all the greater because certain people would accord these councils the right to negotiate contracts directly with the employer, outside of union [channels] and thus in possible opposition to the union. This would in effect entail the death of collective bargaining. (Resolution of Comité Confédéral National, December 1979)

This traditionalist position, which opts for contract over association, is the expression of a coherent doctrine. It rests however on an implicit gamble, namely, the belief that wage-earners, despite their generally higher level of education, will not push for some sharing of responsibilities. Within the French context, then, Force Ouvrière has analyzed the situation in a way exactly opposite to the view of the CFDT. According to FO, the future of modern society does not depend on what goes on within the enterprise but rather outside it—in the development of "leisure time." In this FO also differs from the social democratic tradition, which has promoted comanagerial formulas.

Force Ouvrière's strategy, in the context of the crisis, does not seek to augment trade union power through codetermination rights within the enterprise as compensation for wage moderation. Its line rather can be characterized as a certain corporatism in wage matters, albeit moderated by economic realism. This path, however, introduces a rigidity into global social negotiations and leaves wage-earners ill-prepared to reason in terms of an exchange between sacrifices and advantages.

Current economic difficulties will undoubtedly necessitate a rethinking of collective bargaining structures. Force Ouvrière's leadership views this eventuality with great misgiving, as André Bergeron's statement in March 1980 shows:

> I do not think that one can envision any "grand design" in the short or long-run because no one knows what precisely will occur. The important thing is to preserve the essentials [of the system] which, in my view, are our contractual structures. These permit relations between those who rule and those who are ruled over with the aim of obtaining agreements. (*Revue Dirigeant*, March 1980)

Force Ouvrière and the New Regime

The strategy described here was facilitated by a specific context within which parties and unions operated until May 1981. The CGT and CFDT, by emphasizing the need for a change in regime, indirectly aided FO to occupy the strictly trade union terrain. Has the May 1981 political reversal, by creating a new configuration of forces, jeopardized FO's position?

The present situation does not represent a complete change from the past; rather it retains a certain ambiguity due to the complex nature of relations that FO has had with the Socialist Party since 1971. Force Ouvrière for a long time had been close to the SFIO, since these two organizations shared a common political perspective, namely, the third-force strategy, and a common clientele. Force Ouvrière moved progressively away from the refurbished Socialist Party in the 1970s, however, as the latter sought rapprochement with the PCF. While many Socialists within FO followed the leadership's direction in this respect, a substantial number did remain within the renovated Socialist Party after 1971. Although it cannot be said that FO militants formed the core of Mitterrand's party, they nevertheless did participate in the party's factional conflicts, supporting the reformist and laïc currents, and in the designation of the party's presidential candidate, preferring François Mitterrand to Michel Rocard who was considered too close to the CFDT.

It is possible to situate the membership of FO on the political spectrum with respect to trade unionists as a whole. A 1974 poll, which analyzed the working-class vote for the second ballot of the presidential election, showed that FO members had cast 52 percent of their ballots for François Mitterrand and 48 percent for Valéry Giscard (SOFRES poll, *Nouvel Observateur*, June 1974). In the May 1981 presidential elections the FO vote essentially mirrored that of the French electorate as a whole: first-ballot voting preferences showed 33 percent intended to vote for François Mitterrand, 12 percent for Georges Marchais, 23 percent for Valéry Giscard d'Estaing, and 17 percent for Jacques Chirac (SOFRES poll, *Nouvel Observateur*, 13 April 1981). In purely statistical terms, therefore, FO can be said to lie on the center-left of the political spectrum. This situation plays an important role in elections where pluralities are on the order of 1–2 percent, and explains why the FO and PS leaderships found it mutually advantageous to mute any criticisms of each other despite important strategic disagreements (Mitterrand, 1980, pp. 129–30). As long as the left was in Opposition, this situation primarily benefited Force Ouvrière, which could maintain ties with the Socialists while simultaneously pursuing a strategy of trade union independence. The events of 10 May, however, altered the situation somewhat.

François Mitterrand's victory initially both surprised and worried the FO leadership. As was the case with most observers of the French political scene, FO leaders did not foresee that a left victory could emerge from disunion. The confederation, in accordance with past practice, issued no recommendations to its members as to how to vote. Although the immediate post-electoral period was characterized by a certain resigned acceptance of Mitterrand's victory on the part of the FO leadership, this soon gave way to a more nuanced attitude.

At the level of the federations satisfaction with the outcome prevailed over any misgivings. The policies pursued by the Giscard regime had engendered discontent and apprehension in certain federations, notably the important civil servants' federations. At federal congresses delegates expressed hopes that the trade union movement might regain its rightful place and that a new impetus be given to social dialogue.

The confederal leadership felt obligated to take these sentiments into account. It voiced approval for the inevitable and healthy alternation in power, while stressing the difficult tasks that awaited the new government. Although FO applauded the initial social reforms decreed by the Mauroy government, it reaffirmed its concern for the maintenance of contractual arrangements. Moreover, FO refused any representation within the executive, in contrast to CFDT and FEN, several of whose leaders were appointed to political or staff positions. In sum, the first two months of the new regime were a period of watchful waiting for FO; until the June 1981 legislative elections FO's attitude was on the whole positive with respect to the government's major orientations.

The first real disappointment predictably came with the appointment of four Communist ministers on 24 June 1981, a decision which FO immediately condemned (*Le Monde*, 26 June 1981). The presence of Communist ministers, particularly heading the Civil Administration and Health Ministries, sectors where FO has important federations, was resented as a potential source of difficulties. In a somewhat parallel fashion the presence of former CFDT officials in the new government was perceived as an additional affront. By the summer of 1981, then, FO felt that its organization was directly threatened.

This situation engendered a critical distancing of FO *vis-à-vis* the government. André Bergeron on 13 July 1981 defined the confederation's position thus:

> Today we are more than ever convinced that one cannot have one foot in the government and another in the union movement ... We defend the specific interests of the working-class. The government has very little room for maneuver given the world economic crisis, which did not come to a halt on May 10th. As a result, there will be, sooner or later, differences of judgment between the government and the union movement. While we do not seek disagreement [with the government] for its own sake, we must remain what we have always been. I remind you that our moderation was greatly criticized in the past. Today some of those who so reproached us may have to commend our behavior. (*La Lettre Sociale*, no. 255, 13 July 1981)

In the medium term FO is placing its bets on an inevitable crisis between Communists and Socialists. Force Ouvrière leaders believe that the pivotal role that the Confederation could then play would be appreciated by the President and would permit a political reequilibrium.

There are important sources of concern at the present time, too. While FO has no objection in principle to nationalizations, it does question the role that trade unions are to play within the nationalized firms. The CGT and CFDT, albeit from differing perspectives, demanded the setting up of shopfloor or office councils, equipped with structures empowering them to enter into accords with the firm. Force Ouvrière fears both a politicization of the enterprises, which would mean CGT domination, and the erosion of the union's preeminence, considered the essential condition for contractual arrangements.

The submission of the Auroux report in September 1981 somewhat allayed the fears expressed that summer. Nevertheless, Force Ouvrière objects to amending the law of 11 February 1950 on collective bargaining agreements to authorize unions representing a majority of workers to veto collective bargaining agreements. This would jeopardize the tactics followed until now by FO and could introduce a real split between the union and the Socialist regime.

The guiding thread of FO's attitude since the summer of 1982 is vigilance that the conditions which permit its type of trade union practice are maintained. Numerous examples can be cited. On 27 July 1981 FO was the first to sign the agreement on a reduced workweek, thus attempting to integrate these negotiations within its strategy of "progressing rapidly from the concrete [situation]." To cite another example, the government's intention to institute "new rules for the determination of wages" in order to counter inflation ran into opposition from FO, which has always been hostile to any form of incomes policy. Nor does FO accept the principle of compressing the wage hierarchy.

The last major issue of concern to Force Ouvrière is the reform of social legislation in light of the important responsibilities that FO has had since 1967 in the joint administration of social insurance funds. FO has always rejected the principle of elected administrators. Worse is the climate of mistrust that has arisen between FO and the Ministry of National Solidarity, which has been more influenced by the analyses of the CGT and CFDT. André Bergeron confirmed this in October 1981:

> We do not feel at fault. This is why I want to repeat to the government, that we neither be treated as a scapegoat nor ignored with respect to the projects now being considered. We will fight. (*FO Hebdo*, 21 October 1981)

None of these issues has been resolved in any definitive manner. It is evident, however, that unease is growing among the confederation's leadership. At the meeting of the National Confederal Committee on 9–10 September 1981 André Bergeron commented:

> I said yesterday how impressed I was by your commentaries. If I followed your lead, we would pass into the opposition even more resolutely than under the previous government. But we will do nothing of the kind as it would be a mistake. (*FO Hebdo*, no. 1682, 16 September 1981)

Could FO thus become an Opposition trade union in the future? This is not likely given the present conjuncture, but could occur if the government's policies were radicalized.

At the present time, while FO is taking some dissenters into its ranks, the aim of FO's leadership, many of whom are PS members, is rather to establish a regular interaction with the government in order to promote its views. With this perspective in mind, FO has approached the CFTC and CGC seeking to establish a reformist coalition on specific points that would create a balance of forces to influence governmental policy. Nor should the international dimension of trade union action be forgotten. Force Ouvrière shares the majority of foreign policy orientations put forward by Mitterrand, so any potential growth in international tension would be a factor favoring solidarity with the PS and a rapprochement with the CFDT.

At the present time the social situation contains too many uncertainties to proceed further with this analysis. Force Ouvrière now represents a tradition sufficiently established to be assured of survival. In the final analysis the evolution of French politics, contrary to present appearances, will undoubtedly become of lesser concern to FO than the problems that its conception of trade unionism will face with the evolution of Western societies.

6

The CGC and the Ambiguous Position of the Middle Strata

GEORGES BENGUIGUI AND
DOMINIQUE MONTJARDET

In a book devoted to the French workers' movement and its responses to the current economic crisis it may seem anomalous that a chapter should be devoted to middle management and supervisory personnel (*cadres*). But, as we shall attempt to show, this anomaly is more apparent than real, since the workers' movement is in many respects a movement of salaried as well as blue-collar personnel. In attempting to forge new strategic coalitions or deal with such problems as wage structures, management methods, workplace hierarchy, and workplace struggles the workers' movement cannot avoid dealing with salaried personnel, whether as partners or adversaries. For this, organized labor, like industry, needs a strategy. Thus it is appropriate that a study of the workers' movement analyze organizations and groups representing managers and supervisors.

Salaried employees are affiliated both with the major French trade union confederations and with an independent organization, the Confédération Générale des Cadres (CGC). The present analysis will focus on this group, in part because it has few real counterparts in other countries, and in part because it enjoys considerable influence among the middle strata in France. Indeed there are few countries in which a large union exists solely to represent managerial and supervisory personnel. That the CGC is representative of such personnel cannot be denied. This is particularly true of private sector firms, although within the private sector there is considerable variation in rates of membership, reasons for joining, types of organization, and forms of action depending on such variables as the branch of industry, the firm involved, the terms of the organization's charter, and so forth.

Nationally, in the 1982 elections for technicians' and supervisors' representatives to the labor conciliation boards (*conseils des prud'hommes*), the CGC did considerably better than its rivals, garnering 41·5 percent of the vote among middle managers and supervisors, compared with 17·5 percent for the CFDT, 13 percent for the CGT, 11·7 percent for FO, and 9·1 percent for the CFTC.

The period from the end of World War II until the 1960s was a particularly good one for middle strata in France. Seen as playing a key role in the growth of the economy, the "economic miracle" of postwar recovery, they were hailed as "the leaders of the modern age," to cite one of the many terms of eulogy. Their numbers increased considerably and their income grew faster, generally speaking, than that of blue-collar workers. Apart from enjoying a favorable position in the labor market, middle strata were instrumental in shaping the new patterns of consumption. This situation did not begin to deteriorate in any serious way until the end of the 1960s when the first signs of economic crisis appeared.[1] (However, talk of a "malaise des cadres," associated with changes in the structure of industrial firms, was heard even earlier.) Accordingly this chapter will be concerned primarily with the CGC's strategy from the end of the 1960s until now.

The CGC was officially established at the time of the Liberation, in October 1944. It subsumed four other organizations. Within a few months still other organizations joined the new group, in particular the Chambre Syndical des VRP (an organization representing sales and marketing personnel). From the outset the CGC, in keeping with traditions sanctioned in particular by the Labor Charter of the Vichy government, defined itself in negative terms: its membership was to include those who were neither workers nor employers (thus inadvertently making common cause with certain Marxist writers who also define this group of workers in negative terms, as consisting of those who are members of neither the proletariat nor the bourgeoisie). Accordingly it should come as no surprise that the CGC's strategy can be analyzed in terms of the relations between the group it represents and two other key social actors, organized labor and organized business. (To this list we must also add the state, for reasons explored below.)

Our discussion is in three parts. First, we describe the main issues involved in the CGC's relations with the other three actors mentioned above. Secondly, we look at changes in those relations over time. Finally, we attempt to interpret these changes.

The CGC and the Key Social Actors

Relations with the Workers' Movement
In order to distinguish itself from the major labor unions, all of which possessed middle-strata organizations, the CGC stressed three different themes. In each of these three areas the positions of the unions not only differed from one another but varied over time.

Pay structure　For the CGC the preservation, and indeed the accentuation, of a hierarchical pay structure was a categorical imperative, the founding principle of the organization and its *raison d'être*. At the 1969 CGC Congress it was stated that

the economic justification [of a hierarchical pay structure] lies in the economic value of the labor contribution. It is beyond doubt that the contribution of a skilled worker, foreman, technician, engineer, or supervisor has greater economic value than the contribution of a manual laborer or unskilled worker ... Coupled with the economic justification is a moral justification. Indeed, it is fortunately the case that a man's pay is commonly seen as a reward for his personal effort, intellectual ability, or moral qualities, and it is perfectly legitimate that this should be so. Last, and perhaps not least, is the social justification for a hierarchical pay scale. In a strictly egalitarian society personal advancement would have no meaning ... Given the economic, moral, and social justifications of the hierarchy of rewards, its maintenance is clearly in the general interest.

As André Malterre, former president of the CGC, put it: "Our organization has always favored a hierarchical pay structure, not only in order to protect the purchasing power of supervisory personnel but also as an indispensable prerequisite to the preservation of intellectual and moral values, a sense of individual responsibility, and a spirit of initiative and creative enterprise" (Malterre, 1972). It should be noted, moreover, that one of the main activities of the CGC is to produce a yearly survey of the pay structure.

Quite similar to the CGC's position on the pay hierarchy is the position long held by the CGT, though presumably the two groups have different reasons for holding their respective views. At the UGICT–CGT Second Congress, held in April 1967, its secretary-general asserted: "Defense of the pay hierarchy is coming to be an important issue for more and more categories of workers, not only as a way of defending their standard of living but also as a way of expanding the scope of the class struggle."[2] In May 1970, following a meeting with the CGC, the UGICT–CGT secretary-general declared that "there is no fundamental disagreement between the CGT and the CGC on the following points: hierarchy ..." Henri Krasucki, leader of the CGT, wrote that "to make demands anti-hierarchical in character, to make hierarchy the main issue, is counterproductive: it sets one group of workers against another" (*Vie Ouvrière*, 17 June 1970).

The end of the 1970s saw a change in the official CGT position. In 1977 the UGICT–CGT demanded that wage and salary differentials be reduced by means of differential raises favoring the worst-paid workers; in other words, pay classifications were to be revised within the framework of a unique pay scale running from the manual laborer to the chief engineer (*Le Monde*, 9 January 1977). The CFDT has long been critical of the pay hierarchy. In its view the ratio between the salary of the company president and the lowest-paid workers should be no more than six to one. On this point the two largest unions are in fundamental disagreement with the CGC.

Authority of supervisory personnel   As far as the CGC is concerned, the term "hierarchy" refers not only to pay but also to authority. Hierarchy is a fundamental part of the structure of societies in general and of industrial firms in particular. Supervisory personnel are of course employees of a firm, but they are not like other employees, given the fact that they exercise authority, delegated by the employer, who authorizes them to take certain initiatives. They are the "leaders of the new age," as the title of one radio program, specifically aimed at middle managers, suggests. Authority, exercised within a hierarchy, is what by definition justifies the supervisor's superior position. The workers' movement threatens this authority in at least two ways. On a daily basis workers challenge their "bosses," big and small, on matters of discipline, work organization, safety, and so on. Middle managers frequently complain that the normal hierarchy is by-passed by union delegates, who in some cases have direct access to top management. This, they say, makes a mockery of their authority. (To deal with this problem as well as to undermine the unions some large firms have reinstituted strictly hierarchical procedures for dealing with all personnel problems.) To make matters worse, management personnel have on occasion been sequestered by workers. The number of such incidents has been on the rise since 1968, and labor unions, particularly the CFDT, do not always condemn them when they occur. More generally, supervisory authority has been challenged by union attitudes toward the firm.

Both the CFDT and CGT have called for industrial democracy, worker self-management, and an end to the "monarchical system." Though the unions are careful to emphasize that there will be a role for supervisory personnel in the firm of the future (particularly as agents of technical and social innovation), many middle-level managers see the call for democratization of industry as part of a larger threat to establish an egalitarian society, which they regard as the root of all evil. Writing in *Le Creuset*, the journal of the CGC, in late 1970, CGC president André Malterre cited the following CFDT position (Thirty-fifth Congress, May 1970): "The struggle to democratize the exercise of authority leads to the demystification of the role played by present-day supervisory personnel and thus strikes at the underpinnings of authority in the capitalist system." Malterre comments,

> So we are forewarned. For the CFDT, the attack on hierarchy is a blow against authority in capitalist society and a strike at the capitalist model of economic and social development ... In such a battle compromise is out of the question. The CFDT has made this position its own. It is up to us to defend our vision of industry and society based on the human values of work and enterprise.

When the CGC refers to what it calls democratization, it means measures aimed at increasing the participation of management and supervisory personnel in the decision-making process.

Competition for representation of supervisory personnel   To the extent that the CGC considers its goal to be, in part, that of providing technicians, foremen, and managerial and supervisory personnel with their own distinctive form of representation and organization it clearly cannot tolerate competition, whether from trade unions or rival independents like the UCT. The CGC is particularly wary of competitors, owing to its great difficulties in gaining state recognition as a representative body at the time of the Liberation. At that time representativity was used as a basis by which a limited number of unions were granted certain special privileges. Various criteria were used to determine whether or not a particular organization was representative: size, attitude during the German Occupation, longevity, and so on. The CGC had to conduct a campaign of demonstrations and strikes from 1944 to 1946 in order to persuade the government to declare it a "representative" organization. It is the ambition of the CGC to be regarded as a true confederation on a footing of equality with the trade union confederations. In this respect it differs from the Fédération de l'Education Nationale, whose membership is far larger than that of the CGC. It is the view of the CGC that supervisory personnel are, by virtue of their qualifications and responsibilities, workers of a distinctive kind, not to be confused with the other employees of a firm. The fact that the leading labor confederations have affiliates that claim to represent managerial and supervisory employees runs counter to this view. Hence the CGC is unalterably opposed to these affiliates and does not hesitate to characterize them, rather contemptuously, as *groupuscules*.

Relations with employers
The main issues in CGC–business community relations partly parallel the main issues in CGC–union relations discussed above.

Hierarchical pay structures   The number of supervisory personnel has increased to the point where supervisory salaries can no longer be regarded as a negligible portion of total labor costs. Management is therefore concerned to keep these salaries down to a "reasonable" level. In some firms management has come to the conclusion that, in order to maintain the authority hierarchy, some reduction in pay differentials is essential (particularly in the area of fringe benefits). The pay hierarchy has thus in some cases been attacked by management, particularly through the so-called wage fund technique, promoted at one time by the government (with the *contrats de programme* and *contrats de progrès*). Each time this has happened the CGC has needless to say responded with all the vigor at its command.

"Concertation"   The CGC maintains that supervisory personnel possess important technical, social, and economic skills and that they are consequently in a position to play a major role within the firm: "Supervisory and managerial personnel stand between those who wield economic power and the bulk of the workforce. They are an intermediary group." Furthermore, the members of this group, "by virtue of their role within the firm, are more conversant with economic problems than are ordinary workers. What is more, some supervisors have been trained in economics in the universities and Grandes Ecoles" (Malterre,

1972). According to the CGC, the key role played in this area by managerial personnel is not recognized by employers. It is therefore important, says the CGC, that employers appreciate the value of joint efforts to make use of these skills and the importance of establishing the organizational structures needed to make this possible. The issue should be seen in the context of a broader demand for joint undertakings at all levels in both the economic and social domains. The slogan for all of this is *concertation*, a word that the CGC claims to have introduced into the economic sphere. In July 1974, after several years of discreet negotiations, the CNPF and CGC issued a joint statement (not an accord—the difference is important). This included, in particular, the following pronouncement:

> In order to achieve both social and economic progress, firms should enlist the support of the personnel they employ, particularly in managerial and supervisory capacities, by involving them in the decision-making process. Such a partnership can succeed only by avoiding systematic confrontation and working toward the goal of expanding the firm within the existing economic context.

The leading industry association within the CNPF, the UIMM, translated this general statement in the following way: "This recommendation," we are told, "is the fruit of lengthy and delicate discussions between partners attached to the *market economy and liberalism*, and as such concerned to strengthen the internal cohesiveness of industrial firms" (italics in original). The managerial unions affiliated with the CGT and the CFDT both denounced this statement, the former as "a misguided action" and the latter as a "fraud and an illusion." The truth of the matter is that, with respect to ideas about how firms should be run, the CGC in the late 1960s was largely in agreement with employers. Proof of this assertion is provided by the CGC proposal for industrial reform issued in 1969, that is, the year that saw the departure of the CGC's dissident minority.

Employment issues Another issue between the CGC and employers is that of employment. The economic crisis has been accompanied by a steady rise in layoffs of supervisory personnel, for whom unemployment has become as pressing a problem as it is for other kinds of workers. This has been the issue on which, for the first time, the CGC directly challenged employers. In 1973 the CGC proposed legislation that would allow employee representatives as well as stockholders to file suit to remove incompetent company executives. This was a particularly bold proposal, given the fact that the CGC had never before questioned the employer's legitimacy or power to make decisions. The CGC asked for a limited prohibition against layoffs of supervisory personnel between 50 and 60 years of age and requested that "a summit conference be held with the government on the question of employment."

Although the CGC rarely demonstrates at plant sites, when it does so the issue of employment is generally involved. The CGC never condemns capitalism as such, however, limiting its criticism to the excesses of capitalism, which it says can be overcome only by concerted economic action. What the CGC wants, in other words, is "a market economy whose excesses are corrected by the actions of labor organizations and the state guided by intermediary bodies" (Malterre, 1972, p. 96).

Relations with the State
Since its inception the CGC has come into conflict with the government over two major issues: the question of representativity, which was discussed earlier, and the question of social security and retirement.

Retirement benefits   The 1945 law establishing the social security system made contributions by supervisory personnel to the new plan obligatory and did away with the prewar retirement plan available to these higher-paid employees. The CGC immediately asked for the establishment of a separate, autonomous retirement fund to be administered by the beneficiaries. After a period of indecisiveness, the government finally agreed in 1947 to set up a supplementary retirement fund limited to managerial and supervisory personnel under the auspices of the social security system. Subsequently the government has more than once been tempted to take over this supplementary fund, which controls significant capital resources. In addition, the CGC has become involved in bitter disputes with the government over the level of social security payments by supervisory personnel. It is worth pointing out that, as far as the CGC is concerned, social security is merely an insurance plan not a means of redistributing income.

Direct taxation   For all governments, middle management is the ideal tax base. Managerial and supervisory personnel have relatively high incomes and relatively few opportunities for fraud compared with other occupational groups (farmers, merchants, professionals). Since its inception the CGC has complained about the burden of direct taxation falling on its members, a burden that impinges directly on their standard of living, reduces their differential pay advantage, and therefore leads toward the egalitarianism so feared by the CGC. The CGC says that its members are willing to make sacrifices if other relatively well-off social groups are also willing.

Incomes policies   In the ongoing battle against persistent inflation various governments have periodically made use of incomes policies of one form or another. Almost always these policies set a limit to the total wage fund while at the same time increasing the pay of the worst-paid workers, thus implicitly freezing the income of better-paid workers. As we saw earlier, the CGC has always vigorously opposed this kind of policy, because it undermines the hierarchical pay structure and diminishes the importance of contract negotiations between employers and employees, such negotiations being a key tenet of the CGC position.

The Evolution of the CGC

If we think of the labor movement, employers, and the state as the vertices of a triangle, then the evolution of the CGC between the late 1960s and 1982 might be thought of as a migration from vertex to vertex along this triangle. At the outset the position of the CGC was quite close to that of the employers: CGC broadsides spared both capitalism and the business community. The CGC's main problem was to establish the distinctive character of supervisory personnel, and its demands fell accordingly into three fundamental categories: preservation of the pay hierarchy, preservation of separate retirement funds for supervisory personnel, and reduction of the burden of direct taxes. Essentially these demands were directed not at employers but at the state. Little that was revolutionary was involved in the CGC's conception of the industrial firm. Industrial reform it saw as "less a seizure of power, which can only benefit a few, than a transformation of human relations at every level, involving both those who wield authority of various kinds and those who carry out their commands" (Malterre, 1972, p. 94, 1969). Employers are well aware of the CGC's attitude, and the CNPF has on occasion backed the CGC and urged supervisory personnel to join. On the issue of concertation, of great importance to the CGC, the CNPF dragged its feet for a number of years and in 1974 won agreement to a rather insipid declaration on the subject, a mere statement of intention, a recommendation rather than an accord committing both parties to specific actions. The "concertation committees" proposed by the CGC were not even mentioned. So great were the compromises made by the CGC that the joint statement has to this day not been implemented.

Given the CGC's rejection of class struggle and "subversive" activity as well as nationalization of industry, and its acceptance of the market economy and of a concept of economic planning that reduces the plan to no more than a vast market survey, it is clear that, ideologically speaking, the CGC at this point in time stood fairly close to the business community, particularly to that segment of it influenced to some degree by "modernist" ideas. What this shows is that up to 1974 priority was given to relations with employers. In that year however, in other words, with the beginning of the present crisis, we can begin to detect the first signs of a change in the CGC's position, some of which were touched on earlier (for example, the proposal to remove incompetent executives). The shift was at first quite tentative, however. For example, Yves Charpentié, André Malterre's successor as head of the CGC, wrote that the aim was not "to rake corporate executives over the coals but rather to help them to open their eyes" (*Le Matin*, 21 February 1978). A firmer new tone toward business was evident at the "Estates General" organized by the CGC in November 1980. In the meantime the leadership of the organization had changed: a new team led by Jean Menu had replaced Charpentié and his group with the express purpose of "resyndicalizing" the CGC.

While negotiating discreetly with the CNPF over the joint statement on concertation, the CGC was also involved in negotiations with the UGICT–CGT. As early as 1970 the president of the CGC had made it clear that a tactical accord with the CGT was possible. "We are closer to the CGT than to the other unions," he added, "on such issues as the defense of supervisory personnel and taxes." Following lengthy and difficult negotiations a text acceptable to both parties was approved. In May 1974 the UGICT–CGT announced that negotiations were continuing. In July 1974 the joint statement of the CGC and the CNPF on concertation was published. The CGT–CGC accord was never officially signed. The proposed agreement had always been tactical in nature, and the flirtation between the two groups ended abruptly. With the CFDT things never even got this far. In the eyes of the CGC the CFDT was virtually the devil incarnate.

Matters stood differently with Force Ouvrière and the CFTC, with which the CGC found considerable common ground: all three favored negotiated contracts, concertation, participation in management, the Common Market, anti-communism, and so on. Within the CGC there was sentiment in favor of a reformist alliance with FO and the CFTC against the "revolutionary" CGT and CFDT. Still, it was not until the Menu group came to power in the CGC that meetings with the other two organizations were held with any frequency, and even then no real alliance resulted. The CGC has been developing a new strategy that takes more account of other workers. It should be noted, however, that a joint communiqué issued in March 1982 by the CGC, FO and CFTC is critical of government but not of business, even though salient points of dispute with the business community remain unsettled (employment and reduction of working hours, for example).

Prior to the election of François Mitterrand, two dates stand out as particularly significant in CGC–government relations: 20 May 1970, in the Pompidou presidency, and 29 January 1979, during the presidency of Valéry Giscard. These are the only two dates since 1946 on which the CGC staged protest actions at the national level. The first of these two actions was aimed at certain measures proposed in the context of the Sixth Plan, which the CGC interpreted as an attempt to "bludgeon" its members into submission. The second followed an increase in social security payments. Both actions were intended, among other things, to protect the separate retirement funds and to protest against the burden of income and social security taxes. On several occasions—in 1970, in 1979 prior to the elections to the European Parliament, and in 1980 before the 1981 presidential elections—CGC leaders threatened to back candidates opposed to the majority then in power. This may seem paradoxical, given that the overall philosophy of government of the ruling majority corresponded fairly closely to that of the CGC (which in 1969 called for calm following the social upheaval of 1968). The fact of the matter is that the CGC's action should be interpreted as a pressure-group tactic intended to remind the government that its own interests could best be served by serving the interests of that part of the workforce that most nearly shared the government's philosophy.

Following the election of Mitterrand, the CGC adopted an attitude of benevolent neutrality. But it quickly came to the conclusion that the Socialist economic policy was incoherent and that Bills proposing new rights for industrial workers represented a threat to supervisory personnel, on whom the tax burden was again judged to be disproportionate. (This is so bitterly resented by nearly all managerial personnel that even those who belong to the CFDT asked in February 1982 for a two-year moratorium on further tax increases.) Faced, moreover, with the threat of losing its officially sanctioned monopoly as the representative of middle management, the CGC moved increasingly into opposition, though now it no longer had an alternative set of policies to propose for dealing with the persistent economic crisis. Meetings between the CGC and the Opposition political parties (RPR and UDF) resulted in communiqués vehemently critical of the left-wing government, whereas a meeting with the Socialist Party ended with a statement recognizing the disagreements between the PS and the CGC.

During the 1960s and early 1970s, then, the position of the CGC was apparently fairly close to that of the business community. Not until the onset of the economic crisis did the CGC begin, on rare occasions, to voice criticisms of business policy. With right-wing governments in power, the CGC generally attempted to exert increased pressure from within, but it was not until the advent of the Barre Plan that the CGC really took the offensive. In the May 1981 presidential elections a fair number of middle managers voted against the incumbent president. After the victory of the Socialists, the CGC at first seemed willing to go along with the new government. Very soon, however, its attitude changed radically. Although the business community has not regained its former favor in the eyes of the CGC, that organization's keenest arrows are now reserved for the left-wing government.

Interpretation

In our view the evolution of CGC is best interpreted in terms of a combination of two factors: internal conflicts due to the heterogeneous nature of the organization, and external forces associated with the economic crisis that began in 1974.

During the period of interest here the CGC was shaken by a number of extremely serious internal conflicts. In 1966 G. Nassé, then secretary-general, resigned his post, and in 1967 Nassé and his friends were eliminated from the leadership of the organization. In 1969 the group representing the petroleum industry was expelled from the organization and the group representing the nationalized electric and gas utility (EDS–GDF) withdrew. This led to the formation of a new organization, the Union des Cadres et Techniciens (UCT). The minority faction that founded the UCT drew its membership mainly from large, modern firms in both the private sector (petroleum, aerospace) and the public sector (utilities). It criticized the CGC for its conservatism, its stubborn attachment to the traditional triad of pay hierarchy, retirement benefits, and tax reduction, its closeness to the business community, and its lack of a comprehensive social vision. The minority accused the CGC of being Poujadist. The UCT therefore attempted to put forward a new program in which middle managers were assigned the "historical mission" of making society more just and humane (Donnadieu, 1970).

With the departure of the minority faction, the CGC came closest to identifying its position with that of business in its published program of industrial reform. Apart from the modernist faction responsible for this document, there were two other factions in the CGC. A conservative faction was headed by CGC president André Malterre, an avowed right-winger. Malterre drew his support mainly from the sales and marketing personnel, who were not officially recognized as "cadres." The federation that represented this group had a disproportionate number of votes in the CGC Congress. With the departure of Malterre in 1975, the conservatives retained control of the CGC, electing Yves Charpentié as president. Charpentié came into conflict with the third faction in the organization, which might be called the "corporatist" faction and which had earlier attacked Malterre. Its leader was P. Marchelli, head of the federation representing the metals industry, one of the largest and most active federations in the CGC. Marchelli also drew support from the federation representing the banking sector, which had long flouted Malterre's advice by recruiting members among the clerical personnel.

The corporatists were critical of the conservatives and the Charpentié group for adopting a middle-class outlook according to which "cadres" were defined more by their place in society and their social status than by their job, their place in the firm. They also accused their opponents of being too conciliatory toward the government. The "middle-class policy" had culminated in 1977 in the creation of so-called Groupes Initiative et Responsabilité (GIR). A project of Charpentié's, these groups included officials of professional groups, peasants, craftsmen, owners of small businesses, and physicians. Rumor had it that this was a political initiative inspired by supporters of Jacques Chirac. The corporatists, on the other hand, saw themselves as industrial workers, to be sure workers of a very special kind, but still workers. They criticized the conservatives for a lack of energy and aggressiveness and for being overly preoccupied with lobbying activities.

This is where the effects of the economic crisis come into play. Like other workers, supervisory personnel were faced with a sharp increase in unemployment and renewed threats to their standard of living (with the Barre Plan). Shared by a majority of middle management, these concerns enabled the corporatists, who saw themselves as the champions of this stratum of the workforce, to win control of the CGC in April 1979. Even earlier, in January 1979, the outgoing leadership was forced to follow the corporatists' lead in calling for anti-government demonstrations. Pressure on the government mounted with the advent of the new leadership (which called for an Estates General of supervisory personnel in November 1980, threatened to run its own candidate for President, and so on); Giscard's failure to win reelection in May 1981 was not lamented by the CGC. Still, as we have seen, within a year the CGC had gone back to attacking the government as a first priority, with criticism of the business community a distant second.

In conclusion, what should be noted is that each step in the evolution of the CGC has been a defensive reaction, not an offensive maneuver. The aim was either to defend the traditional triad (pay hierarchy, retirement benefits, tax reduction), that is, to uphold the distinctive position of the group's members, or else to promote employment and maintain purchasing power. The CGC has no medium- or long-range views to offer. It has no new view of the middle-management role to propose to its members, unlike the UGICT–CGT or the UCC–CFDT, which make much of scientific and technological progress.[3] Its arguments are generally couched in economic terms aimed at legitimating its specific demands, while social and political considerations are played down. The very group it represents, middle management and supervisory personnel, is ambiguously defined and heterogeneous in nature, and this forces the CGC to define itself as broadly as possible and largely in negative terms. It embodies no real project for the future. It is not a social movement; rather it is a pressure group, and this fact explains why it has so often wavered back and forth. In conceptual terms the CGC is halfway between a group representing a "profession" in the English or American sense and a trade union. Nevertheless, it would be a mistake for the labor movement or the current left-wing government to neglect the CGC, as is shown by the results of the 1982 cantonal elections, the 1983 municipal elections, and by various industrial conflicts that have erupted.

Notes: Chapter 6

1 It was during the 1960s that the CGT and CGDT became serious about reactivating their affiliates for managerial and supervisory personnel, at the same time that these personnel came forward to play a leading role in a number of important industrial conflicts (Société Neyrpic, for example) and sociologists began to take an interest in this social group.

2 At its 1969 Congress the CGC echoed these remarks, declaring that rejection of the pay hierarchy would "threaten to create a situation in which the value added by highly skilled but underpaid labor would accrue not to consumers or other workers but ultimately to investors, who would benefit from a higher return on capital."

3 In this area the only real contribution made by the CGC was a pamphlet entitled "La novotique" published in 1981. It was generous, vague, and apparently not very widely distributed.

PART THREE

"New Problems"

7

The Decomposition and Recomposition of the Working Class

JEAN LOJKINE

If one is to believe the overwhelming majority of recent sociological studies, the French working class is ailing. Increasingly divided into antagonistic or disparate groups at the place of work and residence, decomposed or diluted by various levels of stratification, the working class allegedly has lost all unity. As a consequence it has also lost its historical capacity to enter the political arena as the leading actor in the struggle for social change.

In this respect the collective work *Crisis and Future of the Working Class* (*Faire*, 1979), which brings together Edmond Maire, Bruno Trentin, and Socialists and historians close to the PS and CFDT, has the merit of revealing the link between such pessimistic diagnostics and the new strategy of the reformist workers' movement. For example, according to Pierre Rosanvallon:

> In the present situation we can no longer accept as given the very concept of the working-class. To speak of class is to speak of unity, these are one and the same. Today, however, the world of the workers is characterized by fragmentation and disintegration. (*Faire*, 1979, p. 24)

Workers are depicted as divided according to whether they have stable employment, the nature of their social benefits, the level of wages, and forms of collective organization (not to mention sexual, ethnic, or generational cleavages). Hence, for these authors, the "old myths" of working-class unity no longer hold in the face of the current decomposition: whether those myths be the recomposition of a "collective worker" grouped around skilled workers (a theme emanating from the PCF and CGT), around technicians (core of the "new working-class" theories of the 1960s—Mallet, 1963), or around semiskilled workers (central to the "mass worker" theory prevalent in Italy in the 1970s—Gaudemar 1980).

In fact what these authors question is the capacity of workers to overcome their divisions *through collective forms of identity tied to the process of production*. In contrast, Rosanvallon argues that production is dominated by the logic of capital which today divides the working class. Therefore, the unity of workers must be "built on a basis other than that of the factory" (*Faire*, 1979, p. 35) by rearticulating problems of the workplace and of the social environment (*cadre de vie*). Similarly Maire clearly favors working-class action based on "a conscious project for transforming consumption patterns and ways of life" (*Faire*, 1979, p. 70). As Touraine (*Faire*, 1979) observes, this signifies that working-class action at the workplace will be secondary to "new social movements" arising out of the consumption process or the milieux of administration and communications. From that point on working-class unity, the idea even of a "class" of workers, loses any significance. It is replaced by a social constellation in which the new wage-earning middle strata and especially intellectual workers will play a hegemonic role.

The political and strategic stakes are apparent in any research bearing on the working class. If it is true that the working class is no longer united in production, at the site of its exploitation and hence formation of its identity, then it is nothing more than a dominated class or a collection of marginal strata. As such, it may be capable of periodic revolts but incapable of intervening in decision-making arenas, of elaborating a social project pertinent for the ensemble of dominated strata.

Our task here, it should be understood, is not to "demonstrate" the revolutionary or nonrevolutionary nature of the working class but simply to contribute to the debate, in a scientific manner, some elements that may shed light on the reality of today's working class. Nothing could be worse, in our view, than a defensive and "workerist" reaction of the workers' movement to the findings of sociological research.

A False Debate: Working-Class Division or Unity

All serious scholars have stressed the incoherence of any debate which attempts to reduce the problem of working-class unity to the contrast (albeit mythical) between today's division and yesterday's unity. If there is a historical constant as old as capitalism itself, it is the process of decomposition and recomposition of the working class. This plays itself out as a function not only of the different stages or phases of capitalist development but also of the specific organizational forms of the workers' movement.

As early as 1845, in his *Condition of the Working Class in England* (1961), Engels related Great Britain's economic boom (stemming in large part from the generalization of factory legislation and the domination of industrial capitalists) to the differentiation within the working class. On the one hand, there were the "protected" sectors, unionized factory and construction workers, who obtained "durable" improvements in their living standard. On the other hand, there was the great mass of workers who made only "provisional" gains and were constantly being thrown back to their original condition "by the influx of crowds of unemployed workers held in reserve, by new machinery which continually replaces workers, and by the arrival of rural workers themselves increasingly replaced by machines" (1961, p. 394; see also Lojkine, 1972, p. 146).

Marx in *Capital*, within the context of his analysis of the workings of the capitalist economy, also drew distinctions between workers. First, there were "workers subject only to occasional unemployment" (*the floating surplus population*). Secondly, there were workers suffering from chronic underemployment (*the latent surplus population*, principally rural). Thirdly, there were workers with extremely irregular employment (*the latent surplus population*). Finally, there were those trapped in the living hell of pauperism: the chronically unemployed but able-bodied, children on forms of assistance and "demonetized" people (the aged, victims of industrial accidents, and workers with outdated qualifications).

Active workers are differentiated as a function of their qualifications, working hours, and form of pay. Here Marx, as well as Engels, juxtaposes the working-class aristocracy (foremen, supervisors, and full-time factory workers) and the large mass of workers with precarious employment (Mouriaux). The interest of their analysis does not lie in these, usually secondhand, descriptions but rather in the relationship Marx and Engels constantly attempt to establish between the *movement of capital accumulation* and the *structure of class*. On this point Pialoux (1981) is correct in insisting that these differentiations—contrary to the claims of contemporary students of the "segmentation of the labor market"—are not *givens* and *immutable*. It is thus illusory to juxtapose an "active army" characterized by stability and skills to a "reserve army" characterized by instability and lack of skills since, as Marx pointed out in his analysis of the relative surplus population, the reserve army is already present within the active labor army. A large number of individuals who belong to the relative surplus population are in fact overexploited laborers in archaic or declining sectors.

The privileged situation of a fraction of the working class can also be jeopardized by the process of capital restructuring. Engels, in the preface to the 1892 German edition of *Condition of the Working Class in England*, pointed out that collapse of the English industrial monopoly would threaten the status of the British working-class aristocracy: "[the English working class], including its privileged and directing minority, will some day be brought into alignment with workers abroad." Contrary to what Engels predicted, this did not bring about the "automatic" ascension of socialism in Britain. Nevertheless, without falling into economism, the relationship between the long-term dynamic of the economy and the internal structure of the working class cannot be ignored.

We must still specify this dual historical movement. Otherwise the process of decomposition–recomposition of the working class would be reduced to a quasi-mechanistic perpetual movement of "continuous restructuration" [*sic*] while no light was shed on the major historical phases of restructuring of the capitalist mode of production—classical and monopoly stages (simple monopoly, state monopoly capitalism and its crisis, and so on). Here Pialoux's analysis lacks rigor, in so far as it fails to link the process of internal restructuring of the working class to a precise understanding of the historical evolution of capitalism (with its national specificities) and of the role played by the workers' movement.

Engels by contrast, comparing the twenty-year era of rapid growth of English capitalism with the period of chronic stagnation beginning in 1876, shows how the transformation of the working class (in this case, the formation and subsequent decline of the British working-class aristocracy) can be linked to the major cyclical movements of capital accumulation (Engels, 1961, p. 394; see also Lojkine, 1972, p. 146). The newly formulated Marxist theory of overaccumulation/devalorization of capital (Boccara, 1977; *Cahiers de l'Histoire de l'Institut Maurice Thorez*, no. 31, 1979) should provide the framework within which to articulate a precise periodization of the economy with a global analysis of the working class, in its demographic, cultural, and political evolution and according to national, regional, and local specificities (for the latter see Trempé, 1971; Chenu, 1982).

We have not yet undertaken the task of linking the major phases of capital accumulation with the process of decomposition/recomposition of the working class. We have, however, studied the principal factors of differentiation and recomposition of the working class at the local level (Bleitrach *et al.*, 1981). The chief merit of our research, in my view, has been to discredit any economistic analysis which is limited to putting forth a simple correspondence between morphological factors (branch of economic activity, demographic changes, and so on) and class structures. We found that each new phase of capitalist accumulation corresponded to a leveling of past gains and the resurgence of new factors of heterogeneity. The structure of the working class, in both Lille and Marseille, is profoundly marked by the weight of the dominant branch of economic activity (the port and naval shipyard in Marseille, cotton and flax production in Lille), the form of mobilization of manpower (continual Mediterranean immigration in Marseille, the early halt of Belgian migration to Lille), the degree of laborforce mobility (high for the Marseille metalworker, low for the Lille spinner), or the sexual division of labor (the majoritarian status of women in the Lille textile industry and the close correspondence between task and salary differentials and the male/female division). However, the concrete form that these two class structures took historically escapes any morphological determinism.

There would seem to be a world of difference between the native Provence worker (highly skilled, owning his house, and working in the docks) and the Italian laborer (sleeping in the open and accepting miserable wages). Yet the Marseille workers' movement was able to overcome these divisions in a durable fashion and counter the different forms of corporatism and racism engendered by periods of recession (notably during the great depression of the late 1930s). Similarly in Lille the weight of paternalism in the textile industry did not prevent women workers from joining the CGT in the early 1900s or from participating in struggles, especially in the cotton mills (where women worked the looms). Despite all this, the differences among kinds of economic activity had a strong effect on the forms and particularly the degree of recomposition of the two working-class groups. In Marseille the pauperized mass of immigrant laborers would be transformed into a working class that was relatively well-paid and protected by collective accords. In contrast, the textile worker in the Lille region up until World War II would be subject to precariousness of employment and indigence.

Craft workers in Marseille (be they skilled workers in the docks, sugar refineries or steel mills) brought immigrant laborers into their union and political battles. In contrast, male spinners in Lille, despite the efforts of the minoritarian PCF and CGTU, demonstrated a long-lasting hostility toward their female competitors. However, this cannot be explained solely in terms of the differences in branch of economic activity between Marseille and Lille. In contrast to the Lille working class, the Marseille working class would be able to circumvent the different forms of corporatism that stemmed from the recruitment policies of employers. Yet in the United States, or Hamburg, the simple combination of migratory flux in the docks and craft structures in the shipyards presented an insurmountable obstacle to overcoming corporatist divisions. This relates to the role played by specific forms of working-class organization and class consciousness in the recomposition of the working class.

From the Workplace to the Residence: Unity and Division of Global Forms of Reproduction of the Working Class.

The workplace, consequently, is the locale *par excellence* of working-class formation and of working-class divisions; nevertheless, it cannot be separated from other milieux of class reproduction, such as the labor market and the place of residence. This is true both for the forms of reproduction of the laborforce and for the forms of collective solidarity. The working class is not defined solely by its place in the process of production (in the narrow sense of the capital–labor relationship in the firm) but by its place in the ensemble of relations of production in the broad sense of the term, that is, relations of production and of circulation, distribution, and consumption. Simply put, just because the working class is defined in the first instance by its ability to create surplus-value, that is, to produce, does not mean that it will not have a specific place in the consumption process and, more generally, in styles of life and culture. In other words, the problematic of working-class unity and division can never be reduced to problems arising from the coexistence of different categories of manpower generated by the firm or the market. On the contrary, there is always a profound connection between the movement of the laborforce as such and the specific forms of "the working world," of its vital space in the broadest sense of the term. In our opinion this point is absolutely crucial if one wants to develop a coherent analysis of the current crisis of working-class neighborhoods and their "ailments" or of the new problems posed by collective working-class action in the workplace.

Returning to our historical examples, both the division and various forms of unification of the working class are closely tied to types of urban organization. Thus in Marseille (from the first phase of industrialization in the nineteenth century up until the 1950s) the lack of an employer policy with regard to working-class housing favored a diffuse occupation of the urban space by different waves of immigrants. This in turn produced a very heterogeneous city, spread over a large area, where immigrants, uprooted and "free" to sell their labor power, were able to establish various systems of collective solidarity, ranging from the extended family to village communities. These systems of solidarity would serve to preserve consciousness of their roots and help them adapt simultaneously to forms of employer exploitation (through clan and clientelist practices) and to forms of working-class resistance.

In Marseille, as in the Paris suburbs, the "working-class fortresses" which developed between the 1930s and 1950s were formed not by isolated firms but by a network of production units intermingled with residential systems. The extreme labor mobility, notably among steelworkers, derived from a certain residential stability, in terms of family life and political and union activity. The extended family thus functions more as the crucible of class identification, of the transmission of life experience than as the milieu of integration and confinement (Bleitrach and Chenu, 1979, p. 30).

Nothing comparable can be found in Lille. Here the workforce, predominantly female, indigent, and precariously employed, lived in an area where employment was highly compartmentalized. Migrations did not engender a social and cultural mix, conducive to genuine urban diversification as in Paris, Lyon, or Marseille, but rather reinforced working-class division and dependence on cyclical fluctuations in the market for cotton and flax.

There are no similarities here with the stream of immigrants that ceaselessly entered the Marseille port area. Real immigration from Belgium came to an end by the turn of the century. The dominant characteristic of Lille workers would become their residential stability and proximity to their place of employment. The owners of the Lille mills implemented a series of paternalistic policies which sought to exert control over the working-class family (all members often working for the same firm). If the Lille urban area was not a mining town or factory town, neither was it (up until the 1950s) a major city propitious to cultural mix. The city was more a jumble of neighborhoods, each with a distinctive character. Neighborhoods bordered but were unaware of one another.

It is this specific form of working-class space that is shaped in a contradictory but simultaneously complementary way by a system of Catholic and employer social assistance and of worker mutual aid (dominated by reformist currents). Working-class resistance in Lille was thus marked by employer repression at the workplace and reliance on neighborhood associations and municipal administration. The most advanced fraction of the working class—the steelworkers of Five-Cails and the railwaymen of Hellemmes—were isolated within this system of sociability, which was simultaneously compartmentalized and cut off from struggles at the workplace. This fraction thus could not play the catalyzing or unifying role exercised by the steelworkers of Paris or Marseille.

The Current Crisis and New Forms of Working-Class Division: How Can Potential Outlets Be Found?

The historical example cited above serves to relativize the current forms of division, segmentation, and decomposition of workers as a group. It does not, however, explain these nor indicate how to overcome them.

The various forms of collective solidarity forged by groups of workers in the nineteenth and first half of the twentieth century rested in essence on the professional and cultural autonomy of craft workers, in particular skilled workers in metallurgy. It is precisely this dual autonomy which is today destroyed. On the one hand, this stems from a new division of labor in the workplace with the Taylorist splitting up of tasks and the development of mechanization. On the other hand, it derives from the destruction of past nuclei of working-class cultural autonomy (the neighborhood and the extended family) with its sexual division of tasks between male militantism and female organization of family life.

Serge Mallet (1963) in the 1960s thought he had found a new catalyzing group within the working class: the technicians of automated industries would replace the "professionals" of yesteryear. However, an examination of the major worker struggles in 1968 or the 1970s suggests that it was more often the semiskilled (OS) rather than technicians who challenged the Taylorist division and parcelization of work. In fact only recently has the problem of the relationship between technicians and manual workers come to the fore. This is due to the fact that widespread automation of production and of research and development is only just beginning. Lacking an analysis of the contradictory position of technicians within the working class, Mallet in part overlooked the tendency of capitalism, through crisis, to accentuate the process of Taylorization and overexploitation of the laborforce.

It is for this reason that the growth of the semiskilled strata and their struggles seemed, to many observers, categoric proof that Mallet's theses were erroneous. This obscured the other tendency, however: the development of new forms of skill tied to automation. In point of fact the theories founded on a recomposition of the working class around the "mass worker" completely ignored the real diversity of positions and qualifications in favor of an abstract and utopian conception of a working-class collective, which denied any technical division of labor. From the OS on the production line to the systems operator there was only one type of laborer, performing work that was simple, homogeneous and standardized (Coriat, 1979a). This missed altogether the innovation that automation represents with respect to mechanization, even if capitalism also tends to adapt the new forms of automation to the Taylorist division of labor.

It is none the less true that current working-class struggles, as well as the majority of sociological research, tend to stress working-class division rather than unity. Thus we have stable workers protected by collective agreements vs workers on part-time, workers in large factories vs workers in firms performing subcontracting, and so on. The same is true with respect to working-class social environments. The old neighborhood communities are replaced by new units for nuclear families. Weekend car trips seem to portend the demise of community life. And the new place of women at work puts into question the former sex-based separation between militant and family life.

Still more serious, divisions of the labor market appear to be deepening through the segregation of housing and social environment. The number of ghettos where the families of the marginalized (often immigrants) reside are growing at a fast pace and entail a complete disintegration of working-class bastions. Here fear, violence, and individual withdrawal are replacing the former associative networks.

Certainly the "tough" or the youth "gang" is not an invention of the 1970s crisis. Marseille in the 1930s, with Sabiani and the gangs which reigned over the port, was an earlier version of today's waves of delinquence. Yet one can reasonably ask whether existing working-class organizations have the means to overcome ethnic and generational cleavages and forge a new solidarity that represents the aspirations not only of the working-class but also the whole of urban wage-earning strata. This is all the more pressing since, more than ever before, the working class cannot be treated in isolation from other wage-earning strata.

The Danger of Theoretical Workerism

An analysis of the dual process of decomposition and recomposition of the working class in all its complexity today implies, in our opinion, a double effort. On the one hand, this process must be linked to a global analysis of the crisis, by dialectically articulating an economic and "anthronomic" analysis, an analysis of the modes of production and reproduction. We will return in a later section to this critical point. On the other hand, this process must be linked to the whole process of restructuring social classes, notably the peasantry and traditional petit-bourgeoisie and especially the new wage-earning middle strata (Eizner and Hervieu, 1979).

A common defect of current efforts to ascertain the forms of working-class recomposition is the radical separating out of fractions of the working class from the totality of working-class and wage-earning strata. Thus anthropologists exalt those forms of solidarity linked to previous working-class cultures (in contrast to so-called "bourgeois" or "petit-bourgeois" culture). They fail to take into account the limits of these systems of sociability: where the woman was excluded from public and professional life and burdened with household tasks and the couple submitted to the "classical" and patriarchal norm of the extended family. Similarly the legendary figure of the "exalted" Parisian, spearhead of the Paris commune, risks obscuring the less glorious side of working-class life in the 1870s, namely, alcoholism, prostitution, and the often tragic fate of children (Poulot, 1980). As for the "mass worker," this new mythical figure implies a dual rupture with the skilled worker (perceived as privileged) and with technicians and engineers (placed in the camp of management and the bourgeoisie).

The "undifferentiated," "homogeneous" worker, without recognized skills, highly mobile, easily replaceable, without any real or permanent organization for struggle and defense, this "multinational mass worker" is considered the product of the merging of four groups: uprooted farm laborers, women, the "young," and immigrants (Coriat, 1979b; Gaudemar, 1980). The struggle against Taylorism and Fordism is said to be organized around this "mass worker." In point of fact, as Pialoux (1981) shows well, the postulated homogeneity of this "mass worker" is totally contradicted by any serious study of the diversity of status and qualifications of workers in mass-production industries. Moreover, Italian authors themselves admit today that this "laboring persona" is split up into a "multitude of partial and contradictory images and workers' struggles fragmented into thousands of marginal episodes" (Gaudemar, 1980, p. 97).

In essence theoretical workerism has two faces: (1) a mythical glorification of the past leading to the conjuring up of ahistorical, intangible, and normative working-class figures (from the "craft worker" to the "mass worker"); and (2) a systematic anti-intellectualism which is nourished by mechanistic contrasts between "working-class experience" and theoretical or scholarly understanding, between manual and intellectual, between those who produce and those who conceive.

These sociological analyses, fed more than commonly believed by attitudes still dominant in the *entire* workers' movement, introduce an arbitrary cleavage within the working class between skilled and semi-skilled (OP and OS) on the one hand, and technicians on the other hand, thus masking the objective rapprochement under way between manual workers and certain intellectual workers. In this respect the definition proposed by Freyssenet (1977) of working-class qualification ("degree and frequency of intellectual activity that a job demands") seems to share this theoretical workerism. As Dubar (1980, p. 47) rightly points out, this definition mechanistically emphasizes the opposition, at all stages of the machine age, between manual and intellectual tasks, although the evolution of productive forces has profoundly altered the definition of "manual work" and "intellectual work." Thus capitalist automation is not characterized, as Freyssenet believes, by "the concentration of intellectual activity in offices of research and development." Rather it is characterized by a dual movement of a development of certain intellectual aspects of manual work and a devalorization of the major part of intellectual labor itself in research bureaus.

Similarly the emphasis placed by certain anthropologists on past working-class communities and cultures (forgetting their sexist and paternalistic nature) tends to conceal real social liberation brought about by the construction of single-family housing, the emancipation of the couple, and new forms of sociability open to confrontation, exchange, cultural mix, and individual initiative (Verret, 1979).

Elements to Identify Existing and Potential Forms of Working-Class Recomposition

We have no intention of questioning the depth of the crisis that today threatens the working class and its organizations: divisions between statutory and temporary workers, employed and unemployed, natives and immigrants; and so on. Certainly such divisions are not new but the gravity of current unemployment levels does not facilitate efforts by the workers' movement to overcome the cleavages.

We believe, however, that the concept of "crisis" implies not only the destruction of old structures but also the birth of new ones. It is precisely these new forms being born in the midst of the crisis of state monopoly capitalism that we will attempt to analyze briefly here. We will emphasize a crucial aspect of the current economic and social crisis, that is, *the confrontation between the capitalist system and the new potentialities inherent in existing forms of automation*. Automation today is no longer confined to certain managerial activities or continuous flow industries (petrochemicals, cement) but extends to discontinuous production industries, privileged sites of working-class concentration, and organization of the workers' movement (metallurgy). The current capitalist response to these initial forms of automation (layoffs of OS and OP, intensification of work, divisions of statutory workers and part-time workers in subcontracting firms, and so on) has fostered the belief among many sociologists (Coriat and Linhart) and working-class activists that automation is just a new form of Taylorism and capitalist exploitation. In my opinion this is a grave mistake that runs the risk of misperceiving the *revolutionary stakes* of current technological changes, were the revolutionary workers' movement to grasp the new technological potentialities in order to propose and implement a different organization of work, a new system of qualifications, and a new style of administration (from the shopfloor to the firm).

Already the preceding technological phase (that of mechanization of mass-production industry) revealed the real albeit limited alternatives to the Taylorist division of labor (job rotation, recomposition and enriching of tasks) in those locales where worker struggles challenged the capitalist organization of work. The very nature of the current crisis (a crisis of the efficacy of the whole of capitalist productivity) and the novelty of the potentialities offered by the initial forms of automation (breaking with the mechanical principle as such) allow further progress to be made. Contrary to the myth of the "factory without people," the automation of entire production sequences and the computerization of the most simple and standardized modes of regulation and control of machines implies a high degree of qualification (both technical and social) for operators. The gravity and cost of breakdowns today assigns an important place to *preventive control* and thus to *breakdown avoidance*.

Contrary to technical and technocratic myths prevalent at the beginning of automation, capitalist elites themselves have recognised the total ineffectiveness of the old Taylorist system in running automated systems. In today's world the combination of unskilled or semiskilled operators and an external maintenance service has proven unprofitable. This is the source of the interest in new "productivity missions" to Japan among European and American businessmen. It is the massive skilling of operators and an integration of work collectives into management of the firm that explains in large part the productivity gains of Japanese industry. None the less, the Japanese "quality circles" are essentially capitalist adaptations to the new technological levels: the economic criteria remain the rate of profit, capital accumulation, and overexploitation of the laborforce.

Taking a different perspective (an alternative calculation of costs that would stress human development and economize on capital expenditures), the French workers' movement could take advantage of the switch to automation to link new working-class skills to a transformed organization of work, resulting in a changed relationship between manual labor (in the workshop) and intellectual labor. Even today the proper functioning of automated sequences requires multivalence of programmers, maintenance workers, and repairmen. This tends to diminish the former cleavages between production and maintenance or between programming and production in so far as numerical control and microprocessors allow the operator to program his or her own work.

Not only does the presence of highly qualified technicians become a necessity but also the relationship of the direct producer to the machine becomes more and more abstract and entails the use of intellectual faculties (attention, deduction) and of capacities for initiative and responsibility (given the cost of equipment). The current division between executants and planners is thus not ineluctable any more than is the precariousness of employment (through subcontracting and temporary work). It can therefore be demonstrated that true social efficacity could be achieved through regularizing the status of workers, putting an end to hierarchical compartmentalization, and eliminating subcontracting.

Even the "disappearance" of the OS does not inevitably mean their dismissal. Real professional training—nearly nonexistent now for this category of workers—would allow them to become skilled workers in their own right, overseeing and controlling the new automated systems (Lojkine, 1982).

May 1981 to June 1982: Where Do We Stand?

It is important when attempting to ascertain the "new potentialities" of automation not to entertain the illusion that there is some "necessary" recomposition of working-class unity "under the effect" of automation (a trap to which theorists of the "new middle class" or the "scientific and technical revolution" have fallen victim). This for two reasons: first, capitalism has demonstrated (and will continue to do so) that it can adapt perfectly well to new forms of automation provided the mass of laborers can be forced to accept new forms of self-exploitation. The Japanese "quality circles" offer ample evidence. Secondly, one can no longer speak *stricto senso* of a new recomposition of the "working" class, if one means by that only laborers directly engaged in production. *For this thereby eliminated the central stake of the next twenty years*: the alliance between productive and unproductive laborers *at the workplace* (supervisors, engineers, technicians, white-collar employees) and *on regional and national terrain* (educational workers, health workers, researchers). We thus prefer to speak of a new recomposition of the *collective laborer, both productive and unproductive*.

Twenty years hence automation will in effect have reduced those workers directly engaged in production of material goods to 10 percent, and possibly even 2 percent of the working population in the advanced industrial countries (Bell, 1973). The "that's enough" (*ras-le-bol*) attitude of assembly-line workers at Citroën, Renault or Peugeot will force mass-production firms to robotize fabrication and assembly processes and try to adapt Taylorism and capitalist profitability to the new imperative of automatized production.

Everything thus depends, in France as elsewhere, on the capacity of the workers' movement—bringing together manual workers and wage-earning middle strata—to elaborate a global strategy corresponding, at the workplace and in milieux reproducing the "general conditions" of production (the city and, especially today, the region), to *new criteria for management* and to a new type of growth. This new growth cannot be based on the liberal solution (treating wage payments as unproductive "costs") nor the Keynesian solution ("the relaunching of production through consumption" which does not address the cost of capitalist management of the economy) (Boccara, 1982; *Economie et Politique*, June 1982).

The Battle for New Criteria of Management
In 1981 the rejection of the "austerity" policy of the right brought to power a left government in France. This government has put forward two major structural reforms that may tackle the problems of the late twentieth century if, that is, workers mobilize not as in the past to criticize and resist but rather to suggest and administer in a new way their workplace, their office, their town, and their region themselves. The two major reforms are the nationalization of the key industrial and banking groups that dominate the economy and the law on decentralization of local collectivities (communes, departments, and regions).

An intense class battle has been waged within the new nationalized public sector over how this sector will be administered. Will it continue as before: according to "the laws of the market and international competition," which led the previous elite to serve certain "bastions" and abandon entire sectors of our economy (such as machine tools or certain data-processing areas) to American, Japanese, or German firms? Alternatively will it aim at "reconquering" employment, national economic independence, and human fulfillment?

At this writing the new conjunctural measures, notably the "wage and price freeze," display the same ambiguity as the previous attempt by certain Socialist leaders to "fund" the reduction of the working week (to 39 hours) by reducing wages, in the name of "work-sharing" and "solidarity in the crisis" (dear to the CFDT). The rejection by the CGT and a large number of CFDT locals of a new austerity policy put a halt to the first effort at "work-sharing." The recent OS strikes are not just a "rejection of [dirty] work" but also a rejection since 10 May of any reduction in their purchasing power.

The issue today is whether the government (predominantly Socialist) will, under the pressure of class struggles, opt for a new economic logic entailing a genuine reduction of capital's dominion. Or, on the contrary, will the government institute a new "state monopoly capitalism" where once again the public sector will serve as the "crutch" for private monopoly capital?

In our view the telling factor will be the capacity of the workers' movement, in the large sense, to utilize its new rights for direct expression by wage-earners (as well as the new economic rights of the works committees) and the laws on decentralization and planning (with the new role for the works committees at the regional and local levels) in order to promote a new mode of management of our society.

We are currently confronting neither "social democracy" nor "post-capitalism" but rather a contradictory sociopolitical process which, in one year, has engendered new perspectives. The social forces fighting for socialism have gained ground, but capitalism still governs the workplace and shapes the dominant ideology.

8

Trade Unionism and Technology

GUY GROUX

Technology, Ideology and Society

Up to the 1970s trade union discourse about technology was largely ideological in nature. Technology was seen as "a progressive force, an agent of social transformation" and as a "tool for transcending capitalist society"—transcending capitalist society being one of the constant preoccupations of the major workers' organizations in France. This preoccupation explains the "class-based trade unionism" of which the CGT is a prime example. The influence of Marx is undeniable, though it is often more implicit than explicit in formal discussions of technology. The notion of productive forces comes up in this context, particularly the contradiction that Marx says exists between the productive forces and the social relations of production at certain historical junctures.

This ideological norm crops up repeatedly in CGT pronouncements on technology. An example is provided by an article published in December 1981 in the CGT's official organ, *Le Peuple*, which informed its readers that "rapid technological progress, and its application in industry, is a crucial factor in challenging existing relations of production and social relations, of which technology is both cause and effect" (Obadia, 1981).

Other theories have influenced the thinking of the CFDT. One was popular in the 1960s, the "new working class," according to which new actors were emerging in conflicts affecting French capitalism at that time. Prominent among these new actors were technicians and engineers who, it was said, were being "radicalized" by the use made of technology within the capitalist system of production. The influence of this idea on the CFDT can be seen not only in its attitude toward class alliances (or class fronts) but also in its criticisms of capitalist implementation of production technologies.

Union discussions of technology have characteristically looked upon society as a totality. Labor critiques focussed on the social implications of technology and not merely on its associated ideology; in short, they were societal and not merely ideological in nature. The CFDT's current position on the nuclear industry, as well as the CGT's current views on the more general question of energy, still reflect this once-dominant theme in labor discussions of technology. For the CFDT, what is at stake in the nuclear issue, beyond questions of industrial policy, is the environment and the safety of the public. The CFDT's demands in this area, based on those of the FGE–CFDT, are quite general in nature: a moratorium on further nuclear development together with democratic discussions involving all concerned social groups (*Syndicalisme*, no. 1878, September 1981, p. 12). This position, typical of the CFDT, extends well beyond the boundaries of the firm to embrace all society. Despite differences between the CFDT and the CGT on this issue, the same can be said of the latter union. Thus, when the Economic and Social Council adopted the Le Guen Report on energy-related problems in October 1981, the CGT's confederal bureau stated that

> this report ... comments on many basic issues, from the need for national independence with respect to sources of energy to the satisfaction of popular needs and the reconstruction of our industrial base. It raises questions about our oil supply that deserve particular attention from the government and the National Assembly. (*Le Peuple*, no. 1117, October 1981, p. 76)

Implicit in the unions' "societal" critiques is the need to have recourse to the state, though the type of recourse envisioned varies from one union to the other. Indeed the need to rely on the state is a prominent feature of this type of criticism.

Union criticisms of the ideology and social consequences of technology have little to do with the labor process as the basic material component of economic production, and this may explain why the production technologies associated with Taylorism faced little real opposition from the leading workers' organizations (see Borzeix in this volume). This may seem paradoxical. To be sure, the unions did take steps to confront this paradox in certain periods. During the economic reconstruction that followed the Liberation, for example, the CGT made a major effort to deal with the issues of industrial modernization, productivity increases, and upgrading technology. It tried to get the newly organized works councils involved in these issues, as is shown by the writings of Barjonet and Lebrun for the journal *Travail et Technique* in the late 1940s. Later some conflicts involving technicians, at the CEA (Atomic Energy Commission), for instance, raised questions about the technological aspect of certain management decisions (Pesquet, 1968; Tripier, 1970). During the 1960s such disputes, involving technical personnel, partly foreshadowed new approaches by the unions to technological issues (Mallet, 1963; Bon and Burnier, 1966). The new union outlook focussed on the organization of labor and economic production.

Technology and the Organization of Work

It was not until the 1970s—more precisely in 1975—that the unions' analyses of technology began to take full account of the material effects of technology on the organization of work. No longer did discussion center exclusively on ideology or on the social consequences of technological change. Now the focus began to shift to the labor process itself and hence also to social conflict in the workplace.

The earliest and clearest manifestation of this change was due to the CFDT. Edmond Maire (*Cadres-CFDT*, no. 290, September–October 1979, p. 4), in a discussion of 1974 strikes in the banking industry and the PTT, defined what he called "a neo-Taylorism of the service sector" and went on from there to discuss the evolution of debate within the unions over the course of the 1970s in the following terms:

> When the question of semiskilled workers became the pressing issue of the day, Taylorist organization had been gaining ground in French industry for some twenty years. By contrast, change is taking place today at a much faster pace. Computers have thus far made only limited inroads into the workplace—and already they are being questioned by workers. It is to be hoped that such questioning will persist, and we for our part will try to see that it does. For we do not want to be subjected once again, thanks to the computer, to the homogenizing totalitarianism of Taylorism.

Clearly for Maire the issue is not the computer as a tool but rather its consequences (under capitalism) for the organization of work. Later in the same article he notes that "it is possible ... to move away from Taylorism and make computers a genuinely progressive tool." This approach to technology treats technological progress both in itself and in terms of its effects on the labor process.

As for the CGT, the change in outlook came more gradually and must be deduced from its later positions on technological questions. The essential change was this: the CGT ceased to look upon technology primarily as part of the "productive forces," with all the ideological and social connotations implicit in the term. It also ceased to view technology primarily in the context of large, high-technology firms, as it had been inclined to do previously. Instead the primary concern became one of examining technological issues on a case-by-case basis, looking at individual firms. The remarks of Obadia (1981) are most suggestive in this regard:

> To begin with, we cannot overemphasize the fact that, with respect to these issues (computerization and automation), we cannot stick to the rhetoric of five or ten years ago in relation to advanced high technology sectors. The time of mass production and widespread distribution of these new technologies has begun ... We must lead the battle to insure that science and technology serve the cause of social and economic progress, not only in general, but case by case in the firms. (Obadia, 1981, p. 10)

The fact that Obadia's article was published in December 1981 is in many respects indicative of the way in which the CGT views its own position in relation to the political changes that took place in France in 1981. But this would be an overly narrow reading of CGT policy, reducing the policy to "political opportunism," by viewing it as a response to changes made at the governmental-superstructural level. Instead Obadia's article must be seen as part of a long, slow evolution of the CGT's approach to technological issues. As early as the late 1960s the CGT, which at that time based its position on the notion of "industrial democracy," published articles interpreting technology to a large extent in terms of its place in the production process. In 1975 the UGICT–CGT planned a major debate on the subject of automation in industry (*Options*, no. 102, 1975). Lastly, the economic and social conditions prevailing in the 1970s obviously exerted tremendous influence on the CGT's discussion of technological issues, and for that matter on the CFDT as well.

Historical Changes in the Discussion of Technology

As we have seen, until the 1960s union discussions of technological questions remained largely ideological in nature. The stakes were defined in terms of the social impact of technological change, and discussion of these issues often revolved around attempts to find "political" solutions.

By contrast, current union discussions of these questions arise from more immediate objective concerns and typically relate to such burning questions of the 1970s as the economic crisis and its effects on employment. The crisis hit, as we shall see, at just about the time when certain sectors, primarily the service sector, were being restructured by the introduction of new technologies. Stated another way, technology was beginning to preoccupy the unions because of the threat that it posed to jobs already vulnerable to heightened international competition in the early years of the crisis (1973–5). Despite the recent slowing of investment in industry, technological change has had a major impact on the restructuring of the economy in the wake of the crisis. As the unions see it, technology may in certain circumstances reinforce the effects of recession on employment. In this view the effects of recession and technological restructuring are similar and mutually reinforcing, both ultimately threatening jobs (Nora and Minc, 1978).

The other main topic in trade union discussions of technology is the effect of technology on working conditions. In the wake of the workers' movement of May 1968 numerous challenges were raised to the existing organization of the workplace and concomitant working conditions. In this respect the 1971 strike of semiskilled workers at the Renault plant in Le Mans still plays the role of a symbol and a precedent. Faced with a growing number of disputes in which working conditions were involved, both the CGT and the CFDT had by the early 1970s made working conditions a primary object of union activity (CGT, 1972; Durand, 1977; Dassa, 1978; CFDT, 1978c; and Dubois in the present volume).

The impact of computerization first began to make itself felt in this context, with the unions charging that computer systems would profoundly alter both working conditions and skill requirements in the manufacturing and service sectors. Thus technology became a central issue in what the unions considered to be one of their primary areas of responsibility. This explains how technology came to be incorporated in and helped to sustain ongoing union discussions of working conditions. No longer would these discussions focus exclusively on Taylorism and the problem of semiskilled workers. Now they could be expanded to embrace the modernization of the labor process and to include other occupational groups, such as office workers concerned about the introduction of computerized office systems.

To sum up, then, the main topics of the "new" trade union discourse remain quite traditional, namely, employment and working conditions. Examination of the literature shows beyond any doubt that these new concerns were shared by both the CGT and the CFDT. Though the causes of discussion were the same, however, the effects on the strategies of the two unions were not, and their respective positions have not moved closer together. Here we see the consequences of the primacy of ideology in the French labor movement, coupled with the practical consequences of the fact that each union has its main roots in different sectors of the economy.

From Union Strategies to Shopfloor Activities

In fact the strategies of the CGT and CFDT are strongly dependent on two factors: one objective, namely, the sectors of the economy in which their respective memberships are most firmly rooted, and the other subjective, namely, their respective ideological orientations.

That there are strategic differences between the CGT and CFDT with respect to technological issues is obvious. These differences affect the way in which each union analyzes technological questions. At first glance the CFDT's discussions of these issues seem better defined, more developed, informed, and thorough than those of the CGT.

It should be noted, however, that these differences are not due solely to the respective ideological positions of the two unions. They also result from differences in rank-and-file support. Broadly speaking, the CGT is based in heavy industry, whereas the CFDT's strength lies primarily in the service sector. Automation and computerization have made few inroads in heavy industry, with the exception of chemicals. Compared to its competitors, France undeniably lags behind in this respect. The Bureau d'information et de prévision économique (BIPE) lists the following figures for the number of computerized robots per 100 workers in each of the following countries: France, $0·7$; Italy, $0·9$; West Germany, $1·1$; United States, $1·6$; Japan, $6·0$; and Sweden, $8·0$.

By contrast, in the service sector, the use of computers was well established. In 1970, 20 percent of all computers used in France were in banking and insurance (Janco and Furjot, 1972, p. 184). With the introduction of so-called distributed data-processing systems in 1974–5, the automation of office work advanced yet another step. The total number of computers in France increased by nearly 30 percent in 1978 (*Cadres-CFDT*, no. 290, September 1979, p. 23), while the number of people employed in banking began to level off as early as 1977 (CGT, 1981, p. 21). Given the CFDT's strong presence in the service sector, it is easy to see why it should have been the first to raise the issue of automation.

But this line of analysis can take us only so far. In fact there are also ideological reasons for the differences in approach between the CGT and the CFDT, differences that extend to the formulation of technology-related issues and their implications for trade union theory and practice. Today the issue of technology is mainly a question of where technology is introduced into the labor process and what new kinds of technology are involved. Computers themselves are not at issue but rather the way in which the labor process is computerized. It is also important to consider management options in introducing new technology and to ask how the unions can influence such decisions through the bargaining process, short of actually participating in them. The leadership of the CFDT clearly seems to have moved in this direction, especially since 1978 (see the chapter by Mouriaux in this volume).

The problem, as CFDT leaders see it, is for the unions to try to influence management decisions concerning technology in a variety of ways, including not only questions of employment but also the organization of the workplace, skill requirements, investments, choice of equipment, and so on. In this connection the position of the UCC (the CFDT's union of managers and technicians) is important, and it has been adopted at the confederal level as well (*Syndicalisme*, 4 October 1979, p. 7; *Cadres-CFDT*, no. 295, September—October 1980, p. 8). The main point is for labor to go beyond protest and denunciation and to formulate genuine counterproposals (discussed by Huiban in this volume). This poses a challenge to one of the most basic traditions of the labor movement in France. The influence of ideological and historical tradition has been strong in French labor's struggles for higher wages and better working conditions. What is more, labor has traditionally reacted to and frequently opposed management decisions with respect to industrial policy and technology. In this regard the historical example of the Lyon silk weavers was more than a symbol, it was a parable containing a hidden lesson and laying down an example of correct conduct for all workers.

Ultimately the real issue is whether the unions will develop new strategies similar to comanagement strategies of the sort adopted in Germany by the Deutscher Gewerkschaftsbund (DGB). If the logic of the new union position is pushed to the limit, then it may eventually run counter to some traditions of the French workers' movement.

For obvious historical, ideological, and sociological reasons, the CGT has been extremely reluctant to move in this direction. Over the past few years, despite some revision of the CGT's traditional positions and a tentative new spirit of pragmatism, the union has firmly refused to participate in management decisions. Indeed this refusal has been raised to doctrinal status. In regard to the new technologies the CGT has in some respects shown itself to be more pragmatic than in the past, but this pragmatism has been coupled with frequent references to socialism. In the words of C. Korsakissok (1980, pp. 16–17), "computers will in the future, when certain conditions have been met, become a potential tool of self-management, a tool that promises workers control of their work and their workplace."

To be sure, the CGT's unwillingness to exert influence over management decisions in regard to technology has in practice not been unwavering, particularly in some nationalized firms. Nationalization (along with the change of government) may be regarded by the CGT as a reason for union participation in certain kinds of decisions, as Yvette Harff has shown. The CGT's attitude toward the nationalized sector in the period 1944–8 is a precedent that could serve as an ideological reference

Unlike the CGT, the CFDT makes no distinction, implicit or explicit, between the public and the private sector in its discussion of technological issues and strategies for dealing with them. As a hypothesis, therefore, one might suggest that there is a correspondence between the attitudes of the unions toward the new technologies and their ideological positions with respect to comanagement. To investigate this hypothesis further one might want to consider its implications for industrial relations. For instance, certain federations of the CFDT, such as the metalworkers (FGM) (see interview with G. Granger in *Syndicalisme Universitaire*, no. 820, March 1982) and the chemical workers (FUC), now seek negotiations involving discussion of productivity gains and linking new technologies, issues of employment, and duration of work. Clearly this approach could, if carried far enough, lead to bargaining of the type associated with comanagement.

Appearances to the contrary notwithstanding, ideologies are never abstract phenomena, as Gramsci showed. An ideology is always a product of material facts, even when it is a "distorted reflection" of those facts. In the area that interests us here, however, there is apparently a wide gulf separating what the unions say from what they actually do in the firm.

In the Firm: The Resistance of the Actors

First, there is a gulf between what the unions say and what they do with respect to labor disputes. Strikes have hit highly technologized firms in industry, above all in the service sector. Ray (1981) has written about strikes in 1979 at a number of insurance companies. Analyzing labor disputes is always a complex business, and when technological issues are involved it becomes even more complex. In various highly technological firms, including banks such as the Crédit Lyonnais, insurance companies such as UAP, the government statistical agency (INSEE), and the Postal Service technological innovations have been the occasion of labor disputes. But the issues in such disputes were generally quite traditional. A good example is the issue of video display terminals (VDTs). Worker grievances emphasized eye-strain and the need for relief periods but not the VDT equipment itself. In the insurance industry women keypunch operators have asked for an end to productivity bonuses (CFDT FGSL, 1980). Computer operators have struck over questions of job classification and working conditions, for example, compulsory shiftwork in a dispute at the Société Générale (*Le Monde*, 25 February 1982). In 1973 there was labor unrest lasting more than a month in the cement industry, already highly automated. But the issue of production automation never arose in either the labor agitation or the ensuing negotiations.

The printers' strike at the Paris newspaper *Le Parisien Libéré* was intended to protect existing jobs and benefits accorded to journeymen printers under collective bargaining agreements covering the Paris press. There was no formal criticism of the paper's management or investment in technology under its owner M. Amaury. By contrast, West German printers staged a lengthy strike in 1978 aimed mainly at automatic typesetting systems and succeeded in protecting existing jobs. Briefs (1980) also reports that 1978, which saw more mandays lost to strikes in West Germany than any year since 1971, was dominated by protests against the introduction of computerization and microelectronics, especially in the steel and metals industries.

A last example is the nuclear power industry: union demands focussed mainly on job safety, attacking safety programs instituted by EDF's management. A prime example is the La Hague plant (*Syndicalisme*, no. 1844, 15 January 1981). A recent study of EDF employees belonging to the CFDT turned up similar results (CNAM research report, March 1982).

To sum up, our examination of labor disputes has shown that the main issue has not been technological innovation in itself but rather the effects of innovation on working conditions, job classifications, and skill requirements, all in all a rather traditional set of labor issues. There is no particular type of conflict or set of new issues associated with technology as such. In the conflicts we have studied workers' suspicions have not been directed specifically at technological progress, and it is not technology *per se* that they have refused to accept. In cases where unions have put forward counterproposals technology has not been the main concern in the majority of cases. Rather the fundamental issue has continued to be the traditional exploitation of labor: technology is seen by workers simply as one prop along with the production hierarchy, Taylorism, management supervision, and piecework.

If, however, we look in purely formal terms at the kinds of demands that arose in labor disputes during the 1970s, we run the risk of confusing cause and effect. For the reason these demands remained traditional in character has to do with the organizational and ideological factors that to a large extent shape the structure of union sections within the firm. The gulf between what the unions say, determined largely at the national level, and what they actually do in particular firms is best understood in relation to these factors.

In the first place it is important to point out that technological innovation affects different occupational groups in very different ways.

Technology often results in deskilling, as in the case of clerks employed in the insurance industry (Lobjeois, 1979, p. 30). But it can also lead to reskilling and even to upgrading a worker's skill level or to retraining in some new field.

Furthermore, the introduction of new technologies into a work system entails a variety of consequences for existing workplace relations, often creating new conflicts or leading to power struggles among the personnel involved. The responses, in terms of issues, interests, expectations, and strategies, vary widely from one occupational group to another. Draftsmen, whose work can be radically transformed by computer-aided design systems, are likely to look upon such systems in quite a different way than technicians in a test lab will look upon automated testing equipment, for example.

Thus labor disputes in which technology is a primary issue will tend to be limited to a specific occupational group This runs counter to the traditions of the French labor movement, whose ideology and organizations have traditionally assumed the unity of all workers, whom the unions are presumed to represent. The "unity of the working class" is in fact one of the central values of the French workers' movement. Tactically this value is reflected in the idea of mass mobilization, which stands in sharp contrast to action based on a narrowly defined occupational group. Organizationally French trade unionism is of the industrial type, to be distinguished from craft unionism as practiced in Britain: the membership of the French unions encompasses workers of all types.

Furthermore, we should not lose sight of the fact that discussion of new technologies by union locals is relatively unusual (CNAM research report, March 1982). This is due in part to the fact that workers at the local level are concerned primarily with wage demands and related issues and depend tactically on mass mobilization. Technological issues are of limited significance in both respects. It is difficult, moreover, for union locals to evaluate the relative significance of the many contradictory factors involved in determining the impact of technological innovation on worker status and workplace organization. The difficulty is exacerbated by the fact that the automation of production is generally carried out in phases, and it is always difficult to foresee how the process will evolve from one phase to the next.

In the service sector, for example, computerization first came in the form of large, mainframe computer systems. But in 1974–5 these began to be replaced by microprocessors in systems sometimes referred to as "distributed" data-processing. These are, in a formal sense, decentralized systems based on computer terminals distributed throughout a company, though generally still dependent on a centralized data-processing department. More recently UNIVAC systems equipped with "Mapper" software have changed the way people in the United States are thinking about the relationship between the local terminals and the central computer or data bank, since programming can now be done at the local terminals. In each phase of the computerization process existing workplace organization will, therefore, be modified to one degree or another. The new technologies are quickly making some types of organization obsolete. But union procedures for organizing worker demands generally depend on the existence of formal, durable systems of workplace organisation.

Because discussion of technological issues by union locals is so sketchy, labor is in a poor position to contribute much when it comes time to negotiate over the introduction of new technology. In only a few cases has there been any discussion between labor and management concerning technological innovations. We shall have more to say below about the reasons for this. In a few firms management has agreed, in response to union pressure, to meet with employee representatives on a regular basis in order to look into problems arising from the use of new technologies. This has happened, for example, at Assurances Générales de France (AGF), where management has accepted a CFDT proposal to devote one meeting each year of the company's works council to problems relating to office automation. Discussions range widely and include such topics as investments in new technology, choice of equipment, impact on employees, and general working conditions (such as the amount of time an employee is required to work at a video display terminal). As one union member involved in this experiment notes, however,

> while the increased access to information and documents has proved important, difficulties remain. The language used by management representatives (like the head of the data processing department) is deliberately specialized and technical and helps to preserve the power of management while enabling them to claim that they are always willing to engage in dialogue. (Lobjeois, 1979, p. 31)[1]

Finally, mention must be made of ideological resistance at the local level to certain implications of technological issues in the area of industrial relations, especially in the case of union locals affiliated with the CFDT. When it comes to labor–management relations, technological issues can never be considered in isolation from other issues. Questions of the ratio between total labor costs and investments always come into the picture, as do considerations of the costs and benefits of productivity gains. At the same time technological issues force the unions to attempt to influence management decisions and, therefore, lead to the formulation of counterproposals to management policies. But many members of union locals look upon such a strategy and its associated negotiations as policies associated with job-oriented trade unions (like those in the United States) and contrary to their desire to seek socialism and self-management (CNAM research report, March 1982). Hence they will often refuse to support such a strategy and really grapple with the issue of technological innovation.

Beyond these problems arising from the labor side, union discussion of technological issues is hampered further by management and the business community. All union discussion of these issues is premissed on the belief that management is willing to negotiate in earnest (and possibly to change its mind) rather than merely for the sake of form. There can be no hope of influencing management decisions unless management is willing to discuss in advance the technological changes it hopes to make.

In fact nothing could be more doubtful than management's willingness to negotiate on this score. There are many reasons for this: technological, financial, and institutional to begin with, but also political and ideological. In the French system, in fact, it is the latter that determine the former.

To start with the technological reasons, we have seen that the present pace of technological development means that any given technology is likely to become obsolete fairly quickly, so that firms must plan their investments carefully. What is more, the installation of any new technology involves a complex decision-making process involving many different actors: company executives, project leaders, production supervisors, representatives of equipment manufacturers, as well as in many cases consulting engineers and works councils. The inclusion in this process of any new actor, especially a union, is often seen by the other parties involved as a cause of delays and even dysfunctions. Then, too, today's investment decisions reflect a very high rate of turnover of capital, in part owing to the rapid rate at which modern technologies become obsolete.[2]

Institutionally labor contracts in France usually cover an entire branch of industry. For historical and political reasons, the business community is firmly attached to this system. Its opposition to the Auroux reforms stems from the fact that they encourage company-level contracts (Reynaud, 1978: and Erbès-Seguin in the present volume). There is in fact reason to doubt the appropriateness of branch-wide negotiations as far as technological issues are concerned. In terms of both planning and organizational consequences the installation of a computer system primarily affects the company in which it is installed, as a labor as well as a production unit. Negotiations are, therefore, most likely to succeed at this level. But employer opposition to negotiating at the firm level casts doubt on the usefulness of this option.

Politically the unions began discussing technological issues during the second half of the 1970s, a time when the business community in France was attempting to use the economic crisis as a pretext for shifting the balance of power in its favor. As part of this strategy employers attempted to circumvent the usual system of labor–management negotiations. One obvious manifestation of this was the attempt by employers, sometimes openly avowed, to put an end to the unions' usual functions within the firm (as at Peugeot-Sochaux and SNIAS-Marignane, to cite only two examples among many: see *Le Monde*, 9–12 March 1982).

Finally, the work of certain German sociologists such as Klaus Dull (1982), who was able to observe the evolution of labor–management relations in a system in which the unions (here the DGB) openly participate in comanagement with employers, strongly suggests that employers will actually negotiate only over personnel issues such as job classifications and qualifications, hiring and firing, safety issues, and job descriptions. Management is quite reluctant to sit down with labor to examine issues pertaining to the organization of the workplace or investment in fixed capital; but the new technologies by their very nature raise such issues. What is more, employer reluctance very quickly develops into open hostility whenever the issue of investment decisions is raised. By contrast, British employers take a fundamentally different stand according to J. Evans (see proceedings of UCC–CFDT colloquium "Changements technologiques 1980–90 et évolution du rôle des cadres" in *Cadres-CFDT*, no. 297, February–April 1981), who reports that agreements have been signed in various British firms regarding consultations with employees about the introduction of new technologies. But French employers, whose attitudes have been profoundly influenced by their history and ideology, are certainly closer in this respect to their German counterparts than to the British.

Conclusion: Union Rhetoric and the Appeal to Leviathan

Given the built-in resistance to discussing technological issues at the local level, it may be confidently predicted that such discussions, if they progress at all, will do so at the confederal level (which, at least in the case of the CFDT, is where they originated). The rhetoric that will emerge from such discussions will, therefore, be a rhetoric of the union hierarchy and not of the rank-and-file.

Even at this level, however, we sense the influence of what is, by comparison with the situation in the United States and Britain, one of the structural deficiencies of the French labor movement. It is of course possible that within working-class organizations new social actors with a direct stake in these questions will emerge. One possibility—for obvious reasons—is among managerial and supervisory personnel who join the CFDT or the CGT (on the CGC see Benguigui and Montjardet in this volume). Owing to their position in the firm, these personnel can contribute in important ways to union analyses of technical questions. This view is enthusiastically supported by the UCC and, somewhat less enthusiastically, by some members of the UGICT. As the references cited here indicate, these unions have already written extensively about the implications of technological change. For them, union discussions of these issues are "custom-made," by virtue of their esoteric content and because they are addressed to union functionaries.

Still it must be admitted that the role played by these personnel in the unions is at best a peripheral one. This is due not only to ideological and historical factors, such as the traditional anti-hierarchical ideology of the French workers' movement (see Mouriaux, 1980), but also to more objective causes. Managerial and supervisory personnel often play a role in the firm that prevents their engaging in any real union activities. Because they do not participate in the pursuit of traditional worker demands, rank-and-file union members often regard them as peripheral to their true concerns. At various levels of the union hierarchy we encounter similar tensions between ordinary workers and supervisory personnel, tensions resulting from the different ways in which the two groups press their demands (*Cadres-CFDT*, no. 301, November–December 1981, pp. 46–59). The latter frequently waver back and forth between calling for social reform and defending their own interests as an occupational group, both activities traditionally disapproved by French labor ideology (though not always avoided in actual practice: the CGT Printers' Union is a case in point, despite its ostensible commitment to a revolutionary ideology). Hence the fact that union discussion of technological issues is carried on largely by the organizations representing these personnel helps to keep those discussions confined to the union hierarchy, without reaching the rank-and-file. This is one more difficulty standing in the way of any reappropriation of such discussion by the locals.

At the present stage of economic development the importance of this issue, heightened by the current economic crisis, cannot be overemphasized. The fundamental paradox of the situation is that confederal union discussions of technological issues acknowledge that technology is a basic economic fact, whereas union activities at the local level reflect little consciousness of this fact. Admittedly technological discussions within the union hierarchy are voluntarist in nature. But such discussions will surely continue precisely because they deal with economic realities, whatever contradictions may be involved.

The political change that took place in 1981 will also help keep technology on the agenda: new opportunities have emerged for the labor movement. Technology is one of these, particularly in so far as publicly funded research may now be made available for use by the unions. The CFDT has proposed the creation of an institute on working conditions to promote "coordination between scientific researchers and human factors experts in the various government ministries" and thus aid the works councils and health and safety committees fulfill their tasks (*Le Monde*, 13 January 1982). The Auroux report led to a revision of laws pertaining to the use of expert advisers by works councils, which can henceforth hire scientific counsel. Consulting services in the areas of science and technology are being expanded. And so on.

If such developments flourish, it will mean more than a shift by the French workers' movement away from its traditional ideology of class struggle and toward comanagement; at stake is a major change in the relationship between the unions and the state. Put another way, this would imply a redefinition of the relationship between certain union confederations and the political authorities in a new and durable political context. It would mean a profound revision of the relations between union and governmental hierarchies, a revision based on new technologies whose importance in the coming years is recognized by both groups. It would mean a major change for French labor, an open break with the historical tradition of a movement all of whose organized representatives have always wished to avoid participating in government. But at the same time it would perpetuate another characteristic of the

French labor movement, namely, its habit of turning to "political" solutions, to the government; in short, its predilection for calling upon Leviathan. If such changes do come about, the state will once more become an "obligatory transitional phase."

This is the ultimate paradox, a paradox characteristic not merely of union discussions of technological issues but of the French workers' movement in general.

Notes: Chapter 8

1   In this regard the Auroux laws may facilitate unions' activities in this domain. The works committee can henceforth demand expert assistance, in this case concerning technology and data-processing. However, these outside experts will have limited possibilities compared to firm management. For example, the head of the data-processing department cited above not only designs plans but assures their execution and evaluation.

2   Technological obsolescence is not recent. But at present, as the case of data-processing makes clear, the process has accelerated. Certain Marxist economists have provided excellent descriptive analyses for the 1960s and 1970s—for example, Baran and Sweezy, 1966; Mandel, 1969; and Gorz, 1971.

9

Trade Union Positions on the Organization of Production

ANNI BORZEIX

"Production is management's concern, organizing it is not our depart-ment." These words were spoken as recently as 1980 by a CGT militant at a trade union seminar (a session in which CGT metalworkers discussed new forms of workplace organization). The sentiment they express is not simply the view of a backward-looking minority, fiercely defending posi-tions from another era. Many militants share it.

Still, trade union doctrine has undeniably evolved since 1927, when Lucien Rabaté asserted, at the CGT's Metalworkers' Federation Fourth Congress, that "we can't stop assembly lines, any more than we can stop the rain from falling." He went on to say:

> Our position is quite clear. We are for the principles of scientific management including the assembly line and production norms. These principles correspond to a certain stage of development of the capitalist regime: Trying to thwart technological progress would not be truly revolutionary.

No union today in France would argue that "scientific management" is a manifestation of technological progress and, as such, that it must be accepted. Instead unions deny that there is anything neutral about Taylorist methods, which are held to be based on principles that are neither objective nor ineluctable. Taylorism, once viewed by labor as a potential ally (the target in the 1920s being the use of Taylorism under capitalism, not scientific management methods in themselves), has for the past fifteen years or so been one of the French unions' favorite objects of attack.

It is not merely the destructive and degrading effects of Taylorism that organized labor has criticized but the underlying principles of scientific management. Thus production lines, piecework, shiftwork, hierarchy, deskilling, robotization, fragmentation, and the sacrosanct division be-tween manual and intellectual labor are all seen as technological choices rather than the product of inexorable fate. Against them workers can and must rebel. Responsibility, initiative, autonomy, and an active in-terest in one's work should no longer be limited to a minority. In short, unions now see Taylorism as the root of all evil, it must be eliminated.

This change in view did not come about spontaneously, nor did it take place overnight. It can only be understood in the context of strikes for better working conditions waged by French workers in the period 1968–75. In these struggles a group of workers previously looked upon as playing only a minor role, even within the labor organizations, emerged into the limelight: semiskilled production-line workers, whose lives are governed by piecework quotas and production speedups. Unlike traditional labor heroes such as miners and steelworkers, assembly-line workers had no special skills or long organizing traditions to draw upon and yet for a time they became the spearhead and the symbol of a strike movement that focussed public attention on the inhuman conditions in which a large part of the working class is daily forced to toil. Without the rebellion of the semiskilled, the change in theoretical doctrine would probably never have taken place.

The strikes of the 1970s clearly brought working conditions back to the forefront of labor–management concerns. Since then there have been endless negotiations, lists of demands, various experiments, and much proposed legislation, all of which have received national attention: the issue of working conditions became an item on the national agenda. While this development forms the background of this chapter, my real purpose is to ask whether the highly offensive strategy for dealing with the so-called capitalist organization of production—the strategy to which union leaders gave their blessing—was actually carried out.

So long as "rationalization" seemed a natural part of the development of the productive forces, organized labor saw its purpose as one of wresting from management compensatory material benefits such as higher wages and bonuses or shorter working hours. The organization of production remained, quite logically, outside the sphere of class struggle. For more than fifty years this ideology dominated trade union thinking on the subject.

Apart from a pile of trade union brochures and position papers, what remains of this legacy today? Has trade union practice followed changes in doctrine? Have words and actions evolved in tandem? These questions are even more crucial since the accession to power of a left-wing government, which has cast the whole issue in a new light. New rights have been granted workers: shop councils, for instance, in the newly nationalized firms; while workers in private firms employing more than 200 people have been given the right to discuss working conditions during working hours. Will this be enough to involve workers and their representatives in the organization of production, as certain unions hope, or will these matters remain "management's concern"?

Fieldwork on Union Action: Sample and Method

In pursuing these questions I shall make use of an empirical study carried out in 1977–9. The purpose was to discover the relationship between theory, as set forth in printed materials emanating from union federations and confederations, and practice, as it was actually observed in the workplace. In the course of this study information was gathered concerning the activity of union militants with respect to working conditions and the organization of production. The study considered how union organizers went about their business, the purpose of their efforts, their impact, and the results achieved.

The information gathered was diverse in a number of respects. In the first place the study looked at a number of different sectors of the economy and regions of the country. Plants in the automobile, electrical machinery, electronics, foodstuffs, and textile industries were included, located throughout France. The plants studied employed from 100 to 15,000 workers.

Firms were chosen to shed light on union action with respect to working conditions and the organization of production. The first four firms on the list had experimented with new forms of organization. The changes introduced, which ranged from "work-enrichment" schemes to "semiautonomous work groups" or "modules," provided an excellent opportunity for on-the-spot study of the tactics adopted by the unions in response to management initiatives of this type. In two other cases the background against which trade union tactics were deployed was quite different. In these plants change was initiated by the workers, after open conflict with management over issues of work life and conditions in the workplace. The other eight firms included in the study had not conducted experiments with work organization or experienced serious labor conflicts and so are more representative of industrial situations in general. This provided some idea of union positions in normal settings in firms operating on a routine, day-to-day basis.

I have tried to approach my research as a three-dimensional object, looking first from above, using published union documents, then from within, using interviews with active militants, and finally from below, using interviews with rank-and-file union members and nonunion workers. By comparing these various views I have come to the results and conclusions outlined below.

Unions' Reactions to Experimental Forms of Work Organization
Let us begin by looking from above and consider trade union strategies toward what are commonly called "new forms of work organization" (I say "commonly called" because there is still considerable debate in France as to the proper classification of these kinds of experiment, which have in common their anti-Taylorism and the fact of their having been introduced by management). The CGT and the CFDT differed sharply on these issues in the early 1970s. The CGT at that time was skeptical of, and hostile toward, what it regarded as the latest capitalist device for increasing productivity by integrating workers into the firm. The CFDT, though wary, was—in keeping with its self-management ideals—more receptive and more interested than its rival in experiments that might point the way toward less alienating work in the future. But if the two trade union confederations differed sharply as to fundamental principles,

the advice they offered their members was strikingly similar. It can be summarized in two words: vigilance and pragmatism.

By the time I began my study the two unions had drawn much closer together. The CFDT had backed away somewhat from its initial curiosity, while the CGT had watered down its criticism. Both unions agreed that, despite certain dangers and abuses associated with the new organizational forms (such as the absence of job guarantees, frequent increases of workload, and lack of improvement in wages or skill ratings), they were preferable to the Taylorist systems they replaced. Notwithstanding certain serious and very real dangers, the reorganization of the work process (job enrichment and formation of semiautonomous working groups, for example) represented the first chink in the armor of scientific management. It made more sense to enlarge that chink than to patch it up. The pressing need in the eyes of both the CFDT and the CGT was to attack head-on the highly complex but absolutely fundamental issue of the content of deskilled labor. The debate over new forms of productive organization provided the occasion for such an attack, even if they fell far short of providing an acceptable alternative.

In examining how union locals reacted to experimental reorganization in the four firms where this was tried two points emerge. First, the locals had no clear strategy, that is, with any degree of consistency, rigor, and continuity. Once the experiments are under way, the unions' positions change over time, as preconceived ideology gives way to pragmatism. Union attitudes also vary from place to place, depending on the nature of the experiment in question (many different things were tried) as well as on the consequences for the workers involved. In two cases we found, as expected, that the CGT was hostile on principle and the CFDT cautious but optimistic, but in two other cases the opposite was true. Furthermore, the tactics of the locals were no more uniform or consistent than their official positions. With respect to reorganization plans, local union attitudes ranged from active support to violent opposition, including refusal to work under the new system—and we are talking here about locals affiliated with the same national confederation.

This wide range of responses, this diversity at both the rhetorical and practical level, suggests that union behavior in this regard cannot be understood simply in terms of changes in the organization of production considered in isolation from other factors. A complex set of parameters must be taken into account in order to interpret the pattern of positions observed. Broadly speaking, these parameters include: (1) the manner in which the experiment was introduced (before or after negotiations); (2) the strength of the unions in the firm, their cohesiveness, and the influence of union leaders; (3) the nature and history of labor–management relations in the firm; and (4) the attitude of wage-earners toward the new system.

In sum there is not one union strategy but a whole range of strategies. Or perhaps it would be better to say that tactics change daily in response to the specific situation in each plant. The unions must accommodate to a web of objectives and constraints, of which experimental changes in the organization of production are of only secondary importance. It is this fact that explains why union militants are so divided on these issues. The logic of their action must be sought elsewhere; their view is at once too limited and too sweeping to focus exclusively on these mini-reforms, which in many cases affect only a small number of workers.

The Organization of Production: A Concept with Many Meanings
The second conclusion of the study is that a gap exists between the doctrinal position taken by trade union federations and confederations on the issue of reorganizing production and the attitudes taken by the union locals. The first indication that such a gap exists is semantic. The concept of "organization of production" has no single meaning. One group with which I was in close contact while doing fieldwork for the study, the CFDT Metalworkers' Federation, wavered between two extremes in its interpretation of the concept (and the same is no doubt true of other federations). On the one hand, federation officials interpreted "organization of production" largely in macroeconomic terms, involving such issues as the restructuring of industry, industrial planning policies, and new technologies. On the other hand, they gave a very narrow—perhaps overly narrow—definition of the term, as revolving almost entirely around questions of workplace reorganization.

Union locals, from their standpoint within the firm, interpret the concept in a way that is at once less macroeconomic and more sweeping. For union representatives, it includes far more than a few experimental programs for reorganizing the workplace. Such experiments, in their view, are merely the tip of the iceberg, and their importance may be overstated. But nevertheless such experiments do have more immediacy for them than industrial policies, which involve technical and economic issues quite remote from their concerns as local union leaders. Their view is perhaps more microeconomic and surely more pragmatic than theoretical. Accordingly their image of the organization of production is more "systematic" than might at first sight appear, for their interest is focussed on the way in which the various parts of the productive system fit together and interact. Among their primary concerns, for example, is the interaction between the way work tasks are parceled out, the way pay is apportioned, and the way in which management handles promotions, raises, skill levels, and other personnel matters. Another major concern is the relationship between health and safety issues and the mechanisms of social control associated with particular forms of hierarchical stratification and technical division of labor.

Leaving aside linguistic ambiguities, what we have here are two different ways, less contradictory than complementary, of looking at the organization of production. At any rate they are different enough to create misunderstanding and incomprehension on both sides.

Turning to the more specific problem of workplace reorganization, it seems that another reason why different people hold different views is that they perceive the issues in different temporal contexts. Some union federations show great interest in these experiments as well as eagerness to stimulate further debate about them in part because of their farsighted outlook. If these federations are less quick to condemn such experiments once and for all than are most local trade union militants, the reason may be that federation leaders look beyond present achievements to future possibilities. The farsightedness of some federation leaders, aware of the possible future value of this type of experiment, stands in sharp contrast to leaders at the local level, who seem to want to look beyond today, leaving to others the anticipation of tomorrow. As they see it, autonomy, cooperation, solidarity, and responsibility in the workplace remain remote, utopian objectives, a rhetoric of dreams in which they only half-believe. Local leaders see innovations in the workplace chiefly as a subtler, more refined way of increasing productivity while decreasing employment with the workers' consent, rather than as an embryonic model of a new way of organizing work. Thus we have two visions: one giving prominence to potential for the future, the other to tangible results here and now.

Between Model and Reality

The second stage of my study had a different focus from the first. Attention was shifted from plants experimenting with new forms of workplace organization—where new forms were the exception rather than the rule—to plants operating routinely according to new forms of work organization. The opportunity to shift viewpoints was given me by the unions themselves: two federations asked me to participate in projects they had undertaken which had a direct bearing on my subject. The CGT had begun research into changing working conditions in the garment industry, while the CFDT was preparing a seminar for militants in the metals industries whose purpose was to increase union involvement in issues concerning working conditions. Collaboration on these two "action research" projects took me on a year-long journey during which I was able to observe union practice from the inside.

Along with the new approach came a new focus for the research, since my collaborators in the unions planned to look at working conditions in general and not merely at the experimental "new" forms of work organization. The further one gets from union headquarters and the closer to the shopfloor, the less the term "organization of production" is used. Local militants refer, almost exclusively, to working conditions. Whether this is due merely to a difference of vocabulary or to a difference in views remains an open question. Regardless of the answer, the central question can be summarized as follows: why is it that union leaders invariably look upon actions to change working conditions as a test? Why are such actions viewed as both a challenge and a crucial necessity?

A few minutes spent leafing through post-1968 union publications is enough to show what an important place the theme of "better working conditions" has come to occupy. Until the beginning of the economic crisis it ranked among the top priorities for both the CGT and the CFDT. The importance of the issue is reflected among other things in the lengthy negotiations carried on from 1972 to 1975 between unions and management representatives, the long list of demands drawn up for those negotiations, the plant reform proposal prepared by P. Sudreau, and the numerous bills submitted to Parliament. Bear in mind that up until the economic crisis the period was marked by numerous strikes against piecework, assembly-line work, nightwork, toxic environmental conditions, and so on. "Our health is not for sale" was the slogan of the day, a rallying cry and an objective of many labor disputes.

Paradoxically however, despite all this tumult, the unions have not had an easy time, to judge by reports from militants themselves, in their attempts to take charge of the working conditions issue. In most plants militants have encountered difficulty in mobilizing workers on this subject except during periods of open conflict, difficulty in moving from individual resistance and rebellion to collective action, and from short-term actions to more sustained involvement. Militants remain doubtful; moreover, about how to give their activities the "aggressive" character that they so often lack and so urgently need. Finally, almost everywhere union members themselves express a feeling of uneasiness, a feeling of inability to come to grips with the real problems, an acute awareness of the gap between theory and practice, model and reality, what could or should be done and what actually is going on.

Changing Work Conditions: A Challenge for Trade Unions

The difficulties reportedly met by the militants are many, as are their explanations of those difficulties. A few examples will help to clarify matters. To begin with, militants complain that such institutional devices as works committees, health and safety committees, and committees to improve working conditions all too often provide an inadequate framework for action because worker representatives elected to sit on these bodies lack needed technical competence, arguments, and information. Another problem with these bodies is that management can effectively thwart union attempts to act through them, if it so chooses. Militants have trouble making full use of the extensive legal resources open to them, which are so complex that only a small number of legal "experts" can hope to master the welter of rules, procedures, and mechanisms of control and intervention theoretically available to workers.

Another major concern of union leaders is that the issue of working conditions is no longer the exclusive province of the unions. Militant action has been hampered in recent years by management initiatives in the area of so-called "social policy." Union leaders feel that they have been caught off-guard and forced to fight empty-handed, having been outflanked by management on these issues. The trade unionists lack the necessary time, skill, and imagination to turn the situation around. Management has got off to a head start by offering workers attractive benefits, not only higher pay but also increased autonomy in setting hours, organizing the workplace, and so on, thus confusing the issue and allowing employers to encroach on what has traditionally been a trade union issue.

A third source of uncertainty for union leaders is the type of relationship with workers. Except in acute crisis situations—open rebellions in the wake of some flagrant injustice, accident, or serious illness—the unions have been marking time on the issue of working conditions. All too often union efforts in this domain become bogged down owing to lack of worker involvement in the struggle for better working conditions and improved health and safety. The fact that workers have no legal occasion to express their grievances directly on these matters together with the fact that too often, due to the way union representatives are elected, there is no permanent union presence at the shopfloor or production-line level, is no doubt a serious drawback in this regard. But the trouble may well lie deeper. Perhaps it may be the very principle of delegating authority that is responsible for landing the unions in the rut in which they now find themselves. If workers do in fact exhibit a "welfare mentality," as has often been charged, might the reason not be that organized labor has all too faithfully adhered, in its own organizational structure, to the model of parliamentary representation?

Many union militants not only question their role and the legitimacy of their action but also harbor doubts about the wisdom of certain union demands. There are glaring signs of disparity between some of the desires and aspirations of the workers and the positions defended by the trade unions. How, for example, can the workers' desire for increased income from bonuses, overtime, and so forth, or their desire to spend as little time at work as possible (or to work 9- and 10-hour days in order to have 3-day weekends) be reconciled with concern about their health, safety, and physical well-being? How can the unions pursue the specific demands of specific occupational groups while at the same time trying to achieve "unity" by pressing issues that are often so general as to claim the active support of no one? Finally, how can the unions bridge the gap between such highly radical, even subversive, demands as "more free time" or "reorganize the workplace" and the ludicrously inadequate, or at least watered down, versions of these demands that actually reach the negotiating table?

Clearly, then, the issue of working conditions is not like other trade union issues. The "more offensive posture" desired by union militants is putting organized labor to the test. The challenge is aimed, to begin with, at traditional forms of organization and modes of representation at the company level, along with familiar ways of doing things, carrying on negotiations, and waging union campaigns within the firm. But it contains the potential for something far broader. At stake are not only traditional union values (that is, priorities for action and ways of analyzing and interpreting events) but also the very relationship between unions and the workforce as a whole. This could cast doubt upon the legitimacy of the trade union movement and its associated tactics, representative institutions, and forms of behavior. Short of thoroughgoing serious internal reform, the unions run the risk of remaining too cautious, weak, and limited in outlook to achieve tangible results. There is also a danger that in spite of themselves the unions may veer in the direction of co-management as a way of overcoming their problems, thus abandoning the class-based trade unionism to which most militants remain steadfastly attached.

Built-In Ambiguity

Union militants explain their own difficulties and contradictions in a number of ways: conjunctural, structural, and ideological. But beyond this web of self-rationalizations, what else can be said? What interpretations—at a more theoretical level—can be offered of the gap between model and reality, between preaching and practice?

To understand the reasons underlying all these doubts and questions that so obviously beset union action in this particular field reference to union action *on* the organization of production is not enough. What must be done rather is to pay heed to the way in which trade union practices are inscribed *within* the organization of production. For it is there that we may hope to discover—this is our hypothesis—the principle that governs the production and reproduction of those practices. Looked at in this way, the organization of production takes on a new significance. It is not merely a new target of union action like wages or jobs but rather the basic principle governing social division of labor within the firm. In other words, the crucible in which all union practices, whatever their object and purpose may be, are formed and acquire a meaning. It is not merely one area of union activity among others but, in a much more fundamental sense, the social space that nourishes and shapes militant tactics and within which those tactics produce their effects.

Despite appearances, the relationship between trade unionism and the organization of production is in no way constant or immutable. It varies from one historical period to another (the advent of Taylorism, for example, profoundly altered the previous equilibrium). It also varies according to the type of production (batch industries organize production in different ways from process industries, for example), the country, and the system of industrial relations. Certain facts are well known: unions exercise considerable control, for instance, over the organization of production in some areas, such as the printing industry and among longshoremen. But much remains obscure. A comparative history of the relationship between trade unionism and the organization of production remains to be written.

As we have seen, over the past fifteen years the class-based trade unions in France have been vehemently critical of forms of work organization based on a strict separation between conception and execution. But if we look only at official declarations and union programs, we are likely to fail to see anything beyond the unions' explicitly stated purposes—the actors' intentions, their political aims. The very real antagonism that comes to the surface in times of overt labor conflict (when organized labor can express its opposition to the organization of the workplace by halting production) should not obscure the fact that the unions' activities are, for the most part, carried on while the plant is running "normally." The importance accorded to periods of open conflict is deceptive, because it tends to obscure the periods of routine.

If we look not only at the way in which union doctrine evolves over time but rather at the unions' everyday activities—the routine practice as opposed to the exceptional situation—we find that the relationship between trade unionism and the organization of production can no longer be thought of exclusively in terms of antagonism. Understanding should make room for the dual nature of trade unionism, its built-in ambiguity: trade unions are an oppositional force, but they are also an integrating force—they are at the same time a source of order and a fountainhead of resistance. That the place of the unions in the firm has been won by struggle, that their hard-won legitimacy is subject to endless dispute, does not alter the fact that wherever unions exist, wherever they are recognized as "legal" institutions, their rights and duties are codified, embodied in law. Thus in their own way unions contribute to the process of social control within the firm. While attempting to organize workers on a "class" basis against the effects of the capitalist system, unions are also taking part in everyday routine negotiations. In this sense they objectively help the system they reject to adapt and to reproduce itself. Their function is dual: opposition and regulation. Contradictory though these two vocations may seem in theory, in practice they are complementary.

The Institutionalization of Organized Labor

The equilibrium between these two functions is inevitably precarious. It is affected by the ebb and flow of worker mobilization and by changes in the balance of power between labor and management. Our assumption here is that trade unionism within the firm at the local level is becoming increasingly institutionalized. For a variety of historical reasons (including the relatively small percentage of French workers who belong to unions as well as the increasing legal recognition accorded to organized labor since 1968), the importance attached to the institutionalized aspect of trade union activity has apparently grown enormously. And this to the detriment of the other role traditionally played by organized labor, namely, that of directly representing the interests and aspirations of the workers' community.

Militants have apparently (if our assumption is correct) been spending too much of their time acting as mediators and negotiators (particularly within representative bodies) and been too caught up in internal union activities to effectively express the will of the rank-and-file groups they represent. (Given the small number of union members, responsibility for organizing meetings and other activities falls to the same few people.) On the whole, union delegates would appear to be too "different" from other workers, a breed apart rather than "ordinary" workers.

This occupational distance is often combined with sheer physical distance: the union delegate moves more freely in time and space and shoulders greater responsibilities (while enjoying greater privileges) than workers who must stick close to the shopfloor. By virtue of his functions and his status in the firm he becomes an outsider, a "personality" who stands apart, physically as well as socially, from the workers' groups that he is supposed to defend. If this view is correct, the French union delegate is not in the best position to represent these worker groups (which the CGT calls the "work collective" and the CFDT calls the "homogeneous group"). Their opposition is, of course, multifaceted, diverse, and often ambiguous. Opposition does not rule out participation or cooperation within the framework established by the current organization of production. The real task at hand is not to assert that this opposition exists but to weld together its various parts, fragmented as they are by the existing division of labor.

In view of the foregoing it would seem far too simple to attempt to analyze the relationship between trade unionism and the organization of production in terms of either pure antagonism or complete subordination. The relationship would rather seem to be one of *de facto* institutional connivance and complicity. It can be argued that opposition to the system is too broad a principle to provide an effective basis for action. Lacking concrete points of reference, broad-gauged opposition may have become more symbolic than real, more rhetorical than effective, more sporadic than continuous. This would explain part of the difficulty that militants have reportedly faced in coming to grips with the concrete issues that come up in relation to working conditions. The unions' preoccupation with their institutional role might very well help to explain the feeling of one union federation leader that

> in this area the labor movement is hampered by both its globalist and its corporatist tendencies. We have not been able to cope with and fully make use of the place where primary worker solidarities develop. We believe too readily that there is no class dimension to shop floor relations, where corporation reigns supreme.

This hypothesis must be seen against the background of another—still sketchy—interpretation, which attempts to explain the reluctance (or perhaps the inability) of the unions to cope with "the place where primary worker solidarities develop." For the present I can do no more than offer an outline for further research. The main point is to draw a parallel between two phenomena that are usually considered separately.

To begin with, the French Marxist tradition generally accords a secondary (not to say marginal) place to the labor process, primary attention being focussed instead on organization of production. The corollary of the central importance given to economic—or rather macro-economic—factors in this tradition seems to be the emphasis placed on problems of "the realization of surplus value," to the detriment of problems relating to the content of work.

The second point is that organized labor views the working class in two very different ways: on the one hand, that class is said to be exploited, submissive, dominated, divided, and fragmented by the labor process; on the other hand, it is said to be rebellious, active, firm, united, and conscious of its own purposes in struggle. Although these two contrasting pictures may well describe different phases in the life of the working class, what is lacking in this dualist view is an explanation of the transition from one phase to the other.

The forces that stimulate collective action remain poorly understood and quite often little, or badly, exploited. At first sight there might seem little in common between this dualist view of the working class and the point made in the preceding paragraph about the French Marxist tradition. But in fact, if there is any hope of getting beyond this Manichaean view of the matter, trade unions must recapture, in both theory and practice, a whole aspect of the reality of the workplace, which might be called the "real" organization of production (to borrow a term from Butera, 1977, who says that the "real" organization is to be distinguished from both formal and informal organization. It is based on the principle of "self-regulated cooperation," meaning a certain type of relationship among workers characterized by interdependence among members of the workgroup).

Cooperation in the workplace, counterorganization, and informal arrangements by workers to flout management-established rules are often neglected or ignored by unions, basically because they lend themselves to contradictory interpretations. Sometimes they are seen as signs of individual resistance to the rules of scientific management, a mild form of rebellion, or protection against imperious and often absurd work rules. Less frequently they are said to betoken the existence of a collectively self-regulated system and to show that workers themselves consent to their participation in the productive process. On rare occasion dialectics are brought in to show that while doing so workers are trying, in fact, to reappropriate space and time in the production process.

The hypothesis outlined here is that the labor movement, by its reluctance to recognize this ambivalent reality of the labor process and by its all too common refusal to see this kind of behavior as more than a manifestation of individual cleverness or, even worse, of class collaboration, is depriving itself of a potent tool that could be used to mobilize its "troops" and advance the cause of labor in challenging the existing organization of production. By neglecting the crucial role of the workplace in the labor process and by hesitating to recognize any "class dimension" in what goes on there, organized labor is preventing itself from challenging the organization of production "from within," at the shopfloor or production-line level. This would explain in part why counterproposals put forward by labor over the past ten years have been so inconsistent, not to say feeble.

It is necessary to reconsider the foregoing ideas in the light of the changes initiated in France since 10 May 1981. Three major innovations relate directly to the topic of this chapter. First, it has been made mandatory for labor and management to engage in negotiations concerning not only wages and hours but also working conditions and work organization. This is expected to revitalize the labor movement by once more mobilizing workers (though few if any signs of such mobilization have been evident thus far). A second innovation came in response to a longstanding union demand: the right of workers to voice their opinion—directly and not only by means of their union representatives—on the subject of working conditions during working hours. This innovation promises to change the relationship between union militants and nonunion workers and, beyond that, may restore the unions to their former position in the working world. Finally, shopfloor councils have been set up in all nationalized firms. These councils will provide opportunities for experimenting with new forms of worker participation in, and control over, the management of production. These three steps clearly have the potential to revolutionize, if one is optimistic, or to modify, if one is less optimistic, the picture sketched above of trade union practices in France. Will they be enough to enable the unions once again to restore to the shopfloor its so-called "class dimension?" This remains to be seen.

10

The "Problem" of Women

JANE JENSON

Introduction

In the complex situation of the 1970s one of the items on the agenda of both the CGT and the CFDT was the "problem" of women. This was by no means a new issue for either because both, and the CGT in particular, had in the past paid considerable attention to the needs of working women and their place in the unions. However, the old problem took on some striking new manifestations in these years. New analyses appeared, then disappeared. New reforms were demanded, and old ones were pressed harder. The responses "to women" divided the CGT and CFDT, then drew them closer, then divided them again. The issue created internal turmoil and at time acted as a lightning-rod for conflict. The story of the two confederations' changing positions on the "problem," in fact, very closely parallels the ebb and flow of general strategic positions within the CGT and CFDT.

One of the more remarkable changes in Fifth Republic France is the rapidity with which the participation of women in the salaried laborforce has increased. There was a major rise in the overall rate of participation as well as a change in the rates of several notable categories. With the rate of 39 percent of French women in the paid laborforce in 1980 came an increase in the numbers of married women, women with young children, and women in the age group 25–40.[1] Moreover, predictions about the laborforce of the 1980s attributes most of the projected increase to new female workers (OECD, 1980, table 16, p. 59).

It is to be expected, then, that the feminization of the laborforce would have had an important impact on the French union movement. Moreover, it was the characteristics of the female workers which shaped the unions' responses to the feminization of the laborforce. One characteristic was the location of working women at the bottom of the wage and skill hierarchy. There were also many women in those sectors of the economy most touched by economic crisis and change. Women formed a large percentage of the laborforce in old and declining industries, like textiles and clothing. At the same time women were disproportionately hired to fill the low-paying, unskilled, and monotonous jobs of the rapidly expanding tertiary sector.[2] In the 1970s women's marginal status and their failure to overcome the weight of historic inequality, discrimination, and double burden (*double journée*) in capitalist society placed them "at risk" when economic crisis arrived.

Both the CFDT and the CGT included descriptions of the needs of women, as marginal workers, in their analyses of economic crisis. They emphasized both the marginal status of working women and the threat posed by the state and capital's initiatives to encourage women to give up the search for employment outside the home. Both confederations described women as disproportionately located in the category of the superexploited (*surexploité*) and listed them, along with youth and immigrants, as workers requiring special union attention and state programs for training and other measures to overcome their disadvantages under conditions of economic crisis. At the same time the unions strengthened the traditional left demand that society assume part of the burden and costs of childbearing and rearing rather than leaving all responsibility to individual women and families.

However, it was not only the increasing presence and more difficult situation of women in the labor market which colored the unions' understandings of the female third of their membership.[3] Nor was it only the changes in the working environment brought about by the presence of so many, and increasingly militant, women in the workplace, although their militancy was crucial in changing rank-and-file attitudes. The effects of other factors than these must be included if the positions of the two largest confederations in the 1970s and 1980s are to be understood.

Simultaneously with the rising participation rates of women came two political events which were profoundly important in shaping the ways that unions interpreted *la condition féminine*. The first event was the appearance, by the beginning of the 1970s, of an important new social movement which challenged the unions' existing analysis of women's condition under capitalism, in particular the extent to which the oppression of women by men could be reduced to the effects of class exploitation.[4] The women's movement, despite all its acknowledged variety of political positions and practices, asserted that, no matter the specific effects of capitalism, women experienced domination due to historic practices of male supremacy and the sexual division of labor. This movement was important because it profoundly touched women who were also included in the unions' constituency, especially that of the CFDT. Therefore, many of the themes first raised and popularized by the women's movement were introduced into the unions. This introduction of new themes came via rank-and-file militants who were simultaneously active in their union and in one of the many women's groups (*groupes-femmes*) which appeared in Paris and the provinces after 1968. The themes were also introduced at the top of the confederations by leaders who incorporated them into their own understandings.[5] Therefore, the confederations' responses to the "problem" in these years were different than they might have been if the women's movement had never enjoyed the influence that it did.

At the same time the second political event—that of the fluctuating fortunes of Union de la Gauche—also had a crucial effect on how the unions came to understand the situation of women. In fact, as this chapter will show, it was the strategic response of each confederation to the changes in electoral fortunes of the left which was *most* important in determining the evolution of their positions on women workers. As chapters by Mouriaux, Ross, and Schain show, the story of the unity and disunity between the CFDT and CGT is a complex and twisted one. From the postwar high point of consensus reflected in the unity-in-action accord signed in 1974 the relationship deteriorated to its current low point of disunity and distrust. Moreover, the CGT–CFDT relationship very clearly tracks that between the left parties, primarily because of the nature of the connection between the CGT and the PCF and the demands that allegiance places on the CGT for strategic change as political conditions alter.[6] Therefore, following closely on the signature of the Common Program in 1972 came the agreement for unity-in-action in 1974. The later outbreak of interconfederal hostilities corresponds in time to the breakdown of Union de la Gauche in the fall of 1977 and the electoral war between the Communists and Socialists which has been waged ever since. Moreover, what will emerge here is that the twists and turns of both confederations' positions on working women are also dependent on the meanderings of party strategy.

Pre-Crisis Analyses

Demands for the improvement of women's wages and working conditions and the struggle for the right to work are not new to the CGT. That confederation has represented an important source of counterideology to the argument that women's place is in the home, that women's lives are exclusively defined by childbearing, and that when women work their salaries are, and should be, supplements to those of their husbands. Instead the confederation has placed the right to work and equal pay at the top of its lists of *revendications* when mobilizing women. It has conducted frequent campaigns to organize more women; and, very important for the ideological struggle of the postwar period, the CGT's discourse has celebrated the beneficial effects for women and their families of participation in the paid laborforce (Guilbert, 1974a).

The conceptualization of women which the CGT used was that, except for a few specific disadvantages and needs, they shared the concerns of all workers interested in social change. Therefore, except for a few specific *revendications,* women's needs were completely covered by the CGT's general program. The specific disadvantages were of two types. In particular, wages, training, and access to employment were restricted by rapacious capitalists and an ideology celebrating the family and childbearing (*natalité*). Unions, therefore, should insist on the right to work and higher wages. A second type of disadvantage and special need related to women's maternal role, which the CGT tended to assume affected all women. Childbearing and the sexual division of labor implied special provisions for leave, childcare, and early retirement. The recognition of these distinctive characteristics of working women was the rationale for some separate mobilizational efforts. Beginning in 1952 the CGT published a magazine for women which in 1955 became *Antoinette*. National Conferences of Salaried Women, established in 1948, provided female and male militants an opportunity to consider the needs of working women.

The CGT's interest in working women rose even more after 1961, when the PCF began to devote more attention to women workers and the CGT became an increasingly important organizational resource for the party. In the 1950s the PCF had approached women primarily via the Union des Femmes Françaises (UFF), around themes of maternity, bread, and peace.[7] But the rising levels of salaried women led the PCF to judge that effort insufficient and a series of new initiatives were undertaken.[8] More attention was paid, in the union and party press, to the situation of working women. In addition, the 1962 "Women in Modern Society" International Colloquium, in Prague, was followed in 1964 by a *Semaine de la pensée marxiste* on the theme "Women of the twentieth century" (PCF, 1965). Other events quickly followed.

The report of the CGT's 1973 National Conference of Salaried Women provides a good indicator of the CGT's traditional positions.[9] While the CGT definitely advocated salaried and well-paid work for women, it did see real differences between the situation of men and women. Throughout this period the conceptual link between "women" and "mothers" remained very close. Thus, seeming to accept the inevitability of the traditional gender-based division of labor, the CGT argued that women's retirement age should be set at 55, with additional benefits for each child raised. The reduction of the workweek and flexible working hours were considered especially important for women, because of their family responsibilities. Much attention in the program was given to the rights of working mothers, including the reform of the restrictive abortion and contraception legislation which was demanded for them.

There were two primary sites where struggle for the reforms advocated in 1973 would occur—the workplace of course and the electoral arena. Much effort was taken in speeches, especially those of the leaders of the confederation, to explain the advantages of the recently signed Common Program of the United Left. It was argued that only with the Common Program could "real change" occur. In fact the Conference Report bears a strong resemblance to *Femmes: quelle libération?* by Madeleine Vincent (the member of the PCF's Bureau Politique charged with work with women) which was written to explain the terms of the Common Program and their implications for women (Vincent, 1976).

What was not included in 1973 was much attention to fundamentally changing women's, or men's, attitudes and behavior in the family or in society. Thus, according to Georges Séguy's very optimistic Preface, it was the *patronat* and reactionary politicians who held the backward ideas about women and transmitted them to women in order to maintain a docile workforce. However, working women themselves had, especially since 1968, begun to abandon such ideas and were moving forward into greater union and political militancy, which would result in an increase in support for the real route to change, societal transformation put into place by Union de la Gauche.

In 1973, moreover, the report displayed a good deal of defensiveness about the CGT's traditional approach to women. For example, Christiane Gilles compared the CGT's positions to those of its "detractors" whom she claimed advocated *égalitarisme intégral* (CGT, 1973, pp. 21–2). According to her, the CGT's demand of special reforms for women was based on an understanding of the "real situation" of working women. Scientific study indicated that mothers' and fathers' roles in childrearing differed and it was presumptuous (*bien présomptueux*) to assume that they could be the same. In sum,

> the increased participation of women in wage labor, and the struggle against the multiple discriminations which afflict them are far more effective in promoting a better conception of married life and the division of responsibilities within the family than to preach complete egalitarianism. (CGT, 1973, p. 21)

Two general observations emerge very clearly from this report and other material. The first is the unwillingness to take up matters traditionally considered to be "private," touching on family and marital relationships. The assumption made by the CGT was that improvements would follow automatically from social or political change or result from the goodwill of the workers. It was in fact only capital and right politicians who created and maintained the ideology which made the emancipation of women difficult. The CGT analysis laid no blame for the subordination of working women on working men. Moreover, the Confederation's emphases on bread-and-butter unionism coupled with political solutions orchestrated by the PCF, which were so visible in its general economic analysis, were also present in its thinking about working women.[10] The program of *revendications* was a compilation of short- and long-term demands to be achieved by struggle in the workplace and by large-scale popular mobilization. The demands nicely meshed with the logic of the Common Program. The CGT confined itself to a traditional workerist focus—even encompassing the demand for abortion reform in the interests of working mothers—while aiming to mobilize the enthusiasm for overall political change which it saw as the responsibility of the PCF and other left formations. In a larger way the CGT's positions on women were derivative of its reading of the evolution of events in the partisan arena and in particular the ways it could best match its own union strategy to the needs of the PCF.

The CFDT's ideas about the "problem" of women were quite different at this point in time. After years of opposition and then at best lukewarm commitment to women's right to work, by 1970 the CFDT had a full-blown theory which made women's liberation a foundation-stone.[11] The public unveiling of the CFDT's strategy of *socialisme démocratique et autogestionnaire* at its Thirty-fifth Congress included several clear statements about women's place in capitalism and in socialism and about the contribution that struggle to liberate women could make to the process of constructing socialism.[12] These followed from the CFDT's triptychal analysis, emphasizing the combined weight of economic exploitation, social reproduction, and ideology for the maintenance of capitalism. Superexploitation of women, the centuries-old social relations of gender-based domination, especially in the family, and ideology all contributed to the contemporary inferiority of women. Action to overcome it would have to proceed on all fronts simultaneously. The working documents of the 1970 Congress included special attention to the liberation of women, derived from the CFDT's notions about alienation inherent in capitalism. In addition to poor working conditions, low salaries, and vulnerability to unemployment, the heavy weight of old ideas kept women subordinate not only to capital but also to men. In other words, working-class men and their organizations also participated in the reproduction of women's subordination, via behavior in the family, in the workplace, and even in unions.

There were two major implications of this analysis. The first was that any proposed reforms should attack both the economic and the cultural roots of the subordination of women in capitalist society. More concretely this perspective implied two loci of struggle. The first was in the labor market both to eliminate the conditions which prohibited women from achieving equality as workers and to promote activities which, because they were linked to the *type de développement socialiste*, would lead to the progressive liberation of all women. Obviously the central condition for moving toward this goal was that women achieve some measure of economic independence via salaried work. The second arena of struggle was in the state and civil society around those reforms—in childcare, education, reproductive policies—which would destroy the sexual division of labor and liberate women from sole responsibility for childrearing. Moreover, for the CFDT, there were many ways that success in the first arena was dependent on some achievements in the second.

The second major implication of the CFDT's analysis was that struggle to move toward the liberation of women was essential to the process of creating a democratic and *autogestionnaire* socialism. Real change of women's condition, just as that of all workers, could not wait upon some decisive moment of rupture or upon political change brought from the top. According to the CFDT, its task was to begin immediately to create change, and the inclusion of workplace and society-wide struggle for women's liberation was a necessary ingredient of that beginning because it did so much to advance the democracy of one group of working people.

However, while focussing on liberation, the CFDT was not very explicit in its national-level documents about how the project would actually unfold. The CFDT refused to develop a specific program of reforms for working women.[13] Moreover, no separate organizational arrangements were made to contact working women or identify and promote potential union militants. Indeed in 1971 the women-only Commission Confédérale Féminine (CCF), inherited from the CFTC, was abolished and replaced by a mixed commission to deal with issues of particular concern to women (Maruani, 1978). Nor was a separate press for women unionists inaugurated. This lack of separation was based on a desire to end the "ghettoization" of CFDT women and the discussion of issues of interest to them. If women's liberation was an integral part of the process of creating a socialism based on democracy and *autogestion,* then it could not be shunted into separate actions.

The CFDT's analysis reflects the greater importance of the *soixante-huitard* influence in that confederation. From the political positions of these groups came much of the CFDT's emphasis on democracy in all social relations—economic, political, social, sexual—and on *autogestion. Autogestion* as a notion about how to make change was well suited to the ideas of the women's movement about the importance of consciousness-raising and creative problem-solving for discovering the route to liberation. The ideas and personnel of parts of the women's movement which came out of 1968 were often more comfortable with the discourse and politics of the CFDT than those of the CGT, with its heavy emphasis on bread-and-butter unionism, a longstanding distrust of "feminists," and its pride in its past record (Andrieux and Lignon, 1981, p. 1069; Lozier, 1980a, p. 10).

Economic Crisis and Unity-in-Action, 1974–7

These were, then, the positions of the two confederations in the early 1970s when they stood poised for the period of greatest unity.[14] Of course this experience coincided with the heyday of Union de la Gauche and the popular mobilization which brought the left parties to the brink of victory in the 1978 legislative elections. Each confederation was subject to new pressures from economic and political circumstances. For the CFDT, much of its post-1970 theoretical propositions and strategic direction had been founded on assumptions about the continued health of capitalism. The arrival of economic crisis made those assumptions somewhat problematic and the CFDT foundered for a bit in search of new understandings of a leaner economy and as a result came strongly under the influence of the CGT. At the CGT, because it was using its considerable resources to back the Common Program, the union experienced many of the same changes that the PCF did in the period of intense competition on the left. One consequence was that the CGT was forced to move some of its own positions closer to those of the CFDT. The CGT could not permit the CFDT to appear, by virtue of its hypermilitant actions, to be the only truly radical Confederation. In the same way the CGT could not afford to leave to the CFDT that large and important group of working women who believed profoundly that there was more to women's inferior status than the ideas of capitalists and politicians and that this subordination could never be voluntaristically overcome by appealing to men and women's sense of fairness or by hoping that it would disappear as more women entered the salaried laborforce. Therefore, changes occurred in the discourse of the CGT, especially in the magazine *Antoinette,* where discussions of rape, sexism, division of labor in the household and childrearing, and so on, began to appear (Maruani, 1979, p. 60, 1980, p. 49; Simon, 1981, pp. 22–6).

In this kind of environment, in June 1974, the CGT and the CFDT signed the most detailed unity-in-action agreement to date. In December of that year a supplementary accord, "Sur les revendications des femmes salariées," was signed.[15] It reflected the same balance of interconfederal influence as the general agreement, being more heavily weighted toward the traditional themes and reforms of the CGT. Indeed its very existence, as a document specifically addressed to women, reflects the willingness of the CFDT to compromise. Nevertheless, it also included some important changes which seem to reflect the competition between the two confederations. It demonstrates in fact substantial movement on the part of the two. The CFDT did accept some of the CGT's emphasis on specific reforms which differentiated men and women workers (although not the retirement age of 55 for women). Meanwhile the CGT accommodated some of the CFDT's emphases on the ideological and social bases of relations of subordination, including acceptance of the two-arena argument which reproduced almost directly the CFDT's 1970 statement.

But this was only the beginning. The CGT's evolution continued, this time mostly as a result of changes in the PCF which were felt simultaneously within the CGT, primarily because the new ideas were carried into the union by some of its Communist members. The PCF was, by the middle of the 1970s, engaged in a process of partial Eurocommunization which privileged struggles for democracy and it went so far as to argue that efforts to extend democracy were anticapitalist in the current conditions of state monopoly capitalism (Ross and Jenson, 1983).[16] The implications of this part of the Eurocommunist analysis were that greater attention should be paid to all efforts to advance democracy and that a process of generating ideas about and support for the construction of socialism in a decentralized and nonhierarchal way was needed. A second aspect of the PCF's Eurocommunism was its criticism of the experience of the Soviet Union and Eastern Europe as a model for socialist France.

These two theoretical changes together opened up a good deal of space within the PCF for reconsideration of old verities. If changing relationships to make them more democratic was anti-capitalist, then surely efforts by women to end age-old subordination qualified as anticapitalist. If "existing socialism" had brought economic change without altering gender relationships very much, it was crucial to ask how that outcome could be avoided in France. This space for theoretical reconsideration was amply used and new work appeared which argued for the absolute necessity of a double struggle—against capitalism and against the subordination of women—all the way through the process of making socialism.[17] This theoretical argument, which included commitment to the PCF's version of *autogestion* by 1977, implied greater attention to noneconomistic mobilizational efforts and the incorporation of many themes which had been popularized by the women's movement. It also implied greater emphasis on democratic procedures for the elaboration of programs, rather than relying on top—down practices of democratic centralism.

The Eurocommunist thrust was carried into the CGT to meet up with the already present rethinking that had begun to change *Antoinette*. The Sixth National Conference of Wage-earning Women, held in the spring of 1977, represents the high point of the CGT's new understanding of women. That Conference was widely celebrated as a beacon of a new CGT, one which was less exclusively economistic, more democratic and creative in its search for solutions, and one which emphasized the need for serious attention to the oppression of women, rather than merely the expression of voluntaristic hopes that it would be overcome as women entered the salaried laborforce. While *Antoinette* had earlier given evidence that some change was in the wind, the Conference itself was the most coherent public expression of change.

A simple comparison of the Fifth and Sixth Conferences makes some of the difference clear. The 1973 report was presented in the traditional way, with the speeches of the CGT leadership reproduced entirely. Appendices gave the CGT's program of reform and the book was prefaced by Georges Séguy, who presented a summary of the themes and issues raised and pointed out the importance of the Conference for women and the CGT. The report of the 1977 Conference, *Les Questions qui font bouger,* provides a sharp contrast (CGT, 1978b). One immediately apparent difference is the greater use of the word *femmes* rather than *travailleuses* in the discourse. Secondly, no complete speeches were reproduced. Instead parts of the interventions of top leaders were interspersed with those of the ordinary delegates and the explicative text, printed in boldface type, was kept to a minimum. In other words, the analysis of the CGT was presented as if it were emerging from the words of the rank-and-file. Moreover, while Georges Séguy prefaced the book again, by 1977 his words were in poetic form!

Of course it was not only style which differed, the content was different too. The theme of the domination of women by men as a group was stressed. This subordination was examined, its historical roots debated, and its reproduction considered. Many interventions utilized an analysis of women's situation which was new to the CGT and very reminiscent of the contributions by some of the top leadership to the PCF's Eurocommunist rethinking of the problem.[18] The Conference also considered the behavior of the CGT *vis-à-vis* women workers and militants. This particular issue was important because it pointed out one of the implications of this new analysis. It admitted of possible divisions within the working class, between men and women, an admission which shattered a favorite CGT assumption about the organic unity of that class.

This idea, plus the notion that struggle against superexploitation was only part of the struggle for liberation of women, was a central contribution of the Eurocommunists within the CGT in alliance with those who were influenced by the women's movement's formulation of issues. In the process of developing this analysis the propositions of the CGT came to resemble more closely those of the CFDT. There was also increased agreement between the two confederations on programs of demands, as the CGT paid more attention in *Antoinette* and other public organs to cultural and social change and was less narrowly economistic in its approaches, all in the context of unity-in-action.

Turning Point: Post-1977

The rapprochement of the two confederations was short-lived. As the events of the electoral arena in 1977–8 began to force apart the United Left, the unions were caught up in the conflict and began to distance themselves from each other more explicitly. Moreover, as the PCF lost its strategic gamble that it made about Union de la Gauche (as the Socialists' support increased faster than its own) it beat a hasty retreat away from unity into sectarian isolation. This new strategic line, explicitly developed in response to the defeat of the spring of 1978 and consecrated at the Twenty-third Congress in 1979, left little room in the party for the Eurocommunist current (Jenson and Ross, 1979; Fiszbin, 1980). However, the strategic retreat was neither immediately perceived in its full consequences nor completely accepted, and a major conflict was touched off within the PCF. Throughout this period of conflict those whose Eurocommunism had included a commitment to democratizing gender relations, theoretical acceptance of a double struggle of women and the working class, and criticism of the experiences of women under "existing socialism" found themselves on the front line of the internal battleground.[19] Thus one of the first casualties of this change in line was the PCF's own openness on women's issues. For example, a June 1978 meeting at Argenteuil reflected a return to more traditional discourse about women as workers and mothers, and the denial of radical credentials to the women's movement as well as to the Socialists.

This conflict generated by Communist strategic change entered the CGT too, although it was translated into specifically trade union terms and raised the topic of the Confederation's strategy and its relationship to political parties. Conflict over the positions of the CGT in the run-up to the elections of 1978 sparked a more comprehensive consideration of CGT–PCF relations and the longstanding strategic predilection to leave the role of mastermind of "real change" to the Communist Party. In many public expressions of this conflict, especially involving top leadership of the CGT, there was a split among the Communists within the union. The dispute eventually narrowed down to one between those who wished to keep the CGT as a mass organization ready to carry out in the workplace and in large-scale popular demonstrations a kind of defensive unionism that would be useful to the PCF's new strategic position, and those with another view of the confederation's purposes. The advocates of "proposition force unionism" wanted the CGT to begin acting to propose reforms in sectors and industries rather than reacting defensively in the face of capital's actions (see Huiban, in this volume; Ross, 1981, ch. 10 and conclusions; Mouriaux, 1981a). Such proposition force unionism entailed decentralization of decision-making to the actual participants in each sector and thus was one way of moving toward a more *autogestionnaire* type of union activity. According to these proposals, the new unionism which was advocated was strategically separated from the partisan arena, so that the confederation would not be dragged into interparty conflict. It was also a unionism in which rank-and-file militants would define and organize struggle and in which the outcomes of such definitions were democratically determined. Thus it gave to the rank-and-file, if it so desired, the power to move away from the traditional, strict economistic focus of the CGT. Moreover, it was essential for proposition force unionism to work that the militants be able to express themselves creatively, confidently, and democratically. There was no room for a silent or subordinate segment of the organization. All militants had to be available for involvement.

In many ways, then, the proposition force proposals were intertwined with the themes that had been identified with both the Eurocommunist and the women's movement's analyses of women (Leger, 1982, p. 42). There was the same emphasis on democracy as a form of relationship and in decision-making. There was similar attention to other concerns than just material ones. There were echoes of the theoretical openness which had promoted creative thought rather than reliance on old models. Moreover, there was more than merely a thematic overlap between the Eurocommunists and the proposition force unionists. There was substantial overlap of personnel, at the rank-and-file level, among union *permanents,* and in the top leadership. This doubling-up of the themes and personnel was of great consequence when the CGT began to follow the PCF into sectarian workerism and new pro-Sovietism after 1978.

The conflict within the CGT eventually resulted in the elimination of most of the top leadership which had advocated greater independence from the PCF in favor of more straightforwardly trade union initiatives and a more democratic internal life for the CGT. This vicious internal conflict also caught those who had drawn the logical consequences of Eurocommunism for the "problem" of women.[20] In particular, the Soviet invasion of Afghanistan in 1979 and the Marchais candidacy in the presidential elections of 1981 were points of particularly vicious and public conflict as Communists within the CGT, as well as non-Communists, became increasingly critical of the PCF's stance and strategy and the CGT's seemingly uncritical official loyalty, especially in the election campaign.

The appearance within the CGT of this combat over the strategy of the confederation, its political role, and its internal life was felt in the major institutional focus of new thinking about women—the offices of *Antoinette.* As its director, Christiane Gilles, became visible as a critic of the PCF–CGT relationship as well as some other official positions of the CGT (particularly on the Afghanistan question), the magazine came increasingly under attack. For example, *Antoinette* and its editors were singled out by several Unions Départementales as not having worked hard enough, and perhaps even having tried to sabotage the CGT's efforts in the 1981 election, and for not having combated the "anti-Communist campaign" supposedly rampant in the country. The emphasis placed on work with feminists and nonunion women's groups at the 1977 Conference of Salaried Women (the report described above was edited by the journalists of *Antoinette*) was criticized by 1981–2 as reformist, as insufficiently focussed on the class struggle, and as pro-CFDT. Finally, in the spring of 1982, just before the Forty-first Congress, eight journalists including the editor-in-chief were fired by the CGT and a whole new team replaced them at *Antoinette*. The criticisms made of this group of CGT *permanents* was very similar to those made of members of the top leadership throughout the post-1977 years which finally resulted in the dramatic resignations (including Christiane Gilles's) in the fall of 1981.

Thus by 1982 one of the major institutional spaces for new thinking about and approaches to women was "taken in hand" after it came out on the "wrong side" of the intense internal combat over strategy, over party–union relations, and over relations with other organizations of the women's movement and the CFDT.

However, the consequences of this change for the CGT's positions are complicated to assess. The Forty-first Congress documents do exhibit a concentration on the right to work as the only major reform necessary to alter women's economic and social position. At the same time, however, *Antoinette* retains many of the emphases familiar to its readers of the last decade. The first issues produced by the new team of journalists and editorial group continued to give major space to themes of sexual harassment as a legitimate trade union concern, to new forms of contraception including "the pill" for men, and the difficulties created by the "macho" nature of soccer during the World Cup (*Antoinette,* no. 207, June 1982, no. 208, July and August 1982). Thus the feminism of the CGT is isolationist rather than interested in cross-class and pluralistic alliances. It is much more concerned with working conditions than social attitudes. However, now it does consider that working women are legitimately concerned with sexual harassment and assaults on their dignity and that contraceptive technique is both worthy of CGT attention and of concern to working men. Thus the effects of several years of strategic conflict are seen in the new isolationism of the CGT and its position close to the PCF. This has meant a return to the right-to-work theme as the focus for mobilizing women. However, in a time of union crisis and declining memberships, the CGT cannot afford to leave the CFDT complete control over "feminism." Therefore, the CGT retains some of its emphasis on changing ideas and on more "personal" politics, even if the actual content of these themes is more economistic than previously.

Therefore, what the long-term consequences of the flirtation with new approaches will be is still unknown. The experience was too brief for any of the real potential problems (which as we will see below the CFDT did begin to encounter) to emerge and be adequately confronted. Therefore, it remains an untried experiment to solve a problem which continues. The rates of participation of women continue to rise, despite the economic crisis. The effects of superexploitation of women have not disappeared. The militancy of women workers continues to be noticeably high and to bring them into conflict with their union leadership. The themes and issues raised by the women's movement remain pertinent and unresolved. Yet much in the CGT in 1982 resembles an earlier CGT. Its failure to sustain modernization, because of its continuing dependence on the swings of partisan strategy to which it has been a captive, will no doubt be a costly factor for the organization in the 1980s.

The CFDT was not aloof from the events which so dramatically buffeted the CGT. It too was forced to take stock after the debacle of the 1978 elections and the breakdown of unified action with the CGT, and an internal debate of some magnitude and hostility was touched off within that confederation. The reconsideration, which resulted in the *recentrage* strategy elaborated at the Thirty-eighth Congress in Brest, had effects for the CFDT's understanding of working women in two ways. The first affected the possibilities of conducting effective struggle to achieve the CFDT's stated goal of instituting a new type of "socialist development" which would begin to liberate women and be more than reformism. The second effect was directed toward the internal life of the CFDT and its ability to incorporate women militants into the leadership of the union at all levels, in order to begin translating some theoretical promise into actual outcomes.

Recentrage can be described in a number of ways, because it was introduced in a somewhat confused way and elaborated by members of the CFDT in somewhat contradictory terms. *Recentrage* was presented as a response to the judgment that the CFDT had in recent years, and especially since 1974, been too much oriented toward "political" solutions and too little focussed on "trade union" solutions. A leftward reading of this critique was that the CFDT had mistakenly ignored its fundamental principle enunciated in 1970, that movement toward socialism could begin immediately as a result of well-designed trade union action, and instead had begun to wait upon political solutions in the electoral arena. Thus in a general way this analysis shared some of the themes of the proposition force unionists of the CGT and they were all heavily influenced by the leftist Italian unions' understandings of how trade unions could and should behave in crisis (Mouriaux, 1981a; Caroux, 1980; Andrieux and Lignon, 1981, p. 1070 ff.). A rightward-reading of *recentrage* was that the CFDT had not only been too "political" but that it had been too radical as well and that it should in the future return to more "centrist" and traditional trade union concerns with wages and working conditions. The impression that this second reading was a more correct one was reinforced by the appearance in leadership positions of the organization of many people aligned with the more conservative, less *gauchiste,* leaders of the confederation, as well as by the continuing response of the CFDT to the economic crisis.

However, debate did continue within the organization over the meaning of the new strategy, a condition which makes conclusions about it difficult to make with confidence.

In addition to a new analysis—whether of a left or right variety—a new strategy for action appeared. In place of mass demonstrations that had united thousands behind unifying and simplistic slogans in the days of unity-in-action the CFDT would switch to the use of small-scale, very specific local actions. These localized struggles would build up to larger ones only if they sparked responses from workers in other plants or sectors with similar needs. Thus, the *recentrage* strategy reflected a reconsecration of the traditional organizational decentralization of the CFDT. Of course this new strategy had a good deal of potential for women workers who wanted to raise new kinds of issues in their trade unionism. It gave the rank-and-file space to be as creative as it wished without relying on the single decisions of the top leadership. New forms of militancy could be developed to push new kinds of demands. If the reforms were well chosen and pressed, they might very well begin the process of transformation which the CFDT's theory saw at present in the actions of trade unions. However, because it was a decentralized strategy, it left the initiative to the responsibility of the rank-and-file. In a situation which the CFDT acknowledged underrepresented women, the decisions made by local unionists at the base could never be guaranteed to live up to this potential.

Moreover, there was also a less optimistic outcome possible from the new strategy. It was that neo-corporatism would emerge in a workforce under intense pressure from high rates of unemployment and economic restructuring (Adam, 1981b, p. 1049). The CFDT recognized that one of the consequences of economic crisis was the segmentation of the labor-force into a multitude of kinds of workers—full-time and part-time, well-protected and vulnerable to unemployment—and that capital's strategy was to maximize this segmentation. The CFDT's concern, in contrast, was to overcome this fragmentation and "remake the social fabric" into a more unified whole (Andrieux and Lignon, 1981). In this light the fundamental demand for improving women's condition in the laborforce was the elimination of a gender-based division of labor by the encouragement of the complete integration of women into all employment categories (*mixité*).

However, a union strategy of decentralizing struggle and avoiding large-scale or national-level direction and negotiations provided little guarantee that such decentralization would not lead directly to neo-corporatism on the part of workers who had jobs and wished to guard them. Moreover, there was some evidence that such neo-corporatism had begun to emerge (Adam, 1981, p. 1053). In addition, since women were disproportionately in the categories of the unemployed, part-time work, or in sectors which were undergoing deskilling, they were particularly at risk from a strategy which might encourage neo-corporatist reactions from the employed, predominantly male workers. There was little evidence that the CFDT had developed any effective mechanisms to overcome this higher risk that female workers ran of being excluded from the laborforce, in one way or another. It was difficult for the CFDT to do so, given its longstanding refusal to promote special *revendications* for women and clinging to the more general emphasis on *mixité*. Moreover, the decentralized stucture of the union made it impossible for the leadership to impose such special efforts, even if they had been developed. Therefore, while working women were always included on the lists of those segments of the workforce which had to be reintegrated into the social fabric, the actual procedures for doing so remained undefined. Moreover, as the internal balance of the CFDT shifted toward the right, in response to the disillusionment with the CGT's antics in electoral politics, the chance that reforms would surpass reformism became less likely.

It was the CFDT's recognition of just such problems with its policies in the 1970s which led to the second kind of change in the confederation's analyses in recent years. From the mid-1970s on, discussion took place at the highest levels of the union about the CFDT's failure to live up in concrete ways to the promise of its theoretical analysis for changing *la condition féminine*. This attention to the real experience of women, as opposed to theoretical expectations, did not occur in isolation. It was part of a more general increase in attention to internal organization, as the leaders interested in *recentrage* attempted to regain control over the internal workings of the union. Along with this emphasis came concern to provide a more concrete unionism and a less ideologically abstract one, in order to demonstrate to the French working class that CFDT could provide the same if not greater benefits than the CGT. Thus the discussion of the CFDT's experience with women was fitted into the new strategy after 1977 (although such discussions predated 1977 by several years).

The Thirty-seventh Congress, for example, was notable for its discussion of the failure of the CFDT to accomplish its goals in any concrete way and it was recommended at that time that federations and local unions be encouraged to reinstate separate women's commissions in order both to provide training-grounds and havens for timid female militants and to revitalize the process of discussing women's trade union needs (Laot in CFDT, 1978d). Within the confederation self-criticisms were frequent and strong. For example, the decision to hold a Conference in 1978 on Women's Work and Union Action was motivated by the recognition that women were not being "heard," nor were they present within the CFDT as much as they should be (CFDT, 1978d, *passim*).

After years during which there was a striking absence of women in leadership positions of the CFDT (only one woman was elected to the Executive Commission during this time) and as the CFDT continued its rethinking of the pre-1977 strategy, at the Brest Congress suggestions were made for the development of an "affirmative action" type of program, or a "quota" system (*Nouvelles CFDT,* no. 7/81, 27 February 1981). After much discussion, the idea of a strict quota was rejected in favor of a more flexible approach which was formalized in the propositions of the Thirty-ninth Congress at Metz (*Syndicalisme Hebdo,* June 1982, pp. 23–5). A goal of 25 percent women elected to leadership positions, including at least eight women in the Bureau Nationale and a substantial increase in the Executive Commission was set out by the resolution of the Congress. The logic behind the resolution was that a necessary condition for the protection of women's needs in a time of economic crisis was at least the presence of *militantes* at all levels.

However, as both the experience in other countries with affirmative action programs and the situation of the CGT which has always had a very respectable number of women in leadership positions show, the presence of women may be a necessary condition for change but it is never sufficient. Accompanying this improvement in numbers must come other guarantees, from strategic actions of all sorts, that women's particular needs will be taken into account in union planning and action. In this area of course the CFDT leaders who promoted the resolution on *mixité* ran up against the traditional themes of union decentralization and democracy. A CFDT with a heavily localized emphasis continues to run the risks of neo-corporatism described above. However, it also has somewhat improved its chances for pushing forward in more concrete ways on its theoretical analyses, if more women begin to appear in leadership posts.

Conclusion

This chapter has traced the effects of the new conditions of the 1970s on the two French labor confederations, which forced them to rethink their understanding of women's situation in capitalism, in socialism, and in the unions. One of these new conditions was very obviously the appearance of more than 1 million additional working women in the salaried laborforce in the decade. These women made demands on the unions to meet new needs. And women workers were very militant in their actions against capital, so that it was difficult to ignore their demands. A second new condition of the 1970s was the influence exerted by the women's movement which challenged the unions to incorporate an understanding of women's subordination to men into the existing analysis of the superexploitation of women by capital. The story of the unions in these years is one of reaction and adjustment to these new pressures at the levels of theory and practice.

However, what this chapter has shown also is that the notions each confederation developed about *la condition féminine,* as well as the mobilization practices *vis-à-vis* women, were drawn from its general strategy and changed as that strategy changed. Moreover, given the well-known weight of political factors on the French union movement, much of the strategic change was a response to changes in the partisan arena. That is, the unions' positions followed not only from secular changes in laborforce participation and from the militancy of female workers but also, and much more directly, from the overall strategic situation which the unions faced. More specifically, the extent to which the CGT and CFDT were able to enunciate an analysis of women's situations which incorporated the themes of oppression as well as exploitation depended on the extent to which, in the case of the CGT, it was able to move beyond narrow economism in *all* strategic realms, and in the case of the CFDT, the extent to which it placed at the forefront a developed commitment to a concretized program for *socialisme autogestionnaire*.

For the CGT, new emphases on changing families and social relations were intimately connected—in theory, in strategy, in personnel—to the Eurocommunist proposition force current. Therefore, once the post-1978 political situation resulted in the CGT being drawn into ever more defensiveness and proximity to the isolationist and workerist strategy of the PCF, and that current of strategic thinking was eliminated from the CGT, new understandings of women were altered too. They were caught up in the internal battle and disappeared, to be replaced by more traditional approaches. For the CFDT, the impossibility of unity in action for the post-1977 years and the disenchantment with "political" solutions, opened up the possibility of two readings of the *recentrage* strategy. To the extent that a leftward-looking reading was credible, the logic of women's liberation in the context of the construction of *socialisme démocratique et autogestionnaire* maintained some promise that union would indeed promote real change in French working women's situation. To the extent that *recentrage* really meant a move to the center and a return to a laborist (*travailliste*) perspective, the context of economic crisis and the emergence of neo-corporatism in the male working class held out less promise.

Notes: Chapter 10

1 Guilbert, 1974b, 1974a, p. 179, reports the statistics for change over time. Laot, 1981, appendix 12, gives some of the same statistics and updates them to 1980. For comparative figures, which place France in perspective, see OECD, 1975.

2 The unemployment rate for women has been higher than for men but in recent years the gap has grown larger. For example, in 1977, women were 54 percent of those looking for work: INSEE, 1979. For the rates during 1975–80 see OECD, 1980.

3 While it is notoriously difficult to obtain precise figures for union membership in France, both confederations claim approximately 30 percent of their members are women.

4 The synthetic literature on the French women's movement is not very large. For an overview of the different groups active after 1968 see Guadilla, 1981, chs 2 and 3. For more general discussions see Albistur and Armogathe, 1977, tome II, p. 665 ff.; Rabaut, 1978, chs 14 and 15; Jenson, 1982; Leger, 1982.

5 Jeanette Laot of the CFDT provides a good example of the kind of movement between arenas of action. She was the only woman on the CFDT's Executive Commission and at the same time a cofounder, *à titre personnel,* of the *Mouvement pour la libéralisation de l'avortement et de la contraception* (MLAC). For a discussion of the problems this double role created within the CFDT, see Laot, 1981, pp. 88–92.

6 For an historical overview of the several stages of the PCF–CGT relationship—whether the CGT was a transmission belt or a relatively autonomous actor—see Ross, 1981.

7 For only one example of the themes that the PCF used see PCF, 1957, which was a report of *Journées nationales sur le travail parmi les femmes* in which women were

assured that they wanted peace and well-being for their families and children. They were exhorted to join the PCF "pour la grandeur de la France; pour le bonheur de vos enfants," even if not for their own!

8   As Jeanette Vermeersch said, the earlier opportunistic orientation had underestimated the importance of working women and the PCF had left *le problème féminin* to the UFF exclusively, which was an error: 1964, p. 43.

9   The following paragraphs are drawn from CGT, 1973, which includes a report of the Conference, a preface by Georges Séguy, an opening speech by Christian Gilles, a closing speech by Henri Krasucki, and an appendix with the CGT's program for women.

10 For a discussion of the general economic strategy and response to crisis of the CGT see Lange *et al.*, 1982.

11 Laot argues that the old ideas continued within the CFDT and emerged at times. She gives an example of the discussion around the CFDT's advocacy of the right to work principle: 1981, pp. 87–8.

12 These paragraphs are drawn from the summary of CFDT doctrine in CFDT, 1978b, pp. 234–8; and Laot, 1981. For a very good analytic discussion see also Maruani, 1979, pt I.

13 Laot, 1981, ch. 2, goes through several issue areas to explain the opposition to specific *revendications*.

14 For a general discussion of these years of unity-in-action see Ross, 1982, chs 8–10; Lange *et al.*, 1982; Mouriaux, 1981a.

15 The agreement is reprinted as an appendix in Laot, 1981.

16 In the words of the Twenty-second Congress of the PCF, "le socialisme c'est la démocratie jusqu'au bout."

17 The best summary collection of this work is in CERM, 1978. Although only published in 1978, several of the chapters had been written and circulated several years earlier. For a discussion of how a single Commission Féminine in a Parisian section attempted to implement some basic Eurocommunist principles, and the troubles this created, see Jenson, 1980.

18 This was especially true of the speech of J.-L. Moynot, whose chapter in the CERM book dealt with many of the questions he raised at the CGT Conference.

19 Henri Fiszbin, in *Les Bouches s'ouvrent,* 1980, details several examples of this process in which women active in the leadership of the Paris Federation were faulted for their work with women: see, for example, p. 67.

20 Sometimes the process became impossibly difficult, as the suicide of Georgette Vacher in the fall of 1981 poignantly demonstrated: Simon, 1981, ch. 2 and pp. 61–3.

11

Trade Unions, the Environment and the Quality of Life

MICHELLE DURAND and YVETTE HARFF

General Introduction

During the last decade the French working-class movement was forced to confront a number of major challenges coming in rapid succession and with a cumulative effect. The first confrontation was with the radical protest movement of May 1968 and the subsequent questioning of industrial society itself. This took a more concrete form with the emergence of the ecological movement, the rejection of exponential growth with its negative consequences, and a proliferation of actions that sought to preserve the quality of life, the social environment (*cadre de vie*), and a certain lifestyle. Some authors were led to proclaim the "logical" demise of the traditional working-class movement and "face-to-face class confrontation" and its replacement by a more general calling into question of industrial society both in its technocratic mode of operation and its end-products (Vidal, 1978; Touraine, 1977; Gorz, 1982).

Since 1974, however, after the first oil shock brought growth to an abrupt halt and the economic crisis set in throughout Europe, the workers' traditional struggles for employment and the maintenance of living standards once again came to the forefront. Yet the number of factory closures and the magnitude of the recession in certain regions of the country would lead the unions to adopt an increasingly clear stance against the technocratic solutions to the crisis that the state and *patronat* sought to impose.

Finally, in the realm of politics, after the period of great hopes and disappointments brought on by the Union of the Left and its defeat in 1978, the unions suddenly found themselves facing new dilemmas with the coming to power of the left in May 1981. While the unions may expect some of their demands to be granted in this new context, the real questions remain to be tackled and have become the locus of debates within the left.

It should be pointed out that this period was marked by a relatively large independence of social movements from the political sphere. The events of May 1968, for example, were followed by a landslide vote for the right in that year's legislative elections. Inversely the left electoral victory in 1981 was not preceded by any major strike movements. While localized strikes have appeared as a result of the recession, more generalized movements, such as national days of action, have lost favor, as government statistics show. Certainly mounting protest in those regions most threatened by the recession (Lorraine, Vosges, Nord, Brittany, Corsica) should not be discounted. The fact that these conflicts remain localized, however, indicates that they do not always work in the left's favor. What we have, then, is two forms of democracy which function independently of each other. This is doubtless representative of a technocratic state where no apparent connection exists between grassroots social movements, the aspirations of civil society, and the exercise of administrative authority.

In this chapter we will examine the trade union confederation positions on the major political choices relative to the organization of social life: choices bearing on the quality of life and general social needs, on regional development (*aménagement du territoire*), and on the economic options for national development. This chapter draws upon previously published research (Harff and Durand, 1977) and attempts to understand the evolution of union positions on these themes in the subsequent period that has been marked by both economic crisis and political change.

The Strategic Orientation of the CFDT and the Emergence of Cadre de Vie Themes

What led the CFDT to take up problems originating outside the workplace and incorporate them into its demand package? How did these themes first enter into the confederation's official debates, later become one of the components of its strategy, and finally develop into one of the most original aspects of its actions?

For the CFDT, these themes came to be integrated into a line of action that had been slowly developing over the past years. If the confederation took up such issues first in May 1968 and to a greater extent thereafter, it was because the confederation recognized the possibility of thus imparting to its social project the greatest scope and expanding its natural field of action. In order to understand this ideological assimilation we must examine the long process of cultural development which is proper to the CFDT.

Several stages in this process can be distinguished. We will not describe at length the initial period (1940–59) during which the CFTC moved from "social corporatism" to "democratic planning." We do wish to indicate, however, how the union's basic inspiration and its internal factional disputes produced a new type of trade unionism which approached the totality of social organization, first in its discourse and then in its praxis.

In this first period the confederation's line derived from, on the one hand, a general consensus among the membership on the values of the ideal society as defined by Christian personalism and, on the other hand, the factional conflict between two opposing conceptions of trade unionism and of the union's role in social evolution. There was consensus, first of all, around the idea of a future "society for mankind," around the quest to achieve a "civilization which would affirm the superiority of the general over the particular interest." The establishment of a new form of democracy, the primacy of law, and the flourishing of the human persona would replace the class antagonisms that stemmed from the conditions of production.

Notwithstanding such common values, which helped to maintain the organization's unity over a long period (until 1964), the confederation's internal debates in the post-Liberation era pitted two currents against one another. The majority current stood for social catholicism, adhering to the *Quadragesimo anno* encyclical of 1931 which stressed the primacy of the professional organization as the guarantor of allegiance to the church's social doctrine and the spirit of social corporatism. The minority current opposed the majority on several grounds:

- trade unions should manifest autonomy with regard to the state, governments and political parties;
- trade unionism has a distinct mission *vis-à-vis* the working class: the unity of the trade union organization should not be based on any community of religious or moral body of thought but rather on this mission;
- the existence of class antagonisms, which are to be accepted as a "structural fact," provide the justification for the trade union's vocation of working to transform social structures.

It was precisely this evolving preoccupation with effecting a change in social structures which led the confederation gradually to take up the whole range of social issues, including at a later date those of the social environment and quality of life. In contrast, for the CGT, the same principled stance in favor of changing social structures led logically to the seizure of political power and not to trade union action.

It was during this period that the CFTC began to move in the direction of a unionism grounded in a social critique. The action model of Christian trade unionism was seen as a mode of social integration within a value system. Inversely, in order to constitute the CFTC as a workers' movement and not a "subsystem of values outside the working class," the minority faction sought to take the concrete situation of the working class as its point of departure. Jean-Paul Sartre (1947) in 1939 had theorized that consciousness is a projection of being outside the self. Similarly one can say that in this period the working-class consciousness expressed by the CFTC "minoritaires" was projected outside the organization itself, outside its ideological system, and thus beyond any dogmatism. Henceforth the field would be open for the construction of

⌐a new type of trade unionism, derived from reflection on the union's "action practices" and confrontation with the "other experiences" of the working class.⌐

The minority's holistic views toward working-class concerns were actualized through the report on *democratic planning* presented by Gilbert Declercq at the Thirtieth Congress in 1959 (CFDT, 1971, pp. 64–96). This opened up a *second phase* of reflection and action for the confederation. The idea of democratic planning derived from a critique of liberalism as incapable of promoting harmony or social and political progress. Not only did liberalism result in social injustice; but it also excluded the possibility of making collective choices democratically, as reasoned choices could supposedly only occur at the level of the individual.

In contrast the concept of democratic planning was based on two guiding ideas:

- the economy should be centralized by means of a coherent yet voluntary plan and investments steered in the public interest;
- this plan should be elaborated through democratically established criteria, which presupposes that the political conditions exist to assure the participation of workers in determining investment and production objectives.

The report presented at the Thirtieth Congress thus proposed democratic structures at all levels of the economy: firm, branch, regional, and national.

From this point on, these positions would lead the CFTC to develop action in two directions. First, it would reject existing structures and propose democratic alternatives at all levels. Secondly, it developed an interest in the different domains of economic planning and spatial organization, thus stimulating reflection on the varied aspects of social existence. Not until 1964, the year of the CFDT–CFTC schism, did the confederation really go into action on these issues. From that point on, however, a plethora of actions were launched which confronted economic and political realities at both the national and regional level.

The campaign "against regional decline" served to focus the confederation's discourse and action on those decisions that reached beyond the sphere of the workplace. This touched on problems of industrialization, urban development, housing, public transport, parks and recreation areas—in short, all decisions bearing upon *aménagement du territoire*—(regional and local development).

Each regional situation underscored the failures inherent in centralized industrial development. In the provinces an awareness of regional underdevelopment and a fight to maintain employment coexisted with a struggle to preserve regional cultures. In juxtaposition to the reality of labor migrations was held up the conception of economic decentralization. This line of action in favor of regional development, which coincided with the often futile efforts of governmental authorities to decentralize industry, nourished within the confederation a growing appreciation of the different modes of development and their increasing power ׀in determining ways of life and cultural behavior.

The inverse situation prevailed in the Paris metropolitan area: here the damage caused by industrial and urban concentration was most keenly felt. In 1965, the year of a political debate on Paris in the year 2000, the CFDT's regional affiliate for Paris (CFDT URP) launched its first campaign to "Live Better in Paris." The campaign took up three themes that would prefigure the forthcoming debates on the quality of urban life.

First, the CFDT URP considered the issue of an economy of scarcity and pointed out that free collective goods diminish with growth. The URP's slogan was: "They expropriate the air, water, quiet and rest from workers in order to sell them at the price of gold."

Secondly, the URP took up the issue of housing for workers—housing was too costly, small, and far from Paris. The URP pointed out overcrowded housing conditions and analyzed the evolution of the housing market itself, where the private sector was gaining while public housing (HLM and Logeco) fell off. The URP noted that, in comparison with other countries, France was behind both in terms of prices and total habitable space. The CFDT called for new projects, such as the creation of a national public housing service that would provide rental housing available to the general public. It also called for putting an end to real-estate speculation by public expropriation of urban land holdings, an improvement in the quality of construction, and a program to rehouse Parisians living in slum conditions.

Thirdly, the URP examined the problem of transportation. It asserted that "Parisian mass transport is still in the horse-and-buggy era; mass transport is slow, noisy, uncomfortable, overcrowded and unhealthy." This diagnosis suggested the need for a Parisian transportation network: this was the origin of the theme "priority to public transport."

These demands bearing on the quality of life in the Paris metropolitan area directly addressed the choices to be made in urban policy. The relevant public authorities were evidently the prime interlocuteur targeted by this action.

A new phase of CFDT policy occurred when it sponsored, in April 1966, a National Conference on Residential Living and Urban Planning. The Conference adopted a series of proposals for institutional changes, notably public appropriation of lands necessary for rational development of the social environment, in particular, urban land holdings. A city real-estate office, where representatives of the communities within the metropolitan area would have a majority, would be responsible for elaborating and approving (in liaison with national and regional representatives) urban development projects and plans. The office would be authorized to appropriate all urban lands: (1) through regrouping lands owned by public agencies; and (2) through purchase of all land within the boundaries of the metropolitan area, at its current use value. Land where buildings had already been constructed privately would also be included—the buildings would in turn be leased to their current owners (CFDT, 1966). This marked a new stage in the evolution of the CFDT's orientation. Housing for the working class was not viewed solely from the standpoint of demand; rather the confederation put forward a counterplan and the means to implement it. The CFDT stressed that the amelioration of housing conditions was a legitimate realm of trade union concern. The right to housing was basic to society.

Beginning in 1967, however, the urban phenomenon in general came under discussion among CFDT militants (CFDT, 1967). Moving from the previous standpoint of the consumer and the consequences of urbanization on daily life, the CFDT now sought a democratic policy of urban environment. The analysis was no longer confined to the consequences of urban policy as a form of power within the city environment. It is noteworthy that this analysis emanated primarily from the construction federation; thus self-analysis of professional activity could stimulate action. With respect to the later debates on urban development and the social environment (mobilizing issues arising out of the May 1968 movement), these CFDT positions represented a considerable advance toward the elaboration of an urban policy and the means for its implementation.

The idea for a counterplan developed out of the CFDT's critique of the role exercised by the state, which had become in principle the architect and motor of urban planning. The state had the human resources and institutional structures (at the national, regional, and local level) and levers (urban redevelopment plans, construction licensing agencies, the land-use law of 1967, and so on) for intervention in this domain. Yet state action encountered two sorts of obstacles: (1) private ownership and parcelization of urban land; and (2) the high value of urban land holdings which derived not from improvements undertaken by owners but rather from zoning regulations and infrastructure sponsored by public authorities. For this reason, the CFDT proposed more radical measures, such as the collectivization of urban land, to disassociate landownership from usage rights. In order to circumvent any centralizing or authoritarian tendencies inherent in collective control over urban land holdings the confederation proposed major decentralization of planning and decision-making authority as well as a greater role for local authorities and the general public, at all stages of elaborating or implementing urban projects.

The counterplan strategy involved a new conception of relations between the "union" and "political" spheres:

> Clearly, when we speak of the necessity [for the union] to be present in all arenas, including the political, where workers' interests are at stake ... we do not intend "to engage in politics," that is ... to act in a "partisan" manner.

Asserting that its actions were to defend the quality of life of workers, the CFDT would engage in social critique of economic policy, regional planning, and urban policy. Likewise, decision-making structures and administration would be subject to CFDT scrutiny. The scope of the confederation's discourse thus extended to the social system in all its dimensions.

We have not yet specified whether the CFDT's emphasis on democratic planning was oriented toward prescribing immediate objectives for action or rather outlining the elements of a long-term social project. In fact we find a two-pronged strategy that would be characteristic of the third phase in the CFDT's evolution. The CFDT thus rejected any separation of immediate objectives from its *projet de société*. Immediate objectives (demands) constituted a cultural element which would in part define the future. The *projet de société* would be prefigured through conflictual action. In accordance with these principles actions undertaken on behalf of democratic planning were to affirm the autonomy of the confederation's project *vis-à-vis* existing structures and pave the road to democratic socialism, the goal officially adopted at the CFDT's 1970 Congress.

Toward Autogestion

The third phase of CFDT evolution (from May 1968 to the 1973 CFDT Congress) was devoted to elaborating a *projet de socialisme autogestionnaire*. In the span of a few weeks in May–June 1968 the "May movement" transformed social conflict from a struggle restricted to the workplace into a national debate over society itself. All the social, cultural, and institutional dimensions of centralized industrial society became targets of social criticism. In the CFDT's view the new aspirations that emerged were a counterpoint to capitalist power that had become more and more technocratic, a reaction to capital's hegemony over the organization of social life. Furthermore, over the years the CFDT had carefully scrutinized the bureaucratic and technocratic experience of East European societies. Thus it was well-prepared in 1968 to propose a project for self-management. Yet it would be two more years before the confederation would opt in favor of socialism (endorsing a report presented by its president, André Jeanson, at the Thirty-Fifth Congress; see CFDT, 1971, pp. 125–41).

Significantly, only following the Thirty-fifth Congress did the CFDT officially elaborate the concept of *cadre de vie*. In fact, so-called qualitative demands and new forms of actions took shape within the perspective of constructing a *projet de société*. The debates and actions bearing on the quality of working life, which proliferated after 1970, were designed to be the crucible of cultural creation, the preview of the new development model. The Thirty-fifth Congress proclaimed a strategy of rupture:

> In conclusion, it is through the class struggle intrinsic to all domains of the capitalist system that workers and their union organizations, in the course of day-to-day action, challenge the existing system, work to make the rights of man prevail over those of property, oppose unilateral determination of working conditions by public or private employers, and will [ultimately] succeed in shifting the balance of forces to favor another type of development. (CFDT, 1971, p. 129)

In April 1971 the CFDT established a commission to "define the demands of workers relative to the social environment and prepare a strategy for action." These themes thereafter were progressively incorporated into the Confederation's overall strategy. First, the CFDT abandoned the concept of "environment," perceived as too restricted in scope, in favor of *cadre de vie* (translated here as "social environment"—*translator*). *Cadre de vie* is defined as "the structural organization of space, of the different milieux, within which workers live both inside and outside the workplace" (CFDT, 1971, p. 127). Secondly, struggles in this domain would be represented as efforts to conquer control over a previously imposed social environment. This was gradually extended to mean the whole of social and cultural conditioning.

The CFDT elaborated a strategy for control that corresponded to this political definition of the social environment: control over the expansion of industrialization, over the extension of capitalist logic to all sectors of social life, and over the tendency toward centralization of decision-making. The Thirty-fifth Congress is an appeal for the exercise of citizenship in the short and long term. The transition to a socialist society cannot be effected without citizens' active participation in the construction of the "new society." The confederation's strategy of action relative to the social environment must be understood as an integral part of a more general strategy of constructing a counter *projet de société*. These long-term perspectives for transforming social structures constituted an integral part of the CFDT's *projet autogestionnaire: "autogestion* entails the administration of the firm by the workers and also of the national economy and polity by the people" (CFDT, 1971, p. 131).

Finally, the attention given by the CFDT to these qualitative demands derived from its three-tiered analysis of social structure: society as economic organization, hierarchical organization, and dominant ideology (that is, a set of norms and values which legitimate the socioeconomic organization). The three levels—economic, social and ideological—constitute the structure of capitalist society "though they are not separable nor is any one determinant in a permanent fashion." Under these conditions, then, the CFDT formulated an original strategy for struggle which, through conflicts over immediate objectives, "attacks capitalism at all levels and in all arenas" (CFDT, 1973, p. 12). Unlike the CGT, the CFDT does not link all problems to the system of capitalist exploitation and production but also takes account of cultural models.

Autogestion and Crisis

The fourth phase (1973–81) of the CFDT's evolution was characterized by the emphasis given to elaborating an alternative development project despite the crisis. Contrary to expectations the economic crisis did not sway the CFDT from its pursuit of this alternative development. In fact, this project was closely tied into the CFDT's project of socialist self-management (*socialisme autogestionnaire*), in which development would be decentralized and any new choices relative to production would be democratically elaborated at the local, regional, and national levels.

The CFDT has thus not abandoned its opposition to the spread of private automobiles, despite the importance of the auto industry in the national economy. The crisis and threat of plant closings forces workers to be vigilant *vis-à-vis* production decisions and quality (Harff, 1981; Durand, 1981; Casassus, 1980). While the CFDT may want new jobs created, it does not want any type of jobs, any type of production. The confederation continues to encourage struggles for workers' control over production; the most prominent example is the CFDT demand that health and safety committees be given authority to halt dangerous production processes. The CFDT also has participated in struggles to "live in the countryside," which address not only the fight for jobs but also the defense of regional lifestyles (as illustrated by the long struggle conducted by the farmers of Larzac against the extension of a military base).

However, it was the anti-nuclear struggle that acquired the greatest visibility and in which the CFDT invested the most effort both in action and research. Why did the anti-nuclear struggle take on such important symbolic value? For one thing, the problem of energy source, central to any civilization, may be an appropriate terrain on which to force a debate over the direction of development. A more important factor in the French case, however, was the "all nuclear" policy launched by the Messmer government in 1974. This policy, which sought to provide cheap energy to the major industrial sectors within the perspective of continued linear growth, symbolized everything the CFDT opposed.

First, the program would foster a highly centralized energy policy. According to the forecasts of the Barre government, nuclear-generated electricity produced by a single type of reactor would account for 30 percent of primary energy consumption and 73 percent of total electricity output by 1990 (Ministère de l'Industrie, 1981). In the CFDT's view such a program entailed not only economic risks but the political risk of an unsafe and secretive society dominated by a police state.

Secondly, the program was perceived as fraught with peril because of the haste with which it was launched, the precipitous choice of sites, and the choice of fast-breeder reactors. Fast-breeder reactors are fueled by plutonium, which is extremely hazardous and whose utilization requires technical mastery of the entire combustion cycle. In 1976 the CFDT opposed the construction of a fast-breeder reactor at Creys-Malville (the first in the world for commercial production of electricity) and demanded a nuclear moratorium and national debate. This nuclear policy, furthermore, carried sociopolitical risks, since plutonium is also used in the fabrication of nuclear weapons; the export of such reactors might thus encourage foreign nations to become atomic powers. Finally, there were ecological risks associated with disposing of the waste products, which remain radioactive for thousands of years.

Thirdly, the construction of nuclear plants and the management of reprocessing facilities (at La Hague) were gradually delegated to private corporations. This privatization both increased the likelihood of risks to increase profits and diminished the possibility for controls. The three-month-long strike at La Hague in 1976 over this issue did not meet with success, however.

Fourthly, and most important, the policy had been imposed by a technocratic power structure linked to the major industrial concerns. The aim was the pursuit of development as defined by the imperatives of international competition rather than by local or regional needs. For example, the decision to choose the "tout nucléaire" option was taken by the PEON Commission, where Electricité de France and several private firms are represented, and the Central Planning Council, which is directly responsible to the President.

We should note in passing the CFDT demands bearing on working conditions in this sector: observance of existing legislation (*Journal Officiel,* 30 April 1975), nuclear monitoring devices for all workers, creation of radiation safety services independent from the production apparatus, occupational safety studies carried on outside the official hierarchy, and maintenance of state control over the industry. The inspection and research conducted by workers in this sector should also be mentioned. Such issues were central to CFDT actions, as demonstrated by the major strike at La Hague, the exposure of fissures in steel reactor tanks, and the risk-analysis done for all stages of the production process (CFDT SNPEA, 1975; see also the CFDT films *Condamnés à réussir* on La Hague and *Le Dossier Plogoff*).

In response to the Seventh Plan of 1975 the CFDT proposed an alternative to the "all nuclear" program. The CFDT position was based on a rejection of the linear notion of progress tied to economic growth and on the principle of decentralization. The CDFT called for a diversification of energy sources and criticized "the reasoning of EDF which chooses 'all nuclear' after having chosen 'all electricity' as the starting point." The CFDT advocated better development of existing energy resources: (1) hydroelectric, which was still underexploited in France; (2) coal, where production could be revived; (3) gas, where utilization could be expanded through bilateral accords with other nations; and (4) oil, albeit maximizing independence *vis-à-vis* the multinationals and establishing more egalitarian relations with producer countries. The CFDT also wanted more research and development in geothermy, solar, and biomass—forms of energy which could be used locally in contrast to the technocratic mode of distribution of nuclear energy.

With regard to future evolution of primary energy use, the CFDT forecast for 1990 was 220 million tons of oil equivalent, that is, about half the increase predicted by the Barre government (which forecast 242 million tons). Nuclear energy was to account for 30 percent of total energy consumption by 1990 in the Barre Plan and only 13 percent in the CFDT Plan. Similarly the CFDT wanted to limit the nuclear component of total electrical production in 1990 to 30–35 percent, while the Barre government in contrast put this at 73 percent in 1990 and 84 percent in 2000.

It should be pointed out, however, that the confederal positions seem to be poorly reflected in the attitudes of union members. Thus, according to a 1977 Louis Harris poll, 41 percent of CFDT members supported construction of nuclear plants. In similar fashion, although the CGT officially endorses nuclear energy, 46 percent of its membership opposed such construction. This finding supports the previous observation as to the separation of the union and political arenas. The union membership does not line up politically with the confederation; rather the confederation is divided by politics.

The CFDT and the Left Government

With the left's ascension to power in 1981, the CFDT hoped for a major slowdown of the nuclear program. The cancellation of the Plogoff plant and initial government moves in July 1981 to suspend construction of new plants seemed to indicate that the nuclear program would be reconsidered. The CFDT did not let up its pressure on the government, however. It promoted a national petition that called for a halt to the nuclear program, opening of a public debate, and initiation of regional consultations. On 26 August 1981 Edmond Maire warned:

> If the nuclear program elaborated by the right is pursued, then the socialist government will have chosen continuity as the easiest route, and we will once again experience a type of growth that wastes energy while economizing manpower ... A balanced industrial policy will have been sacrificed in favor of an export policy serving a few privileged bastions.

In October 1981 the National Assembly voted on two Bills concerning the nuclear program: one sponsored by the Mitterrand government, the other by a Socialist deputy favorable to the CFDT viewpoint. The government Bill carried, thus setting into motion a program to build six new nuclear plants in 1982–3. A third reprocessing unit would also be built to augment the capacity of the La Hague plant.

Under these conditions what are the chances of some future turn toward a new type of development? It is still too early to tell, since the industrial strategy of the nationalized firms is not yet known. The major axes of the interim plan—return to a 3 percent growth rate, revival of a competitive industrial sector by stimulating investment, promotion of growth more self-sufficient in energy and raw materials—do not seem to indicate any effort to reorient growth. Such a possibility might emerge from the decentralization and democratization reforms and from the possibility of a reorientation of research. The Economic and Social Council's report on the interim plan stressed that "the development of research and technology is undoubtedly one of the most potent levers at our disposal for getting out of the crisis." This poses the question of the use and orientation of science: either its expertise, legitimacy, and power for social exclusion will be employed to support centralized, authoritarian decisions (in which case the distance between the orientation of science and the aspirations of civil society will increase) or, alternatively, efforts will be made to democratize choices bearing on development.

In this regard an analysis of economic choices is revealing. Are we, on the one hand, heading toward a dual economy in which an internationally competitive sector and a domestic economy, characterized by a more harmonious but less profitable development, would coexist—with a growing disparity between the two? Or, on the other hand, will we move in the direction of a society characterized by work-sharing, highly standardized production, more leisure, where all creativity is not directed by industrial society? This would seem to be the American model. A form of civilization—European civilization—seems on the verge of disappearing.

This is not the development option proposed by the CFDT. The CFDT insists on a type of development that would be adapted to regional needs. We can predict in this context that the struggles taken up by the CFDT will have the following axes:

• attaining greater democracy within the firms, especially in nationalized concerns where union independence will be a major issue;
• promoting democratic "concertation" on development orientations and options at all levels of society.

To conclude this section we cite Edmond Maire's query: "Will governmental power become the sole motor of change or can [administrative] decisions be coordinated with the autonomous action of social forces mobilized to achieve major transformations in society as a whole?"

The CGT Approach to the Problem of the Social Environment

The CGT's approach to the problem of the social environment can be understood through examining its analysis of social needs and its critique of social policy and planning. Social needs are defined in two ways. First, societal progress in all domains redefines both levels of demands and rights (leisure, for example). Secondly, social needs are connected to transformations in the workforce engendered by economic development (community services become needs with the increase in the number of working women). Prior to the 1960s, such transformations were accepted as givens and whatever difficulties wage-earners encountered in their social existence were attributed to the "deficiencies" of governmental action. Starting in the 1960s, however, the problem came to be formulated in a different fashion. At its Thirty-third Congress the CGT lamented working-class living conditions engendered by economic development: specifically, the growing segregation of workplaces from residential neighborhoods and the consequent increase in commuting time.

Two texts—one in 1964 pertaining to regional development policy, another in 1966 prepared for a debate on urban redevelopment—clarified the CGT's position. These show the importance attached at that time to such problems, notably labor mobility at the regional level and quality of life in urban areas. In the latter case, in addition to listing the problems of fatigue and the diminution of free time, the CGT discussed the consequences of the degradation of social life in residential areas on the periphery of urban centers.

These documents also illustrate which changes brought about by economic development the CGT viewed as acceptable. The CGT defined urban growth as intrinsically linked to development, an inherent phenomenon of modern civilization and therefore beyond any challenge. Hence the issue was formulated in terms of existing obstacles to bringing about a mode of urban development that would allow wage-earners to adjust to a new way of life and even make some material and cultural progress. The CGT criticized the fact that regional development policy concentrated public facilities only where employment was already growing and thus forced workers to move to these localities. The CGT asserted that the "working population" was made available to the major capitalist firms and therefore "subject to [capital's] locational decisions and interests."

For the CGT, regional development policy should entail first and foremost orienting development itself: "[taking as a starting-point] evaluation of the needs of the populace, an inventory and utilization of all the natural and human resources in the area" in order to develop each region. However, in this period, it was not the approach to wage-earners' daily problems or even to regional and national development that distinguished the CGT from other organizations but rather its mode of analysis and strategy.

The Broadening of Union Concerns within the CGT Strategy

A debate emerged, in particular between the CGT and CFDT, over the issue of democratic planning. The two sides viewed planning as a process with the potential of both eliminating the negative fallout of economic development and shaping development to become a factor favoring progress in the conditions of existence. The CGT, however, did not believe that real influence over developmental options flowed logically from decentralization, heightened participation of social actors, or administrative reform because these did not alter capitalist logic. Nationalizations and a change in regime were necessary preconditions for real progress.

The struggle for a more harmonious regional and urban development was relegated to the political domain in the future. Trade union action at present could only be defensive in character, tackling the effects not the root cause. For example, addressing the problem of the poor locations of industrial and commercial concerns, the CGT advocated reimbursing workers for travel costs and reducing working hours.

The strategic options defined at its Thirty-fourth Congress (1963) would compel the CGT to go beyond such defensive measures. At this Congress the CGT committed itself to working for regrouping working-class organizations (parties, unions, and other associations) around a program of reforms with the long-range goal of bringing about a change in regime. This strategic choice had two effects. On the one hand, the

CGT expanded its conception of what constituted social issues, as a consequence of the debates within CGT federations on what reforms were needed in their respective domains. On the other hand, the CGT drew a clear distinction between immediate demands, that is, those realistically attainable through trade union struggles, and what it termed "democratic objectives." This distinction in effect eliminated from the union's action program any discussion of desirable transformations in social and occupational life. Such themes would appear in confederal texts only following the May 1968 events.

Shaping CGT Strategy after May 1968:
The Idea of Cadre de Vie *in Confederal Discourse*
The CGT's Thirty-seventh Congress (1969) witnessed a certain innovation in the CGT's position on health, education, housing, and leisure. This broadening of CGT perspective was not only the product of incorporating pre-1968 discussions into the official texts but also a reflection of the rethinking that had occurred on the federal level since May 1968. There was a discernible change in the CGT approach to social needs. The problem of access to health, cultural, and recreational services took on a broader meaning as nonmaterial and nonfinancial considerations were taken into account. Community services, while always considered important, were no longer viewed solely as the means for satisfying needs but also analyzed for their potential impact on lifestyle and social relations. Finally, demands for improving residential living were put forward for the first time. Questions, too, were raised on preventive health care, industrial damage, and pollutants in urban areas.

Only in the areas of health and housing were concrete reform proposals laid out. Nevertheless, this Congress did open up debate between organizations on reform objectives and encouraged CGT locals to undertake joint action with other unions in pursuit of these goals. Essentially the strategy elaborated at this Congress would guide CGT actions until the 1977 rupture of left unity.

Mobilization on the terrain of the social environment began after this Congress. The orientation of CGT action was specified in the following passage:

> The Congress calls upon all confederated organs to initiate or participate in actions which aim at requiring that a portion of rent income be utilized to maintain and improve building stock, to combat real estate speculation ... [and] to struggle against displacement of workers [by demanding that] urban renewal projects include public housing to re-locate workers in the same area.

The 1969 Congress laid out the essential elements of the CGT's line on problems of the social environment (more fully developed after the 1972 Congress). Certainly workers were to be mobilized at the workplace around demands directly addressed to management, for example, firm participation in promoting public housing, culture, and sporting activities. More important, the union was to reach outside the sphere of production and seek accords with other organizations, associations, or movements on common objectives.

The CGT's action in 1973 on the issues of housing and the social environment was typical in this regard. At the national level an appeal endorsed by six organizations (including tenant, family, and self-help organizations) was launched. At the local level meetings and debates often brought in a wider range of groups, in particular the left parties (PS, PCF) and the other union confederations (CFDT, FO, FEN). It should be noted that while the CFDT often participated at the local level, it declined to sign the national petition.

In a parallel fashion, protest over the government's regional development policies began to be linked to fights over employment. In 1971, in conjunction with actions against job cutbacks, especially in the Paris region, the CGT came forth with the triptych "housing–jobs–transport." This would be echoed in the Râteau conflict of 1974:

> Workers of the Paris region have had enough of so-called regional development policy which puts them out of work, pushes them further [outside Paris], and turns the country's center into a monster ... They want well-planned cities where diversified employment will reduce the insanity of commuting.

Trade union action with regard to the social environment was not considered merely an epiphenomenon. Issues pertaining to public facilities and land-use planning (although always considered important to workers) were converted into demands that could be integrated easily into CGT strategy. While this was a domain in which political reform was demonstratively necessary, it was also an excellent terrain for rallying popular forces into action. In fact, this would become one of the major axes of left unity, especially in the 1972–4 period leading up to the presidential election.

In contrast mobilization on industrial and urban damage which developed throughout Europe at this time could not be so easily integrated within the CGT's action program (not fitting the confederation's major preoccupations, approach, or strategy). At the Thirty-eighth Congress (1972) the new line was defined in a report under the chapter heading "Cadre de vie." However, while broadening its perspective to include environmental concerns, the CGT would stress the need for an "ideological struggle" against attitudes "questioning industrial society."

Cadre de Vie: Arena for Critique of Capitalist Development and Rejection of Anti-Industrial Challenges

In the early 1970s the issues of the social environment, the natural environment, and "quality of life" generally received a strong popular response. The CGT, however, chose to remain outside this shift toward popular awareness of such problems, characterized as it was by a questioning of industrial civilization and supported principally by the ecological movement. Until 1971 neither environmental concerns (in their ecological dimension) nor rejectionist attitudes toward urban life and industrial society were seen as relevant for the working class. The CGT position can be seen, therefore, as a reflection of the differences in the social composition of the CGT and CFDT base. Initially, at least, the weak echo of environmental concerns within the CGT had sociocultural as well as ideological roots.

The CGT at the time concerned itself only with noxious effects (*nuisances*) that directly touched wage-earners in residential areas. For the CGT, this entailed broadening the scope of demands bearing on housing conditions (living space, soundproofing, and so on). In practice this meant that the themes and perspectives developed by other movements working in areas of the social environment remained unknown or alien to the CGT.

Beginning in 1971 the environmental debate began to take on European dimensions. In 1972 the international workers' movement began to mobilize; a conference was organized in April 1972 at Oberhausen by IG Metall (Germany), the WFTU (1972) published a document entitled *Dossier on the Environment and Workers*. The environmental issue was given political recognition in France (nomination in 1971 of a ministerial delegate to the Prime Minister's office in charge of environmental protection, creation of a Ministry for the Environment in 1973). A new orientation in economic, industrial, and social policy seemed to be occurring (following the April 1972 declarations of Sicco Mansholt, president of the EEC Commission). The CGT was thus obligated to take a position and did so by incorporating environmental problems into the polemic over economic growth.

The CGT thus would mobilize against perceived threats to living standards rather than out of concern for the environment as such. The CGT's initial texts denounced the publicity accorded the warnings emanating from ecologists and the MIT research team as a psychological campaign designed to foster acceptance of lowered living standards. Pollution was depicted as only one of many concerns workers had about the environment: "workers know that housing and working conditions are part of their environment and that culture, leisure activities and tourism should be inherent components too." Mansholt's proposals were categorically rejected; for the CGT, it was unthinkable to accept a type of planning that, under the guise of new "quality of life" criteria, jeopardized working-class living standards.

The CGT elaborated two new objectives of trade union action: (1) "to make workers aware of the real causes of the environmental crisis"; and (2) "to exert through struggle … pressure on employers and the government to halt pollution and end the waste of resources." It is within this perspective that the CGT added the chapter on Cadre de vie to the program put forth at the Thirty-eighth Congress (1972). What was new at the level of demands touched on industrial pollution: enforcement of effective pollution standards, controls exercised by health and safety committees, and business contributions to damage settlements. Another new element was the criticism of "industrial and urban damage (*nuisances*)," which seemingly echoed those challenging economic development but put forth a very different analysis: "it is not modern life which is responsible for *nuisances* but rather the anarchic nature of a system based on profit, which wastes natural resources and neglects fundamental human needs."

The cleavage within the left, between the CGT and PCF on the one hand, and the PS and CFDT on the other, over the issue of *dégâts du progrès* (damage wrought by progress) would become particularly evident in battles in the realm of social environment. United action was achieved on such issues as the pollution produced by the Péchiney chemical plants, the red tide in the Gulf of Gascogne, and the myriad problems of Fos-sur-Mer (ranging from inadequate housing and services to pollution). Differences broke out, however, when it came to joining with the ecologists, as was the case in the Larzac struggle. The CGT held back on or actively opposed battles fought on the theme of "protecting ways of life," perceived as contradicting the working-class need for economic development. The slogan "Live, work, and decide in the countryside" (found on both sides) pointed to the need for industrial development. For the CGT, however, the choice in favor of industrial development was incompatible with any alliance with movements that opposed or disregarded this option. The priority given by the CGT to unqualified support for development (and, after 1974, to combating redeployment of national production abroad) stalemated the CGT-CFDT debate on the *dégâts du progrès* and social needs. Whether it was overreliance on the automobile or overconsumption of medical care, the CGT gave scant recognition to the problem and insisted on the union's duty to defend access to consumption and health care. Criticism of distortions in lifestyle or health care were seen as "blaming" workers and pushing them toward acceptance of austerity measures.

Beginning in 1973–4 the debate would center on the nuclear question. For the CGT, this issue invariably tied into the choice in favor of development. The CGT criticized the policy reversal in favor of "all nuclear" following the oil shock, as it had the previous policy of "all petroleum," for reasons of national independence and the need to exploit other energy sources (coal or new energy forms). The CGT did not perceive the ecological problem of the nuclear power industry as different from that of other dangerous industries. It called for a slowdown in the nuclear program because the accelerated pace did not permit resolving problems encountered during production. Nevertheless, it opposed the call for a moratorium, which by halting construction under way would entail delays without resolving the security questions that might arise during operations. It demanded instead a democratic debate through the media on energy policy, including nuclear, in all its dimensions: objectives and needs, means and resources, and the generic problems of each energy source.

The demand for a public debate stemmed from the difficulties of confronting anti-nuclear activists in the field. During the 1975—81 period the ecological movement made considerable gains through anti-nuclear struggles by mobilizing local populations affected by the siting of nuclear plants. The CGT charged the anti-nuclear activists with playing on people's fears in order to foster an unconditional rejection of nuclear energy. The CFDT, which supported these struggles, was portrayed as entertaining "utopian illusions" on the possibility of doing without nuclear energy and simultaneously developing the regions and answering their needs. This was seen as particularly true in the case of the Plogoff plant in Brittany. Convinced that development in Brittany necessitated nuclear energy, the CGT could only "speak out against obscurantist arguments ... which have deliberately spread confusion among the population [by associating] nuclear plants with the image of Hiroshima."

The Recent Period: Toward Incorporation of Environmental Issues

The rupture of left unity in 1977 over actualization of the 1972 program was bitterly received by the CGT, which had mobilized all its forces around "support for the Common Program." The rupture engendered a self-critique at the Fortieth Congress (1978) and debates on union praxis. A colloquium on the legacy of the May 1968 events, held just prior to the Fortieth Congress, appraised the period just ended and in particular analyzed the gaps that may have developed between new aspirations and problems and the way in which the CGT approached them (*Le Peuple,* July 1978).

The CGT recognized that actions relative to social environment issues had to be conducted in a different manner: intervening at levels closer to local concerns, giving latitude to participants to define their own needs and specific demands. In addition, social issues should be debated within the workplace, linking demands concerning life within the workplace to those arising from without. The UGICT (the CGT's cadre affiliate), at its Congress which followed shortly after the CGT National Congress, explicitly accepted the term "quality of life."

Within this framework a colloquium was held in 1979 on health (treating *nuisances* at length) and another in 1981 on housing. At these two colloquia considerable emphasis was placed on the need to overcome past passivity whereby actions were merely symbolically supported. The objective now is to mobilize wage-earners to act on the basis of their own demands and, in the case of pollution, to propose concrete solutions. We see, then, that the push in favor of democratization of trade union action was simultaneously a striving for greater efficacy in proposing solutions that would reconcile the exigencies of both development and environmental protection.

The question of nuclear energy would also be subject to debate. The CGT had previously issued several texts on energy policy and nuclear power. The text brought forth in 1979, "in the spirit of the Fortieth Con-

gress," was designed specifically to be the basis for debate on all problems relating to nuclear energy. This document, more complete and
coherent, dealt in particular with establishing the conditions necessary to
"resolve problems as they arise" and to effect "democratic control" in
order to guarantee the security of local populations and nuclear sector
workers.

The May 1981 political change, quickly hailed by the CGT as "porten-
ding something other than crisis management," would not alter the new
orientations set at the Fortieth Congress but rather accelerate the evolution toward a broader approach on environmental issues (now including
problems of energy conservation and resource waste). It was not so much
the CGT positions that changed but rather the context of the debate. The
rapprochement of the positions of the PS (once in power) with those of
the PCF and CGT on the subject of nuclear energy, the relaunching of
economic growth, and the use of scientific and technological advances to
solve environmental problems, created a more favorable context for
CGT actions on problems of the social environment, pollution and
energy/raw material waste at the level of production.

The discussion opened up in 1980 on waste and ways to reduce it
without affecting working-class living standards continued after May
1981. The analysis itself was not particularly original: the CGT, although
opposing attacks on "consumer society," was not ignorant of such
problems as overreliance on private transportation and the declining
quality of products. The novelty consisted in setting the trade union a
new task of controlling waste at its source. This was how the role of
consumer protection was defined for INDECOSA, the consumer
organization created in 1979 by the CGT. The CGT called for the left
government to grant works committees new powers to oversee products
with regard to quality, price, and waste.

Another new axis of CGT action came with the 1981 initiative of CGT
members and PCF deputies active in environmental associations to
create a national movement for environmental protection, open to all
those who desired "reconciling economic interests and protection of the
natural environment" (*Le Monde,* 3 December 1981). (This idea was
launched by Camille Vallin, a Communist senator from the Rhône,
longtime president of an association combating pollution and working to
defend the natural environment in the Rhône valley.) The aim was to
stimulate "the intervention of the forces of labor in environmental
struggles."

It would be difficult to predict at this point in time what concrete form
such new orientations may take. Many obstacles stand between confederal objectives and militant mobilization. Control of inflation is now
a more pressing concern to union militants than control of waste. The
current employment situation, too, is not conducive to raising questions
of production from a health or environmental standpoint. For example,
the CGT's recent actions to stem the decline in production of French
cigarettes shows that the CGT has still not reached the point of
elaborating industrial counterproposals that would reconcile employment

and public health imperatives. However, to the extent that the CGT links environmental protection and the fight against waste (at the level of the social environment and of production) to economic revival, we can expect that these new orientations will weigh heavily in future union action.

Conclusion

By the end of the 1970s ideological debates came to be closely tied to the practical choices to be made within the context of reviving growth. The differences between the CGT and CFDT are no longer so sharp. The two confederations are closer in certain respects in their analysis of the effects of the mode of economic development on the natural and social environment. Where they differ is on questions of lifestyle and social needs and, therefore, on the logic of this "new growth."

The debate is no longer over conceptions of "quality of life" but rather over the implications of union support for or criticism of current industrial policies. Thus the CFDT believes that supporting the revival of the automobile or nuclear power industry would entail the abandonment of its perspective for rupture with the logic of industrial development. In contrast, the CGT believes that attacks on the auto lobby would amount to accepting European and international economic restructuring. Similarly rejection of the nuclear option would entail abandoning regional development oriented around basic industries. The entire debate within the French labor movement currently revolves around the question: "is there a choice between different roads toward a better 'quality of life'?"

PART FOUR

Forms of Mobilization

12
Collective Action and Union Behavior

DENIS SEGRESTIN

The typical French scholarly approach to trade union issues in terms of congresses and official strategies obscures what is really occurring at the grassroots. Many rather superficial analyses depict unions as perpetual prey of crisis and faction. The fact is that ideological divisions affect rank-and-file practice only to a limited degree. While there are many different labor organizations, practice is far less varied. What is more, practice varies little over time and is not much affected by other sorts of change.

Despite economic crisis and political renewal, traditional union action and forms of mobilization remain remarkably constant except in relatively minor respects. There are, however, indications that real change may be in the offing; moreover, certain changes are vital to the survival of a labor movement that finds itself, in the 1980s, facing the prospect of irreversible decline.

The Enduring Tradition

It is reasonable to suppose that workers who join unions and participate in collective action share certain attitudes and patterns of behavior which have exerted a powerful influence on the evolution of the labor movement. The converse of this statement is more doubtful. Consider two contrasting views of the labor movement. According to one, each union fashions its own ideology, from which derive certain tactics, strategies, and practices. According to the other view, which I share, there is a dominant pattern of practices with deep roots in the history and sociology of the labor movement, and which shapes the relationship between unions.

The dominant pattern of practices itself is not shaped in any fundamental way by ideology, nor even by any clear view of the purposes of collective action. Revolutionary acts figure in the history of the French workers' movement, but this does not mean that joining a union requires the development of revolutionary consciousness. The fact is that the ideological context is not incompatible with the adoption by workers of attitudes shaped primarily by their identification with a group, their sense of themselves as being a collectivity. On this view labor practices spring initially from certain stable social representations supported by institutions (such as trade unions) that help to give visibility, cohesiveness, and internal stability to the community of which individual workers are members and in terms of which they define themselves.

The basis of all collective action is the consciousness that individuals have of being *actors* involved in social relations. Through a process of *social integration* individuals acquire a "capacity for mobilization." The effects of the integration process are more immediate than those of processes of alienation or exclusion.

The foregoing remarks do not imply that the "revolutionary context" counts for nothing. In fact it counts for a great deal, because the integration process in question extends beyond small groups to embrace the "class" as a whole. More precisely, the collective interests of workers are not defined by "occupational" or other restricted groups. Such groups serve rather as loci where workers become aware of "standing on the same side of the barricade" as their comrades, that is, on the side of the working class. As a result of this process of integration, working-class practices are not shaped by the aims of any specific group but rather integrated into a broad social movement that aims to comprehend the whole of society.

The workers' movement, then, carries with it a way of life, and with this way of life are associated certain political representations, at once simple and paradoxical. On the one hand, the vast majority of workers who participate in collective action have little to do with "politics." It is striking to observe that even among the members of the leading French unions, polls show that a majority of both male and female trade unionists rate their interest in politics as "minimal" or "nonexistent."

On the other hand, when the same people are asked whether they consider themselves "right-wing" or "left-wing," there is a strong polarization toward the left, a polarization that increases still further as one moves closer to the working class as such, that is, closer to the "core group" whose working-class status is most clearly marked in terms of collective identity and "communities of reference."

These results show that the attitudes in question are at once much less and much more than a way of situating oneself in the political spectrum. Much less, because the statement "I am on the left" is at bottom merely a way of identifying oneself socially rather than a positive act. But at the same time much more, because in the final analysis it is these attitudes that shape social relations, that impress themselves on the face of society: on the one side stand the workers, on the other the bosses and their allies. Behind these sentiments, moreover, is the feeling that workers have of belonging to a progressive group welded together by history and shaped by destiny.

Ultimately these attitudes and feelings form the foundation of the French-style "mass- and class-based labor movement," sometimes associated, not entirely wrongly, with the tactics and modes of action of the traditional metalworker. The traditional *metallo* was a skilled worker, inclined to remain in his job for a long period, who participated in collective activities, going out on strike or signing his union card with the attitude of a man who has chosen to signify his membership of a specific occupational community, to signal his acceptance of the norms governing that community, and to express his solidarity with those who speak for him and, beyond that, for the working class as a whole.

A man who joins a union for such reasons is acting individually but with the conviction that what he is doing reflects the attitudes of a majority, indeed all, the members of the group to which he belongs. He is moved by the most immediate forms of solidarity, but his feelings are less deep than those associated with true personal commitment. Psychologically the costs are small and so are the rewards. A man who takes out a union card does not appreciably alter his relationship to the community. The man who does not join or who fails to renew his membership does not jeopardize his status, so long as the continued existence of the community affords him the opportunity to demonstrate that he is still a part of it. These remarks explain why only a minority of the working class actually belongs to a union; they also suggest that, as far as attitudes are concerned, this fact is relatively insignificant.

The history of the labor movement is obviously an important factor in explaining why this pattern of behavior has become so common, to the point where nowadays it influences segments of the working population which at first sight would seem to be quite different, culturally speaking, from the typical worker in the metals trades. It is as though the objective consequence of the growth of the CGT has been to extend the legitimacy of this dominant behavioral pattern, thereby gradually imposing on workers generally a model of action rooted in skilled workers of the industrial trades.

It is worth adding that the CGT has been able to improve that model of action. Besides promoting this model in its ideology pronouncements, the CGT has literally embodied the model in its own *organization*. By way of illustration we need only mention the CGT's loyalty to traditional occupational structures, its caution whenever immediate forms of solidarity are threatened, its way of papering over differences between its words and its actions, between its active militants and the mass of the rank-and-file, or between the confederation as a whole and its constituent bodies—all of these are so many signs of the symbiotic relationship that has grown up between the CGT's organizational logic and the logic of collective action that prevails among the rank-and-file.

This presumed "harmony" has of course never been tranquil. It is a harmony frequently disrupted by stormy outbursts, of which there has been no shortage in the history of the French workers' movement. Broadly speaking, however, if it is true that the CGT has always played the leading role in that movement, it is also true that the behavioral model it embodies has been a constant influence on the behavior of individual workers.

To be sure, signs of instability in this model have been gathering now for some fifteen years. Union pluralism, which prior to 1960 was a pluralism in name only, in practice inhibited by respect for the notion of working-class unity, became a reality with the rise of the CFDT and its insistence on alternative sources of legitimation. On another level pluralism threatened to establish a link between ideological choices and union tactics and thus, except where concerted action was possible, to thwart the traditional dynamic of mobilization.

Along with this came a crisis in working-class identity, characterized by a new type of action and new attitudes toward unions. Technological progress, the gradual disintegration of key groups within the working class, the current economic crisis, rising unemployment, new personnel policies—all of these have been cited at various times as causes of a widespread crisis of confidence in traditional working-class action. Depending on the author, the crisis is taken either as the herald of a new age or as the death rattle of the old labor movement and its associated social dynamic.

Considerations of this kind figure in the approach taken by the CFDT, a union well placed to establish itself among new types of workers isolated from traditional working-class identities. Loud and clear was the CFDT denunciation of forms of action which it wished to see changed or abandoned altogether. The union practiced what it preached, adopting new tactics more concerned with achieving specific *objectives* than with simply expressing solidarity with the working-class community. Implicit in this change of tactics was the existence of militant activism at the grassroots, indispensable for bridging the gap between different echelons in the movement.

What were the results of the CFDT's new approach? Undoubtedly there was a renewal of militant trade union consciousness, which manifested itself in new issues and the development of new forms of action at the grassroots. A comprehensive assessment, however, must in all honesty acknowledge that the labor movement's overall logic of collective action was not really affected. The traditional class-based type of action retained its validity, and continued to transcend difference between unions.

Many illustrations of this assertion spring to mind. Consider the question of structural reorganization: one of the CFDT's goals was to attack corporatism, for which purpose it proposed redrawing the boundaries defining which union federations represent which occupational groups (for example, rather than a railway workers' federation the CFDT proposed a transport workers' federation; rather than separate unions for journalists, printers' trades, and cultural bureaucrats, it proposed a union for workers in the audiovisual and cultural fields). The purpose of moving away from structures based on differences between status was to facilitate the tailoring of union tactics to serve broad political objectives. But this confederal program, which clashed with the ways in which workers have traditionally acquired their social identities, ran into determined corporate opposition from the occupational groups affected.

Similarly, when the CFDT attempted to encourage action by non-contract and part-time employees and other "marginal" workers usually excluded from union membership, or again when it attempted to invoke the solidarity of the working class (as in 1981—2) over the problem of wage compensation when the Socialist government reduced the length of the workweek from 40 to 39 hours, it met with widespread lack of comprehension on the part of workers accustomed to enter into action in order to acquire benefits already accorded to more fortunate workers. The only alternative was to tolerate a *de facto* split between practice and preaching, coupling progressive rhetoric with actions that continued to be based on fairly stable and well-integrated occupational groups.

The Problem of Forging New Communities of Action

If, as we have seen, traditional class-based collective action remained fundamentally unchallenged, this does not mean that there was no change whatsoever in trade union practice. The labor movement in fact had to cope with a certain crisis, but a crisis limited, in my view, to one aspect of the broader question, namely, the problem of forging new communities as a basis for new practices.

One striking indication of this crisis may be seen in strikes, to which much attention has been devoted in the past fifteen years, by semiskilled workers, often immigrants, and strikes by women; as the great tide of the traditional trades-dominated labor movement began to recede in the early 1970s these new forms of labor action emerged like hidden reefs. Also typical of the phenomenon were strikes by office workers in banks and insurance companies: "semiskilled pencilpushers" in an environment traditionally dominated by a veritable ideology of careerism and professionalism, these white-collar employees suddenly became visible as the old system, in which they had no part, crumbled around them.

Actions staged by these kinds of worker were not so much precursors of new labor tactics as signs of crisis, in as much as they involved occupational groups that took it upon themselves to fight with whatever resources they had at their disposal, without reference to the rest of the workforce or to "working-class solidarity." Unions generally played a minimal role in these actions, or at any rate a role that depended on the ability of organizers to regain influence among the workers by virtue of their performance under the gun.

Yet these actions certainly involved the existence of new "communities of reference," which some observers immediately took to represent alternatives to traditional worker groups. The specific problems of immigrant workers are today seen as a legitimate issue of social conflict, one taken into account by the unions themselves. Feminism has had a similar influence on the action of women in the workforce, an influence so profound that some commentators have argued that, in the future, collective action must depend on new forms of collective identities and thus must inevitably involve the social system as a whole, rather than being confined to the workplace and workplace relations.

The truth is much more subtle: analysis shows that workers have not been quite so ready to shed their identity qua workers and that labor, even in its most alienating forms, continues to have a profound effect on the collective identity and collective actions of the workforce. "Women's struggles" in the workplace are just as much struggles of "women workers" as they are feminist struggles.

Broadly speaking, there has been no sweeping change in the logic of collective action. Manifestations of "feminist" and "immigrant" identities, whatever their significance for large-scale social change, may for our purposes here be regarded as signs not of renewal of the labor movement but rather of its decay, calling for a reconstitution of working-class solidarity and for a closer relationship between unions and the realities of working-class life today.

In my view similar caution is in order when it comes to explaining and interpreting the recent increase in the regional dimension of conflict. Local issues have again come to the fore in the wake of the job crisis. Commentators are prone to take it as proven that the resurgence of "regional struggles" involves either a return to the roots of anarcho-syndicalism (following the collapse of a labor movement dominated by the mythology of work and skill) or the creation of new links between union activity and political action at the local level.

In fact, however, true regional conflicts are much rarer than is commonly believed (union organizers who have attempted to breathe new life into regional and local union groups know how difficult it is to achieve mobilization at this level). What is more, it is difficult to see how such conflicts can bring about a general renewal of the labor movement. Regional labor conflict relies, even more than other forms of labor conflict, on social integration rather than a conscious ideological program. The success of actions based on the slogan of "living and working in the region" has had nothing to do with the efforts of unions to rethink the jobs issue or to combat mass layoffs by promoting alternative solutions to develop industrial activity at the local level. Success has come rather, because workers are attached to their roots and to their collective heritage.

More precise analysis of strikes has shown that workers look to the region as a true community of reference to the extent that the region sustains notions of "local interdependence" *vis-à-vis* an outside adversary. Regional communities can be mobilized—and not only around problems of employment—if the regional social system remains strongly integrated in the face of threats of fragmentation as, for example, when textile magnate Marcel Boussac ceases to dominate the Vosges and is supplanted by a board of directors in Paris, cut off from local issues and problems; or when local employers, the traditional powers in a semirural area, must contend with a multinational corporation headquartered in Italy; or, again, when a company like Alsthom in Belfort is shaken by economic troubles that threaten to undermine an industrial tradition on which the local social equilibrium had been based.

If mobilization does occur, it brings into play mechanisms which, broadly speaking, rely on age-old social representations, more pre-industrial than postindustrial in nature. For example, when middle management and supervisory personnel take part in such conflicts, they do so because they share a paternalistic conception of their role as one based on a hierarchical order of legitimacy and not because they understand the major trends that are shaping the evolution of the supervisory role in modern industry.

Similar remarks could be made about labor action centered on individual firms. It should not be forgotten that the recent economic crisis has hit hardest at the employees of firms faced with mass layoffs and threatened plant closings, threats that bind employees of these firms into a kind of community. Just as a few years ago unions seized on the theme of the "new working class" and linked concerns about technological change to demands for participation or self-management, so today the firm has emerged as the new organizational community of the moment. But the conditions in which this has occurred suggest that there has been no real break with the classical trade union model. Because of the deteriorating economic climate, industrial action aimed at specific firms has increasingly become synonymous with a certain "shrinkage" of class-based actions. "Company chauvinism" has replaced demands for maintaining employment and "shop corporatism" has impeded movements to achieve more broadly based solidarity.

What conclusion can we draw, then, other than that this is a time of crisis, of fragmentation in the labor movement, of stalemate on a broad front? The least we can do is to try to look at the problem in a broader perspective.

In the first place, the logic at work is not purely corporatist in nature. The size of a group does not strictly determine the kinds of issues it will approach through collective action. Traditional worker communities are capable of dealing with new problems once they get beyond the first stages of crisis in which those problems initially come to light.

Whatever the size of the community, be it centered on a particular firm or a region, its members must cope with certain fundamental problems. One such problem is whether, in a context of systematic delocalization of capitalist management, a locally based social movement will be able to change the rules of the game. Since regionalization and decentralization are the order of the day, now that the Socialist government is in power, this is a major issue, even if such local initiatives are based on traditional or outdated views of society. This question is related to the question of structural reorganization of the labor movement: there is no current institutional structure in France for dealing with regional issues, no local regulatory bodies with real power to deal with management.

Another fundamental question is whether, at a time when traditional lines of distinction between trades are breaking down, the labor movement can seek to restore its lost unity by concentrating on organizing particular firms. It would be a significant development if such a shift (or a related shift to plant-based organizing) were to occur at a time when there is not only significant risk of layoff and unemployment but also a move afoot by employers to "individualize" the workforce and break down the traditional distinctions between one kind of worker and another.

Here it is worth noting that the labor movement and the left government elected in 1981 share certain common concerns: the government program includes a plan to "reconstitute labor unity" and preliminary steps have been taken to limit the use of temporary or limited-contract labor.

If this is seen in conjunction with the decision to nationalize some of France's leading industrial firms, the question arises whether what is taking place is not some kind of broad movement organized around the firm (notwithstanding the admittedly defensive character of "company chauvinism" in the 1970s). It would seem that the workers' movement is reappropriating a community—the community of company employees—that has over the years been abandoned by business. Just as the traditional trades came to dominate the labor movement at a time when they ceased to be the basis of the logic of production, and just as regions have begun to mobilize as employers abandon them, so too may the industrial firm become a key element in the social fabric, a stimulus to reunification and collective action and not merely the basic cell of the industrial system. The "workers' rights" promulgated by the government should promote a new idea of "industrial citizenship" and strengthen the hand of the unions within the firm.

This new movement should be seen as aimed at developing a "labor community" within the firm rather than a labor movement organized around individual firms. The latter would require a combined social and economic strategy as well as a political and social context in which labor tactics could be seen as aiming at both the reaffirmation of class solidarities and at influencing management decisions, as has occurred in certain phases of the Italian labor movement. Such a context is lacking at present: organized labor in France remains rigid and divided, and current economic prospects do not promise to involve the rank-and-file in decisions at the company level.

In the final analysis the foregoing remarks reinforce the earlier assumption concerning the development of labor community within the firm. For with "direct expression" of grievances and shopfloor councils, it is at the company or plant level that the united working class must find representation of its interests as opposed to the interests of management.

Collective Action and Political Change

One characteristic of the dominant class-based action is an assumption that the working class is necessarily opposed to the government. Mobilization is a matter of maintaining class identity rather than attaining specific objectives and as such might be called "intrinsically irresponsible" if the term were a neutral way of describing a social dynamic and not a political and moral condemnation. Traditionally the unions did not consider economic constraints in formulating their demands: their function was that of a socially legitimated countervailing power to the economically legitimated power of the employer.

But the French labor movement underwent two successive trials, the effects of which were cumulative and raised fundamental questions about the internal logic of the labor movement. The first of these was the economic crisis, which raised the possibility of a contradiction between traditional union tactics and the need for responsibility and realism. The second was the election of a left-wing government in 1981 with widespread support from union members and other workers. Did these two "trials" shake forms of action? Never really challenged by "militant activism" in the past, the traditional tactics no longer seem suited to the current economic and political situation. Will there be reform?

It is worth noting that the problems raised by the economic crisis that began in 1973–4 were similar in nature to the problems raised by the recent change of government. Because of the crisis union militants became more willing to take economic realities into account in formulating union policy and demands. Unions came to assume that the employment crisis was real and that the future of certain firms and even entire industries was threatened, necessitating steps toward industrial reconversion and job retraining, even if they continued to evince a certain hostility to these policy shifts.

The CFDT certainly went further in this direction than other unions, initially in limited ways (the case of Lip having given the signal that change was necessary) and later with a major shift in policy indicated by the term *recentrage*. In various ways, however, the CGT underwent similar changes, abandoning when necessary its traditional kinds of demand. In 1977–8 the "counterproposals policy" served as a model of an alternative union strategy that could be adopted in conjunction with a left-wing government program (see Huiban in this volume).

The question is to what extent action at the rank-and-file level followed these changes at the confederation level. The least that can be said is that changes at the grassroots were far less clear-cut than changes at the top. Even the most favorably disposed commentators on trade union activities acknowledge that workers did not greet the "industrial plans" with wholehearted enthusiasm. In 1978–9, for example, when the unions tried to organize a counteroffensive against the dismantling of the steel industry, they found themselves face to face with a workers' movement unwilling to bother itself about "counterproposals." Angry workers did not pause to examine the state of the steel industry, preferring instead to demonstrate at steel mills and blast furnaces (Noiriel, 1980). The effect of the "plans" was less to mobilize than to demobilize.

More broadly, the shift by unions to more "responsible" strategies seems to have produced greater divergence between rank-and-file movements and top-level analyses of conflict. The unions have learned to negotiate dispassionately on the basis of an assessment of the respective interests of both labor and management, independent of what is happening with the rank-and-file. By contrast, worker mobilization has in many cases been associated with hopeless causes, its only purpose apparently being to "show the colors" of the working class.

These developments have lent credence to the idea that mobilization is sometimes pointless and that victory can sometimes be won without it, whereas as recently as a decade ago the "balance of power" between unions and management was seen as the decisive factor in every advance of the French labor movement. Another consequence has been a perverse but (given the bitter division within the French labor movement) predictable interpretation: namely, that the split between, on the one hand, strategies of "coping with the issues" and, on the other hand, strategies of "support for the rank-and-file" in some sense reflects the division of labor between the CFDT and the CGT. The CGT opted for "mobilization at any price," apparently abandoning when necessary any hope of seriously influencing either issues or outcomes. The CFDT, on the other hand, was tempted to experiment with new forms of negotiation in order to avert mass layoffs or to determine how a reduction of work time should be organized. The effect of this strategy was to sidestep the issue of mobilization, which was seen in some cases as the one sure way not to succeed. In January 1981 a CFDT publication gave this significant estimate of the situation: "The CGT would apparently rather see a plant closed and occupied by a few militants (often not employed there) proudly proclaiming 'No layoffs!' rather than a plant reopened with a good percentage of its jobs saved." It may well be that this perverse interpretation is itself responsible for the fact that behavior has not changed much.

Since the May 1981 presidential elections and the installation of a left-wing government, not much has changed. Basically the unions still see themselves as operating independently, in keeping with their traditions. This is even more true given the different relationships between the leading labor organizations and the government. The CFDT seemed, in the beginning at any rate, to be more directly linked to the Socialists, whereas the CGT, which in spite of Communist participation in the government found itself with a free hand, continued to see itself as vigilant watchdog, a "powerful combat force ready to press workers' demands."

Nothing, therefore, threatened to undermine the dominant pattern of union practices, whereas the changes envisioned as late as 1977 under the *Programme Commun* would have necessitated major tactical changes. Had the left stuck to the *Programme Commun*, the CGT would either have had to repudiate its support for the program and insist on its independence as a union or else risk becoming a sort of "official union"; this would presumably have meant that the time had come for adopting radically new tactics designed to "accompany social change" and mobilize support for the policies of the government.

In 1981–2 such a "new spirit of responsibility" does exist in certain sectors, especially where the Communists have direct ministerial responsibility, as in transportation. But even there nothing like a general switch to new kinds of practice has occurred. The situation is more one of watchful waiting and preservation of the status quo. The CFDT was the first to have understood this clearly and to have moved away from its identification with the new government in order not to lose contact with its rank-and-file.

Change has been peripheral at best, owing in part to the high expectations of the new government, in part to the fact that for too long there has been a divorce between the state and the social forces. It is true that some groups of workers, in certain types of firms, have expected or demanded that they be given new responsibilities: middle-management personnel, civil servants, and employees of nationalized industries may be more disposed than other workers to invest collectively in new modes of management and new types of union activity. Doubtless there is some change in the fact that unions can now pursue their traditional aims by looking to an alliance with the government against management. Certain of the CGT's activities in late 1981 openly took this course.

Still the most important point is that the 1980s have begun without any real revolution in the attitude of the rank-and-file toward the labor movement and its action and there are good reasons to think that this is a source of both strength and weakness for the labor movement.

In the absence of any real impetus toward social change, workers continue to tread well-beaten paths or to resign themselves to the status quo. The real issue for the future, and the indispensable prerequisite for any real change in union practices, is that of creating conditions in which workers can once again become *actors* in the full sense of the word. Perhaps this will become possible when the economy turns itself around once again and the game of politics, so prominent a part of the French scene for so many years, recedes into the background.

13

The Strike in France

PIERRE DUBOIS

The left's accession to power in May 1981 did not give rise to any mass social movement, as had occurred in 1936 and the immediate postwar years. Strike activity in the latter half of 1981 and early 1982 remained at the low ebb of the past several years. The conclusion of this chapter suggests several possible explanations for this relative decline of strike activity. In our opinion the economic crisis should not be regarded as the decisive factor; rather the ongoing division of the two major trade unions is of paramount importance. In the new political conjuncture, the CGT and CFDT, whatever their past differences, are both trapped between two reefs; while they want to avoid hindering, through strikes, a government favorable to wage-earners, they also wish to promote economic and social change by means of mass mobilization.

This chapter presents a limited survey of the numerous studies on strikes and outlines the main thrust of these analyses. A contrast will be made between the statistical approach, relying on national data sources, and the monographic approach. Statistical analysis, notwithstanding the limitations imposed by source reliability, does show the growing divergence between economic fluctuations and patterns of strike activity. Furthermore, statistical analysis points to the growing influence of the sociopolitical context. Where this method is less reliable is in pinpointing the locale of strike outbreaks. Here the monograph excels: it suggests that strike propensity is not really linked to any particular professional categories but rather related to the homogeneity of the laborforce at the individual workplace, that strike activity is preceded by unionization, and that strikes break out at a particular point within a cycle of extremely diverse forms of struggle. The monograph also shows how the demand strategies, negotiations, and forms of action adopted by the various actors are articulated.

The Importance of Strikes

The industrialized countries have kept statistical records of strike activity for over a century. Exhaustive data for France have existed since the beginning of the Third Republic, so specialists are well situated to measure the quantitative importance of strikes and the evolution of strike activity.

The importance of strikes in France can be determined from three indicators: the annual number of conflicts; the number of workers involved; and the number of days lost due to strikes. The average annual number of conflicts for the past decade (1970–80) is approximately 3,500, with a minimum of 3,104 in 1979 and a maximum of 4,350 in 1971. An average of 3,500 means that less than 10 percent of industrial and commercial establishments are affected by strikes each year (taking into account that several conflicts may break out in the same factory).

The number of strike participants in this ten-year period has varied from 501,000 in 1980 to 3,814,000 in 1976. Although labor inspectors are instructed to record the number of strikers at the height of the conflict, it is difficult to assess the reliability of this indicator. For example, it is often difficult to determine the number of real strikers in certain conflicts; to illustrate, workers laid-off temporarily can be included when counting all those who have stopped working. *At any rate, excluding exceptional periods (strike waves), strike participants never exceed 20 percent of all wage-earners.*

The number of man-days lost to strikes during this ten-year period has oscillated between 1,700,000 in 1980 and 5,000,000 in 1976. This figure is evidently linked to the number of strike participants and the duration of the conflicts. The margin of error is thus certainly higher than that for the other two indicators, since the time between the strike outbreak and the resumption of work can be spaced out. The volume of days on strike is clearly less than 1 percent of the annual number of days worked.

The first question that needs to be asked is how the importance of strikes has evolved over the long run. Annual variations in the three indicators chosen are significant enough to render any judgment as to a long-term tendency problematic. The tendency is clear as regards the number of conflicts: there has been a steady growth over the past century with an *historic maximum* of 4,350 conflicts reached in 1971 (excluding the years 1936 and 1968). The tendency is less clear with respect to the number of strike participants: while they have been much more numerous since 1945, no clear pattern can be discerned. As regards the number of man-days lost there has been a decline relative to the interwar period, but again no clear pattern shows up in the postwar period. In other words, the thesis prevalent in the 1960s of a withering away of conflict and a decline in strikes has no empirical basis. Compared to thirty years ago, there are more frequent strikes and a greater number of participants yet a fewer number of days lost (that is, strikes are shorter). Moreover, this does not take strike waves into account. Overall there has been a noticeable drop in the number of strike participants since 1978 in relation to the preceding period: the average for the years 1970–7 was 2,346,000 and for 1978–80 only 724,000. This is also true for the number of days lost: the average for 1970–7 was 3,715,000 (or 214 days for every 1,000 wage-earners) and for 1978–80 only 2,503,000 (or 138 days for every 1,000 wage-earners).

The major annual variations led some specialists in the field to put forward the hypothesis of a *strike cycle* (Goetz-Girey, 1965) or to focus their research on *strike waves.* Shorter and Tilly (1973) suggest that a strike wave exists when the number of strikes and strike participants for any given year exceeds by 50 percent the average for the preceding five years. The question remains as to how these variations in the importance of strikes and long-term tendencies are to be interpreted. Most studies have examined annual variations in strike activity in terms of the economic conjuncture and long-term trends in strike activity in terms of the sociopolitical context. Certain interpretations, however, have attempted to combine analysis of both the economic and sociopolitical contexts.

The General Context of the Strike

Are strike movements, in the short and long run, sensitive to the evolution of the economic context and/or the sociopolitical context? With respect to the former, it can be asked both whether the economic conjuncture has an impact on strike activity and correspondingly whether strike activity has repercussions for the economic conjuncture.

Economic Fluctuations and Strike Fluctuations

Is it theoretically and statistically legitimate to correlate conjunctural economic indicators and strike activity indicators? An objection of a theoretical nature is that this type of analysis presupposes a line of causality, that is, strikers are somehow mechanistically influenced by the economic conjuncture.

If we accept the hypothesis that it is *consciousness of the conjuncture*, to employ Michelle Perrot's terminology (1973), which influences strike activity, then an objection of a statistical nature must be posed. All such analyses proceed from establishing correlations, usually of an annual nature, between certain economic parameters and strike indicators, with each being considered at the same point in time. This procedure is not valid, however, if the argument is that workers anticipate or react to conjunctural movements, which implies a time lag. In other words, the correct method would be to correlate monthly statistics with some temporal separation; this type of work has not been conducted to our knowledge. Shorter and Tilly set aside this problem, although they acknowledge it exists. They claim, for example, that no correlation can be found between the number unemployed and either the annual number of strikes or strikers for any period examined. They admit that this does not take into account any relationship of a time-lag nature, although they acknowledge that the impact of underemployment is greater after a year's time than in the short run.

For the period up to 1890, Perrot (1974) found that economic expansion and recovery are favorable terrain for strikes; workers tend to call strikes when their purchasing power is relatively good. For the 1890–1914 period, Andreani (1968) observed that the number of strikes increases in periods of growth and decreases in periods of contraction. For the 1914–62 period, Goetz-Girey (1965) noted that "conjunctural factors have had less importance since World War II than in the interwar period"; for Goetz-Girey, "it is not inflation but an acceleration of the rhythm of economic expansion that is favorable to the growth of social conflicts" (p. 137). For the 1950–71 period, Scardigli (1974) confirmed that no correlation exists between inflation and strikes.

The interwar and postwar periods differ with respect to the link between economic production and strike activity. In fact, two contradictory tendencies show up in different years. On the one hand, a positive correlation sometimes appears between production and strike activity, that is, if production sharply increases, then strikes become more numerous (as workers seek to increase their share of the pie and perceive themselves in a favorable position for successful action). On the other hand, a negative correlation can also show up, that is, if production increases, then strikes diminish (as less strikes erupt because of layoffs and as employers are more willing to cede to wage-earner demands). In other words, the results obtained by Scardigli strongly indicate that *the influence of the conjuncture is not strictly determinant* but rather always mediated by the decisions of the actors involved.

Several scholars have attempted to analyze the conjunctural factors that produce strike waves. Soskice (1978) proceeds in this fashion in attempting to interpret the resurgence of strike movements in the majority of European countries that occurred in the late 1960s. According to Soskice, attention should be directed to the events of the early 1960s. Inflation, balance-of-payments problems, and a fall in the rate of profit led governments to institute deflationary policies (such as the stabilization plan in France) and wage–price controls (in France an incomes policy conference and the Toutée-Grégoire procedures for setting public sector wage guidelines). Correspondingly the employer response was to carry out rationalization at the plant and company level. What followed was an increase in the unemployment rate, moderation in the growth of real wages, erosion of wage differentials, and an increased workload. In a certain sense the policies proved successful: the rate of profit rose, balance-of-payments problems were eased, and inflation slowed. Economic recovery was partially achieved, so that the unemployment rate began to decline (by early 1968 in France).

The unions in the various countries, however, had been locked into medium-term contracts (two to three years' duration), and consequently wages lagged when the economic situation began to improve. The explosion of the late 1960s stemmed from the disparity between the slow rise in wages and the amelioration of the economic climate generally. Such a situation is evidently not unique to this period. What Soskice ignores is the influence of phenomena of a strictly sociopolitical nature (specifically, in the French case, the left's electoral gains in 1965 and 1967 as well as the CGT–CFDT accord on united action signed in early 1966).

In sum, it is clear that *the economic conjuncture influences strike activity in conflicting ways*. Analyses show that the economy has less influence now than in the past and can no longer be considered the decisive factor; sociopolitical factors have assumed greater importance. Before analyzing the impact of such factors on the frequency of strikes, we will pose a different question: the impact of strike activity on the economic conjuncture. In particular, to what extent do strikes bring about a drop-off in production?

Every major strike (whether of long duration or in a key industrial sector) inevitably gives rise to assertions of the type: "the pursuit of the strike amounts to sabotage of the economy." That strikers seek to disrupt production by means of a work stoppage is self-evident; but is this really what happens? The answer given to this question is often biased. Those who see sabotage everywhere are proponents of limitations of the right to strike, while the defenders of the labor movement's traditional arm tend to minimize the strike's disruptive economic impact.

Where does the truth lie? Because of their low volume, strikes do not appreciably disrupt production at the national or even branch level. In the worst case strikes result in production delays, that is, a drop-off followed by a catching-up. France in 1968 serves as the best example of this phenomenon. Compared to April 1968 figures, production fell 31 percent in May and 21 percent in June 1968. An initial catching-up was registered in July with a veritable surge coming in the last trimester. As a result, notwithstanding the most important strikes ever witnessed in France, average industrial production in 1968 was 4·5 percent higher than in 1967. In contrast, at the level of the firm, strikes can often engender an irreparable drop in production or at least a serious slowdown in expansion.

Nevertheless, despite the weak economic impact of strikes, the hypothesis can be advanced that strikes today are more disruptive than in the past. This is due, on the one hand, to the growing integration of the production process and, on the other hand, to the forms of action adopted by strikers. Strikers now more often select disruptive methods. Moreover, they are aware of the stratagems through which production can be recouped after the resumption of work (overtime, speedups, and so on) and have, in some cases, resisted such methods.

The Sociopolitical Context and Strike Movements

No one would deny that strikes are linked in some way to the sociopolitical context; however, many contradictory hypotheses have been put forward as to the exact nature of that linkage. A distinction first needs to be made between the linkage of strikes to specific sociopolitical events and linkage to the general sociopolitical structure. The latter formulation focusses on the role of trade unionism within the nation or, put another way, the nature of the country's industrial relations system.

As regards such sociopolitical factors as elections, changes in government or ruling coalition, the nature of the parties in power, and international events, research based on monthly strike statistics can be carried out without major difficulty. None the less, certain stereotypic views are still commonly held in this domain. The most prominent example is the erroneous impression that strike activity in France drops off in pre-electoral periods. Even if unions attempt to restrain strikes in such periods—which is not always the case—strike activity does not necessarily diminish. Even during wartime, while strike activity does decrease, it does not disappear altogether.

With respect to the relationship between strike intensity and the political orientation of the parties in power, every possible combination has occurred in France during this century: strikes in 1920 broke out after a clear victory for the right (which resulted in the so-called "blue horizon" chamber); those in 1936 after the victory of the Popular Front; those in 1947–8 after the departure of the Communists from the government; and those in 1968 without any change in the ruling coalition. In recent years, strike activity has tended to increase as the left was on the upswing and when the two major union confederations (CGT and CFDT), united by an accord on joint action in labor disputes, gave support to the Union of the Left strategy. The intensity of strikes was thus relatively greater from 1967 to mid-1968 and again from late 1970 to mid-1977.

The hypothesis that the overall sociopolitical structure influences strike movements was put forth years ago in nearly identical fashion by Knowles (1952) and by Ross and Hartman (1960). According to this argument, as trade unionism becomes accepted, it gradually acquires political support, usually from left parties. As the union begins to adopt reformist objectives, strike movements decrease in average duration and diminish in intensity. This, then, is the thesis of the increasing institutionalization of conflict (trade union objectives are negotiated through recourse to regulatory or grievance procedures) or even the withering away of conflicts. A contrast was drawn between the low propensity to strike in northern Europe and the continued high conflict level in southern Europe, where the trade union movement is divided and contested by employer groups because of labor's political objective of a more or less revolutionary nature.

This thesis should have been swept away by the wave of struggles in the late 1960s, especially as strikes broke out even where conflict had been most institutionalized. However, the thesis was not discarded but rather altered. The reformulated argument held that the strikes of the late 1960s had taken place as a result of important flaws in the system of peaceful conflict resolution, especially at the level of the individual firm. At the firm level, especially in France before 1968, trade unions had not been accorded legal status and negotiation remained underdeveloped.

In order to ward off any recurrence of such strike movements public authorities gambled in the early 1970s on recognizing plant-level union organs and promoting negotiations within the firms. The hope was that such changes would bring about a decline in open conflict. The spread of union representation was indeed facilitated, but no progress took place in two critical areas: (1) the right of workers to hold union meetings at the workplace during working hours was not granted; and (2) the legal protection accorded unions proved of limited utility for reinstating union representatives subject to discriminatory layoffs. Progress in the realm of bargaining structures did not go far enough either. Firm-level agreements were facilitated and works committees given new rights to information and consultation, yet such legal rights by no means endowed workers with codecisional or veto power.

How can we explain the fact that during the first half of the 1970s conflict remained at past levels (in terms of the number of strike participants and days lost) and even increased (in terms of the number of disputes)? Were the changes simply insufficient or rather was their ultimate goal—the pacification of conflict—fundamentally challenged? The radicalization of union ideologies and methods (to be examined below) lends support to the latter answer. Hence it can be said that whatever hopes were placed in trade unions as agents of conflict institutionalization in France were disappointed. As a consequence, a different, albeit more traditional, approach to dampening industrial conflict was taken in the latter half of the 1970s: anti-union repression.

The Locus of Strike Outbreaks

The strike is a phenomenon of limited economic significance; its sociopolitical causes and consequences are of much greater import. We thus agree with the hypothesis of Shorter and Tilly (1973, p. 859) that "strike movements represent the spearhead of political action by workers in France, and, consequently, their periodicity is regulated by national political crises rather than by fluctuations in economic activity." At any given point in time, however, the general economic and sociopolitical context is the same for all firms. How can we explain, then, why strikes break out in some places and not others?

Any attempt to utilize national strike statistics in tackling this problem is complicated by gaps in official records. While the size, activity, and site of the firms hit by strikes can be determined from these records, no information is provided on the firm's viability, composition of the workforce, level of unionization, or history of past conflict. Case-study research indicated that such parameters are essential to our understanding of this problem. Three questions must be answered: (1) do strikes break out more often in larger plants?; (2) are certain occupational groups more prone to strike than others?; and (3) are strikes more likely in unionized or nonunionized plants?

The Higher Propensity to Strike in Large-Scale Plants
A higher strike propensity in large-scale plants shows up in all studies which rely on national data sources (Shorter and Tilly, 1973, 1974; Scardigli, 1974). The research carried out by Dassa (1978) is of particular interest because data is provided on strike propensity among firms of a similar size; thus in 1976 strikes affected $0 \cdot 5$ percent of firms with 10–49 employees, $4 \cdot 5$ percent of firms with 50–199 employees, $15 \cdot 4$ percent of

firms with 200–999 employees, 29·0 percent of firms with 1,000–5,000 employees, and 22·0 percent of firms with over 5,000 employees.

What is the significance of this trend? Is it the concentration of workers that predisposes them to strike once every three to five years? Other possibilities include a greater exploitation of workers in large-scale factories and/or more effective union penetration.

The Propensity to Strike among Various Occupational Groups

Information on which occupational groups strike is not systematically recorded in official records. Specialists often utilize the variable of industrial sector, although all firms within a given sector do not have the same labor mix with regard to sex, age, skill levels, and seniority, and there is no reason why strikes should break out in those plants most representative of the sector as a whole. Moreover, as with firm size, the type of industry does not tell us very much unless other factors are considered.

The best-known study relating the type of industry to the propensity to strike is that of Kerr and Siegel (1952). The authors noted a high strike propensity among miners and dockworkers in eleven countries. They suggest that this is a function of the social niche occupied by such workers; grouped together in isolated and cohesive communities, they readily engaged in social revolt. Kerr and Siegel also point to the nature of the labor performed by these workers. This theory was later rejected by all specialists in the field. Shorter and Tilly, for example, found that strikes occur more frequently in polyindustrial than monoindustrial geographic areas. Moreover, the weight of different industrial sectors in strike activity seems to vary over time.

A reference to the industrial sector does have the merit, however, of undermining hypotheses hastily constructed around certain spectacular struggles. In the early 1970s Serge Mallet (1975, pp. 87–106) among others stressed the development of strikes by women, semiskilled workers, and immigrants. These groups were said to form a *"new* new working class" which struggled for workers' control.[1] This theory does not stand up to the facts. Desrosières (1972), for example, found that "conflicts appear more frequently in those sectors with a high capital intensity and high skill levels; inversely, [strikes] are less frequent where workers are less skilled and the percentage of women is high."

Rather than analyzing strike propensity among different occupational groupings in search of those most prone to strike (especially as statistical studies yield contradictory results), one might alternatively examine the characteristics of the workgroup. In our study (Dubois *et al.*, 1976) of worker reactions in mass-production industries we hypothesized that individuals were not predisposed to protest or strike depending on whether they belonged to any given occupational category but rather on whether they belonged to a homogeneous workgroup. The findings largely confirmed our hypothesis. Protest is stronger among homogeneous workgroups than among heterogeneous ones (where semiskilled and skilled laborers, men and women, young and old, veterans and newcomers, French and immigrants, and the stably and precariously employed work side by side). Since current hiring practices foster such differentiation within the workgroup, an additional obstacle inhibits the emergence of protest action.

Danièle Kergoat (1978) adopts a relatively similar perspective. She examined a number of firms over a time span sufficiently long to capture the phases of ebb and flow in combativity, thereby reducing the possibility of hasty generalizations made on the basis of a particular conjuncture. Kergoat attempts to understand the genesis of working-class practice in terms of the relation between the flux of combativity and the internal dynamic of the workgroup. Her analysis stresses the process of differentiation occurring within the working class. The change in the nature of the demands put forth is not reflective of any evolution in the majoritarian or hegemonic class fraction but rather stems from the ongoing tension between and within different groups.

Her rejection of any global approach to this problem should not be read as acceptance of the theory of a working class which is fragmented, divided, or torn by corporatist temptations, where each group supposedly has its own specific demands and forms of action. For Kergoat, this view represents a false alternative; homogeneity—heterogeneity and decomposition—recomposition are but different dynamics of a single reality. Analysis of the internal contradictions of the working class has little meaning unless combined with an analysis of class restructuring. The working class is made up of groups which not only oppose and confront one another but also ally and manifest solidarity during the gradual process of restructuring by means of unifying demands, common reference to a class culture, or ties outside production (the family or residence). One thus sees the temporal dimension, overlooked by statistical studies.

The Higher Propensity to Strike in Unionized Firms

That strike propensity is higher in large plants and in certain industrial sectors does not explain why, even in such cases, strikes break out only in a minority of firms in any given year. Is there another necessary condition, namely, trade union presence? Unions are still not present in all French firms; today 75 percent of firms with over fifty employees have a works committee, yet only 50 percent of the firms falling under the labor code have a union local. The role of unions must be understood if we are to choose between competing theses on the outbreak of strikes: one which emphasizes the spontaneity of conflict and another which links recourse to the strike weapon with a strong union presence.

Official strike records often do not contain data on union presence or strength at the firm; scholars must therefore rely on more indirect indicators. Shorter and Tilly, proceeding in this fashion, put forth the hypothesis that "strike movements develop out of a solid organizational base and collective tradition of the working class; they stem much less than commonly believed from the impulsive action of the unorganized and the unaffiliated" (1973, p. 859). Their method is subject to several criticisms; for example, they correlate strikes with the more unionized industrial sectors, regions, and trades but one cannot be certain that strikes break out only in those firms where the union is present. Michelle Perrot (1974) points out that, historically, strike outbreaks preceded unionization in French firms.

In a study of the 1968 strikes (Dubois *et al.*, 1971), based on a sample of 182 firms in the Nord region, workers were found to go out on strike themselves in 15 percent of the cases, strikes were unleashed after a call by union activists in 73 percent of the cases, and the pattern was ambiguous in the remaining cases. The spontaneous strike outbursts (constituting a small minority of cases) occurred in nonunionized establishments and always in the wake of strikes in other firms. Identical results were obtained in two subsequent studies—on strikes in 1971 (Durand and Dubois, 1975) and on labor relations in newly established plants (Dubois *et al.*, 1975). Thus, nowadays, the strike always follows union penetration and not the inverse.

This finding does not imply of course that the longevity of union presence, the degree of unionization, or the nature of the hegemonic union at the particular firm does not influence the shape of the conflict. We have shown that, contrary to the hopes of "conflict institutionalization" theorists, trade union presence has become a necessary condition for the emergence of open conflict. Could they be correct, however, in arguing that unions exert moderation in the course of the conflict? We will attempt to answer this question by examining the forms of action adopted in strikes.

Forms of Action during Strikes

The institutionalization of conflict thesis predicts a reduction in strike activity essentially due to a shortening of strike duration, in turn linked to an increase in union penetration. In this view organized workers no longer throw all their forces into relentless struggles, as in the past, but rather temper their efforts so as to harass their opponents. During this century, then, the situation has evolved from one characterized by few strikes with a limited following yet long duration to one characterized by numerous strikes with a large following yet very brief duration.

In the past several years, however, it appears that the situation is reversing course, that is, by a decrease in average strike volume and an increase in strike duration. Furthermore, there has recently been increased militance in the forms of action adopted. Have these two tendencies occurred against union wishes or with union encouragement? In other words, while a union presence seems necessary for a strike to break out, what role do unions play once the strike is unleashed? This issue will be studied below.

What is the relative weight of extended strikes relative to strikes as a whole and how has this evolved over time? In order to determine the average length of strikes per striker we divided the number of man-days lost by the number of strike participants. We can venture several conclusions based on this relationship: the average duration of strikes, estimated at 16·2 days for the 1919–35 period (Goetz-Girey, 1965), gradually diminished until World War II; since 1952 average duration has oscillated between 1·1 and 5·5 days. A relative stabilization in average strike duration at around 1·5 days took place from 1965 to 1972, and since that time there has been a slight rise (between 2–3 days if all conflicts are counted, more than 5 days if generalized stoppages are excluded).

Average duration, however, does not adequately convey the significance of long strikes. We must instead turn to the results of studies which systematically sampled strike records for individual years. Erbès-Seguin and Casassus (1977) found that strikes of over 7 days' duration represented 12·4 percent of the total number of strikes in 1966–7, 15·9 percent in 1972, and 22·3 percent in 1974–5. Dassa (1978) found that 34 percent of all localized conflicts in 1976 exceeded 6 days.

Strong-arm and illegal actions (occupations, picketing, sequestration) have significantly increased since 1968. Michelle Durand (1977), comparing strikes in 1966 and 1971, noted more frequent disruptive actions in 1971 (also suggested by our research on a more limited number of strikes, see Durand and Dubois, 1975): an increase in the number of repeated stoppages per month and workplace occupations (5 percent in 1971). Sami Dassa (1978) found that occupations took place in 7·7 percent of the cases in 1976.

As stated previously, official dispute records often do not contain information on union representation at firms hit by strikes. Case studies thus must be used to establish the relationship between unionization and forms of protest action. In our study of the 1971 strikes (Durand and Dubois, 1975) we found that illegal action was supported in most cases by at least one of the union organizations represented at the workplace; only in one case out of seven was union sanction altogether refused. Union attitudes toward such actions were highly disparate, varying from one site to another: at some locals union activists rejected strongarm actions, while at others they either supported such tactics or acquiesced. Union support for such actions in 1971 was generally more forthcoming where the CFDT was the sole or hegemonic union and where union locals had only been recently established at the workplace in question. In sum, the toughest forms of protest appear in a wide variety of firms and not necessarily where the union is absent. Thus the thesis positing a general relation between unionization and moderation of conflict does not have universal scope and can in fact be confirmed only in a minority of cases. Only monographs can evoke the extremely complex role that organization plays in the management of conflict (Batstone, 1978). A strong union is one that retains a capacity for potential strike action (which may or may not be exercised), relying on a tight network of activists who can mobilize for the strike.

In a study of industrial relations in newly established factories (Dubois *et al.*, 1975) and a subsequent study of worker reactions in mass-production industries (Dubois *et al.*, 1976) we posited the existence of a cycle of struggles. This cycle of struggles includes such diverse forms of action as strikes, sabotage, absenteeism, withdrawal, self-identification with the firm, and the establishment of representative structures. Almost all firms pass through this cycle. In each phase of the cycle several forms of action occur simultaneously with one form clearly dominating.

In phase 1 individual reactions are prevalent: attitudes of withdrawal and competition for promotion; protest remains latent (as union representation for channeling claims and grievances is not yet in place and any direct action exposes the perpetrator to sanctions). Phase 2 of the cycle follows the establishment of representative structures. This in effect institutionalizes self-identification: the works committee serves to put forward employee suggestions rather than claims or grievances, thus performing an integrating function. Attitudes of withdrawal are less pronounced in this phase, and protest behavior remains individualized. Challenges by workers to the representative structure functioning exclusively in the firm's interest may be the forerunner to phase 3 of working-class reaction: the explosive strike. Without fixed time limits, unplanned, ill-controlled by union organizations, and highly disruptive the explosive strike evidences a flowering of protest. In phase 4, which follows the explosive strike, all worker attitudes coexist; a plurality of forms of action becomes a permanent feature. A revival of withdrawal occurs with the development of absenteeism. A crystallization of self-identification with the firm comes with the emergence of a group constitution in opposition to the leaders of the explosive strike. Finally, a certain routinization and institutionalization of protest occurs as claims are more thought out and linked to coordinated stoppages by the organizations most representative of firm personnel.

Conclusion

When the left came to power in 1981, strike activity was at a fifteen-year low. The level of conflict, already very low in 1980 (1,674,000 days lost), declined even further in the first four months of 1981 (557,000 days lost compared to 667,000 for the same period in 1980). This decline in strike activity affected localized strikes less than generalized stoppages, as the CGT and CFDT publicized their clear-cut divergence on short- and medium-term objectives and ceased issuing calls for common action. A general disenchantment set in; workers seemed to lack confidence in the efficacy of the strike weapon or the union itself. The number of union members declined. The *recentrage* (recentering), which the CFDT adopted at its 1979 Congress with the objective of reversing this tide through opening up negotiations with the government and employers, had no appreciable impact.

The left thus won the presidential and legislative elections in the context of an ebb in unionization and strike activity. In the immediate aftermath of the left victory the union leadership put forward their priority demands. They did so without any interunion coordination or, despite declarations about the continual necessity for struggle, any calls for strike action. The government meanwhile promoted economic and social transformation: a fight against unemployment, an increase in wages for the lowest-paid workers, a reduction in the workweek, nationalizations, regulation of temporary and part-time employment, a lowering of the retirement age, new rights for workers at the workplace, and reform of the social security system. Unions supported certain reforms and complained that others were inadequate or were not implemented quickly enough.

In sum, the events of 1981 were not brought about by any social movement, nor did they generate any such movement. Several possible causes of this historical anomaly can be suggested: the divisions among wage-earners generated in the preceding period (due to the proliferation of different kinds of work contracts), trade union divisions, the rapidity of the transformations effected by the left, a sympathetic response by wage-earners to the managerial discourse on the economic slump and the paralyzing impact of strikes, and continued confidence in the welfare state (why mobilize when decisions are made at the top?). The Socialist government is thus not completely off the mark when it promises business that social peace will be assured.

What will become of the strike in the absence of any social movement? Strike activity remains at a low level: only 755,000 days lost to strikes in the period from September 1981 to January 1982. This is an increase compared to the corresponding period in 1980 (368,000 days lost) but is lower than in 1979 (1,570,000) and considerably below the average for the 1970s. The conflicts that broke out in late 1981 followed the pattern of the preceding three years: localized, fairly long in duration (3·4 days on the average vs 1·7 days for the 1970–7 period), weak in volume (129 strikers per strike vs 617 strikers for 1970–7), and with an occasional resort to plant occupation. In other words, the 1977 rupture in CGT–CFDT united action engendered a cessation of industry-wide and transindustrial conflicts and, beginning in 1978, an increase in strike duration and decrease in strike participation. As the union division has continued, this situation remained unchanged at the end of 1981 and into early 1982.

Have demands remained unchanged as well? The answer is both yes and no. Demands remain unchanged in the sense that conflicts continue over wages, job classifications, working conditions, and employment levels. Some conflicts over employment levels have become, however, more virulent because they involve plants of nationalized firms; here strikers do not accept a continuation of past policy. On the other hand, the legislation sponsored by the Socialist administration has engendered conflicts in response to specific measures. These are not national conflicts, orchestrated by the unions to push for a "good" law or accord but rather localized conflicts, under pressure from the base, to concretize or ameliorate a law or accord or to safeguard privileges previously won.

According to whether they have the former or latter objective, local disputes have a diametrically opposite impact. The furthering of a law or accord aims at accelerating change and is future-oriented. The local conflicts that have broken out at Renault plants can be so classified: Renault, as in the past, being at the forefront of the workers' movement. In contrast, the safeguarding of past gains often has the air of a defense of sectoral interests, corporatism, a nostalgia for the past, and a rejection of solidaristic efforts.

The conflicts which best illustrate this duality are those that broke out in early 1982 over the reduction of the workweek. On the one hand, some conflicts aimed at reducing the workweek beyond the 39-hour level set by the government for 1982, creating jobs in response to the reduced workweek, and circumventing managerial efforts to undermine collective benefits (such as seniority leave or coffee breaks). On the other hand, other conflicts broke out to protect special privileges (such as leave granted to certain occupational categories), obtain complete rather than partial compensation for the reduction in working hours, and prevent the introduction of some flexibility into work schedules.

If the strike now has little economic impact and is less linked to fluctuations in the economy, it continues to have sociopolitical significance. The strike retains many aspects of class war. While it obviously effects some change in the economic condition of wage-earners, the strike can also have political aims or consequences. Even if the major working-class organizations no longer subscribe to the revolutionary general strike, the strike remains a means of political pressure and can still bring down governments.

Note: Chapter 13

1 Serge Mallet, along with Pierre Belleville and André Gorz, in the early 1960s had pointed to the emergence of a "new working class." The role of this group—made up of scientific workers, engineers, and technicians—within the labor movement coincided with a change in the nature of capitalist society. In the early phase of capitalism craft workers, because of their strategic position, dominated the young labor movement. Later capitalism moved into a second phase, with the development of Taylorism and Fordism, and manual workers in the mass-production industries rose to prominence. In the third phase, ushered in by automation, highly trained workers in technologically advanced industries (the "new working class") would become the vanguard of the workers' movement. Dubois's reference here to the "*new* new working class" emphasizes the modification of Mallet's earlier formulations. For further reading on the debates revolving around "new working-class" theory see "Qu'est-ce que la classe ouvrière française," *Arguments*, vol. 3, no. 12–13 (January–March 1959), pp. 2–33; Belleville, 1963; Gorz, 1967; and Mallet, 1975, 1963—*translator*.

14

The Industrial Counterproposal as an Element of Trade Union Strategy

JEAN-PIERRE HUIBAN

> The trade unions have absolutely no power to carry out an offensive economic strategy directed against profit, because they are, in reality, nothing but the organized defense of the work force.
> (Rosa Luxemburg, *Social Reform or Revolution?*, 1906)

> In its daily activities trade unionism coordinates the efforts of the workers and attempts to increase their standard of living in such immediate ways as shortening the work week, increasing wages, etc. But this task is only one aspect of the work of the trade union movement, which is also laying the groundwork for the total emancipation of workers, a goal that can be achieved only by expropriating the owners of capital. It advocates the general strike as a means of action and holds that unions, today centers of resistance, will tomorrow become centers of production and distribution, i.e., the basis for the reorganization of society.
> (Amiens Charter, CGT, 1906)

At about the time of the "Lip affair" of 1973 (and toward 1977 in heavy-industrial sectors) French trade unions developed a reluctance to confine collective bargaining to the social consequences of decisions taken by others and displayed a new desire to exert direct influence in the industrial arena. What caused this development? How did it manifest itself? What does it mean for the trade union movement in France, particularly in the wake of the political change that occurred in 1981? These are the questions that this chapter will attempt to answer (for a more ample treatment see Huiban, 1981).

The Roots of Change

Since the end of World War II, and especially during the 1960s, the

French trade union movement's primary strategy for securing institutional status was to share the fruits of economic growth (Dahrendorf, 1959, discusses the notion of institutionalization). During this period France achieved both a high rate of economic growth and expansion of mass consumption by adopting Keynesian economic policies (Carré *et al.*, 1972). The period saw a shift to a new "mode of regulation," the Keynesian system, which incorporated social and political as well as economic components (see Boyer in this volume; Aglietta, 1979; Buci-Glucksmann and Therborn, 1981). The two primary elements of the Keynesian system are the demand variable and the state, which becomes the agent of economic, political, and social regulation. For the first time, labor and capital, although still antagonistic on the microeconomic and micropolitical level, witness a convergence of their interests at the macroeconomic level of the national economy. Capital accumulation and development of mass consumption are mutually supportive.

The wage labor relation is obviously affected by this development. If the pursuit of growth requires increased demand, increased demand just as clearly requires increasing income, and in particular increasing wage income. Thus a duality is created. At the firm level capital and labor continue to clash over the classical issue of the wage level. At the level of the "nation-state," however, the contradictory interests of capital and labor merge in the common objective of global economic growth. The realization of this objective remains the object of regulation. The nation, understood in terms of its political, economic, and social dimensions, becomes the natural environment in which this regulation takes place, and the state comes to be seen as its central actor.

Trade unionism becomes institutionalized through the operation of this capitalist mode of regulation. The trade union movement is the natural representative of wage-earners in the cycle that leads from a rise in income to an increase in consumption to a growth in output. For this cycle to operate properly the trade unions must be recognized as legitimate negotiators empowered by the workers to bargain over wage increases. It is not the number of members that secures this legitimacy (with approximately 20 percent of its workforce unionized, France has a far lower percentage of unionized workers than many other countries) but rather the recognition of trade unionism within the firm (established in France by the law of 27 December 1968, which authorized union locals in firms employing more than fifty workers). Unions achieved this institutionalization primarily by adopting a strategy of pressing workers' demands, especially demands for higher wages.

In France, although the period of growth did allow a certain increase in the average income of wage-earners, it did not lead to increased participation by workers or unions in either the management of industry or the setting of economic policy at the national level, despite signs in the immediate postwar period that this would ultimately occur. The main responsibility for this failure lies with the state and the business community, but the unions must bear part of the blame. Analysis of the unions' strategies up to the middle or end of the 1970s suggests the coexistence of two basic approaches:

- on the one hand, unions engaged day by day in negotiations for higher wages and better working conditions but did not directly concern themselves with industrial or economic policy-making;
- while on the other hand, they engaged in political activity (both rhetorically and practically) characterized, in the case of the CFDT and CGT, by a sweeping denunciation of the capitalist system, with the objective of enabling political parties with ties to the labor movement to take control of the government.

Thus we see a division of roles in which the state and business community manage the economy and the unions press for higher wages in the social sphere and support the parties of the left in the political sphere. Such a division of responsibilities is an essential feature of the Keynesian mode of regulation. The various actors will accept their respective roles only so long as the system continues to function well, and in particular only so long as wage-earners continue to reap concrete benefits from its operation.

That said, it is not hard to understand why the crisis, which is nothing less than a breakdown of this entire mode of regulation, threatens to undermine the institutionalized position of the trade unions. In this respect it is a crisis of the labor movement. It would seem that the unions, especially the CGT and CFDT, have arrived at a similar view of their current situation, which thereby impels them to seek to participate in the process of industrial and economic policy-making.

The Effects of the Crisis on the Working Class

Much has been written on this theme in this volume and elsewhere, so we shall limit ourselves to dealing with how the crisis has undermined the basis of the unions' old strategies and forced them to define new ones. It is convenient to distinguish between two kinds of effects, though in reality they are not distinct but overlap: one we shall call the "recession effect" and the other the "destructuring effect" of the crisis.

The Recession Effect

Looking at changes in two objective indices will make clear what we mean by the recession effect. To begin with, the number of unemployed workers in France now stands at 2 million. Shocking as this figure is, it does not fully convey the gravity of the situation since it reveals nothing about the number of workers actually losing and regaining jobs—the unemployment flow, as it were. Every worker is faced now with a greater likelihood that he or she will be out of work, and this tends to limit the worker's freedom to pick and choose between different jobs on the labor market (Salais, 1980). The second index of the recession effect is income. Not only has there been a decline in the growth rate, but employers have made use of this change to win concessions from workers in contract negotiations. Instead of a positive-sum game we are now in a zero-sum game (Thurow, 1981). Rather than a struggle over the fruits of growth there is a battle by workers to maintain their standard of living. The idea of forward progress has given way to the idea of maintaining the status quo (Perrot, 1981).

The Destructuring Effect

At a deeper level what we are witnessing is a breakdown of traditional job definitions: "the crisis must be understood as a twofold process, involving a destructuring or restructuring of capital in conjunction with a decomposition or recomposition of the working class" (Rosanvallon, 1979, p. 22; see also Greffe and Rosanvallon, 1978). Together the recession and destructuring effects of the crisis have tangibly altered the conditions affecting labor action. Generally speaking, the decrease in job security and wages has not resulted in increased worker militancy. Instead individual workers have responded in many different ways, and these differences are encouraged by management. According to the CNPF's Yves Chotard (*Le Monde*, 15 June 1979), for instance,

> the aspiration of workers to obtain greater freedom, initiative, and responsibility inevitably leads, in my opinion, to case-by-case treatment of individual workers. I would even go so far as to say that this is the direction in which history is moving.

Union Responses and Demands for Participation

Since 1974 the French labor movement has had to face many challenges: difficult conditions in which to wage strikes or negotiate contracts, an attitude of resignation among workers, a fragmentation of the working class involving the emergence of new, hard-to-organize groups such as youths, the unemployed, and immigrants as well as traditionally neglected groups such as women. At a deeper level the whole institutional status of the labor movement has been called into question by the crisis, as discussed above. In analyzing the unions' responses to these challenges it is useful to distinguish between two periods.

In the period 1974–8 the French, and especially workers, oriented their actions by reference to the coming legislative elections. We saw earlier how the unions coupled demands for higher wages with attacks on the capitalist system as such. This was the unions' tactical approach up to 1978. Because of the political situation emphasis was placed on the political component of labor action, and wage demands were kept moderate.

By 1978, indeed as early as the end of 1977, the entire labor movement had suffered a cruel disillusionment. It was at this point that self-criticism aimed at developing the theoretical foundations for a new strategy first made itself heard, primarily at the CFDT's Thirty-eighth Congress (held at Brest) and the CGT's Fortieth Congress. Criticism was directed first of all at the principles that had governed union representation of the working class. Speaking at the CFDT's Thirty-eighth Congress Edmond Maire declared that "we are still a union dominated by a masculine/industrial cultural model." J.-L. Moynot (1979b) wrote that May 1968 "must be seen ... as the date when the unions began to neglect problems encountered in the production process and in society." The second major line of criticism attacked the previous political strategy, which was now called inadequate or even dangerous. "This neglect," Moynot continued,

> was probably not an inevitable consequence of May 1968 ... but was influenced, and in some ways accentuated, by the adoption and pursuit of the political line embodied in the Union of the Left and the Programme Commun. Everything in France was made dependent on, and in some cases subordinate to, this line. We in the CGT have acknowledged that this influenced our struggles in the workplace and that we had a tendency to sacrifice the CGT's own program to the Programme Commun.

The unions began to cast about for ways to overcome the crisis in the labor movement. It was therefore quite natural that a new idea should emerge at this point, particularly in the CFDT, but also, rhetorically at any rate, in the CGT as well (at both federal and confederal levels in both unions): namely, the idea that the old sharp distinction between employers who manage the business and unions that demand higher wages and better working conditions was beginning to be blurred. "The clearest point to be made," wrote Moynot (1979b),

> is that we have not yet completely overcome the following false dilemma: either we act as though our role were simply to make social demands while leaving full responsibility for economic policy to management and the government, or else we place our faith in the capacity of the right economic program to resolve, in some miraculous way, all the problems that have not been resolved through struggle.

The blurring of the old distinction leads logically to a desire on the part of the unions to help shape industrial and economic policy. The CFDT's position, stated by Edmond Maire (1980a, p. 129), is that "by taking advantage of the government's need to act in this time of crisis, the unions can press for alternative solutions."

Speaking for the CGT, Moynot (1979b) stated that

> as long as economic growth continued, it was possible to think in terms of waging social struggles to correct the adverse consequences of that growth ... But in the current period, it is essential that the labor movement have the capacity to formulate its own industrial objectives in an autonomous way ... With problems as great as those we now face it is absolutely impossible to restrict our ambitions to negotiating over wages, employment, or even working conditions.

Force Ouvrière's leader, André Bergeron, demurred, however, rejecting any attempt by the unions to move outside the traditional social sector: "It is not the role of the labor movement to make up for the deficiencies of the government. We do not need to take the place of either the government or the business community" (*Le Matin,* 17 March 1980). To sum up, then, the need to participate in industrial decision-making was acknowledged by the two largest French unions for the first time in 1977–8.

Signs of Change: A Case Study

It is important to distinguish between different levels of union participation in the decision-making process. It is easy to see that there is little in common between, say, a union local that intervenes in a firm in economic difficulty and a union federation that proposes objectives for a whole sector of industry. From a methodological standpoint, therefore, it is important to ascertain the level of intervention.

Industrial Counterproposals at the Firm Level

In this section we shall consider the case of firms affected by economic developments over which they have little ultimate control. We shall be using the word "firm" in a microeconomic sense and looking at small and medium-sized companies as well as subsidiaries of large companies. In the case of subsidiaries we shall be concerned only with local reactions, limited to a single plant, to decisions taken by authorities not present on the premises.

The relevant union structures, then, are local organizations: sections within the firm or local, even departmental, unions. In fact our interpretation of these cases is shaped largely by their local or single-plant character. Special circumstances in each situation (such as support of local politicians, support of the populace, importance of the firm in the region's economy) will therefore exert a major influence on the course of events.

Finally, it is important to look at the nature of the crisis responsible for the elaboration by the unions of an industrial counterproposal. Examples include bankruptcies or threatened large-scale job losses. Of course the unions need not wait until a plant closure or major layoff actually occurs to propose alternatives to management decisions concerning the product manufactured or the organization of production. They could perfectly well suggest such alternatives while the plant is running smoothly, and indeed this is what the unions have done at the sector level. We did not choose to exclude this possibility at the local level. It is simply a fact that in France to date no such proposals have been made at the local level prior to the onset of an actual crisis. Counterproposals have been reactions to events rather than anticipations of them.

This helps explain a point that may seem to contradict our earlier statement concerning the date of the first union interventions in an ailing

French firm. The first case on record is of course that of Lip, where crisis struck in 1973 (Rozenblat *et al.,* 1980), long before the breakdown of the Union of the Left. While labor unions were still primarily concerned, at the federal and confederal level, with political strategy, union members at the local level had to cope with the first effects of the economic crisis. In 1973–4 the number of bankrupt firms rose sharply (Valet and Albert, 1977). Structural changes did not begin until somewhat later, in 1977 or 1978. It is easy to see why the unions' national strategy might have been unacceptable to workers faced with the loss of their jobs. Counter-proposals made by the unions at the firm level may thus be seen as local correctives to an overall union strategy ill-adapted to the needs of workers in any number of specific cases.

From a study of some forty cases throughout France in the period 1973–80 we have drawn the following conclusions. First, it is difficult to draw a hard-and-fast line between a strategy of counterproposals and a more "classical" strategy of defending jobs. The parties involved in a protracted industrial conflict, including the unions, will frequently raise issues of management policy. At what point it becomes reasonable to speak of a "counterproposal" as opposed to mere discussion of such issues thus becomes an exercise in subtle interpretation. In my view a useful criterion is whether a concrete attempt is made to demonstrate the viability of the firm under some new policy. This usually involves calling upon the services of experts, be they union sympathizers or paid consultants.

The strategic significance of the use of an industrial counterproposal is crucial. In essence what the union must attempt to do is to recreate, in a time of crisis, a situation in which it can act. The aim is twofold: to give workers an objective in order to mobilize them and to find an interlocutor with whom discussions can be carried on in the absence of company owners. This interlocutor might be someone in a position ultimately to take over the firm or to find a new buyer. In this sense the counterproposal is part of an intermediate stage of mobilization, a first step toward finding a solution to the company's problems: "The purpose of the offensive aspect of the proposal is chiefly symbolic. It is a step toward restoring the dialectic of management action and union reaction which the absence of management participation had destroyed" (Mercier, 1976).

The industrial significance of these proposals emerges clearly from their goals. It involves not reforming the economic system as a whole but, more pragmatically, preventing a firm from going out of business and/or workers from losing their jobs. What is needed is a rapid solution that a potential buyer can easily accept and implement. Seldom are such pragmatic schemes supplemented by more innovative ideas such as using layoff indemnities to set up training programs, basing new strategies on detailed analyses of the regional and national economies, or engaging in wide-ranging debate over the kind of development envisioned.

Thus, although the number of cases of intervention of this kind has grown rapidly, no real strategy has emerged, and there has been little progress in developing new managerial approaches to the problems of firms in serious difficulty. This must be seen, in my view, as a consequence of structural limitations on union intervention in such firms: intervention comes quite late in the game, the unions have few resources to assume management responsibilities, and the hierarchical nature of the system of production would hamper them in any case. Firms, especially small- to medium-sized firms, cannot hope to influence the evolution of markets dominated by a few conglomerates and so have little room to maneuver. This gives particular significance to union intervention at a higher level.

Intervention at the Branch Level

Union intervention at the branch level came later than intervention at the firm level. Not until 1977–8 did unions propose alternative economic and industrial plans for the steel industry. Though it came later, this kind of initiative was perhaps even more significant than intervention at the firm level, for it represents a union strategy based on a thorough analysis of the overall economic and political situation. The stakes in this kind of intervention are also far greater: 600,000 workers are employed in the textile and garment industries, for example, and the Rhône-Poulenc conglomerate alone employs 100,000 workers.

Space does not permit a full discussion of all our case studies (Huiban, 1981). Attention was devoted primarily to four industries: textiles, aeronautics, automobiles, and steel (primarily concerning the conflict connected with the steel industry in 1978–9). The specific character of each industry obviously affected the nature of union intervention. Nevertheless, a major lesson, common to all the cases studied, is that two strategies are available to unions seeking access to industrial and economic decision-making.

We shall call the first the strategy of the economic counterplan (ECP). In practice what this means is that unions will supplement their usual tactics with arguments from economics. As before, the goals of such a strategy are, on the one hand, to win concessions from management and, on the other hand, to stake out a position *vis-à-vis* the political parties. Issues are still posed basically in terms of a Keynesian macroeconomic framework emphasizing state intervention (including possible nationalization). Promotion of economic activity through demand stimulus remains the primary focus of policy. This is a highly centralized type of strategy and as such requires no major departure from previous union strategies; nor is its use by unions entirely novel (counterplans of this sort were proposed by the CGT in 1935 and by the CFDT in 1936).

The second type of strategy mentioned above will be referred to as the strategy of industrial counterproposals (ICP). The use of this kind of strategy involves a transition to a new mode for the unions, involving the formulation of proposals rather than the issuance of demands. It also involves the unions in what for them is a new area: responsibility for management decisions. No theoretical definition of this kind of strategy exists, other than the imprecise, often contradictory definitions given by the unions themselves. For conceptual purposes we offer the following definition: an industrial counterproposal suggests alternative means and ends relating to the manufacture of a product, ranging from the conditions of production (for instance, location, choices of investment and technology, workplace organization) to marketing of the final product, coupled with consideration of the purposes of production.

Once we have distinguished between the two types of strategy, we must then consider the degree to which a given union uses each type. The first thing we discover is that the CFDT primarily makes use of the ICP, whereas the CGT prefers the ECP and FO refrains from any intervention in the area of economic or industrial policy. A more subtle analysis is needed, however. Within the CFDT certain federations, particularly in the textile and garment industry, have challenged the strategic choice made by their confederation. Conversely, some members of the CGT—a small minority, it is true—have expressed a desire that their union adopt an ICP type of strategy.

Interpretation and Prospects for the Future

What impact has union intervention had on industrial decisions? What objectives and conceptions of the labor movement inform the two different kinds of strategies? These are the questions this section will attempt to answer. But the answers require working within a clearly defined theoretical framework.

For this I have drawn on the work of John Dunlop (1958), who conceptualizes the institutional actor (that is, the union) in terms of a "system of industrial relations" wherein the actor in question is related to (1) all the other actors in the system; (2) the rules that govern the system as a whole; and (3) institutions and other operational sites.

Using this framework, I shall examine the deeper issues involved in each of the two types of strategy by looking at the following central themes: (1) relations with the state, the parties, and the workers; (2) the quest for ways to extend collective bargaining into the area of industrial policy; and (3) the need for new ideas concerning how the unions might truly institute a democratic process for the formulation of industrial policy.

Redefinition of the Actors: Union Relations with the Parties, the State, and the Workers

The trade union, viewed as part of the system of industrial relations, is defined, on the one hand, by its relations with the political parties and the state and, on the other hand, by the way in which it represents the workers. It is important to see how both aspects of this definition are affected by the adoption of one or the other of the two strategies discussed above.

The first dimension is particularly important in France, where the industrial relations system is closely related to the political system.

Because of this, no union strategy can remain politically "neutral." Indeed the strategies of the unions, including the kinds of strategy we are concerned with here, reflect the unions' respective positions *vis-à-vis* the political parties.

As we have seen, an ECP strategy cannot be implemented without obtaining control of the government. Use of such a strategy therefore requires that the union be subordinated to a political party, which takes the lead in pursuing the strategic goal. Indeed the effect of an ECP strategy is to increase labor's demands on the state. Recourse to nationalization or to demand stimulus at the macroeconomic level requires expanding the powers of the central government in the economic sphere. In all this it is difficult to see any autonomous intervention by the unions, other than in the expression of desires or the imposition of *a posteriori* controls. Power is delegated, by the worker to his union and then, through the workings of representative democracy, by the union to the party and the state. The autonomy of the union is not increased. Rather it becomes increasingly dependent on the party and makes further demands on the state. It is striking that in France it is mainly the CGT and FO that envision the problems of industrial policy in this way. The CGT enthusiastically favors this kind of strategy and FO violently opposes it, but neither union conceives of an alternative kind of strategy.

Use of the ICP type of strategy requires a different outlook, associated mainly with the CFDT. The goal is to broaden the scope of union thinking and action with respect to industrial policy in such a way as to take account of economic and political constraints from the start. Thinking about workplace organization and manufacturing strategy is done without reference to the political parties or the state, as an autonomous contribution by the union, partly for its own use, partly for use in negotiations with other parties. Nationalizations are rarely mentioned. When they do come up, they are regarded as a means, not an end. In this respect the significance of the ICP is very clear: it helps the union to maintain its independence *vis-à-vis* the political parties and reduces demands on the state. The union sees itself as a driving force in social change, change that need not involve control of the government. This is important, because it means that the ICP has a political dimension. As Trentin (1979) puts it, the ICP is a "union strategy which seeks to increase the workers' power in the firm by means of decisions pertaining to production, the control of investments, and decentralization ... and which induces further political effects in society as a whole and in the state."

In the first part of this chapter we showed how traditional labor strategies ultimately proved incapable of responding to the breakdown of traditional working-class identities (more precisely, to the institutionalization of this process by employers). From the standpoint of those who use ICP strategies, a standpoint I share, this type of strategy is among other things an attempt—thus far unsuccessful—to deal with problems previously ignored even by the labor unions. Two aspects of ICP strategies contribute to this goal. First, the offensive aspect:

previous union strategies, preoccupied as they were with defending workers' gains in the face of economic and organizational upheaval, gave *de facto* recognition to existing divisions in the workforce. The transition to an ICP strategy makes it possible to reconsider the exclusion of certain kinds of workers, an exclusion that constitutes part of a sweeping strategy on the part of employers. Secondly, there is the regional aspect of ICP strategies: by emphasizing the intrinsic connection between industrial policies and regional development policies, ICP strategies give geographical considerations their due. It is, moreover, at the regional level that it is possible to restore worker solidarity that has broken down in the industrial system as a whole.

Extending the Scope of Collective Bargaining

The purpose of the ICP (but not, in my opinion, of the ECP) is to extend the scope of collective bargaining to include industrial decision-making. This results in a conflict with the institutional role of labor unions under the Keynesian system that developed in the previous period.

In the wake of demands for autonomy *vis-à-vis* the state what we see now is a renewal of union demands to go beyond the Keynesian system. Paradoxically the unions have come into conflict with a system that excluded them from any role in industrial decision-making while they continue to use one of the key tools of the previous Keynesian phase, namely, collective bargaining. Under the Keynesian system collective bargaining was highly centralized. The conclusion that emerges from our case studies is that this degree of centralism cannot be maintained when the strategic goal becomes greater access to the industrial decision-making process. One of the problems for the unions is to relate the organizational level with which workers identify to the institutional level at which negotiations take place and the economic level at which the effects of decisions are felt.

Consider the following example: suppose that workers identify with a particular department or plant. Suppose, further, that decisions taken will impinge on a particular conglomerate or branch of industry. What is the appropriate level for negotiations to take place? And how can the workers appropriately express their wishes? Difficulties of this kind come up time and time again in the cases I have studied. Different solutions have been adopted in different cases. The fact that these solutions have been shaped by organizational factors—negotiations focussing on a department, plant, company, group, or branch of industry—as well as physical factors—the influence of a company's physical plant, a locality, or a region—shows quite clearly that collective bargaining must be carried out in many different places and that the old centralized structures are no longer operative.

One final aspect of the change in the nature of collective bargaining over industrial policy issues is the inclusion of new participants in the process. Largely ignored in the past, these new participants can acquire a new legitimacy through worker input to the management of the manufacturing process. In the cases we studied such new participants included consumers' groups as well as local and regional organizations representing individuals affected by the industrial activity in question. This broadening of the decision-making process is a step toward greater democracy, which at the same time raises issues of reconciling productivist concerns about preserving jobs with consumer concerns about the social utility of the products manufactured (see Durand and Harff in this volume). The question of democracy leads into the topic of the next section.

Changing the Rules: The Central Problem of Democracy
Union counterplans? Elaborated by whom? And with what degree of participation by workers and rank-and-file union members? Here we touch on an important problem in the functioning of centralized organizations, the problem of democracy. All too often French trade unions have structured their organizations in accordance with very narrow conceptions of representative democracy involving delegated authority. The worker places his or her trust in an elected representative and, until the next election, has no further recourse.

This old problem has recurred now that the unions have decided to become involved in questions of industrial policy. Our case studies suggest that establishing the procedures for elaborating industrial counterproposals is a major strategic issue and, moreover, a challenge that has yet to be effectively met. It is a major strategic issue because it is difficult if not impossible to mobilize workers in support of proposals they had no part in elaborating. The challenge has yet to be effectively met, however, because the unions have not yet shown themselves capable of reconciling proposals made by the rank-and-file with consistent and comprehensive plans for reorganizing an entire branch of industry. In steel, for example, workers criticized union proposals on the grounds that they were submitted to the rank-and-file for approval only after they had been fully worked out.

P. Zarifian (cited in Najmann, 1981), a CGT economist, has argued that

> our conception is that all workers should be systematically included in the elaboration of industrial and social demands, which they debate collectively, at the union's behest, before the final draft of any proposal is made. There should be a free exchange of opinions, and the proposals that emerge from this process should reflect workers' ideas, rather than being a document that workers are asked to support after the fact.

Beyond uttering a pious wish, this is merely recognizing a strategic necessity and pointing to the failure of his own organization, as well as the CFDT for that matter, to abide by that necessity.

The full significance of this issue did not become clear until the reversal of political fortunes that occurred in May 1981, which brings us to our next topic.

Now What?

After the explosion of May 1981, little progress has been made, paradox-ically enough, in the area that interests us here: participation by workers and their unions in the industrial decision-making process.

To be sure, industrial policy is not an area in which decisions are made overnight. But the reasons for caution in fact lie elsewhere. The new state of affairs contains the potential for great progress, but at the same time it throws certain contradictions of the labor movement into relief.

So far our discussion has been concerned with a period during which the right was in power. The strategies adopted by the unions were in a sense opposition strategies. Similarly the results obtained were limited by the intransigence, and occasional pigheadedness, of the previous govern-ment. At that time the notion that unions should not participate in the management of the economy was virtually an article of faith subscribed to by business and government, with the result that union proposals were ignored, regardless of their content. The balance of power has now shifted, but none of the fundamental problems facing the labor move-ment have been resolved. Accordingly much of the foregoing analysis, especially the distinction between ECP and ICP, remains relevant.

Consider two aspects of the government-inaugurated reforms: the expansion of the public sector, and the establishment of new rights for workers. From the standpoint of the government there is nothing con-tradictory in these reforms. The expansion of the public sector—through nationalization—had long been sought by both the CFDT and the CGT, though for different reasons. Nationalization can be a very important means of shaping industrial policy to serve the national interest. Genuine participation by workers in the management of nationalized firms would be an extremely significant step toward participation by workers and their unions in the formulation of industrial policy. But nationalization is also, in its initial stages, an appeal to the state. Both the state and the unions might succumb to the temptation to mistake means for ends, which would take us back to the old model of representative democracy and delegated authority, merely adding another level to the hierarchy of delegation: workers elect experts, paid by the unions or by the govern-ment, and these experts then establish the firm's industrial policy in con-junction with other experts, employed by management or the ministries. The nature of the decision-making process is not altered, even if the end-result may benefit workers to some extent. Recourse to the state would remain the predominant means of action. Centralized decision-making would still be governed by an ECP logic, which would also determine the kind of measures put into effect with popular support. The problem of defining a democratic norm thus remains unsolved: true industrial democracy has yet to be invented. Edmond Maire (*Le Monde,* 26 March 1981) has warned against this mistake:

> We do not want any more nationalizations which are in fact étatisa-tions. Those nationalized industries that now exist must be socialized

at once. Instead of relying solely on the power of the state, nationalized firms must recognize the power of local communities and workers. This will then provide the basis for further nationalizations. We are not in favor of nationalization as a mere symbolic gesture. We want precise objectives to be defined for each firm slated for nationalization as well as a statement of the expected benefits for each branch of industry slated for restructuring.

The ICP strategy moves in a different direction. It offers greater possibilities but also greater difficulties, owing to the need to venture into territory still largely unexplored: namely, giving workers the means to participate in a meaningful way in the preparation of economic and industrial policy decisions. Such a possibility does not yet exist, but some work has been done in laying the groundwork. But moving to the next stage, actually grappling with real issues, is another matter. The observations made above remain pertinent. Workers cannot effectively participate in the decision-making process until they, and their union representatives, have received the necessary training in economics and the required expanded access to information.

These prerequisites are necessary but not sufficient. Another necessary step is to decentralize decision-making in government, business, and for that matter in the unions. Even after a start has been made on all these changes, problems will still remain—especially then, I should like to suggest! Many factors need to be taken into account, including the need to keep French industry competitive in a socialist France, as well as the need to protect jobs while at the same time serving the interests of consumers. In the process innumerable contradictions will inevitably come to light. What is more, there are signs today that some workers and trade unions are clamoring to defend special privileges, which shows that attitudes must change as well as structures. One of the biggest issues of the next few years in France will be reconciling democracy with efficiency in the industrial sphere.

The challenge is a formidable one, for it involves not only the economic crisis but also the social crisis and the crisis in the labor movement.

15
Ideology and Industrial Practice: CGT, FO, CFDT

BERNARD H. MOSS

Contrary to a view that sees trade unions as adaptive or reactive organizations, they play a formative role in the creation of a working class. Their wage and industrial policies not only help set the conditions for capital accumulation but also weld the bonds and shape the consciousness of the working class. Industrial policies articulate the ideologies—values, objectives, and strategies—that prevail in the labor movement and society at large. Trade union mechanisms of class formation are particularly evident in France where at least three major ideological currents—Marxism, social democratic reformism, and a form of New Leftism—vie for influence in the labor movement. Each of the major confederations or centrals, CGT, FO, and CFDT, deploys distinctive industrial policies to advance ideological goals. Drawing upon my research on eight industrial federations of the three unions—Metal, Chemical, Textile, Construction, Agriculture, Health, Railways and Bank—this chapter describes how each central put its ideological project into industrial practice from 1968 to 1982.[1]

CGT

Since World War II the CGT has derived its Marxist strategy from the French Communist Party (PCF). Relations between workers and employers were seen as relations of exploitation, the source of an unceasing struggle between labor and capital that is the major conflict in industrial society. Trade unions, in this view, function to limit the effects of exploitation and to raise the level of understanding for the essentially political battle for socialism. Responsibility for deciding the ways and means of socialism—of securing state power—was left to the political parties, in practice the PCF. Its members predominated on the executive committees of all the federations studied except Metal, which like the central reserved half of its posts to non-Communists—mostly Catholics from the Young Christian Workers (JOC). A strong ideological consensus bound Communists and non-Communists in the federal leadership. There was little evidence of the ideological dissidence that appeared at the summit of the central in 1978.

Following the PCF, the CGT shifted in 1978 from seeking a global political solution in a Common Program of the Left to a neo-syndicalist strategy of *autogestion* or worker control. Between 1968 and 1974 the CGT sought to unite the interests of the working class and middle strata—technical, supervisory, and engineering personnel—and to avoid the extralegal and minoritarian tactics of the extreme left that threatened to divide the working class and frighten people into support of the regime. Once the Common Program had been signed and the extreme left isolated, the CGT apprehended a new danger in the hesitation of the CFDT and the Socialist Party (PS) to commit themselves to the Program. Slowly and ambiguously the CGT radicalized its approach with plant occupations to save jobs and equipment. In 1977 it revised its hierarchical wage policies and admitted that the crisis of capitalism had a social and cultural dimension that required for its resolution greater initiative and cooperation among workers and democratization of the workplace. When the left was defeated in 1978, the CGT turned further toward a neo-syndicalist strategy seeking immediate gains through local struggles and proposing worker control over production and industrial redeployment.

The CGT practices a conception of mass and class unionism whereby class unity and consciousness would emerge from the unification of concrete struggles for material gain. To represent all categories and unite the class it assembled a comprehensive catalogue of demands—on wages, hours, working conditions, pensions, employment—for workers, staff, women, youth, and immigrants. It sought to defend workers' interests by raising the level of combativity and struggle. It reminded workers that gains depended on direct action and warned them against relying on outside intervention—skillful negotiators, automatic cost of living indexes, or third-party arbitrators.

The CGT ratified agreements that afforded real gains without restricting its freedom of action. It favored national agreements that set minimum standards which could be surpassed by local struggles. It combated contracts that bound unions with no-strike, prior-notice, or arbitration clauses. It refused settlements, such as under the Toutée Procedure in the public sector, in which unions were asked to distribute a fixed wage sum to different categories, because they diverted workers away from the struggle with capital. The decision to sign bargaining agreements depended on initial targets, level of worker combativity, state of public opinion and employer resistance. Whether ratified or not, accords were "desacralized"—broken down into positive, negative, and insufficient clauses. Until 1980 probably because of its wider presence the CGT signed more territorial accords than the CFDT.

CGT federations were the most maximalist in the formulation and the negotiation of demands. For the CGT in contrast to the CFDT, it was the level and not the type of demand that made it anti-capitalist. Maximalist demands would heighten the sense of injustice, raise expectations, and spur activism. They would point the way to a level of mobilization or political change, as in 1968 or under the Common Program, that

Table 15.1   *Territorial Collective Agreements*

Avenants signed	1979	1980
CGT	334	176
CFDT	136	184
FO	495	301

Source: Ministère du Travail, 1980.

could conceivably overcome obstacles to their satisfaction. With the exception of the early 1970s, when some CFDT locals were more intransigent, CGT federations were the most exigent in negotiations as well. Their reputation among employers as the most costly adversary was well deserved. CGT settlements were invariably higher than those of other centrals. In metal, for example, the plants and sectors which achieved the highest wages were generally those where the CGT was strongest.

Federations set their minimum wage targets, net of bonuses, at the level of the SMIC—the legal minimum wage—demanded by the CGT. This figure, which in the 1970s, fluctuated between 40 and 30 percent above the official SMIC, represented the minimum requirement for a skilled worker with a family of four in the Paris region. It was adjusted to a cost of living index based on Parisian prices that excluded the deflationary effects of qualitative improvements. During the 1970s the index of the CGT was usually one point above those of the CFDT and FO and three points above the official index.

Despite ambitious targets, federations disposed of wide margins for compromise. Negotiations involved a two-stage compromise, first, to work out a common platform with other unions, and secondly, to reach agreement with employers. Federal targets, which set a national measure of need, had to be adapted to local conditions and aspirations. So long as local unions shared the ideological consensus on general questions, they disposed of considerable freedom in setting demands, planning action and signing accords. But from 1974 to 1978 demands tended to be globalized and set at unattainable levels.

With real wages and productivity rising from 1968 to 1974, CGT federations signed wage accords that afforded increases on their index.[2] Textile approved accords in 1970, 1973, and 1974, when minimum rates rose faster than the SMIC. Employees signed once in the bank sector in 1971. Construction, seeking to raise minimum scales faster than actual wages, authorized regional accords that raised all grades above the SMIC. Local unions occasionally infringed guidelines, but few accords were signed after the wage freeze of 1976. Aiming to raise all grades substantially above the SMIC, Agriculture initialed few national accords in the cooperative sector after 1975. By contrast, in the production sector, where it wished to secure some protection yet disposed of little bargaining power, it displayed nearly the same propensity to ratify departmental accords—with minimums barely above the SMIC—as FO and the CFDT.

Table 15.2   *National Agreements for Agricultural Cooperatives*

Accords signed	*1979*	*1980*
CGT	16 (only 3 on wages)	13 (only one series on wages)
CFDT	28	43
FO	37	60

Source: Ministère de l'Agriculture, 1980.

Table 15.3   *Regional Accords in Agriculture*

	1979		*1980*	
	No.	*% of total*	*No.*	*% of total*
CGT	464	67	564	68
CFDT	569	81	694	84
FO	487	70	641	78

Source: Ministère de l'Agriculture, 1980.

Metal and Chemical demanded minimum scales that would narrow the gap with actual wages. Since the gap between regional minimums and actual wages widened, few accords were signed after 1973. The CGT, which never approved a chemical accord, signed once in petroleum after joint action produced a better than normal settlement in 1979. The CGT often signed for a better than average increase in order to consolidate a successful mobilization as in textile in 1978. After 1973, the CGT signed a diminishing number of accords and increasingly vetoed the legal extension of those signed by FO in the Commission on Collective Contracts.

Political factors made CGT federations even more exigent in the highly visible public sector. In 1970 Prime Minister Jacques Chaban-Delmas, counseled by Jacques Delors, attempted a "revolution" in French industrial relations with pluri-annual *contrats de progrès* that

Table 15.4   *Industrial Action, 1978–80: Reported by CGT Unions*

Local Action (September–December)	*1978*	*1979*	*1980*
Strikes (at least 24 hours)	868	682	1,125
Occupations	54	64	63
Other actions	561	1,712	3,558
All local stoppages*	1,041	1,555	792
Total Actions			
CGT	1,490	2,102	4,842
CFDT	319	471	294
FO	63	118	59

* Ministry of Labor.
Source: CGT, 1980.

offered increases of 2–3 percent—tied to a complex productivity formula—in return for an obligation of social peace, in the end, a three-month cooling-off period. Holding a referendum against the contract in EDF (Electricité de France), the CGT obtained its normal majority. The CGT opposed *contrats de progrès* not only because they threatened its bargaining strategy but also because ratification would imply approval of the government's social and economic policies. When the anti-strike provision was deleted and a new wage guarantee added in 1971, the federation felt compelled to sign. Ratifying guaranteed increases through 1974, it was later chastised by the central for breaching the common front of opposition to government policy.

The political factor was more evident on the railways where, with the exception of 1971, when the CGT signed to avoid isolation, it refused to compromise its demand for 3 percent across-the-board increases. A few months after signing for a better than usual guarantee in 1971, the CGT called a joint strike with the CFDT to protest the unilateral adoption of the new official index and to demand a vacation bonus, demonstrating that its demands were not limited to the terms of agreement. Thereafter, the CGT refused all offers, including the generous one for 1976 that met its basic criteria.

The Socialist sweep of May–June 1981 established conditions for change that were unfavorable to the CGT's wage maximalism. Bowing to the Socialist victory to which it had been forced to contribute, the CGT scaled down its immediate SMIC target to 20 percent and asked its federations to make similar adjustments in platforms where appropriate. Relinquishing claims for across-the-board increases, public sector federations demanded quarterly cost of living adjustments that kept ahead of inflation on the CGT index, with increases for low-wage earners. Metal, which had initiated a critique of its politically oriented maximalism in 1979, abandoned the campaign for a national convention and concentrated on unifying scales in regional accords, fixing medium-term targets at 10 percent differential increases up to the level of managerial personnel. Employees sought a 2 percent increase in the newly nationalized bank sector. Because of the prevalence of low wages in their sectors, Textile, Construction, Agriculture, and Chemicals felt they could not make medium-term adjustments. Nevertheless, with the deepening of the world economic crisis, and the social pause and wage freeze in 1982, even private sector federations came to accept cost of living adjustments with increases for the lowest-paid as more realistic immediate objectives.

Negotiating positions were always linked to industrial action. Asserting that workers could only advance their interests through struggle, the CGT subordinated negotiations to action. Of the three centrals it was the most activist, conducting far more strikes than the others (see Table 15.4). The CGT employed a battery of weapons from delegations, petitions, and stop-work meetings to plant-level, regional, and national strikes. Federations favored the 24-hour national strike for maximum mobilization at minimum cost to strikers. These strikes were called as much to raise issues and spur plant activity as to affect the outcome of specific negotiations.

The CGT's activism—going against the natural tide—became apparent despite the 1974 economic slump and the 1976 wage freeze. Moreover, rather than yield to the mood of resignation and despair— accentuated by private sector membership losses—that followed the 1978 election, the CGT conducted two general strikes at the end of 1978, a march on Paris in March 1979 during the steel crisis and a week of protest activity in September 1979, before renewing unity of action with the CFDT. When unity reached its breaking point over Afghanistan in 1980, the CGT stepped up its strike calls to demonstrate its capacity for independent initiatives. In 1980, a year of low strike participation, it called 127 branch, 56 regional, and 18 interindustrial actions.

During the period of the Common Program the CGT tried to raise activity to the highest and most political level with the one-day interindustrial general strike. These strikes were timed to spur or crown a rising level of activity or to show protest in its absence. They were valued because they strengthened interindustrial solidarity and identified the government as the source of national wage and economic policy and key to successful negotiations. From 1972 to 1978 they were also used to promote the Common Program.

The defeat of 1978 led to a reorientation away from political action toward more plant, regional, and branch activity. At the Fortieth Congress the CGT conceded it had lost touch with workers because of a preoccupation with political issues.

Organizing in sectors that were small-scale and widely dispersed, Construction and Agriculture ceased calling national strikes. Others continued, but they preferred the day or week of action in which the form of action was decided by local unions. Since May 1981 the CGT has restricted its activism to national strikes and the relatively low-level week of action. Unless and until the PCF decides to break with Mitterrand, the CGT is not likely to mount any large-scale general strike as it did so often under conservative governments.

FO

Despite its syndicalist and Socialist origins, FO has represented social democratic reformism since 1968. It tried to defend workers' interests through collective bargaining and social welfare policies. Consistent with its commitment to welfare state capitalism and European integration, it was equally critical of Giscard's free market liberalism and Mitterrand's extensive nationalizations. Arising out of opposition to Communist domination of the CGT, FO attempted to counter CGT strategy by creating stable bargaining relationships with employers and avoiding excessive demands that might destabilize the economy. To encourage collective bargaining FO focussed on the most immediate and negotiable bread-and-butter issues—wages, hours, and pensions. Its concern for obtaining benefits without price instability, its disengagement from agitational and political strikes as well as its minority status led it to set sights relatively low. Employers were willing to sign with FO in order to avoid an accumulation of discontents and reward their most reasonable partner. FO federations did not sign just anything; they could be tough and unyielding about obtaining the bare minimum, especially in the public sector where—all things considered—results were rather good.

Results in the public sector were obtained as much by lobbying—Bergeron's frequent visits to the Elysée—as by collective bargaining. In 1977 FO fought tooth and nail to break the Barre wage freeze, even to the extent of participating in the 24 May general strike. In the end, after several visits to the Elysée and Matignon before the 1978 legislative election, FO preserved cost of living increases for all but public servants.

Reflecting its syndicalist origins, the Railway Federation had originally been more exigent than the rest of the public sector. It refused to participate in the Toutée Procedure and worked out joint platforms with the CGT and CFDT. In 1970 FO and CFDT signed for 2 percent after eliminating the anti-strike provision. But when the government refused 2 percent in 1972, FO struck alongside the CGT. Thereafter it regularly obtained between 3 and 5 percent until after 1977 when it settled for cost of living with increases for the lowest grades. With obvious displeasure, it signed on similar terms in 1981 with Charles Fiterman, Communist Minister of Transport.

FO was reluctant to announce ambitious wage targets. It favored a level of the SMIC that kept up with average wage levels—usually between 5 and 10 percent above the current SMIC. Many federations refused to announce minimum figures. Announced targets varied from cost of living adjustments to alignment with the CGT. Unlike their rivals, FO federations were quite willing to settle on the basis of the official price index, which was usually two points below their own. During the early 1970s they sought increases of 2 percent, scaling it down to 1 percent after the wage freeze of 1976 until 1980 when they accepted a cost of living adjustment.

Reflecting considerable variations FO federations could be classified into two groups with respect to exigency and militancy. Reconstructed in a pragmatic mold after 1947, Metal, Construction, Agriculture and Textile were "contractualists," who refused to announce targets, signed regularly for minimal gains and accepted a moral obligation of social peace during the term of an accord. While resisting arbitration and anti-strike clauses as impediments to bargaining, they were not averse to preambles that linked improvements to social peace, profitability, and productivity. "Contractualists" regularly obtained guarantees that were a point or so above employers' unilateral recommendations.

Metal unions signed accords several grades below SMIC and that allowed the gap between minimum scales and actual wages to widen. Their greatest successes were local pacts that took advantage of the profitability of certain companies. The 1970 SNIAS aeronautical accord fixed a schedule of increases with quarterly—later semi-annual—adjustments that until 1977 kept abreast of inflation. Agriculture ratified minimums at the level of the SMIC. Construction allowed its unions to approve scales that left several grades below the SMIC and that lagged behind those in other sectors—a situation partly remedied by the 1979 upgrading of classifications. Until 1976 Textile obtained real increases. Between 1975 and 1980 it refused its signature four out of thirteen times when offers failed to keep pace with inflation. In 1978 it called a national strike with the CGT and CFDT.

Reflecting the militancy of the prewar CGT, Chemical and Employees shared its conception of accords as temporary compromises in the class struggle. The presence of Trotskyists from Lutte ouvrière and the OCI (Organisation communiste internationale) contributed to the militancy of the bank employees. Aligning their targets with those of the CGT, they signed only once, in 1971. They engaged in joint action on a common program several times and took the lead in the bank occupations of 1974. Chemical went through a socialist and New Left phase before the departure of Maurice Labi in 1972. Less exigent than the CGT, it was the major partner in the petroleum accord that barely kept abreast of inflation. But it signed only once in the chemical sector, engaged in several national strikes with the CGT and was a force for greater exigency, notably with respect to the reduction of working hours, within FO.

Force Ouvrière, the least activist of the centrals, subordinated action to negotiations. Having abandoned agitational and political strikes, FO called national strikes as a last resort to remove obstacles to settlement. Health, one of the only FO federations capable of conducting its own national action, called several national strikes to advance claims in negotiations and to break the wage freeze under both Giscard and Mitterrand. In principle, FO favored the show-down strike of indefinite duration to the one-day agitational strike of the CGT. Despite an official ban Employees and Chemical engaged in joint action with the CGT. Preferring open-ended strikes, bank employees often joined with the CFDT in issuing one-day renewable strike calls. Force Ouvrière "contractualists" rarely engaged joint action on the national level. They were not interested, as were the CGT and CFDT, in achieving mass mobilization for its own sake; they were content to support limited groups of workers without enlarging the scope of action and opposed violent and extralegal tactics such as plant occupations. Force Ouvrière's preference for negotiations over action was reflected in low strike rates, but its reputation for moderation did not exclude greater activism to defend purchasing power under Mitterrand.

CFDT

Always subtle and elusive, the CFDT changed from a fairly moderate social democratic union to a radical New Left movement in the early 1970s. Drawing upon an eclectic mix of Christian, social democratic and New Left themes, it aimed to construct a socialist alternative to the PCF.

During the 1960s this alternative embodied collective bargaining and the counterplan; in the early 1970s worker-managed socialism; since 1978 a return to bargaining within the parameters of a national plan. The CFDT always showed sensitivity for "qualitative" issues—working hours, low-wage workers, grassroots democracy, and women's rights.

It underwent radicalization in 1968 when it took the side of the student movement against the CGT and launched the slogan of *autogestion* or worker-management. It assimilated the anti-bureaucratic and anti-productivist themes of May–June and proclaimed its revolt against all forms of alienation: degradation of the work process, hierarchical divisions of authority, sexual and racial discrimination, and destruction of the natural environment. While incorporating Marxist themes into its analysis, it refused to recognize economic exploitation as the basis of class struggle. Sympathetic to the plight of the underprivileged, it attracted newly radicalized social categories—youth, immigrants, and women—who had been relatively neglected by the CGT. Qualitatively different from the CGT, the CFDT drew elements who were both to the right and the left of the PCF—moderates who wanted to democratize the factory without squeezing capitalist profits and radicals who wanted to give class unionism a more grassroots orientation.

In the political void created by May–June 1968—the absence of a large social democratic party—the CFDT adopted a neo-syndicalist strategy seeking structural reforms outside the political process. This neo-syndicalist strategy concealed divergent ideological approaches, radical and moderate, that largely paralleled the currents dividing the PS, in particular, the CERES and Rocard factions. The moderate CFDT majority, led by Edmond Maire, criticized the Common Program for its quantitative maximalism and political centralism. The radicals basically supported the Program as a precondition for a rapid transition to worker-managed socialism. Local activism and the adoption of worker-managed socialism in 1970 forced upward adjustments of demands and a new alliance with the CGT. Once the original impulse of grassroots radicalism had been spent, moderates reasserted their control. They began to arrest Marxist influence in 1975 and to remove the Trotskyists of the LCR (Ligue communiste révolutionnaire).

The rupture between the PS and PCF, which moderates blamed on the PCF, freed them from the constraints of the CGT alliance and allowed them to begin a major *recentrage* or reorientation—a return to the bargaining of the 1960s. The Moreau report of January 1978 announced an end to political strikes and a return to wage moderation and bargaining at all levels. Qualitative themes—solidarity with the low paid, the reduction of hours and improvement of working conditions—were given priority in negotiations with the CNPF, but worker-managed socialism was relegated to the distant future. The effect of *recentrage,* combated in dispersed order by the radicals, was to bring wage policies closer to those of FO.

Moderates dominated Metal (Jacques Chérèque and Albert Mercier), Chemical (Maire and Jacques Moreau), and Agriculture (Michel Rolant and Jean-Paul Jacquier). The PSU was strong in Hacuitex (textiles and garments) and the Bank; the LCR in Health; and CERES in Construction. Under Fredo Krumnow, Hacuitex had launched the idea of worker-managed socialism. Enrolling a new student generation, the Bank reflected the spirit of May–June. Placed on the defensive by the split in the left, radicals fell victim to their own divisions and lack of a coherent program. After a purge of Trotskyists, moderates took over Health in 1980. Leaders of Construction abandoned the CERES after 1978. Bank and Hacuitex held out against the confederal majority until May 1981 when they began to seek compromise. In 1980 the leadership of Railways passed to a radical caucus, but its voice was muzzled by incorporation within the moderate Transport Federation.

Federations tended to shift between the minimalism of FO and maximalism of the CGT as a function of political alliances. During the 1950s and 1960s they usually signed collective bargaining agreements alongside FO while engaging in joint action with the CGT. The subtle practice of unity and competition with the CGT tended to raise the level of demand. A series of unity pacts—begun in 1966, resumed in 1970 and capped in 1974—tended to bring federal platforms into alignment. At the Grenelle negotiations in 1968 and until 1971 the CFDT was still closer to FO than to the CGT.

In 1970 it signed the *contrats de progrès* because they corresponded to criteria formulated in the early 1960s—indexing wages to prices and productivity and redistributing a wage fund to low-income earners. Traditional wage policies were out of phase with the new radicalism. Inspired by the spirit of May–June 1968 and the entry of the extreme left, local CFDT unions were proving themselves more intransigent than the CGT. This local activism and the adoption of worker-managed socialism compelled a revision of federal platforms and alliances.

After denouncing the accord signed for 1972, public sector federations condemned the *contrats de progrès* as mechanisms of class collaboration and aligned their position with that of the CGT—3 percent increases that kept ahead of prices on their index, a refusal of indexing to productivity, and a monthly minimum of 1,000 francs. Radical federations—Bank, Hacuitex, and Health—outbid the CGT on minimum wages, demanding lump sums of 500 francs or sixty additional points, and urged the central to outbid the CGT on the SMIC. Bank, insisting on its minimum target, refused to sign alongside the CGT in 1971. During the 1970s Hacuitex signed only twice, compared with six times for the CGT. Overall, however, because of the acceptance of differential increases total wage demands remained below those of the CGT.

Despite differences on strike tactics, moderate federations moved into alignment with the CGT as well. Metal, which reached an accord on a national convention with the CGT in 1971, envisaged a merger. Agriculture, the only CFDT federation studied with a plurality in its sector, was least affected by unity of action, continuing to sign for rates below those of the CGT. Chemical took a long time to reach an accord with the CGT in 1976. At the height of unity in 1977 twenty-nine federations had worked out common platforms—with only three refusing unity of action. Once the CGT revised its wage policies toward differential increases in 1977, federal wage platforms became virtually identical.

Recentrage was resisted by radical federations, which maintained maximalist demands and refused their signature. When CFDT leaders expressed preference for bargaining over action and proposed wage cuts in return for a reduction in working hours, widespread opposition—not limited to radicals—forced them to back down. The SMIC target did not drop below that of the CGT until 1980 when the CFDT announced that its figure—5 percent lower—was a long-term and not an immediate objective.

With *recentrage* moderate federations immediately lowered targets and negotiating positions. Agriculture reduced its minimum requirement from 6 to 2 percent and began to sign national accords alongside FO (Table 15.2). Chemical reduced its wage demands by half, but was unable to reach any new national accords. Health, now under moderate leadership, began to sign in the private sector. Metal abandoned the campaign for a national convention, a maximalist demand that lacked credibility after the rupture of the left, and sought limited accords with minimal results. In negotiations with the Union of Metal and Mining Industries (UIMM) it initiated a series of regional negotiations for a guaranteed annual income. The CFDT signed only five of fifty such accords reached in 1980; they were not renewed in 1981 because of their minimal impact on real wages. In 1981 Metal ratified eleven regional wage conventions alongside FO, a practice it had abandoned after 1970. Its 1981 Congress endorsed the policy of seeking results by negotiations. It lowered wage demands to cost of living with increases for low-wage earners and suggested wage cuts in return for a reduction in working hours. As the number of accords ratified by the CGT diminished, the number approved by the CFDT increased (Table 15.1). In 1979 it signed 30 percent of 286 minimum wage accords; in 1980 40 percent of 378.

Despite its undisguised preference for Rocard within the PS, the CFDT shared fully in the Mitterrand victory; it supported his objective of a revitalized Socialist Party that reduced the PCF to an auxiliary role. CFDT moderates and allies invested key economic and labor posts in the Mauroy government—Delors at Finance, Decaillon at Labor, Hubert-Prévot and Rocard at the Plan, and Lésire-Ogrel at Solidarity. The CFDT immediately proposed and the government granted a minimal 10 percent increase in the SMIC. While the government echoed the CGT theme of increasing workers' purchasing power, its wage policies were more in keeping with the CFDT's call for wage restraint. In April 1982 Maire repeated the warnings of Rocard and Delors about inflationary dangers and the need for sacrifices from the better-paid. He approved the social pause of April and the substance, if not the form, of the wage freeze in June 1982. The CFDT behaved as the principal social partner of the Mauroy government and Mitterrand regime.

The trend toward wage restraint was accelerated by 10 May. Metal and Chemical lowered their sights to cost of living plus increases for the lowest grades. Agriculture set a regional target that was minimally above the new SMIC. Former radicals—Hacuitex, Bank, Construction and Health—also debated about making their demands more negotiable. For the first time Hacuitex presented a minimum demand that was 10 percent lower than that of the CGT. Only Railways held to its wage maximalism.

Rather than merely aggregate demands voiced by workers, the CFDT selected qualitative themes that were designed to raise the level of social conscience and solidarity as much as to mobilize for struggle. During the early 1970s it argued that "qualitative" demands concerning wage equality and working conditions posed greater challenges to capitalism than did bread-and-butter demands that were easily digested by the system. In 1978 it engaged negotiations on three priority issues: low wages, working conditions, and the reduction of working hours. In 1980, warning of the dislocation of the working class as a result of the crisis, it focussed concern on the status of temporary, part-time, and noncontractual workers. At the 1982 Congress the main themes were solidarity with the underprivileged—the low-paid and unemployed—and the promotion of women in the union. The "qualitative" issues may have been of marginal material interest to most members, but they attracted new social categories and struck a humanist chord that united workers coming from a Catholic background with the generation of the New Left.

The battle-cry in the 1970s was to reduce wage differentials. Radicals insisted on large lump-sum increases that would tend to collapse the lower wage scale. Moderates generally combined lump-sum and percentage increases in a more maximalist version of FO's *salaire binôme*. Government and management were quite willing to negotiate higher minimum wages for they assuaged the demands of social conscience without imposing substantial across-the-board increases. The CGT opposed lump-sum increases because they tended to divert workers away from the struggle with capital toward differences in their own ranks. While admitting the need to increase low wages disproportionately, the CGT defended percentage increases as a way to unite blue-collar, technical, and managerial personnel. In 1977, in the face of popular demands and constraints arising from the economic crisis, the CGT supported compressing wage differentials from eight down to five or six to one, virtually the same as that of the CFDT. Since 10 May both centrals have stressed differential increases.

The other qualitative issue pushed by the CFDT after 1978 was reduction of working hours. CFDT moderates sought to reduce the hours of the least protected workers and to facilitate new hiring without imposing additional wage costs on employers. To accomplish these reductions they were prepared to call upon better-paid workers to sacrifice income for the sake of the underprivileged and unemployed. The CFDT was most responsive to CNPF proposals for an annual reduction to a 40-hour weekly average in exchange for the removal of daily and weekly restrictions to achieve more intensive use of capital equipment. Hostile in principle to easing daily and weekly restrictions, the CGT and FO required a higher price for settlement—38 and 39 hours, respectively, with full pay.

In the last round of talks in July 1980 the CFDT pressed for an accord that would have reduced annual working time for 15 percent of the workforce while allowing more flexible conditions of night, weekend, shift, and variable hours for all. The opposition of CGT, FO and CFDT federations, many of which already enjoyed the 40-hour week, scuttled the accord. When talks were resumed under the patronage of the Mauroy government, pledged to a 35-hour week, a first-step reduction to 39 hours was unavoidable. The CFDT and FO nevertheless accepted a protocol that went no further than the previous one, particularly since it relegated the contentious issues of flexible hours and wage compensation to the branch level. Because of ideological preference for voluntary bargaining over political intervention, the CFDT refused to take advantage of the new relationship of political forces and chose to negotiate on the branch level where, due to worker demobilization, it would dispose of less bargaining power.

In the absence of large-scale mobilization employment gains were minimal. Having achieved their objective—39 hours with a fifth week of paid vacation—FO "contractualists" were willing to settle for less than full pay on the branch level. CFDT moderates pressed for a greater reduction of working time and employment guarantees in exchange for wage cuts. Agriculture settled for a quota of 12-hour days in return for an annual limitation. After much discussion, Metal and Chemical agreed to wage cuts of 30 and 33 percent for those reductions beyond 39 hours. Some CFDT unions settled for wage cuts with respect to the 39-hour week, a policy encouraged by moderate Cabinet ministers but finally repudiated by Mitterrand himself. Others, including Bank, Hacuitex and Railways, refused to yield on wage compensation. The Congress of Metz in May 1982 passed a resolution calling for hours reductions with full pay up to twice the value of the SMIC, once again overriding confederal leadership on this issue. In its first spurt of activism since the 1981 elections the CGT encouraged demands for at least 38 hours with full pay, advantages that were obtained in a small number of sectors—dockers, truckers, RATP, Air France and so on.

The CFDT traditionally stood between the CGT and FO on industrial action, according it equal weight with negotiations. Lacking a Parisian base and truly national presence, it stressed local and regional initiatives. During the 1960s it led militant strikes at the factory level. After May–June 1968 it conducted long struggles against combative employers, especially in the newly industrialized west, its main bastion. It defended the most exploited categories—the unskilled, immigrants, and women. It accepted the help of extreme left groups and sanctioned the use of extralegal tactics—sequestration, occupation, bottle-necking production. With Lip in 1973, it popularized the factory takeover as a labor tactic. To involve the unorganized, CFDT unions formed strike committees outside of the union structure. While the central moved to restore union control after 1973, local unions continued to work with extreme left groups in independent strike and support committees—Lip in 1973, soldiers' committees in 1975, the Gironde union in 1976. By 1977 the central had isolated these groups while support for independent strike committees within the radical federations waned.

Through unity of action with the CGT, the CFDT was drawn into general strikes. Moderates expressed reservations about "centralized" action, insisting on the need to prepare it with local initiatives and bickering over the timing and themes of demonstrations. They counterposed the Italian practice of "articulated" action arising from plants and spreading to region, branch, and nation. Articulated action was an ideal that no central could program in advance. Implicit in the CFDT position was a traditional distrust of politics, a desire to avoid commitment to the Common Program, and fear of losing its identity. Even during the height of unity CGT federations complained about the absence of CFDT unions from mutually agreed national strikes and action.

With *recentrage,* the CFDT resolved to resist CGT entreaties for general strikes. The new approach was to articulate action with negotiations at the appropriate level—plant, region, branch, or nation. While radicals and public sector federations continued to argue for national action, others reduced their level of activity. The CFDT refused interindustrial action at the end of 1978 and during the steel crisis of 1979 when it condemned the demonstration in Paris as the "march of the cantonals," designed to enhance Communist prospects in local elections. In September 1979 the CGT renewed unity of action on a local basis around the CFDT's priority demands, but results were disappointing. The CFDT conceded its inability to mobilize around issues of substandard wages, working hours and conditions, and Maire spoke of a crisis of syndicalism. Even radicals were caught up in the mood of resignation and inactivity caused by divisions in the left, rising unemployment and aggressive union-busting. They pulled out of occupations and struggles to save plants and employment and condemned the CGT campaign to save Manufrance—an old gun and bicycle manufacturer—as a political gimmick.

The CFDT campaign against the CGT over Afghanistan precipitated the rupture. In June 1980 the CGT condemned *recentrage* as a capitulation to the forces of capitalism and imperialism and asked its federation to refuse concerted action on the national level. Joint action, it concluded, had not prevented *recentrage*, but only served to blur distinctions between the centrals. Contrary to expectations, the 1981 victory did nothing to bring together rival centrals, to reconcile differences, or restore confidence to workers still immobilized by the split in the French left.

CGT: Union of Workers' Control?

During the 1970s as the CFDT turned toward moderation along with the PS, the CGT appropriated its role as the union of worker control. In the 1950s the CGT had conducted fierce battles at the shop level over working conditions and employment. From 1968 to 1974 the CFDT assumed this role while the CGT, fearful of extremists, accused it of dividing the working class and helping the government. When the PS and CFDT turned to the right in 1974, the CGT radicalized its approach. During the 1974 presidential campaign it discovered its own Lip with the occupation to save Râteau, a turbine manufacturer in a Parisian suburb. With Râteau, the CGT shifted its attention from defending jobs to preventing the destruction of industrial capacity, including plant and equipment, that was occurring under the new international division of labor. By 1975 the occupation of plants to save jobs and equipment became common-place. Having placed hopes in the Common Program to arrest industrial decline, after its defeat the CGT began to elaborate industrial propositions for the preservation and modernization of plants threatened with closure.

These propositions linked the preservation of industrial capacity to the modernization of technology and improvement of working conditions. Metal called upon steel unions to suggest ways in which new technologies could be used to eliminate painful and dangerous jobs, reduce working hours and integrate production into downstream industries. Aimed at preserving the steel industry at a high level of capacity, the CGT steel plan challenged the cutbacks directed by the Common Market and Giscard. It made no sense within the framework of existing economic policy but was consistent with the alternative economic strategy of the PCF.

During this period the party was itself adopting a *stratégie autoges-tionnaire* whereby structural reforms prefiguring those of socialism, such as were contained in the steel plan, could be attained by workers' struggles within a capitalist regime. This was precisely the kind of neo-syndicalist strategy, ignoring the importance of political power, that the PCF had previously condemned in the CFDT. In the absence of large-scale mobilization such a strategy could only result in the minimal job protection obtained by CFDT and FO in the July 1979 social convention on steel. Lacking credibility under Giscard, the CGT's strategy at least stood a better chance in the twilight zone—between socialism and capitalism—that emerged after May 1981. The Forty-first Congress in June 1982 endorsed the strategy of worker control, with the formation of shopfloor councils to discuss working conditions, production, and technology, the gradual elimination of all painful, repetitive, and dangerous jobs, and eventually all assembly-line work.

Conclusion

The study of French unionism since 1968 demonstrates how ideological goals were advanced through distinctive industrial practices. Ideology shaped all aspects of policy: the form, nature, and level of demands, willingness to compromise and ratify accords, frequency and type of industrial action, and employment policies. The Marxist-oriented CGT was the most comprehensive, maximalist, and uniform in the formulation and negotiation of demands, and the most activist and political in the use of industrial action. The reformist FO was the most sectoralist and wage-oriented, the most minimalist in the formulation and negotiation of demands and the least inclined to strike. Always stressing qualitative issues, the New Left CFDT shifted between the maximalism of the CGT and the minimalism of FO, depending on political alignments.

During the 1970s the policies of FO were most constant while those of the CFDT—with its radicalization in 1970 and *recentrage* since 1978—least, but the CGT also had shifted away from a focus on political change before 1978 toward local struggles and industrial propositions and from the maximalism of percentage increases to a more modulated bargaining position. Both the *recentrage* of the CFDT and the *stratégie autogestionnaire* of the CGT represented adjustments to the deepening economic crisis, but they were rather belated ones precipitated by a major political event—the split in the French Left. The election of Mitterrand did little to alter previous trends and differences. Industrial policy and practice continued to reflect the ideological division of the French left.

Notes: Chapter 15

1   The federations were chosen to represent a broad spectrum of the workforce—primary, secondary, and tertiary; white-collar and blue-collar; public and private sectors. Open-ended interviews were conducted on three occasions—in 1977, 1980, and 1981 with officials from eight federations each of the CGT, FO, and CFDT. The interviews were supplemented with research in union publications, including federal bulletins, platforms, congress reports, flyers, and so on, for the years 1968–82. The narrative of events is largely drawn from *Le Monde* and *L'Humanité*. For reasons of economy, references are omitted. Readers are referred to other chapters in this volume and to the author's forthcoming book on trade unions and the left under the Fifth Republic. The author wishes to thank the ACLS for the initial fellowship to begin this study, the Auckland University Research Committee for a travel grant, René Mouriaux of CEVIPOF for his advice and assistance, and the trade unionists who accorded their precious time and cooperation.
2   Unless otherwise specified real increases are calculated in terms of the official index.

PART FIVE

The Trade Union Movement, Politics, and the State

16

Relations between the CGT and the CFDT: Politics and Mass Mobilization

MARTIN A. SCHAIN

Introduction

Throughout most of its history the French trade union movement has been sharply divided into competing confederations. Although the strength and support of the rival organizations has changed over the years, except for brief periods before and after World War II, the split of 1922 over the Russian revolution has never been bridged. Indeed, with the deconfessionalization of the Confédération Française des Travailleurs Chrétiens (CFTC) in 1964, the rivalry has become more intense, as the (new) Confédération Française Démocratique du Travail (CFDT) has chosen to compete directly with the CGT on the same ideological terrain, for the same working-class constituency. Interunion rivalry has become an integral part of French industrial relations. From the very basic level of the plant sections, to the industrial federations, to the interprofessional confederations, union organizations compete constantly for members, support, and control of mass action. Furthermore, competition is accentuated by the rules of the game in industrial relations, which give all of the representative organizations the right to negotiate and sign agreements at every level.

Rivalry, however, has weakened the effectiveness of all unions in collective negotiations, and appears to have reduced the attractiveness of unions to large numbers of workers. Thus continuous ideological dialogue among and within the organizations has reflected the intensity, and defined the grounds, of union competition. Ideological dialogue, however, has reinforced the intransigence of employers, and supported their reluctance to accept—in practice—the legitimacy of the unions in bargaining (Sudreau, 1975, p. 25). Furthermore, in the process of collective negotiations, union rivalry has left employers free to choose their negotiating partners, or to refuse to negotiate altogether.

The division of the trade union movement is also cited as a key factor in its inability to organize more than 20 percent of the workforce. While this is a complex question, there is some evidence that in so far as division is regarded as "political," it contributes to a lack of confidence in union organizations (Adam *et al.*, 1970, ch. 2). The reaction is strongest among workers who do not belong to unions, but is significant among unionized workers as well. Thus in a 1970 survey more than one-third of CGT members and almost half of CFDT members agreed that unions were "concerned too much with politics, and not enough with the defense of professional interests" (Adam *et al.*, 1970, p. 158). In another survey, conducted in 1977, 30 percent of the members of both confederations agreed that *their* unions placed "political preoccupations before the interests of the workers" (Louis Harris France, 1977, p. 14).

Thus it would appear that union rivalry is neither advantageous nor popular. It is supported, however, by the dynamics of organizational survival, and "union pluralism" is favored by a majority of members of both the CGT and the CFDT. Nevertheless, in an attempt to overcome at least some of the disadvantages inherent in the division of the trade union movement—to strengthen the ability of unions to bargain and to mobilize workers—the CGT and the CFDT succeeded in negotiating a series of national agreements on joint action and strategy after 1966. These agreements were difficult to reach, and even more difficult to sustain, but they endured through 1979. The agreements survived as long as each confederation was able to conclude that its organization and its most important goals were strengthened by the alliance, even if compromise was necessary. The alliance proved impossible to sustain when both confederations concluded that their organizational survival was being eroded at the base, even as the influence of their elites was being enhanced, and that their political objectives were not likely to be attained.

This argument, and this emphasis, however, is somewhat different from the more conventional argument that union relations are more or less a reflection of political party relations within the French left, and the evolution of the CGT–CFDT alliance was political in the sense that it manifested the needs of the parties rather than the union organizations themselves. It is the point of view of this article that the latter argument is unnecessarily simplistic, and fails to take into account the complex relationships among political parties and trade unions within the left.

Politics and Union Relations

Before 1968

The political evolution of party relations within the left have often been cited as the key to understanding relations between the CGT and the CFDT (Smith, 1981; and Moss in this volume). While this appears to be generally true, especially for the CGT, this emphasis tends to ignore some of the important conflicts between party and trade union strategies and concerns, as well as other dynamic forces in trade union life that have both motivated and undermined cooperation between the CGT and the CFDT.

The period between 1964 and 1968 was marked by both a rapprochement of the Communists and the Socialists on the political level, and increasing collaboration between the CGT and the CFDT on the union level. An important priority for the CGT in the negotiations for the "unity of action" pact of 1966 was the goal of the Parti Communiste Français (PCF) of a union of the forces of the left in support of a popular-front-type agreement:

> the union of all democratic forces, without exclusion in order to elaborate a *common program* in which demands of the working class must find a place ... [The unity] will permit us to go together towards a real democracy and the realization of an economic and social program. (*Le Monde*, 20 June 1964; Adam, 1967, p. 584)

However, collaboration with the CFDT on the basis of broad policy agreements "at the summit" also strengthened the role of the CGT as an independent political force, a role sometimes disputed by the PCF.

As early as 1957 the CGT had begun to revise its orientation toward other unions. By this time the confederation had dropped its emphasis on *unité d'action à la base*—that is, an attempt to mobilize workers belonging to other unions, and to undermine the influence of other union organizations through unity of action committees—and instead stressed agreements with other unions at all levels. Increasingly, in the late 1950s, the CGT sought goals and policy objectives that were at variance with both the objectives of the PCF at the time, and with the indirect role that the CGT was supposed to play in policy development.

Although the CGT continued to emphasize "action" goals, there were clear indications that it was edging toward linking strikes and demonstrations to broader policy. In 1957 the confederation called for nationalization of several industrial branches (two years before the PCF), and during the years of the Algerian War the CGT participated in joint anti-war actions with the CFTC, UNEF, and FEN. In one notable case the union was forced to withdraw its support after a demonstration was openly denounced by the PCF as "adventurist" and "dangerous" (Fejtö, 1966, p. 109; Mallet, 1963, p. 248). The tension between the more independent course being probed by the CGT and the attempts by the PCF to impose limitations probably reached a high point in May 1962, when Maurice Thorez accused the leadership of the CGT of promoting "inadequate and poorly thought out demands ... of seeking unity at any price ... and only at the summit ... [of] frequent violations of the rules of trade union and workers' democracy" (Fejtö, 1966, p. 139). After the death of Thorez in 1964, the CGT pursued its broader version of "trade union democracy" somewhat more easily.

Although the pact with the CFDT in 1966 was referred to as a program of common "action" in support of workers' strike demands, it also contained references to the extension of trade union rights, increased public investment in housing, education and health, as well as demands for guaranteed employment and tax reform (*Le Monde*, 22 January 1966).

Although one of the important goals of the CGT, going into the negotiations with the CFDT, was an agreement on a broad union of the left, this was dropped in favor of other goals that increased the institutional strength of the CGT.

For the CFDT, the agreement with the CGT also served political objectives, but not necessarily those of any of the political parties of the left. Summing up a discussion of "union practice and political objectives," in a research document published by the CFDT, Denis Segrestin stressed that the "historic role" of the CFDT has been "to link union practice directly to the stakes [involved] and to a *projet de société*, union action with a political dimension." In contrast with the CGT the action of local unions is "impregnated with the CFDT ideology and is related to the *projet de société* defined by the whole of the CFDT." Thus Segrestin argues the CFDT strives for a coherence as an independent political force (CFDT BRAEC, 1981b, p. 7).

In its pursuit of an alliance with the CGT during the early 1960s the CFDT (and before it the CFTC), sought to separate unity based on "political" (that is, party) objectives from unity based on agreements on "professional" (that is, job-related) interests. During this period, before 1968, the CFDT pursued its own political objectives, and supported a broad non-Communist left alliance. Nevertheless, in practice, the CFTC and the CFDT did participate in joint political action with the CGT.

By 1966, convinced that unity of the non-Communist left would be a long time coming, some leaders of the CFDT (notably Eugène Descamps, the secretary-general of the confederation), saw an alliance with the CGT as an effective means of by-passing political parties in defining a policy of the left. "Now, incapable of acting for political renovation—the Defferre experience and the [1965] presidential election testify to that—the CFDT, but also the FEN, are developing union action that has an evident political significance" (Adam, 1967, p. 582). That is, it was not the growing unity of the parties of the left that encouraged these leaders, but its failure.

Clearly, by political objectives, the leaders of the CFDT were referring to attempts by the CGT to draw them into a broad left alliance; political objectives for the leaders of the CGT (when they referred to the CFDT) meant the kind of independent political program involving coherence between action and objectives being developed by the CFDT. In their dialogue through the 1960s each confederation resisted the "politics" of the other, while pursuing the advantages of their alliance. The growing dialogue between the Communists and the Socialists after 1965, rather than supporting collaboration between the CGT and the CFDT, frequently became an issue of discord in itself.

For example, Georges Levard, the president of the CFDT resigned in 1967, citing as his reason the symbolic affirmation in the 1966 agreement that the Communists were politically acceptable:

I consider that the entire non-Communist left dishonors itself in affirming that the Communists have approached our conception of democracy in a decisive manner. I can no longer accept to cover up a policy that pretends to ignore this fact. (Lefranc, 1969, p. 195)

During the following year, as the Communist–Socialist dialogue became more intense (at least until May 1968), the CGT–CFDT relationship became more tense, in part because of the attempts of the CGT to draw the CFDT into contact with the PCF. The CFDT was not at all opposed, in principle, to a left alliance, but was most distrustful of the Communist overtures: "We are not in agreement with them," argued the new president of the CFDT, André Jeanson. "They are approaching democracy, but not enough" (Lefranc, 1969, p. 196). Therefore, it is not at all clear that during the period before 1968, the growing dialogue between the parties of the left contributed to the alliance between the CGT and the CFDT. It is somewhat more evident that the tensions produced by that dialogue contributed to the growing discord between the two organizations during the months before the events of 1968.

Nevertheless, for both the CGT and the CFDT there were real benefits in unity of action, but they were less political than organizational. For the CGT, the pact of 1966 ended its national and international isolation. With the support of the CFDT, representatives of the CGT were brought into negotiations with the CNPF, and (ultimately) into the institutions of the European community in Brussels (Adam, 1967, pp. 584–5). For the CFDT, the accord also served as a means of emergence from a different kind of isolation, the Catholic ghetto, and facilitated joint action with other union organizations (notably the FEN). It also strengthened the working-class image of the CFDT as well as the internal changes signified by the deconfessionalization of 1964. These organizational advantages were certainly much more obvious than the fluid political context for understanding both the agreement of the CGT and the CFDT in 1966, as well as the strength of the agreement before 1968.

The Post-1968 Period

The period from 1970 to 1979 was marked by an intense politicization of relations between the CGT and the CFDT, a politicization that was related to, and influenced by, the successes and failures of the Communist–Socialist alliance, but that had a life of its own. In the midst of the political chaos that defined Communist–Socialist relations during the years between June 1968 and June 1971 (the Socialist Congress of Epinay), relations between the CGT and the CFDT seemed far more stable. The 1966 agreement had broken down even before the massive strikes of 1968, and for more than a year after the "events," the confederations went their separate ways. However, the acceptance by the CFDT, at its 1970 Congress at Issy-les-Moulineaux, of the doctrine of class conflict, the condemnation by the congress of the capitalist system, and its advocacy of democratic socialism, set the stage for new negotiations with the CGT (Mouriaux, 1970, p. 1089). On 1 December 1970 the two confederations concluded a new accord on unity of action that, at least in its intentions, went beyond the agreement of 1966:

> This accord marks the movement from purely tactical unity of action to a strategic design that insists on the search for common objectives for the transformation of society. (Edmond Maire, 1973, in *Liaisons Sociales*, 1980, p. 147)

During a period when the parties of the left were barely on speaking terms, the unions of the left were speaking a great deal. Six months before the December 1970 Congress, CFDT leaders had initiated a long series of discussions with the CGT on common action and basic strategy. The discussions went on for two years (Maire, 1973, pp. 82–6). They were also attempting to coordinate their bargaining strategies and their strike action (*Le Monde*, 28 October 1971).

On the other hand, at roughly the same time that the reorganized Socialist Party and the PCF were drawing closer to an agreement on a common program for government, relations between the CGT and the CFDT were deteriorating, largely over relations with *gauchiste* militants in the plants, a conflict that accentuated the basic competition between the two organizations over the new political forces that had emerged during the 1968 events, but over party commitments as well (*Le Monde*, 9 March, 11 May 1972). The CGT was fully committed to the Common Program, while the CFDT chose to emphasize its own version of *socialisme autogestionnaire*.

Moreover, after 1970, the CFDT had its own political agenda for the left, as well as for the trade union movement, and it was in this context that it understood relations with the CGT. If, in the early period, the main objective of the CFDT, in pursuing unity of action, was a reinforcement of both its organization and its working-class credentials, after 1970, its objectives became more frankly political, to influence the evolution of the CGT, and in this way the entire French trade union movement. As Edmond Maire summarized this position in 1980:

> Our aim is an evolution of the entire French trade union movement, in all of its component [parts] ... In 1974, we formulated a great strategic ambition for the union movement, resting on the development of an autonomous approach of the whole of the union movement, at least of the CFDT and the CGT. (*CFDT Aujourd'hui*, no. 46, November–December 1980, p. 8)

In the years after 1970 the CFDT had become an increasingly powerful component of the labor movement, and a more explicit spokesman for socialist change. Frankly committed to a political program, the CFDT sought dialogue with the CGT, not simply to work out a program for union action but to develop a program that would link action to political change. Indeed the great ambition of the CFDT was to draw the CGT away from the Communist Party, and into an independent force of the left (CFDT BRAEC, 1981b, pp. 49–51). Therefore, political differences between the two confederations, and the conflicts and polemics engendered by these differences, were influenced not only by the evolving relationship between the parties of the left but also by the way that the two organizations approached politics.

After the presidential elections of 1974, the parties of the left went through a period of reorganization and reassessment, marked by sharp accusations and polemics through the fall of 1975 (Johnson, 1981, pp. 171–4). The party tensions were reflected in stronger attacks by the CGT against the CFDT. Nevertheless, in June 1974, the two confederations signed a new accord that was meant to "reinforce the *dynamique unitaire* ... in the new situation created by the advance of the united left." The agreement was fairly wide-ranging, once again identifying a number of common objectives, as well as methods of action and "common principles for the participation of the workers in decisions on action." The document was certainly a political agreement in the CFDT sense of an autonomous platform for common commitments. Indeed it served as a basis for the common attack of the two confederations on the *Plan Chirac* and the *Plan Barre* through the spring of 1977.

The Breakdown of the Alliance

For over a decade the CGT and the CFDT had struggled to find some common ground upon which they could build cooperation and augment their effectiveness. In the process the CFDT had clearly moved to the left, while the CGT had moved toward supporting political objectives that were autonomous, if not divergent, from the Communist Party. The process ground to a halt just prior to the 1978 National Assembly elections, primarily because the "strategic ambition" of the CFDT changed, a change partly related to the breakdown of the Common Program alliance of the Communist and Socialist parties in September 1977:

> Never had the two organizations appeared closer, since the CGT no longer hesitated to declare itself *autogestionnaire*. Now the CFDT blocked the dialogue with the CGT on January 11, 1978: the accord being prepared would not be a union agreement, but, in reality, support for the orientation of the PCF. (Mouriaux, 1982, p. 118; *Le Monde,* 13 September 1980)

If unity among the parties of the left had raised questions about party–CGT links for the leadership of the CFDT, the breakdown of that unity presented that problem in even stronger terms.

After the failure of the elections of 1978, the CGT neither abandoned its commitment to an alliance with the CFDT, nor did it move closer to the Communist Party. For the CGT, at least initially, the lack of party unity did not preclude a trade union alliance. During the months after the 1978 elections, when the PCF–Parti Socialiste (PS) split was becoming increasingly bitter, and when the PCF was slowly isolating the dissidents in its ranks, the CGT moved in a different direction.

A month after the elections, Georges Séguy attended the Congress of the (Communist) World Federation of Trade Unions, and launched a series of attacks against the organization, as well as the East European delegates, from the podium of the congress hall in Prague. He accused the WFTU of avoiding objective and critical discussion of the situation of unions in Eastern Europe, and he expressed the hope that the international organization would be able to deal with "pseudo-union organizations in countries where dictatorship rages" (*Humanité,* 18 April 1978). Séguy strongly defended the right to strike ("The superiority of socialism ... cannot reside in the interdiction of the right to strike") even in socialist countries and, finally, withdrew the CGT candidate from the position of secretary-general (*Humanité,* 28 April 1978). At the same time, in both Paris and Prague, representatives of the CGT (together with other union representatives in Paris) were meeting with dissident trade unionists from throughout Eastern Europe (*Le Monde,* 20 April 1978).

In the same spirit the Fortieth Congress of the CGT, and the discussion leading up to the Congress, was marked by an unprecedented critical openness (as well as by invitations to other confederations to attend the congress). Séguy argued (in an autocritique) that indeed the CGT had played too prominent a role in the electoral campaign, and "had distanced itself from the daily preoccupations of the workers" (Johnson, 1981, pp. 245–7; *Le Monde,* 28 November 1978). Thus distancing the confederation from the political preoccupations and connections with the PCF of the electoral period, Séguy asked:

> Basically, the debate has posed to the congress an important question: "How to consolidate unity of action and preserve it from the disturbances of the political environment? How to elevate it to the level of the needs of the hour ...?" (*Le Peuple*, 1–31 December 1978)

The solution, argued Séguy, was a national committee of unity-of-action, in which all of the major confederations would be represented, would exchange views, and would act in concert. The CGT overture, however, led neither to a national committee, nor to a general agreement during the next year, as it might have before 1978, principally (though not entirely) because of the political reorientation of the CFDT.

The CFDT had drawn conclusions about the period 1974–7 that were similar to those of the CGT. The CFDT had been too oriented toward political action, had been too often led "to stake all on political change," and had neglected social mobilization which, in the end, was the principal cause of the failure of the left. Where the CFDT parted company with the CGT was in its analysis of the importance of their alliance. Even before the elections, in January 1978, a working report written by Jacques Moreau on "the general situation and strike activity," had been highly critical of national and centralized cooperation with the CGT that, Moreau argued, had served to demobilize, rather than mobilize, workers (*Le Monde dossiers et documents*, no. 78, February 1981). In April the CFDT national council approved a *recentrage de l'action,* a reemphasis on linking strikes and demonstrations with negotiations at different levels of decision-making, "a search for results, even partial, which would give confidence to the workers once again" (*Liaisons Sociales*, 1980, p. 58). Thus in refusing to join with the CGT in a national day of protest against increases in social security payments Edmond Maire commented: "the solution for problems of workers' demands is not the repetition of grand demonstrations without end, that aim above all to accumulate discontent for future elections, without bringing any real solutions for precise problems" (*Liaisons Sociales*, 1980, p. 50). This theme was repeated, with greater force, a year later at the CFDT Congress in May 1979: "If we want to make of social struggles the motor of all change, then negotiation is the best way to transform conflicts and social mobilization into results" (*Liaisons Sociales*, 1980, p. 51).

The *recentrage* of the CFDT clearly reflected two disappointments: the shock of the electoral loss of 1978, and a disappointment with the strategy of forming an independent union front with the CGT. The leaders of the CFDT had not given up the alliance with the CGT (indeed the new orientation was strongly criticized at the Congress of May 1979), but they had clearly decided to give it lower priority. They also decided (not surprisingly) that a left political majority would not be possible in the foreseeable future. Thus in criticizing the "electoral strategy" of the PS in 1979 Edmond Maire noted: "because of the breakup of the left, because of the choice of the Communist Party to weaken the P.S. before envisioning again the conquest of [government] power, it is difficult to believe that electoral logic can suffice to give a majority to the left" (*Maintenant*, 2 April 1979).

The break between the CGT and the CFDT began to solidify during 1979, as the CFDT flirted with closer cooperation with the government, and the CGT was drawn closer to the PCF. In August, in the midst of delicate negotiations with the CFDT, both the CGT and the PCF announced at the same time that they would lead a great mass movement against unemployment in September. However, the CGT leaders had failed to communicate these plans to their counterparts in the CFDT when they had met only two days before (Johnson, 1981, p. 274). In some ways the political break between the CGT and the CFDT was deeper than that between the PCF and the PS. In March the two parties joined with the CGT and other unions in a march in Paris to support the steelworkers. The CFDT declined to participate, however, and accused the Socialists of favoring the strategic themes of the CGT, of having a peculiar fascination with the Communists, and of trying to assert a Leninist hegemony of party over union (*Maintenant*, 2 April 1979; Johnson, 1981, p. 268).

Under these circumstances it was somewhat surprising when the two confederations reached a tentative accord on 17 September 1979 to support joint demonstrations and strike action that would favor low-salaried workers and unemployed workers' rights. The agreement was even more surprising because just a few days before, negotiations between the Socialists and the Communists had broken down. The agreement proved to have been stillborn, however, since during the months that followed, the confederations were unable to agree on ways of implementing it. The tensions of how to implement the September accord were augmented by conflict over the Soviet invasion of Afghanistan, and—during the following year—by disagreements on policy over Poland. In September 1980 Edmond Maire denounced the CGT as having entered a long *anti-unitaire* period, and of being totally controlled by the Communist Party—"a complete alignment on the policy of sectarian isolationism and the ideological hardening of the PCF" (*Le Monde,* 5 September 1980). Séguy responded that "unity of action has become impossible at the confederal level" (*Le Monde,* 6 September 1980). Before the summer, a CGT report on unity of action had accused the CFDT—as well as other unions—of "using ... union activity for administering the crisis for the greatest profit of the bosses," an accusation that was cited frequently by the CFDT as the final, unacceptable bottom line (*Le Monde,* 8 June 1980).

In denouncing the CGT in sharp political terms the CFDT had also accepted the failure of its own political strategy of the 1970s; by writing the CFDT out of the socialist community the CGT had, in the end, aligned itself with the PCF line that marked the end of a long attempt to develop a united left bloc. For each of the confederations the long conflictual dialogue of unity of action had had a dynamic of its own that was related to, but not always dominated by, the fate of collaboration of the left at the party level. The long-range objectives of the two confederations had always been different, but the special meaning of the breakup of unity of action in 1979–80 appeared to be the abandonment of these long-range goals.

Moreover, the relationship between the confederations appears to have been influenced little by the electoral victory of the left in May 1981. Certainly neither the CGT nor CFDT had seriously expected a Mitterrand victory, and their long-range plans presumed his defeat (Roy, 1981). The hasty Communist–Socialist rapprochement, the entrance of PCF ministers into government, and even attempts by the government to encourage increased union collaboration, however, have resulted in no important change in the position of either confederation (*Nouvel Observateur,* 17 April 1982).

The CFDT activity report, in preparation for its May 1982 Congress, emphasized that any alliance in the future must be built on a basis of "precise and concrete objectives," and no longer on "vast common platforms. In this way partners in collaboration will no longer be predetermined in the name of prior conditions and objectives" (*Syndicalisme,* December 1981, p. 35). Edmond Maire's report to the Congress reacted to the pressure of the government by stressing: "Unity of action must not take place because the parties of the left need it or to create an illusion at the time of Mayday; united union action must be deployed in full autonomy in order to place social struggles in the heart of change" (CFDT, 1982a, p. 23).

In the same spirit, Henri Krasucki, in his report for the Confederal

Bureau for the June 1982 Congress simply noted that while the alliance is more necessary than ever, the CFDT has reaffirmed its previous positions of "recentrage." Although the CGT will participate in a forthcoming meeting with the CFDT, "in order to clarify things as far as possible," the CGT is "for unity of action with all of the representative unions of the workers" (*Le Monde,* 15 June 1982).

Thus it would appear that the breakdown of 1979–80 has been reaffirmed, and that there is little possibility of the kind of understandings and united action that characterized relations between the two confederations between 1966 and 1977. As we have seen, political and strategic considerations have been important in determining the evolution of relations of the CGT and the CFDT through the years. However, we would argue that political and strategic considerations provide us with an insufficient understanding of the dynamics that have undermined solidarity between the two largest unions in France. Specifically, the final break after the 1978 elections, and the surprising lack of impact of the left victory in 1981 on union solidarity cannot be understood without reference to some of the more enduring problems of the French trade union movement, particularly problems of membership, mobilization, and control over mass action.

Union Cooperation and Mobilization

Despite the vehemence of their rhetoric, the CGT and the CFDT have always agreed more easily on the bargaining goals that they should pursue than on how and when to mobilize workers, and how to link mobilization to bargaining and political goals. In the French environment of weak unions, conflict over goals is perhaps less important than conflict over mobilization, because the latter touches on the power and even the survival of a union organization.

The core problem of the French trade union movement is the difficulty unions have in maintaining a stable membership and in maintaining control over the strike weapon:

The difficulties of union action in a worker environment cannot be seen in their quest to be officially recognized, which they won through long national struggles, but in their contact with the base, where the rate of unionization is quite weak, and, in addition, is marked by a strong current of instability. (Sainsaulieu, 1970, p. 1070)

Unstable rates of unionization reduce the authority of union representatives in the bargaining process, and contribute to the uncertainty of the strike process. Indeed, in France, there is a tendency to see the strike as a process with its own momentum and its own independent force, linked to an unpredictable "social climate," rather than as an organizational weapon (Schain, 1980; and Segrestin in this volume).

In effect, every initiative that a union takes in calling, as well as preventing, a strike becomes a test of its power to mobilize, which in turn becomes a key factor in subsequent bargaining with employers or the state. Orders at the national or regional levels for strikes or demonstrations by the confederations or federations are generally intended to be a show of strength at a particular moment, or an exercise to encourage, or to show solidarity with, "struggles in progress." Therefore, national mobilization in France is fundamentally different from similar action in most other industrialized countries. It indicates neither the breakdown of bargaining, nor is it a test of strength, through which bargaining is continued through other means. It usually serves as a precondition for any serious bargaining. Local or plant-level strikes provide opportunities from which advantages can be extracted at many levels, but there is generally little direct connection between strike action and collective agreements. Generally less than 1 percent of the strikes each year are directly related to collective agreements.

In this environment unity-of-action has always been marked by the uncertainties and problems of mass mobilization. A key problem for the CGT and the CFDT has always been how to link agreed-upon objectives to mobilization. A continuing conflict over the years has been whether objectives should be used as mobilizing tools, or whether mobilization based on a wide variety of demands should (indeed could) then be channeled to support agreed-upon objectives.

At the core of every accord between the two confederations has been an agreement on coordinated mobilization that both organizations have calculated would strengthen them individually and collectively—that would enable them to deal more effectively with the problem of control over mobilization. "When an organization is too weak to act alone, engagement in action, and the means to make it effective, supposes a policy of alliances with partners in accord with the essential ends sought" (CFTC, 1964, p. 65). So argued the "new" CFDT in 1964. Complaining that "Since 1960, they [employers and the state] negotiate less and less," Gilbert Declerq concluded that the 1966 agreement with the CGT would encourage mass action (that is, local strikes) with which to challenge this obstinate resistance to bargaining (*Nouvel Observateur*, 19 January 1966). For two years prior to the 1966 accord, CGT—at the confederal level, but especially at the federal level in the public services—actively sought to coordinate its objectives with the CFDT. In fact, in the autumn of 1964, both confederations had set up liaison committees to coordinate the strikes of their federations in the public services; at the same time the metals federations had reached an agreement on the priority of strike demands (with FO joining in) (*Le Monde*, 12 January 1966, 9 February 1966). Therefore, by 1966 joint strike declarations by CGT and CFDT unions had become commonplace, with the emphasis on stimulating and channeling strike activity toward agreed-upon objectives at every level.

The agreement in 1970 presumed that "a high level of combativity" would serve as a firm base from which both greater organizational unity and more effective bargaining could be built. In an attempt to overcome important differences on how workers could be mobilized the accord supported initiatives at all levels. If the CGT favored national demonstrations, and the CFDT was more inclined to accentuate "specific actions, decided by the workers themselves," they agreed that the bargaining objectives that they were seeking "can be gained only through action taken by the *syndicats,* as well as by the federations, department unions and the confederations themselves" (joint statement cited in Echevin, 1970, pp. 1120–1).

If there were doubts about the agreement, they were less about the objectives being sought than process—about the possibility that bargaining would outrun mobilization. For example, a key criticism came from J. Moreau, then of the chemical workers' federation of the CFDT:

> Now we think that today, if we want to take the lead on "qualitative" problems, this kind of bargaining can only be imposed to the extent that there is mobilization. And mobilization can only be organized on the basis of the problems closest to the workers. To say that we are going to act on working conditions means nothing. (Nassé *et al.,* 1970, p. 1055)

The last important agreement on unity of action between the two confederations in 1974 was marked by a concern not only to stimulate action at every level but to reinforce control over mass action through direct contacts between CGT and CFDT unions, and through the establishment of "common principles for the participation of workers in decisions on action" (*Liaisons Sociales,* 1980, p. 47).

Despite their divergent political strategies, what consistently drew the two confederations together from the early 1960s until 1977 were the uncertainties of control over mobilization, as well as the benefits of a common bargaining front. They presumed that in both areas they were more powerful united than separated. While they were generally able to agree on bargaining objectives, however, the uncertainties of mobilization constantly presented problems for how they would engage in action. First, the success of joint strike orders was always uncertain. Secondly, the uncertainties of mobilization frequently generated conflict among militants of the two organizations at the plant level. In both confederations militants argued that the identity of the two organizations was being brought into question by unity of action. Indeed the closer the agreement on objectives, the more important the problem of identity.

Mass mobilization is a delicate process, not easily controlled by union organizations, even when they are united in purpose and in strategy. For example, the agreement of 1966 was followed by a series of brief national strike calls that were, in general, strongly supported. Therefore, both confederations were confident that their "invitation" to increase strike activity in the fall of 1966 would be followed, but the strike level declined. In 1967 the confederations supported national demonstrations in the public sector, but strikes increased dramatically in the private sector instead, for which the unions claimed that their national action had provided the necessary spark. A close examination of strike activity in the private sector, however, does not support this claim (Schain, 1980, p. 200; *Le Monde,* 28 April 1967).

Throughout the period from 1970 to 1977, when unity of action pacts were in force, they constantly broke down in conflicts over how to deal with strike activity and mass mobilization. The 1970 pact collapsed in the spring of 1972 over the decisions by the CFDT to support "adventurist" actions by poorly organized workers. "What is striking ... is the support that [these workers] are given by the unions of the CFDT, always available to support a movement from the base, and less inclined than the CGT to question relations of force or the political impact of the strike" (*Le Monde,* 10 May 1972). The 1974 agreement collapsed slowly, but for similar reasons. The Moreau report, presented to the CFDT leadership in January 1978 stressed that, in practice, action taken together with the CGT has in fact been demobilizing, "insufficient," and even "dangerous" in the sense that such actions do not favor a "mobilization of a majority of the workers" (*Le Monde dossiers et documents,* no. 78, February 1981).

During the next year the problems of mobilization emerged in a more obvious way as a key impediment to the reestablishment of union agreement. Both confederations tended to place great emphasis on the difficulties that their militants were facing at the plant level. These kinds of conflict between the CGT and the CFDT were not new, but the emphasis given to them by each organization was indeed new (*Syndicalisme,* no. 1283, March 1970, p. 100; Maire, 1973, p. 63). Initially the failure of the September 1979 accord was explained in terms of conflicts among militants (*Le Monde,* 2 October 1979, 31 January 1980). Only later did the political rhetoric about "class collaboration" on the one hand, and "party domination" on the other become more prominent. It appears that the final attempt to develop unity of action had failed to generate mass mobilization, and had also failed to overcome the competitive forces among the militants.

There is evidence that agreements between the CGT and the CFDT have always been a difficult problem for militants in the poorly organized union environment of France, where militants are always bidding for the membership and support of a fluid constituency. Thus while we often think of trade union confederations (especially the CGT and the CFDT) as organizing different working-class subcultures, the overlap is considerable, and there is movement of members and supporters between confederations. About a third of the members of the CFDT (compared with a tenth of the members of the CGT) consider themselves to be "Catholics," and 33 percent of CFDT members (compared with 17 percent of CGT members) identify themselves as politically center or right (Louis Harris France, 1977, pp. 5, 8). Nevertheless, in 1970 25 percent of the members of the CFDT once belonged to the CGT (there was not much movement the other way) (Adam *et al.,* 1970, p. 137).

As the two confederations have moved closer together in their commitments to class conflict and opposition to capitalism, agreement on objectives has become easier at the national level; but the task of

Table 16.1 *Attitude of CFDT Militants toward the CGT*

Relations (with the CGT) are:	National level (%)	Plant level (%)
Rather good	53	23
Rather strained	30	66
Sometimes good, sometimes strained	13	9
Don't know	4	2
% =	100	100
N =	47	47

Source: Smith, 1981, p. 51.

developing mass action by militants while maintaining the distinctiveness of their union position has become more difficult. Distinctiveness has been based less on broad programs and objectives as such, and more on strategy, style of action, and specific demands supported at the enterprise level. The confederations, far from imposing their ideological divisions on local activists who are inclined to cooperate on pragmatic grounds, appear to have imposed unity on their local units only with great difficulty, especially in the private sector. At times both confederations have openly complained about the lack of authority of the other (*Le Monde,* 6–7 April 1975, 2 October 1979). As one CFDT militant explained:

At the national level, the relations between the two unions do not correspond at all to the situation at the factory level. In the plants it's continuous, open warfare. And one has the impression that the union headquarters want to give an appearance of unity which is not at all felt by the base, nor even desired by the base. At the national level, the unity which seems to develop is much more political than a real desire. (Smith, 1981, p. 45)

Although CFDT militants interviewed by W. Rand Smith agreed (in 1977) that unity of action at the plant level was associated with higher levels of controlled mobilization, less employer resistance, greater organizational effectiveness and greater strike success, and although they felt that unity was strongly desired by the workers, they also felt that, in practice, unity was most difficult to achieve (in 1974) (Table 16.1). If competitive tensions at the plant level have always been a factor in the relationship between the CGT and the CFDT, this factor has been accentuated by a crisis of mobilization that began to emerge in the mid-1970s, and that by 1977–8 began to have a profound impact on the orientation of both organizations.

The "Crisis of Unionism" and Unity of Action

Since 1978 it has become commonplace to refer to a "crisis" in the French trade union movement. The core problem has been the emergence of secular trends of membership decline, a slowdown of organizational expansion and decline in the distribution of union journals and newspapers. In a larger sense the ability of unions to influence and control mobilization has been brought into question once again. All of this has happened during the same period that the trade union movement has become more institutionalized, and perhaps better protected than any other time in its history. Indeed the problem has been even further complicated by the victory of the left in May 1981, a victory which has given union leaders substantial access to political decision-making and has weakened the political and bargaining position of French employers (Adam, 1981; *Témoignage Chrétien,* 29 June 1981; *Quotidien de Paris,* 11 March 1982). Although it can be argued that these trends are temporary setbacks, related to the *conjoncture,* there are also structural changes that are developing in the workforce that will continue to affect the ability of unions to organize and to control events.

Since 1975 the CGT has been losing membership steadily. In six years the confederation has lost 20 percent of its members according to official figures, and 35 percent according to unofficial figures. For the first time since the mid-1960s the CGT admits to fewer than 2 million members (Kergoat, 1982b; *Le Peuple,* 24 April 1982, p. 120). Similarly since 1976 the claimed membership of the CFDT has declined by 11 percent, losses that are more or less confirmed in unofficial estimates (*Syndicalisme,* 4 February 1982; Landier, 1981).

During the late 1970s both confederations reacted to the membership decline. Beginning in February 1976 the CGT announced a general membership drive—"a battle of recruitment"—and emphasized recruitment among young workers in large enterprises. By the end of 1978 the confederation confirmed that more than a million new members had joined, but "despite the important number of new adhesions, the membership of the CGT remains practically stable." Although they claimed to have recruited more than 250,000 new members each year after 1973, they were losing at least that number each year (*Liaisons Sociales,* 1980, p. 11). "We can conclude that the CGT is an *organisation passoire,*" contended one CGT report ("La politique financière de la CGT," *Le Peuple,* 16–30 June 1979). Similarly in 1979 the CFDT noted an "alarming evolution" of its membership—a "rotation" of 20–25 percent of its membership each year. The confederation had become a "leaky bathtub": "Until these last few years, the leaky bathtub did not empty because the faucet remained open. Today, the bathtub is still leaky, but the faucet is closed" (*Liaisons Sociales,* 1980, p. 52).

Both unions referred to the rise in unemployment as the cause (but not the only cause) of the growing problem. However, this presumed relationship may be exaggerated. True, there has been a decline of union presence (plant sections) in plants with more than 300 workers since 1976 (although in smaller plants union presence continued to grow)(*Liaisons Sociales,* 1980, p. 190). However, a detailed study, based on information supplied by the CGT in its internal publication, *Courrier Confédéral,* shows that, while in some regions there has been a membership loss that corresponds to rising unemployment, in many departments where unemployment has risen there is no corresponding decline in membership; while in still others (such as the Paris region) membership losses have been far higher than the rise in unemployment (Kergoat, 1982b, p. 17).

In addition to the membership decline, there are other signs of malaise in the union movement. Support for the CGT and the CFDT remains high, but it has not increased significantly in recent years and, by some measures, it seems to be eroding. According to results released by the Ministry of Labor, for example, the "big five" national unions (CGT, CFDT, FO, CFTC, and CGC) obtained 82 percent of the vote for factory councils in 1966–7; in 1976–7 support declined to 77 percent; the remainder of the vote went to smaller (often company) unions, and (increasingly) to nonunion candidates. The slow, if steady, decline in the share of support for the major confederations, moreover, is not evenly distributed. The CGC and CFDT have maintained their share, and CFTC and FO have gained slightly. The share of support for the CGT, however, has declined steadily from about 49 percent of the total in 1966–7 to about 37 percent in 1978–9 (Mouriaux, 1982, annex 3). The CGT disputes these figures, but not the trend.

Another aspect of the weakness of support for the trade union movement is indicated by a survey conducted for the CFDT in 1981. Only a bare majority of young workers, according to the survey, expressed support for any trade union at all, far fewer than their adult counterparts, while 49 percent expressed various forms of "distance" from unions:

It is young workers, who benefit the least from collective guarantees, who indicate most often their distance from the trade union movement ... the trainees and apprentices (64%), the temporaries and intermediaries (58%), the workers in establishments with fewer than 50 workers (55%). They are also the most disfavored: unskilled and assembly line workers (52%), workers earning less than 3,000 Fr. [per month] (53%). (CFDT BRAEC, 1981a, p. 56)

Another troubling aspect of the report is that adults most firmly *reject* the unions. While 23 percent of the young workers specifically reject any trade union, the figure is as high as 41 percent for the adults in private industry. Only "disappointment after experiences with failure can explain this difference," contends the CFDT report.

Finally, although the CGT, and especially the CFDT, have often claimed to have a special appeal for young workers, this claim is not supported by the 1981 survey. Both unions are supported by higher percentages of adults than young workers. Moreover, young workers expressed greater confidence in FO than in the CFDT. While none of this is completely new—the results of a worker survey in 1970 show similar patterns—the results were most disappointing after a decade of a massive expansion of union presence (Adam *et al.*, 1970, p. 146).

From 1970 to 1977 the number of plants in which union sections were present more than doubled, but the unions were not able to translate this extensive expansion into intensive increases in membership. During these years the CGT increased its plant sections by 250 percent (from 5,245 to 13,275), while its membership remained virtually stagnant and began to drop after 1977. During this same period, support for the CGT in plant elections fell steadily. Therefore, in a sense, the crisis of membership and support is worse than it appears, since it has emerged during a period when union presence has been more widespread and better protected. Indeed the expansion of union presence may well have masked a long-term decline in the effective membership of union organizations at the plant level. While the number of plant sections of the CGT tripled from 1970 to 1977 (some plants have more than one union section), the membership per section declined by about two-thirds (from 445 per section to 176 per section), steadily declining each year (*Liaisons Sociales,* 1980, p. 190).

Reinforcing the problems that unions are confronting are the important changes in the workforce that eat into traditional trade union sources of strength. Industries in which unions have been traditionally strong— steel, ship construction, textiles, chemicals—are all in the process of being restructured. At the same time the laborforce continues to change, as the proportion of clerical workers, women, and immigrant workers has become more important. In addition, the role of the so-called *marché periphérique d'emploi* (temporary workers) and the underground economy has also grown. All of these structural changes in the laborforce have further weakened areas of union strength, and have posed greater challenges for recruitment and mobilization.

Historically the French trade union movement has gained members as it has become more institutionalized. Thus during three periods—after World War I, during the initial phases of the Popular Front, and during the period just after World War II—membership in the union movement grew as organizations gained influence and access to governmental decision-making and strength in the bargaining process. Membership began to decline (in 1920, 1937, and 1947) as the hopes raised by union power began to fade (Prost, 1964, p. 196; Lefranc, 1950, p. 52).

During the last decade neither greater protection for union presence, nor access to government decision-making and the corresponding political weakening of the influence of French employers, have strengthened the ability of unions to mobilize workers. For the moment what Gérard Adam has argued appears to be true:

> I do not use the word "crisis." It seems to me that we must speak of a change in the mode of influence of the trade unions. The unions are perhaps losing members, but they are gaining in influence, even if it is a sort of influence that is more diffuse. (Adam, 1981a)

However, the unions seem aware that the real problem is the gap between growing (diffuse) influence and declining support, since the effectiveness of the former is related to the growth of the latter in the long run.

Therefore, both the CGT and the CFDT have turned inward, and have given increased attention to the arguments and needs of the militants. Both confederations have concluded that their alliance has become a threat to their identity at the plant level, and that organizational strength at the plant level is hindered, rather than aided, by the kind of cooperation that they engaged in between 1966 and 1977.

For the CGT, this threat was expressed periodically after 1968, when they were challenged from the left by the CFDT, and more strongly at their Congress of 1975 and after (CFDT BRAEC, 1981b, pp. 40–2). A sharper criticism of the alliance with the CFDT, however, appeared during the months leading up to the Forty-first Congress in 1982, when the CGT identified its most important membership losses with a loss of identity encouraged by union cooperation. Workers turned from the CGT when they could no longer see its specificity as an organization of "class and mass."

> It is only when it spoke once again [argued the CGT] in its own language, when it was able to demarcate itself clearly from unions who were seeking social consensus, that the CGT was able to find once again its audience and reverse the decline of its members. (Kergoat, 1982b)

The orientation document for the 1982 Congress stresses that "union pluralism is an established fact, but not an ideal for the CGT ... The CGT intends to work for ...: one working class, one union confronting the only employers' organization." Moreover, "a decisive condition" for unity is the reinforcement of the CGT: "its action, the diffusion of its ideas, the reinforcement of its membership and organizations, the growth of its influence." Only by mobilizing workers itself can the CGT "lead the CFDT and the other union organizations to adopt positions and new behavior favoring unity of action" ("Projet du documentation d'orientation," *Le Peuple,* 16–28 February 1982, pp. 40–2).

Similarly the CFDT, by 1978, had begun to see cooperation with the CGT as a danger to its identity and its organizational strength. The Moreau report, which was linked to the *recentrage* of 1978–9, specifically related the alliance with the CGT to the decline of influence of the CFDT. Less categoric than the CGT, the CFDT, in 1982, viewed the importance of cooperation in a similar way. "It is our ... action that carries the *dimension unitaire.* For we seek to unify the workers through action and for the transformation of society," argued Edmond Maire at the CFDT 1982 Congress. In responding to criticism that the alliance with the CGT was necessary for mobilizing workers, Maire answered that the capacity of the CFDT should not be underestimated, that "it is by being itself, and by inspiring union action that corresponds to the desires of the greatest number of workers, that the CFDT can best lead its partners towards a more unitary attitude" (CFDT, 1982a, p. 26).

While denying that there is a "crisis" of unionism as such, both the CGT and the CFDT have reacted to the problem of mobilization by turning inward, and by rejecting their alliance as a priority. Certainly the breakdown of the alliance between the two confederations after 1978 was encouraged by the failure by each organization to attain the political objectives that it had set for itself after 1966, as well as by the tensions between the political parties of the left. However, we have argued here that the breakdown has been, primarily, a reaction to their organizational weakness, a shift of emphasis from organizational cooperation to competitive efforts at the plant level in the name of organizational survival.

Thus, even now, when the parties of the left are governing, and the government has encouraged union cooperation, the organizational problem discourages the reestablishment of the old alliance. Whatever the success of the alliance in maximizing union influence in bargaining and political decision-making, it is now clearly perceived by both the CGT and the CFDT as having sapped their organizational ability to organize and mobilize workers.

17

From Economic Crisis to Victory of the Left: Workers' Reactions and Union Policies

JACQUES KERGOAT

The question of the links between, on the one hand, the working class and, on the other hand, the institutions which it has provided for itself and the leaders of those institutions is a subject of much controversy. Some observers believe that working-class institutions faithfully reflect the diversity of workers' aspirations. Others believe that only the true inner experience of the working class is worthy of interest: institutional apparatuses are completely alien to the class they claim to represent.

Neither view is entirely adequate, however. Admittedly nothing could be further from the truth than to regard the major unions and their strategies as faithful representatives of workers' concerns. The issue here is not merely that the leadership of the several unions is open to a wide variety of interpretations (bureaucratic, reformist, class collaborationist, Stalinist, corporatist, counterrevolutionary, and so on), thus allowing various interpretations of the unions' political programs as well. Rather the point is that the union leaderships have, as institutional entities within capitalist society, achieved some measure of autonomy with respect to pressure from the rank-and-file, even if union leaders as individuals did not consciously seek to bring about such a state of affairs. The union organizations themselves recognize that this autonomy exists: they justify it by the need to interpret the precise significance of what workers are doing. Yet experience shows that this interpretation is always shaped by certain assumptions peculiar to each union confederation, that is, by that confederation's political strategy.

Before proceeding with the argument, three remarks are in order. First, working-class organizations do not perfectly mirror the wishes of the working class, but at the same time there is no impenetrable barrier between one and the other. What the working class does (or what segments of the working class do) obviously has an influence on the attitudes of unions as well as their decisions and strategies, the *raison d'être* of the unions being to appear to represent the working class. If the distance between representatives and represented becomes too great, the workers may decide to seek new representatives. Short of this dire remedy, any (perceived) major discrepancy between the views of the workers and the positions of the unions injures the credibility of the unions *vis-à-vis* their interlocutors from other classes of society. Every labor organization, especially unions, must take account of what workers are doing. But it is wrong to think that one can analyze the behavior of workers in some "pure" form, independent of the strategies of labor organizations: the various union leaderships' political strategies influence the behavior of workers.

It is axiomatic—at least for a materialist approach to these problems—that the behavior of workers is in the first place determined by the concrete situation in which the working class finds itself, a situation understood in terms of wages, jobs, working conditions, and threats to basic freedoms that the working class has managed to win. Hence worker behavior is also shaped by the policies of business and government, compounded of varying proportions of unemployment, austerity, industrial restructuring, and repression. In the last instance, however, it is overall political conditions that overdetermine the behavior of workers, affecting not only the way they view their present situation but also their hopes and expectations for the future; in other words, their perception of the strategic situation.

The interaction of these three factors determines the behavior of the working class, the degree to which it organizes, and its level of militancy, as well as its level of consciousness (Kergoat, 1982a). During the period that extends from the beginning of the economic crisis to just after the May 1981 presidential elections we notice changes in each of the three factors in question, namely, union tactics, economic and social conditions, and the strategic situation or balance of power between the classes. The weight to be attached to each factor also changes with time. In this way we can describe three successive phases in the period 1974–82 distinguished by varying levels of militancy, organization, and working-class consciousness.

Worker Reactions to the Economic Crisis: Fall 1974 to Summer 1977

Two contradictory assumptions are commonly made about the effects of economic crisis on the behavior of workers. On the one hand, it is often thought that economic crisis "radicalizes" workers. On the other hand, it is frequently said that crisis mutes worker responses. Neither hypothesis is invariably true. In fact, the relationship between economic conditions and worker reactions is mediated by a number of specific variables (Kergoat, 1979–80). This conclusion emerges clearly from an analysis of working-class reactions in the period 1974–7.

Degree of Militancy

Taking the annual number of strike days as an index of the level of social conflict, we find a striking result: the figure for each year in the period 1974–7 exceeds the figures for every year since 1963, except of course

1968 (see Boyer above, Table 1.1). The rate of participation in strikes remained high (35 percent in 1974, 34·5 percent in 1975, 29·8 percent in 1976 as against 34 percent in 1973) and the average length of strikes increased (from 2·03 days in 1974 to 2·74 days in 1975 to 4·12 days in 1976, as against 1·72 days in 1973). Other indices yield the same results: for example, this was also a period of impressive mass demonstrations, especially that of 7 October 1976.

Looking beyond these overall statistics, we find that the picture varies considerably from industry to industry. It is immediately apparent that the degree of militancy is highest in the branches of industry most directly affected by the crisis. But the form taken by the social consequences of the economic crisis is not without effect. In some industries the increased number of layoffs places a damper on the militancy of workers: generally these are industries whose decline is not due solely to the 1974 crisis, such as textiles, leather goods, and printing, among others. In still other industries the crisis simply puts an end to worker militancy: these are generally relatively unstructured industries such as construction.

Looking at the problem from another angle, we find that the crisis particularly affected the militancy of female workers: women in fact resisted the attempt to drive them out of the labor market and showed a new determination to defend their right to work. Throughout the period in question there was a spate of long, bitter strikes led by women in companies with a majority of women among their employees. Looking at the figures industry by industry, it is clear that there is no correlation—despite persistent myths to the contrary—between the percentage of women employed and the reluctance to engage in industrial conflict. Indeed in one branch employing a high percentage of female workers, clothing, the onset of the crisis tripled the frequency of strikes.

By way of contrast, the crisis pointed up ambiguities in the behavior of young workers. The number of unemployed youths tripled. Many of these were not dismissed from jobs but faced difficulties finding initial employment. Youths in this situation cannot readily make use of the strike weapon or any other form of collective response, given the dispersal of the unemployed. Where youths did face layoffs, these occurred in situations that made mobilization difficult, often involving individual layoffs from very small, nonunionized firms. Union attempts to enlist young workers met with little success, moreover.[1] Not until all possibility of employment in a particular industry or region was exhausted—as in the case of the steel industry in Lorraine, for example—do we see an explosion of anger among young workers. Nevertheless, militant attitudes (toward supervisors, speedups, and so on) did persist.

Immigrant workers responded to the crisis in a variety of ways. Where the crisis had an impact on wages and working conditions but did not threaten jobs, the militancy of immigrant workers did not flag: this was true of Parisian sanitation workers and subway cleanup crews as well as throughout the service sector. By contrast, where jobs were jeopardized militancy did decline, as in the construction industry. Still, whatever "demoralization" there may have been was not lasting or profound.

Throughout the period worker militancy was evident in struggles waged outside the firm, as is shown by the long strike at Sonacotra (a government agency operating immigrant worker hostels).

The Level of Organization
Generally speaking, the crisis does not seem to have adversely affected the level of working-class organization, which remained stable or even increased. But the situation differs from labor unions and political parties.

Union membership increased only slightly, no more than $0 \cdot 5$ percent overall, with slight increases in CFDT and FO enrollment compensating for losses by the CGT. Party membership increased much more, rising 30 percent from 1974 to 1976, thanks largely to worker enrollment. The increase came exclusively from organizations participating in the *Programme Commun* and benefited mainly the Socialist Party. The extreme left stagnated, largely because of the decline of the PSU.[2] It is difficult to provide much detail about the new recruits; one noteworthy fact is an increase in the percentage of female workers joining unions.[3]

The Level of Consciousness
The bourgeoisie elaborated its own ideological response to the crisis in which two concerns were paramount. The first was to deny that the different classes of society have different interests. The division between classes was replaced by a division within the working class: "We're all in the same boat" and therefore the "well off," that is, in this case workers with job security should sacrifice to help the less fortunate. The second concern of the bourgeoisie was to promote resignation and passivity in the ranks of workers: the crisis, it was argued, depends on objective factors, such as oil prices over which no one has control and is therefore a matter of fate to which everyone must submit. In short, while capital in the abstract may bear some responsibility for the crisis, actual capitalists are blameless.

How did the working class respond to this ideological persuasion? Unions lost some ground in professional elections, but this can be explained by a decline in CGT enrollment that predated the crisis. However, working-class organizations, especially the Socialist Party, scored well in political elections. This upward trend peaked in the 1977 municipal elections, when the Communists and Socialists won control of a majority of cities over 100,000 population and two-thirds of cities over 30,000 population.

Other signs also confirm that the working class maintained a high level of consciousness. For example, there were ongoing debates within working-class organizations (particularly concerning union tactics), and certain radical ideas were increasingly translated into reality, such as "soldiers' committees" linked to the workers' movement. (The number of such committees increased from 70 in 1975 to 97 in 1976. See Docre and Mars, 1979.)

Obviously the determining factor here was social and economic conditions. With the onset of economic crisis, the working class became the object of wide-ranging attacks. But these attacks called forth resistance and militancy sharpened by working-class struggles in the wake of May 1968. The bourgeoisie's policy was still uncertain, moreover. The scope of the crisis had not yet been fully appreciated. The government fought fires wherever they broke out. But its efforts to stimulate the economy were insufficient to curb unemployment and fell far short of a comprehensive plan for restructuring the industrial base. Maurice Papon, a leader of the RPR and secretary of the National Assembly Finance Committee, characterized the policies of this period in the following terms: "The government's so-called structural reforms amount to setting up field hospitals to dispense emergency treatment" (1978 Finance Committee report on proposed budget).

By comparison workers' struggles reaped considerable benefits: the percentage of conflicts that ended without gains by workers declined from 62 percent in 1966–7 to 42 percent in 1972 to 38 percent in 1974–5 and only 30 percent in 1976. Wages increased faster than inflation: 14·8 percent in 1975 and 15·1 percent in 1976. During the lull in the crisis in the spring of 1976 French employers were the only ones in Europe who had not restored their pre-crisis rates of profit. Workers justifiably felt that they had staved off the government offensive and that capitalist restructuring of the economy had not yet opened any deep wounds. On the contrary, the first scratches had provoked a strong response. Throughout this period union leaders did not directly oppose overt struggle, their policy in this respect having evolved since May 1968.

The Socialist Party, born from the remains of the old SFIO and baptized by François Mitterrand at Epinay in 1971, understood that its only hope of growth lay in challenging the influence of the Communist Party among workers. To accomplish this it had to repudiate its old "center-left" allegiances and sign a pact with the Communists. For their part, the Communists saw no hope of guiding the increasingly restive working class without some sort of political alliance that held out hope of future victory. Thus in 1972 the *Programme Commun* was signed by the two parties. Like it or not, the union confederations had to conform to the new status quo (except for FO—concerned to preserve its independence and hostile to the PCF and CGT; we shall have little to say about FO in this period). As a result their policies became increasingly similar; this evolution was formalized in 1974 with the signing of an accord between the CGT and the CFDT. Workers saw this new state of affairs as restoration of unity, hardly reason for discouragement, and when the economic crisis hit the unions found themselves facing a highly combative rank-and-file. Union leaders were not at this time directly opposed to strike action but merely sought to ride the current while avoiding any initiative that might enable scattered strikes to spark a mass uprising. With the unions following the workers rather than prodding or restraining them, it seems clear that worker behavior was determined primarily by economic and social conditions in this period. Beyond the complex diversity of responses the repercussions of the crisis are fairly clear:

increased militancy, increased level of organization, maintenance of a high level of consciousness. By the beginning of 1977 conditions seemed ripe for the development of a major working-class offensive. What happened at that point cannot be understood without analyzing the policies adopted by the leaders of the major working-class organizations.

Economic Crisis, Worker Responses, and Union Policies: Fall 1977 to 10 May 1981

It quickly became clear that the initial electoral advances of the left, combined with rising militancy among workers, threatened to launch a movement that the traditional leadership of working-class organizations would have difficulty controlling. Union leaders at the time were advising workers to wait for the coming elections and avoid compromising the outcome by taking intemperate actions or making unusual demands. As the months went by, however, there were growing signs not only that a victory of the left in the March 1978 legislative elections was becoming more and more likely but also that such a victory might come about as a result of a rising tide of strikes, a mass movement whose dynamic the traditional left-wing organizations might be unable to control. How did the Socialist and Communist Parties respond to this situation?

The Socialist Party believed that it would soon triumph at the polls. But it was increasingly worried about the economic situation that it would face upon coming to power: the Socialists feared that a number of promises made in the *Programme Commun,* negotiated in a period of strong economic growth, could no longer be kept. Or rather they feared that, owing to the high degree of working-class mobilization, they would be forced in order to keep those promises to go further than they wanted to go—in other words, to abandon the market economy. The call for new talks to "update" the *Programme Commun* may have aimed to replace those promises with more moderate objectives.

The concerns of the Communist Party were different. The Communists were also afraid of reaching power in a time of economic crisis, a period in which the *Programme Commun* seemed obsolete and hopes for the PCF program of "advanced democracy" seemed dim. Above all they feared being obliged to preside over a program of austerity in a situation in which they would be subordinate to the Socialists and would face active opposition from extreme leftist groups that had done quite well in the recent municipal elections and had begun to link up with combative elements in the working class. Most important of all, the Communists felt that instability in France would be fundamentally incompatible with maintaining the international status quo the necessity of which was pointed out insistently by Soviet leaders. They went straight to the heart of the matter and broke off their alliance with the Socialists.

The process of rupture began in late 1977 during discussions over the updating of the *Programme Commun,* and little by little its effects came to be felt by the unions. Initially, however, the upshot was not a breakdown in relations between the CGT and the CFDT. Rather each union expressed its approval of the new alignment of the political parties.

The first open break between the unions came in 1979 at the behest of the CGT, and the CFDT responded in 1980 with a spirited attack by Edmond Maire (delivered at Nantes on 4 September) on the ties between the CGT and the Communist Party.[4] As time passed differences between the two unions grew wider, particularly over tactical questions involving strikes by fishermen, subway cleaners, Manufrance employees, and others. With the approach of the 1981 presidential elections, these differences also took on a political aspect. Neither union asked its members before the first round of the elections to transfer their votes to the surviving left-wing candidate in the second round, despite demands from the rank-and-file (notably CGT militants in Marseille). Indeed the CGT refused to admit the possibility of a vote for François Mitterrand, emphasizing instead the convergence of its program with that of Communist candidate Georges Marchais. Nor did the CFDT admit that a vote for Marchais was a possibility. Furthermore, once it became clear that Michel Rocard would not be the Socialist candidate, the CFDT was at best lukewarm in support of his victorious rival François Mitterrand. The working class approached the 1981 elections in a climate of factionalism and pessimism. What is more, economic and social conditions had changed considerably since the fall of 1977.

The government and business community had begun determined efforts to implement their program for restructuring the economy. At the end of 1977 wages were increasing at the very low rate of 12·1 percent. Allowing for inflation and the reduction in the average number of working hours, this represented an increase in purchasing power of less than 1 percent. In fact, taking defects in the government's indices into account, purchasing power actually declined. For the first time since the beginning of the crisis the government and the business community succeeded in whittling away at the purchasing power of workers.

Immediately following the 1977 municipal elections, it became clear that the government's policy objective was not to create new jobs but to reduce the number of people seeking employment, in part by contriving ways to eliminate them from official unemployment statistics. This was the goal of the second Barre Plan adopted in April 1977, officially dubbed the National Pact on Employment: the plan included, among other things, an expanded early-retirement program, reduced social welfare taxes for firms that hired young workers in 1977, and on-the-job training subsidized by the state. At the risk of stirring up latent racism the government offered assistance to immigrant workers to return to their country of origin. At the same time plans for restructuring industry were announced: first came the April 1977 "steel plan," followed in June 1977 by the merger of Berliet-Saviem with Renault Industrial Vehicles, followed in July by a plan for restructuring and subsidizing the shipbuilding industry.

These plans were arranged so that, in most cases, their social impact was not felt until after the March 1978 legislative elections. When the left lost those elections, full implementation was not long in coming. René Monory, the Minister of the Economy, stated that "up to now we have been temporizing. We've kept businesses afloat. That's finished: whole segments of industry are no longer viable" (*Nouvel Observateur,* 19 August 1978). This policy was partially carried out. From March 1977 to March 1980 the rate of unemployment rose from 3·3 percent to 4·2 percent among men and from 6·2 percent to 8·6 percent among women, while in the same period the inflation rate increased far more rapidly than wage increases. Nor was the business community content with these results: it planned a wide-ranging assault on the whole series of worker gains so as to introduce greater job mobility and wage flexibility. The *Nouvel Economiste* announced on 24 April 1978 that the government had decided to "kill off the indexed minimum wage (SMIC)." On 3 May CNPF spokesman M. Pugo announced that the "notion of an indexed minimum wage is outmoded." The plan at that time was to replace the SMIC with the far more flexible idea of a "guaranteed annual income." On 12 April the vice-president of the CNPF declared in *Le Républicain Lorrain* that "the law stipulating a forty-hour week and regulating overtime, with its narrow administrative restrictions, is no longer adapted to our time." The plan was to replace the 40-hour week with an "annual total of 1,920 hours"; employers could thus schedule the workweek to fit the needs of production.

It proved impossible to put these plans fully into effect. Still, the working class was faced with an attack of unprecedented scope by what *Le Monde* called "the radicalization of the Barre Plan." The government offensive did undoubtedly score some points at a time when the left was demoralized by the results of the March 1978 legislative elections, and this shifted the balance of power between the forces of labor and capital. But if we look at the evolution of worker responses, we find that the decisive factors were not the attacks launched by the business community or the failure of the left at the polls in 1978.

The Degree of Militancy

Broadly speaking, we find a marked drop in the level of worker militancy. Furthermore, this drop was apparently not a mechanical consequence of the left's electoral failure. The symptoms do not emerge fully until 1980, when the number of strike days drops to its lowest level since 1968 (1,674,000 man-days were lost to strikes in 1980, compared with 3,656,000 in 1979, 2,200,000 in 1978, 3,665,000 in 1977, and 5,010,000 in 1976). Worker participation in strikes, which had increased in 1979, dropped again sharply in 1980 (to 29·5 percent compared with 38·9 percent in 1979, 35 percent in 1978, 37·8 percent in 1977, and 29·7 percent in 1976). And the duration of industrial conflicts, which had risen continuously through 1979, also dropped in 1980 (to 4·6 days compared with 5·6 in 1979, 4·0 in 1978, 3·7 in 1977, and 4·22 in 1976).

This shows that it took several years of political division and factional strife in the labor movement before the militancy of workers was affected. That the tactics of division were indeed the cause of the drop in militancy is suggested by a decline in the rate of strike participation: many workers refused to take part in strikes whose outcome was unpredictable owing to the lack of agreement between the unions. At the same time other signs show that worker militancy was not entirely destroyed: the figures for the length of strikes, for instance, show that, even if the average length dropped in 1980 compared with 1979, it remained higher than every other year since 1973 (in other words, when workers did decide to join a strike, they stood firm). There were also major street demonstrations in 1980, notably a demonstration against changes in the social security rules.

Breaking down these aggregate figures industry by industry, we find that the divisive strategy of the union leadership dampened worker militancy across the board: only a few pockets of resistance remained in industries where employment was threatened in a particularly dramatic way, the steel industry in Lorraine, for example, which saw explosive outbursts by angry workers in Denain and Longwy. When we look more closely, however, we find that after 1977 matters are quite different from what they were in 1974–6, when threats to employment were met by militant workers, the more militant in proportion as their industry was more highly unionized. Beginning in 1977 the sectors least directly affected by the policies of the unions, especially the CGT, suffered the fewest consequences of the wait-and-see attitude: these include petroleum, auto sales, construction, wood products, and so on. The marked decline in militancy in 1980 also confirms the assertion that industries where union influence was weakest were least affected by the divisive tactics (construction, wood products, and so on). By contrast, the number of strike days in certain bastions of unionism fell dramatically: the drop is particularly impressive at the highly unionized electric and gas utility EDF-GDF, which experienced 270,700 man-days of strikes in 1976, 42,800 in 1977, 31,900 in 1978, 2,500 in 1979, and 800 in 1980. Other indicators confirm that where union control was weakest, worker militancy had the least difficulty expressing itself. This is true, for instance, of the major mobilization of young apprentice workers against on-the-job training programs. It is also true of struggles waged by immigrant workers as in the case of the subway cleaning crews or the battle of undocumented workers.

Degree of Organization

Throughout this period membership in working-class organizations of all kinds declined. All the left-wing political parties lost members, the Communists most of all.[5] Union membership also dropped: the most dramatic losses were sustained by the CGT, but for the first time since 1968 the CFDT also suffered a slight decline.[6] It seemed that the downward slide might have deep effects on the working class. During the first few years of the economic crisis the number of union sections had continued to grow at a healthy rate, but this rate dropped sharply in 1978 (from 5·24 percent in 1976 to 4·45 percent in 1977 and 2·26 percent in 1978). This loss affected all the union federations (the percentage of union sections affiliated with the CGT, CFDT, or FO went from 77·9 percent in 1975 to 77·6 percent in 1976, 77·3 percent in 1977, and 76·8 percent in 1978). The CGT and the CFDT were especially hard-hit (their joint share declined from 66·2 percent in 1975 to 63·9 percent in 1978).

The Level of Consciousness

Here the indicators are contradictory. Against the division in the workers' ranks the employers' strategy of "fragmentation" was able to score some points. The class struggle suffered setbacks wherever the employer strategy of offering "bonuses" for voluntary acceptance of layoff won out, particularly among some of the more vulnerable members of the workforce: workers of rural origin at Saviem, women workers at CIT-Alcatel, and young workers everywhere. But this was not generally the case.

Contrary to what the figures showing a drop in union membership might suggest, elections to works' councils in 1978–9 do not indicate a marked reverse for the labor unions (the share of the vote going to the CGT, CFDT, and FO decreased from 69·9 percent to 68·9 percent). Elections to the grievance councils in 1979, even more representative, show that, despite the drop in union membership, the idea that only the unions could assure the protection of the workers remained influential, and there was no shift of support to employer-controlled or fascist-leaning unions (workers' unions took 82 percent of the votes: 42 percent for the CGT, 23 percent for the CFDT, and 17 percent for FO).

The March 1979 cantonal elections as well as the elections for representatives to the European Parliament held in June of that year demonstrated that the left-wing parties were holding their own. The slight setback suffered by the left in cantonal by-elections held the following year was not regarded as significant. Within working-class organizations debate was lively, showing no signs of apathy or dejection. There was opposition to downward revision of labor demands and, at the CFDT congress in Brest, to the union's policy of *recentrage*.[7] Discussion later turned on the question of unity, both in the Socialist Party (the Socialist Party Congress at Metz resulted in defeat for the Mauroy and Rocard factions, which had favored moving the party away from its alliance with the Communists) and in the CGT, where there was criticism of the Communist Party (this position was greeted with apathy by union militants and disapproval by part of the union hierarchy—Moynot, 1982a), as well as in the "Union dans les luttes" movement. Finally, social movements outside industry continued to thrive, and there were major demonstrations for the right to abortion and contraception and against nuclear power as well as in defense of the rights of immigrant workers and homosexuals. The part taken in these movements by workers, particularly in the abortion-rights struggle and in demonstrations against the construction of a nuclear power plant at Plogoff, demonstrates that the level of working-class consciousness remained high.

During these four years we find that worker responses were affected more by division between the left-wing parties and within the labor movement than by the offensive mounted by the government and business community or by discouragement in the wake of the March 1978 legislative elections. The division on the left dampened worker militancy and resulted in a marked decrease in the level of working-class organization but did not significantly affect the level of workers' consciousness.

Workers reacted to this situation in two apparently contradictory ways: some once-militant workers adopted a "wait-and-see" attitude, while other workers were "politicized" by growing awareness of the harm done by division on the left. Had the Barre government been able to inflict a decisive defeat on the working class, it seems likely that lasting demobilization would have ensued. But the government drew its strength only from the fact that the working class was divided. Internally weakened by open rivalry between Gaullists and Giscardians and tainted by various scandals, the government was unable to carry out extensive plans to restructure industry as envisioned by the Third Barre Plan. Accordingly politicization won out over demobilization among workers: unable, owing to division within the labor movement, to get rid of the government through industrial strife, the working class turned to the electoral arena and tried to overcome its division in the political realm.

The Left in Power: the Working Class and the Unions Cope with Economic Crisis and the New Political Situation, 10 May 1981 to 10 May 1982

François Mitterrand's victory on 10 May 1981 was won without support from significant segments of the bourgeoisie. The Socialist's good showing in the first round of the elections resulted from a shift of votes mainly from the Communists but also from the extreme left. Analysis of the second-round vote shows that broad working-class support made Mitterrand's victory possible, not votes drawn from various segments of the bourgeoisie. Even the support that Mitterrand obtained from normally Gaullist voters came from working-class areas (Jaffré, 1982).

Although the working class did not vote for the Socialist Party platform, about which it knew little, it did expect the government to meet its most urgent demand (Kergoat, 1981). For the government, the problem is that most previous experiments with social democratic government in Europe have been carried out in circumstances that allowed substantial economic concessions to be made to the masses, in periods of relatively high growth or when substantial American aid was available (under the Dawes Plan, Marshall Plan, and so on). This is not the case today, which explains why the new government did not receive the support of any segment of the bourgeoisie merely to secure the benefits of a regular alternation of left- and right-wing governments as in other countries. In fact, owing to the crisis and the absence of American aid, any attempt however modest to satisfy the demands of workers would require sweeping anti-capitalist reforms. This was not the course chosen by the government. Immediately following Mitterrand's election, it first opted for a Keynesian demand-stimulus policy, which quickly fizzled. In any case the original plan was extremely cautious. By the end of 1981 the purchasing power of workers had increased 0·01 percent. Household consumption increased 2·3 percent in 1981 (compared with 1·8 percent in 1980), due largely, it seems, to a reduction in workers' savings. As a result industry did not increase output and most of the increased demand went to import consumption, aggravating the balance-of-payments deficit. Not even the 8·5 percent devaluation of the franc relative to the Deutschmark was enough to make French products competitive on foreign markets, which further worsened the balance-of-payments picture.

Socialist leaders expected a worldwide economic recovery to supplement their efforts at home by the end of 1981: this did not occur. Thrown back on its own resources, the government then attempted to stimulate demand by deficit spending while at the same time making concessions to employers. The 1982 budget included 24 billion francs in long-term loans to industry, and the appropriation for financing investment conforming to governmental priorities increased by 35 percent over 1981. In 1982 the government added a reduction in the professional tax of 11 billion francs, froze social security deductions until July 1983, and assumed the cost of financing aid to handicapped adults. Business remained reluctant to invest, however. In the current crisis businessmen in key sectors will invest only if profit rates return to what they consider an adequate level. By attempting to please everyone the government lost all its bets. As a result it suffered a sharp setback in the March 1982 cantonal elections. The left proved unable to hold its wavering "middle-class" electorate, driven rightward by the government's indecisiveness. What is more, some working-class voters, tired of waiting for change, deliberately abstained from voting.

The Outlook of the Unions

Not that the unions did anything to heighten worker impatience. Since the Socialist victory in fact the unions have generally sought to justify the government's slowness to act and have pleaded with workers to be patient. Force Ouvrière leader André Bergeron declared on 10 September 1981 that the government was "going too fast" and on 13 September that it was going "too far." The CFDT leadership frequently sought to persuade workers before the fact that the government would be obliged to compromise with employers. As for the CGT, its leader, Henri Krasucki, observed that the government was "headed in the right direction" and harshly criticized those who attacked its policies as "left-wing crisis management."

Although the unions may all seem to be taking a similar approach to the new government, each has been doing so in its own way and encountering specific problems. Many FO leaders, for example, had close relations with the SFIO in the past and today have close relations with its successor, the Socialist Party. But the union's stand against the appointment of Communist ministers has created some tension between it and the government. It is also worried about various threats to its longstanding policy in favor of contractual negotiations with employers. It fears that the granting of new rights to workers will create organizational structures allowing workers to express their views outside the framework of the union organization. Finally, it fears that reforms in the social security system will put an end to the considerable benefits it has reaped from its agreement in 1967 to manage retirement funds jointly with employers.

The CFDT authorized several of its leaders to serve the government as Cabinet staff members. The suspicion persists, however, that the union maintains close relations with the Rocardian minority within the Socialist Party, which does not necessarily enhance the union's stature with many members of the government. While the union is always quick to stand up for realism and austerity, provided the sacrifices are fairly apportioned, the susceptibilities of its rank-and-file on certain issues sometimes force it to take a harder line, as in the case of the nuclear program.

The CGT has only limited room to maneuver, given the Communist Party's wavering between staunch support of the government and its affirmation that it is the only party that favors "real change." Still, it is not particularly hard for the CGT to maintain, to some degree, an independent voice: as a union with ties to a minority element in the governing coalition, it cannot really act as a "government union." But at least in this initial period, it was able to mount mild protests against the government's policies. By depicting itself as the faithful representative of worker demands, it may hope to recoup some of the losses—in credibility and membership—resulting from its support for the military regime in Poland.

The various union leaderships, then, have their own concerns, which may be distinct from the concerns of the government. Unlike unions in most other European countries, French unions have no organic relationship with the social democratic government. The government is therefore faced with a relatively complex situation, aggravated by the fact that union factionalism has increased since 10 May. This factionalism, coupled with the lack of formal government–union ties, make French labor unions poor instruments for either mobilizing pro-government support or shaping worker demands. If this situation is a difficult one for the government, it is no less difficult, obviously, for the working class, whose behavior is influenced by the economic crisis, the fact that a left-wing government now holds power, and the policies of the various unions.

Level of Militancy

In 1981, unlike 1936, the working class was neither mobilized nor unified prior to the left-wing victory. Nor did the Socialist government take its first decisions in response to pressure from striking workers in occupied factories (unlike the Blum government in June 1936). After the elections the dominant attitude was not "wait and see," it was just "wait." The number of man-days lost to strikes in the first few months of the new regime was even lower than the already low level of 1980 (103,200 in June, 84,200 in July, and 7,500 in August of 1981, compared with 342,000, 111,700, and 16,100 for the same months in 1980). One young worker admirably captured a universally shared feeling when he told a union meeting that "the way to reduce the length of the working week is not for us to go out on strike, because now it's up to the government to pass a law."

By September 1981, however, in the absence of any new laws, the situation had changed: between September and the end of 1981 the number of man-days lost to strikes considerably exceeded the comparable figures for 1980, though remaining below the 1979 levels (September: 111,700 in 1981, 64,400 in 1980, 182,500 in 1979; October: 215,800, 113, 800, and 182,500 respectively; November: 197,500, 55,900, 418,500 respectively; December: 133,900, 62,900, and 169,900 respectively). Finally, in January 1982 the new law governing the length of the workweek was promulgated. It contained several concessions to employers; in particular, only workers receiving the minimum wage were guaranteed that the reduced workweek would not result in any loss of wages. Employers immediately took advantage of every loophole in the new law: some whittled away at the new fifth week of paid vacation, others eliminated coffee breaks to make up for the hour lost each week, and still others tried to make employees work on weekends. Employers generally attempted to win approval for wage cuts to balance the cut in hours. The response of workers was instantaneous: in January and February the number of man-days lost to strikes greatly exceeded the comparable figures for all preceding years (January: 125,000 in 1982 compared with 93,700 in 1981, 135,000 in 1980, 130,000 in 1979, 73,700 in 1978; February: 454,000, 126,000, 113,000, 268,000, and 131,000 respectively).

Not until President Mitterrand disavowed his own government and announced that all wages would be maintained despite the reduction in the length of the working week did the wave of strikes begin to recede. Thus working-class militancy remained high, despite union divisions over the issue (the CFDT approved a reduction of wages to compensate for the lost hour of work). The high level of militancy is also reflected in other indices, notably the number of strikes. The reason why the number of days lost was not higher is that these strikes were relatively short. Given the prevailing political climate, employers did not want to risk prolonged strikes, preferring to reach a quick compromise.

Many anecdotes tell of growing worker recalcitrance in the face of arbitrary decisions by management. Workers took heart from the belief that now "the guys upstairs are working for us," that this time the bosses had lost their grip on power. Worker militancy was directed for the most part not at the government, however disappointing its actions may have been, but at employers (except of course in cases where the state itself was the employer, such as the customs service, telecommunications, and so on).

Level of Organization

The 1981 electoral victory of the left differed from past victories in that it was not followed by any marked increase in the strength of working-class organizations. The Communist Party of course insists that its membership has not declined since 10 May. Though reliable information is sorely lacking, there is reason to doubt the accuracy of this statement. The PCF itself admits that it lost some working-class members in 1981 (at the 24th Party Congress it was stated that 90,000 workers had quit in 1981 and that "several hundred" cells had vanished from industrial plants). It is hard to see what other strata of society the party might have drawn upon to compensate for these losses.

The Socialist Party undoubtedly benefited from the post-election spirit. Surprising as it may seem, however, the party gained more recruits during the presidential campaign than after its victory (it had 159,000 members in 1980, 189,987 on 10 May 1981, and 210,000 in September 1981). The gains came from various segments of society, moreover, and because of the party's weakness in working-class areas it was not really able to translate its advance into solid gains among workers. In any case there was nothing like the wave of new members that joined in 1936 or 1945.

Nor did the unions achieve any significant gain in membership after 10 May. While the exact membership of Force Ouvrière remains somewhat mysterious, it seems likely that the CGT, severely damaged by its support for the military government in Poland, has today scarcely more than 1 million members.[8] The CFDT claims a slight increase in membership in 1981, but it is unlikely that the total exceeds 1 million. It is not hard to understand what is happening: no large-scale social movement preceded, accompanied, or followed the May 1981 elections and, unlike the Socialist Party, none of the three major unions can claim to have played any role in the electoral victory.

Level of Consciousness

If the massive working-class vote in 1981 reflects a high level of class consciousness, the results of legislative by-elections in January 1982 and cantonal elections in March 1982 are more difficult to interpret. In both elections the workers' parties lost 4–6 percent of their vote. Generally speaking, these votes did not swing to the right, though the Socialists undoubtedly lost a portion of the moderate vote that had switched to them in the legislative elections. The crucial change seems to have been still further losses by the Communist Party, especially in traditional working-class communes (the PCF lost 4·2 percent between the legislative elections of 1978 and 1981, and 7 percent between the cantonal elections of 1976 and 1982). Was Poland the reason? Or the mediocre performance of the government? This time, moreover, the portion of the working-class electorate that refused to vote Communist did not support the Socialists either. Most simply abstained. How can these statistics be interpreted?

One possible interpretation is that the abstentions are the first sign of a real decline in the class consciousness of the working class. On this view the abstentions signify not only that some workers are disappointed with the results of the government's actions but also that they have lost faith in the possibility of a real change. Their lack of interest in the political situation is due, presumably, not merely to the fact that it is hard to see any real change but to deeper reasons as well. Poland, it is said, has profoundly affected working-class views: not only does the Polish situation offer definitive proof that "socialism is impossible," it foreshadows what might come of a ruling alliance between the Communists and the Socialists. Such a view suggests that a large-scale demobilization of the working class lies ahead. Other signs of this are in evidence: "agents of change," as the Socialist Party likes to call them, are increasingly hard to find these days. A shift to a more traditional social democratic form of government (that is, a government openly serving the interests of a segment of the bourgeoisie) may be possible, though such a shift would no doubt require a break with the Communist Party. It would also cause despair in some quarters of the working class.

A second interpretation of working-class abstention is that the abstentions are a deliberate warning to the government from the most class-conscious segment of the working class. In this view some workers abstained from voting because they could not simultaneously express their desire to defeat the right and their doubts about the wisdom of some government policies. Poland, and the PCF's position on the Polish question, undoubtedly persuaded some workers not to vote for the Communists. But it would be a mistake to view this gesture as resulting from a decrease in class consciousness and to imagine a defeated and bitter working class using the Polish tragedy as an occasion to mourn its lost illusions. On the contrary, whereas the right was able to exploit events in Hungary in 1956 by leading the protest against them, this time workers have taken the lead in showing solidarity with Solidarnosč. The CFDT, the FEN, and FO have played a leading role in this mobilization, and even the CGT could not remain completely aloof. In the factories discussions have focussed not only on the halt to progress occasioned by the military's seizure of power but equally on the positive role that the Polish working class has played throughout the Solidarnosč experiment.

There has been no lack of social movements in France, but these have not been prepared to defend the government's actions unconditionally, as Socialist leaders might have hoped they would. There are active movements of immigrant workers seeking work permits, women seeking employment, and young people seeking changes in the requirements for military service. Lively debate also attests to a continued high degree of class consciousness among workers. Given the information currently available, I think that the second interpretation of the abstention question is closer to the truth.

A continuing high level of worker militancy and class consciousness coupled with diminished organization: such is the overall assessment after one year of left-wing government.

The blame for the lack of organizational progress clearly lies with leaders of working-class organizations. The problems began in the months prior to the election and have been compounded by the factionalism that has reigned since, particularly among the unions.

By contrast, the continued high level of worker militancy and class consciousness cannot be explained in terms of party or union policies or in terms of the social situation, which for the time being remains largely unchanged. Instead we must turn to the overall political situation resulting from the 10 May elections: the defeat of the right, driven from power after decades of undivided rule, an absolute (two-thirds) majority of Socialist and Communist deputies, and by one of history's ironies a situation in which the institutions of the Fifth Republic ensure that the experiment under way will proceed unimpeded for a fairly long period of time—in short, an unprecedented shift of the balance of power in favor of the working class.

It is this shift that explains the high level of militancy: let the bosses oppose workers' demands—rarely have workers been in such a good position to prevail. The shift also explains the high level of class consciousness. Workers feel that this is *their* government, that they elected it. Expectations are therefore extremely high, and the slowness of change does not discourage mobilization but rather stimulates debate and provokes renewed questioning.

What will happen next? First of all, from what we now know of the Socialists' economic policies, there is good reason to think that they will not suffice to put an end to the current crisis. In fact the government confronted a major choice sooner than it had anticipated. It may meet rising worker demands by moving to more radical policies, in which case it will be led ineluctably away from the market economy as we know it. Or it may move overtly toward the positions of the business community and adopt policies similar to those of its predecessors, albeit with a sweeter-sounding vocabulary, replete with words like "realism," "pause" (prior to the decisive move toward progress), and "priorities." It would then opt for an incomes policy, "a collective apprenticeship in austerity" (to borrow the terminology of Rosanvallon; see his article in *Liberation,* 3 March 1982), a restructuring of industry in the name of technological progress, and a shift toward a "dual society."[9] Many in the government are undoubtedly ready to choose the second course. But it is wrong to think that there are no alternatives or that such a choice could be made without provoking a strong reaction.

Secondly, worker militancy is unlikely to be eroded. Union factionalism put a damper on militant attitudes before 10 May, but the situation today is different because the government is no longer seen as an obstacle but as an ally. Today worker militancy is directed against employers, but tomorrow its target could change, especially if the government is seen as surrendering too much to the demands of business.

Thirdly, working-class consciousness is not the product of a moment and is unlikely to diminish sharply unless workers are decisively defeated and there is a radical shift in the balance of power between classes. The situation today is not the same as in 1936, when the Popular Front's victory followed a long series of defeats for the working class in Europe. The generation of workers assuming power today in the unions and the parties of the left has never suffered a decisive defeat. It is a generation forged by experiences that began with May 1968, a generation that has seen a shift in the balance of class power in its favor, not only in France but in Europe and the rest of the world.

Fourthly, the level of organization remains the great unknown. It is wrong to assume that it will continue to decline or that the traditional working-class organizations will continue to grow weaker. On the contrary, we cannot overemphasize the fact that, whenever the working class becomes more radical, the traditional working-class organizations are the first to benefit, not various protest groups. Workers are looking to the Socialist and Communist parties, the parties of government, to satisfy their demands. They are not going to abandon hope of influencing those parties overnight. Initially this may redound to the advantage of the Socialists. But it is wrong to think that the balance of power within the French working class has shifted definitively and that the PCF now faces an irreversible decline in its fortunes: merely by virtue of its deeper roots in the working class, many workers may turn to the Communist rather than the Socialist Party.

Similarly, any radicalization of the working class would alter the situation with the unions, with many contradictory consequences. Factionalism is today more apparent in the labor movement than in politics, and it could lead to a decline in union influence. But despite everything, the unions are likely to attract new members and create new sections where none now exist.

If that happens, which union will benefit most? The CFDT is not handicapped in the way the Socialist Party is by a lack of roots in the working class. New members might choose different unions in different situations, opting for the CFDT in large firms, say, where workers still remember positions taken in the past by the CGT, while favoring the CGT in small firms, where the CFDT has less support (a 1978 survey shows that, in a sample of 12,049 firms employing 50–149 workers each and having only one union section, the CGT is represented in 7,094 and the CFDT in only 4,036). Force Ouvrière is unlikely to profit much from the new membership; its ambiguous ties to a segment of the working class have not generally helped it grow in periods of radicalization.[10]

Progress in organization will affect not only labor–management relations but also the policies of the union leaderships themselves. Strengthening of the traditional organizations means they will surely tighten their hold on the working class as a whole, but it will also stimulate debate and opposition within the organizations themselves, thereby encouraging the development of organized opposition within the unions and even within the Socialist and Communist parties. Rank-and-file workers might then be in a position to begin moving away from the policies of the official leadership. Such a development occurred in the past, but generally too late to have any real influence on events. The only thing one can say for sure is that the outcome will once again be determined by interaction, interpenetration, and mutual influence between the leadership of the workers' parties and unions, such as they are, and the working class, such as it is.

Notes: Chapter 17

1   A Louis Harris poll sponsored by the CFDT in March 1981 (that surveyed 500 youths aged 18–24) found that only 50 percent of those polled expressed confidence (complete or moderate) in unions to defend their interests. A 1979 poll yielded a figure of 57 percent in response to a comparable question put to workers above the age of 18.

2   In 1974 the leadership of the PSU, headed by Michel Rocard, left to join the Socialist Party. At the same time a number of left-wing factions also quit the PSU, whose membership dropped from 9,000 in 1973 to 2,800 in 1977.

3   According to a 1976 study by the CGT's Centre d'Etudes Economiques et Sociales, union membership increased particularly markedly in industries employing a high percentage of women. The Clothing Industry Federation's membership, for example, increased from 18,000 in 1973 to 25,000 in 1976. The rank-and-file's interest in assuming leadership responsibilities progressed in the same way: the percentage of women in leadership training courses was 16 percent in 1973 and 22 percent in 1976 ("Les femmes salariées," CCESS note, 1976).

4   Contrary to a superficial impression, there were significant differences in the timing of changes in attitudes on the part of the PCF and CGT. Nearly a year after the PCF had begun the process of withdrawal from the Union of the Left, the CGT proposed setting up a National Unity Committee (*Le Peuple,* 1 December 1978). Not until the end of 1979 did the CGT adopt the theme of "ideological warfare" and begin emphasizing the role of reformism in the consensus sought by the right (adducing as proof the CFDT's move to a policy of *recentrage*). Then, in early 1980, the CGT made a statement on Afghanistan, followed in June by a statement on "unity of action" that accused the other major confederations of attempting "to promote a policy of crisis management for the benefit of the business community."

5   Communist Party membership officially remained virtually unchanged from 1978 to 1979 (702,000 to 700,000 members). But Paul Laurent's report to the Central Committee in April 1980 stated that 25 percent of the party's cells were no longer meeting. Most observers believe that the party's membership declined by a similar percentage during this period. As for the Socialist Party, after reaching a high of 180,000 members in 1978, it fell back to 155,000 in 1980.

6   The official figures for CGT membership are as follows: 2,322,055 in 1977; 2,192,862 in 1978; 2,031,163 in 1979; and 1,918,583 in 1980. Actual membership went from 1,719,245 in 1977 to 1,491,691 in 1978, 1,459,215 in 1979, and 1,174,956 in 1980. As for the CFDT, its losses (according to official figures) were less significant but equally steady over the same period: in 1977 the membership was 1,077,071; 1,047,990 in 1978; 1,008,590 in 1979; and 963,220 in 1980 (not including retired members, whose numbers remained at about 75,000 throughout).

7   Strong opposition to the leadership's policy emerged at this Congress. The leadership even found itself in the minority on the question of the reduction in working hours, the majority favoring an immediate reduction to a 35-hour week with no loss in pay.

8   On 12 January 1982 486 union sections, 25 regional and departmental unions, 7 local unions, 23 national unions, and 6 federations called for a lifting of martial law, liberation of political prisoners, and recognition of the union's right to exist, thus showing their disagreement with the position of the CGT.

9   The so-called "dual society" can take two forms: a "sectoral" dualism, that is a dual labor market in which only some of the workers are employed by highly productive firms integrated into the world economy; or a "temporal dualism," that is, a kind of part-time employment in which workers spend less time in regular jobs and more in "free time" activities. Both employment patterns were discussed by a working group

on the future of work under the auspices of the Eighth Plan (see "Réflexions sur l'avenir du travail," Documentation française, 1980). Here of course we have primarily the former in mind.

10 A number of indicators suggest similar interpretations, though none is conclusive. For example, 66 percent of women FO members attend more than three union meetings annually, compared with 79 percent for the CGT and 81 percent for the CFDT (based on figures compiled by Madeleine Guilbert for the CGT in 1976). As for militancy, 40 percent of women belonging to FO have never gone on strike, compared with 27 percent for the CGT and 25 percent for the CFDT, respectively. As for the level of class consciousness, 49 percent of young FO members or sympathizers believe that union activities have little or no effect, compared with 19 percent for the CGT and CFDT (Louis Harris poll in 1981 sponsored by the CFDT). Further, 34 percent of women FO members believe that, in order for female workers to live better, the "system must be changed"; this figure is 63 percent for the CGT and 61 percent for the CFDT. Voting behavior is similar: in 1974 48 percent of FO members voted for Giscard in the presidential elections; only 10 percent of CGT members and 27 percent of CFDT members so voted (SOFRES poll published in *Nouvel Observateur,* June 1974). It seems clear, then, that FO is not organizing the same segment of the working class as is the CGT and CFDT.

18

Trade Unions, Employers, and the State: Toward a New Relationship?

SABINE ERBÈS-SEGUIN

As the economic crisis deepens in the early 1980s the major social issues of the day are also changing in a more obvious way than before. In France as in other industrialized countries the years of plenty brought improvement in the workers' standard of living. But no such improvement has taken place with respect to participation in economic policy-making by the representatives of French workers, whose access even to necessary information about the economy remains limited. The situation of French unions in this respect is quite different from the situation of unions in other nearby countries: German, British, and above all Swedish unions have not been systematically excluded from access to the centers of power. The purpose of the present chapter is not to discuss the relative advantages and disadvantages of the French case but rather to examine the impact on labor–management relations of the left-wing government elected in May and June 1981, after twenty-three consecutive years of conservative governments.

Roughly speaking, during the 1950s and 1960s wages in France were increasingly fixed by negotiation and contract; this in turn was a requisite of the new model of accumulation (see Boyer in this volume). Regardless of any guarantees won by the workers, and regardless of any negotiation over benefits in which employers may have engaged, negotiations invariably focussed on the social consequences of economic decisions taken without participation by workers or their representatives. This is what I shall attempt to show in the first part of this chapter.

Subsequently, with the onset of economic crisis in 1974–5 and further aggravation of the crisis, labor–management relations deteriorated without any accompanying change in the political situation. This resulted in further exclusion of workers from the decision-making process. Then came the political reversal of 1981, whose impact on labor–management relations I can merely suggest.

The Era of Growth: A Prelude to the Restructuring of Industry

During a growth phase that for two decades (1950–70) seemed limitless, there also seemed to be no "technical" limits on the scope of labor–management negotiations over wages and fringe benefits, that is, over the workers' share in the fruits of economic growth. Such negotiations were used by management to prevent workers and their unions from questioning economic choices. Wages and fringe benefits (labor's share of national income) were regarded as the be-all and end-all of worker demands in that other issues, over which management was unwilling to negotiate because of their larger implications, could always be replaced by a discussion of wages. Management, moreover, retained the initiative to take steps to cope with the social impact of economic decisions. Management also had the financial resources to avoid being hamstrung by industry-wide negotiations (except in metals, where negotiations were regionally based). In general, negotiations were carried on at two levels: the national level, where bargaining agreements were general and not specific, and the firm level, where contracts with individual firms showed greater variety with respect not only to wages but also to job classifications and working conditions. Questions about the growth-centered development model were hardly more than symbolic, mainly involving union discussion of social change, nationalization, and participation in decision-making.

Until 1966–7 there was a brief rise in the number of firm-level contracts, often based on the example of some pilot firm (such as Renault). But contracts of this sort gradually gave way to industry-wide contracts at the national level that were eventually written into and extended by legislation (between 1957 and 1964 there were ten such national laws or accords; in 1964–5 there were none; and between 1966 and 1974 there were sixty-seven). This period may be looked upon as marking a turn toward guaranteed minima for all occupational groups in preference to an increase in the standard of living of workers as a group. The change also reflects an increased division of labor between the state and employers, the one providing welfare assistance, the other investment capital. This division of roles was formally acknowledged by the French business community for the first time in 1965 (in a CNPF document amounting to a virtual "charter" of French business). The first national accords amounted to a diversification in the realm of labor contracts that paralleled structural transformations in the productive apparatus (for a detailed study of how this worked in the metals industry see Erbès-Seguin and Casassus, 1977, pp. 152 ff.).

By the late 1960s the signs of what would later be seen first as a structural transformation of the economy and later as a crisis of the system of production had just begun to appear. Restructuring of industry on an increasingly vast scale exacerbated the disparities between, on the one hand, rapidly growing sectors (mainly those producing for export) and regions, in which the size of the workforce increased somewhat and, on the other hand, sectors and regions that were experiencing stagnation and even decline (INSEE, 1974). The impact of these changes on total employment was concealed until 1972 by the fact that surplus labor was absorbed by expanding sectors and by state subsidies in certain other sectors such as steel and mining.

Until about 1971 trade union strategy varied from sector to sector: in some sectors negotiators sought new gains, while in others they were mainly interested in protecting existing wage levels, benefits, and jobs. Where these union strategies were successful they can be viewed as posing a challenge to the exclusive right of management to make decisions: any guaranteed labor share in total production costs can be regarded, in a time of threatened wage rollbacks, as a substantial victory. But the real point is that such a strategy has no hope of lasting success so long as wages remain the central focus of union demands. The management-encouraged trend toward company-by-company negotiations, depending on the economic condition of each individual firm and overall conditions for the branch, coupled with the concomitant trend for government to assume responsibility for guaranteeing minimum wages (which began around 1966–7), made it possible to maintain wages as the main bargaining issue until the crisis had reached a rather advanced stage (see interview with Pompidou, *Jeune Patron,* August–September 1967).

Throughout the period of growth, and for a considerable length of time thereafter, the state's traditional interventionist role was discharged largely through this assumption of responsibility for maintaining the minimum wage. At the same time the state gradually relinquished responsibility for investments, even in the public sector. Thus the state's position was a contradictory one, but the ambiguities in its role were in a sense functional: it withdrew from the economic sphere *per se* while taking on increased responsibility in the area of labor–management relations, specifically in order to protect the victims of economic change.

The social crisis of May 1968 and the political radicalization that followed only added greater visibility to changes whose causes can be traced back to a much earlier time. Indeed as early as 1956 some observers noted a weakening of the planning authority's power to control and direct the economy (Carré *et al.*, 1972). The state's role in planning continued to decrease as the focus of government attention shifted to monetary policy on the one hand, and welfare policy on the other. Among the explicit purposes of the Sixth Plan, moreover, was that of facilitating industrial concentration. Control of the money supply became a primary concern of the government only after the crisis was in full swing, though constant reference was made to the importance of monetary policy.

The state's other social function, the search for a broad consensus, was discharged in a variety of ways. Contracts between the state and its own employees, for example, were held up as an example of the way to achieve a consensus on income (especially worthy of note in this regard is the experiment tried in 1969 by Jacques Delors, at that time an advisor to Prime Minister Jacques Chaban-Delmas). Still, the government's position on the wages of its own employees had to take account of its other main concern, that of controlling inflation, and during the growth phase this led at times to divergences with other employers—who were more concerned with expanding production than with controlling prices. This widened the gulf between sectors even further.

It was only in industries or firms that were experiencing difficulties at a time when the rest of the economy was still growing that workers and their unions were able to challenge the strategies of their employers, in particular by questioning the central role accorded to the wage issue in all negotiations. But this happened only in isolated instances, increasingly common, it is true, after May 1968. With no leadership from the parties of the left, criticism of employers' policies began to emerge in sectors of the economy experiencing difficulties. At the same time new talk, much of it largely symbolic in nature, was heard about social change (symbolic because the discussions focussed on particular sectors of the economy and were not picked up by the political parties). Among the proposals discussed were nationalization of certain firms in the textile and chemical industries, at that time undergoing restructuration; self-management at Lip; and the right to employment, in strikes at Râteau and in the textile industry (Casassus and Erbès-Seguin, 1979).

It is important to stress the change in circumstances surrounding labor conflict that occurred in 1966–7. May 1968 can be interpreted in part as a reaction to the restructuring of industry that was just beginning. Worker demands were treated as economic issues until the political parties lost control of the situation in June 1968. This points up one of the limitations inherent in the political aspect of trade union action, namely, the need to rely on political parties as soon as the conflict enters the political arena. Throughout the initial period of growth, however, we note a growing contrast. On the one hand, there is an increase in the frequency of wage negotiations, encouraged by a situation of economic growth without major structural change but with major gains in productivity. On the other hand, there is an increase in the number of strikes of the type that Shorter and Tilly (1974) call "politically symbolic" but that are really a symbolic means of access to economic issues.

The result is a transformation of labor–management relations. Traditional management strategies for fragmenting worker demands are reinforced by the growing disparity between one branch of industry and another and, within a given branch, between one company and another. More and more issues are dealt with at the firm or even the plant level. Yet at the same time the real locus of economic decision-making moves to a higher and higher level owing to economic concentration, while the range of negotiable issues shrinks more and more from 1970 on, though the degree of shrinkage varies from sector to sector. In consequence worker demands come more and more to focus on broader economic issues, yet in a purely symbolic way as long as the political parties remain unwilling to take up the challenge. The issue of jobs is only the most striking of many examples. The general exacerbation of the situation here described has been, I think, one of the major effects of the economic crisis as well as an important factor in precipitating the political change of 1981.

Steady Change in the Leading Social and Economic Issues

By distinguishing between different subperiods in the critical phase that begins in 1972–3 we can get a better idea of how the positions and strategies of various social groups changed with time. It is important, though, to emphasize that the chronology of these transitional periods is imprecise because the factors at work are contradictory, some looking back to earlier periods, others ahead to the future. These remarks apply in particular to the period that runs from roughly the end of 1974 to the end of 1976.

To begin with, the goals of the government's economic policy changed. This change, which began as far back as 1966–7, quickly assumed a clear direction. For one thing, the state withdrew to some extent from management of the public sector, confirming its neo-liberal leanings. But changes in the industrial structure hit France later and with greater force than they hit other European countries, especially West Germany, and this fact, together with the scarcity of private investment in new plant, forced the state to intervene in a stepped-up but selective fashion in the private sector not only to ease the consequences of the changes but also to accelerate the whole process.

These concerns are explicitly mentioned in the Sixth and Seventh Plans. But the long-term effects of these muddled interventions are doubtful, particularly in the area of jobs. How could the government have supposed that short-term measures would be able to counter effects of long-term structural changes promoted by its own actions? In any case the underlying economic and financial issues had not yet clearly emerged in 1974–5, and certain contradictions between the strategies of the government and those of business are evident. First of all, employers opposed any freeze on prices or credit, whereas the government attempted in early 1974 to introduce an anti-inflationary monetary policy. Even more important, there was disagreement over Giscard's 1975 plan to reflate the economy. This plan included short-term measures to aid firms while leaving them free to pursue their own strategies, but at the same time the official recommendations of the Commissariat au Plan impelled firms to speed up the restructuring process.

Furthermore, new legislation (adopted in 1973 and 1975) aiming at limiting layoffs seemed to run directly counter to the expressed intention of leaving management free to make its own decisions. The main impact of this legislation, however, was to force business to abide by certain legal formalities when making layoffs. Especially after 1978, it was used mainly as a pretext for not hiring as well as for making certain changes in labor contracts. What developed, in effect, was a sort of management right to lay off workers, something quite different from the right to employment demanded by the unions.

As a result by 1975 the lines of future confrontation over economic policy issues were already being drawn. An attempt was made to place these issues on the agenda of the 1978 legislative elections, but the political parties failed to rise to the occasion. For the workers and their unions, the issue of nationalizations (included in the *Programme Commun*) was of the utmost importance, owing to its connection with the issue of employment. But for the parties of the left this issue proved to be a stumbling-block to a pre-election agreement, whereas for the parties of the right, then in power, it was a major target (Erbès-Seguin and Casassus, 1977).

From the standpoint of the unions, the economic crisis is not a sudden or temporary aberration but a sign that the contradictions of capitalism are becoming more visible. The business community at times attempted to promote the notion that the crisis was a disaster that originated outside France. The point of this was to justify a reduction in labor's share of the national product in the interest of restoring profit rates to pre-crisis levels as well as to prevent any change in the status of wages as the central issue in labor–management negotiations, on the grounds that such a change might infringe management's freedom to decide in economic matters. This being the case, workers had no choice but to attempt to gain control of the government as the only ways of circumventing the obstacles thrown up in their path by both business and the right-wing government.

Political considerations, in particular the need to win elections, thus played a large role in shaping the behavior of the conservative parties then in power; up to 1980 in fact these political considerations (stemming from the 1974 presidential elections and the 1978 legislative elections) precluded any major attempt to cut real wages. An important part of this strategy, which brought the political class in power into conflict with a part of the business community, involved short-term measures to stimulate the economy and to aid ailing industries, as we saw earlier.

Allowance must be made, however, for previously existing systems of wage regulation. Pressure exerted by the unions has in the past been very significant in avoiding reductions in real wages, and it remains significant today. In the past the wage level was not the economic policy issue that it is today, but it was the central issue in labor–management negotiations. As the crisis deepened, however, different unions viewed its causes and effects in different ways, and this led to a divergence in union strategies. The CGT held that capitalism was in the process of destroying itself and therefore that the unions should heighten their demands in order to precipitate a political crisis (see article by J.-L. Moynot in *Le Peuple,* 16–31 January 1974).

According to this view, the job of finding a political solution to the crisis was one for the parties, an argument that the CGT used to justify concentrating all its effort on the immediate fight for higher wages. This, incidentally, placed the union on the same side as the more dynamic capitalists, in opposition to the government's efforts to hold down inflation. The CFDT, on the other hand, had still not fully accepted the reality of the crisis as 1974 began. Initially it focussed attention on the social consequences of what was in fact a structural and economic crisis. It did not approve of relying on politics alone to solve problems stemming from the relations of production. Along with a strategy based on the *Programme Commun* (staunchly supported by the CGT, less staunchly by the CFDT), the CFDT developed the concept of self-management, which challenged economic decisions at all levels of the hierarchy and not merely at the top. The union saw, however, that in early 1974 its program was more radical in intention than in content. There were three reasons for this. First, it was difficult to elaborate a unified approach. Secondly, there was a lack of common objectives shared by all workers interested in this kind of change. And thirdly, employers in the private sector preferred to make financial concessions rather than suffer the effects of a strike. But the driving force for change must lie in social struggle. Electoral victories are not enough. In any case it is not the unions that gain power through elections. "Union autonomy can only come from commitment" (*Syndicalisme*, 3 January 1974).

Furthermore, the importance of nationalizations to the unions cannot be overemphasized. Ever since 1945, when the left was strong enough politically to force the nationalization of such profitable firms as Renault, the symbolism of nationalization has been important in France. Nationalizations are seen, especially by the CGT, as a catalyst for structural reforms, an open breach in the neo-liberal system, and a tangible victory for workers, particularly in cases where the state itself invests in the nationalized firm (such as EDF, Renault, and the SNCF).

The attempt to use the state against the liberal system and to exploit the contradictions of that system is a typical example of symbolic confrontation in the realm of economic policy options. But nationalization became a realistic political option when it was incorporated into the *Programme Commun*. The growing political importance of the issue cannot be emphasized too strongly. Nationalization is an issue that enjoys strong support among the union rank-and-file. When the left-wing government that came to power in 1981 decided to go ahead with its nationalization program, it counted on this firm base of support. Still, during the 1970s the unions took different views of this common objective. This may help to account for some of the difficulties that the *Programme Commun* ran into prior to the electoral victory of the left.

Employers, too, were beset by contradictions. The extraction of surplus value from the workers was influenced by two factors between the late 1960s and the late 1970s. These factors dominated labor–management relations and help to explain why the rate of profit did not decline until 1974 in France, in contrast to other industrialized countries. Neither factor is peculiar to France, but the French situation seems to have exacerbated their effects. First of all, the rate of change of working conditions was accelerated: "Taylorism" and "Fordism" were reinforced and wide use was made of speedups and shift work, particularly in sectors considered to be the most profitable—other sectors were gradually abandoned. This aggravated regional, sectoral, and plant-to-plant

differences. At the same time the international division of labor was reinforced. Labor contracts were also revised, and jobs were made
vulnerable to cutbacks in all the usual ways. By the end of the 1970s this
development had assumed unprecedented proportions.

Taken together, all of these factors had a strong effect on labor–
management relations, which varied widely from one context to another.
This corresponded quite well to the objectives sought by one faction of
French business (especially the UIMM, which includes the metals industry,
the toughest of all CNPF member-groups) during the early period of the
crisis (up to 1977–8). Later, employers tended to coalesce around the
common objectives of reducing labor's share in production costs and
above all of attacking the terms of labor contracts, in order to rid firms
of what employers saw as the albatross of workers who could not be laid
off.

The second factor alluded to above was of great tactical importance
during the period in question. This was inflation, and it involved labor,
management, and government in a three-way struggle. It is fascinating
to study the rhetoric that was spun around this theme, particularly by
management and government, and to see how this rhetoric was brought
to bear on labor–management relations (Erbès-Seguin, 1971, 1980, pp.
484–524).

By 1974 the CNPF had taken up where the government left off, using
inflation as an argument against further wage increases at a time when
wages in the private sector were still rising steeply. Because investment
had become increasingly difficult, efficiency could now be improved only
by exerting pressure on labor (see statement by F. Ceyrac, in *Patronat*,
October–December 1974). Yet real wages did not level off and begin to
decline, for the first time since the war, until 1979–80, a sign of the
workers' capacity to maintain the wage level.

The Beginnings of a Long-Term Crisis

This period of uncertainty saw a growing trade union offensive. The
economic upswing of 1975 left business and government in doubt about
what was going on and therefore about what policies to adopt. The
unions were the first to put forward the diagnosis of a structural crisis
affecting the entire capitalist world. The CGT (*Vie Ouvrière*, 4 December
1974) initially proposed a plan to combat unemployment, at the end of
1974. The CFDT argued that "reflation without structural change will in
all likelihood lead to a new surge of inflation" and proposed new controls
on investment and full nationalization of credit, adding that the only way
to end the crisis for good was to change the economic system (*Syndicalisme*, 13 March 1975). The question placed on the agenda by the
unions was the following: to what extent, and under what conditions,
can the current crisis accelerate political change? Meanwhile there were
fewer strikes, particularly in the private sector, than there had been in
the previous period. But the significance of the strikes that did take place
had changed: when the government accused the unions of "politicizing"

labor disputes, it did not mistake the deeper meaning of what was going on (see Jacques Chirac's speech in the Senate, 4 November 1974).

The resulting situation was one that France had never before experienced, given the magnitude of the recession, the accelerating rate of unemployment, and the low level of investment. Business analyses of the situation at this point had two main strands, summarized by François Ceyrac (1975) as follows: France, like the rest of the industrialized world, was faced with an economic crisis not fundamentally different from but

> only longer and deeper than previous recessions. We shall overcome this crisis. But the real crisis lies elsewhere. It is structural. Ultimately it involves the structure of society.

This article may be read as a direct response to the unions: the issue, according to Ceyrac, is not capitalism but "society as a whole." The article is important because it provides a key to the future behavior of the business community: business strategy now aimed at bringing about a short-term recovery, but a recovery not necessarily premised on the same basis as before.

It is against this background that we must view the decisive change that came about at this point in both the rhetoric and the behavior of the business community with respect to the issue that now emerged as the most crucial of all: employment policy. Management of the major industrial firms in France had initially taken the position that the crisis was a temporary one and responded accordingly by reducing hours rather than laying off large numbers of workers. (This happened in the chemicals and glass industries, for example.) But by this point business had come to recognize the fact that at least some aspects of the crisis were persistent. Accordingly it accelerated the pace of industrial restructuring and translated structural change into a reduction in the size of the workforce. This of course meant repudiating what had been the traditional policy of many large firms, a policy of attempting to attach workers to the company (Freyssinet *et al.,* 1979).

Now it happens that in 1975 certain laws were passed concerning layoffs, which had important implications for employers' personnel policies. Union pressure was brought to bear on the legislature, just when employers were attempting to reduce the size of the workforce and, with it, labor's share of the total costs of production. This added even further impetus to employer efforts to challenge the status quo with respect to wages. Between 1976 and 1978 employment issues had a major impact on all elections. The increase in the number of layoffs for economic reasons starting in 1975–6 shows that management reacted quickly to changing economic conditions by adjusting the size of the workforce.

After 1978 this strategy was replaced by a nearly total hiring freeze other than temporary work contracts. This date also marks the beginning of a long period during which the CNPF refused to enter into any comprehensive wage negotiations ("circuses of no practical use to anyone except those who scream the loudest", according to Ceyrac, *Le*

Monde, 6 August 1976), even in sectors reportedly most ready to negotiate.

The period 1975–8 can therefore be seen as a latency period, during which the old status quo in labor–management relations began to fall apart, and with it the existing wage settlement first instituted some thirty years earlier. The fact that in this period labor relations were linked to the political situation doubtless reflects disarray in the labor movement: the temptation was to place hope in a change of government as a panacea for all the problems associated with structural change in the economy. But this state of affairs, which of course culminated in 1981, shows how important the evolution of economic policy issues was. On the left the question of the adequacy of the existing policy, as embodied in the *Programme Commun,* came up as early as the spring of 1977, once again over the issue of nationalizations. It was at this time that the brief economic recovery began to run out of steam, and it is not unreasonable to suggest, with hindsight, that this is when the left really began discussing what it would do once it came to power.

The return to increasingly neo-liberal policies not only reflected the political orientation of the government but also pointed up its incapacity to gain control of the economic situation (see *Le Monde,* 29 August 1979). As for labor relations, the situation was one of naked ideological confrontation. Market mechanisms determined the course of the economy in a climate of international competition, while social legislation protective of workers' rights was increasingly challenged by employers, especially after the victory of the right in the 1978 elections. Temporary labor contracts were used to counter restrictions on layoffs, and there were complaints from businessmen about the system of unemployment compensation and the financing of social security. These initial steps inaugurated a general challenge to the existing wage labor relation. Within three years the left had come to power and had to face the same problems, but the major shift in the balance of political power made it possible to envision new ways of dealing with them.

There are many differences between the current crisis and the Great Depression of the 1930s, most notably in the area of finance. Another major difference is that the unions are now able to exert at least indirect influence on economic decisions through their participation in wage negotiations. But the fact that the social impact of the current crisis has been cushioned for so long should not obscure the significance of the challenge that has been raised to the status quo.

Reformulating the Issues

The 1970s ended with the socioeconomic scene in turmoil. The first challenge to the workers' position came not in the area of wages but in that of jobs. Although the right to employment has never been assured by capitalism in any of its phases, unemployment has until recently been confined largely to particular regions and branches of industry. (The number of unemployed began to rise very slowly in 1963, after a long period of labor scarcity. The children of the postwar "baby boom" did not reach the job market until 1973–4, which unfortunately coincided with the onset of economic difficulties.) Employment, however, now became the crucial issue: an issue in the process of being redefined, as the following signs suggest. First, there have been hard-fought negotiations over a reduction in the length of the workweek, negotiations that have been going on for many years and only began to bear fruit with the election of a left-wing government. Secondly, disputes over job issues have been exceptionally long and have frequently required the intervention of third parties, such as the courts or local political authorities. Only rarely, moreover, have such disputes led to settlements satisfactory to workers. This suggests that the issues involved are crucial and cannot be resolved solely through confrontation at the company level.

Thirdly, the traditional labor collectivity has fallen apart. By "labor collectivity" I mean a production unit that corresponds to a specific geographical location, a clearly defined legal entity, and a clearly defined employer. The breakdown of economic and legal categories that date back to the earliest days of industrial capitalism is probably one of the most important problems of the 1980s (Caire, 1973; Magaud, 1974; Vacarie, 1979; Dourdan Conference, 1982). Finally, working conditions have become the critical issue in labor disputes. A precursor to this development may be seen in the first court decisions against employers for failure to respect safety rules, which were handed down in the early 1970s. These cases created such a furor that they changed the way working conditions affected the exploitation of workers: instead of cutting corners on safety, employers now attempted to induce workers to sign temporary employment contracts. This issue is related to the question of reducing the length of the workweek.

What we are witnessing, then, is very likely a redefinition of what is negotiable in labor–management disputes, a redefinition in which the wage level, and particularly the question of a certain percentage annual increase in wages, will no longer be an effective surrogate for all other worker demands. This change is taking place despite the fact that it runs counter to the virtually institutionalized status of the wage issue. It would appear that over the long run the new central issue will be that of establishing the necessary conditions to ensure full employment: a shorter (and relatively less well-paid) workweek weighed against increased hardships such as shift-work, geographical mobility, and job retraining.

A Conclusion of Sorts: The Left in Power and the Conditions for a Change in Social and Economic Priorities

The accession to power of the French left has not done away with harsh economic realities, but it has opened up the possibility of alternative economic strategies. Two important points about the new constellation of forces should be kept in mind. The first relates to the scope of the nationalizations undertaken in the wake of the elections. Beyond the symbolic function of the move, its grip, as it were, on the French political imagination, the nationalizations are a key element in the government's new social and economic policies. At first sight political considerations would seem to have been paramount in the decision: domestic political factors made it important for the government to act quickly so as to create an irreversible *fait accompli* and to enhance the political credibility of both the President and the Prime Minister. "The state must substitute for the failing private sector." President Mitterrand, at his first press conference (24 September 1981), gave a clear indication of what his strategy would be and left no doubt that responsibilities would be apportioned in a manner entirely in keeping with the traditions of the Fifth Republic: the President would set the overall course, while the government would make the hard economic and social choices.

Beyond the desire to keep his campaign promises Mitterrand stated his determination to prevent firms from "wielding economic and therefore political power great enough to thwart decisions taken in the public interest" as well as his rejection of "an international division of labor and production decided far from our homeland and serving interests that are not our own ... We have chosen to favor efficiency in order to rebuild our industry." Very quickly this became the primary bone of contention between the government and the new Opposition in the period between the fall of 1981 and the passage of the nationalization Bill on 11 February 1982.

Indeed this issue posed a major problem for any future choice of economic and social policy, as well as with respect to the relative power of business and government. Also in September 1981 Prime Minister Pierre Mauroy called for a mobilization on behalf of employment and announced plans to combat unemployment together with selective hiring subsidies for small- and medium-sized firms. These steps are subordinate to the government's big weapon for achieving its new major objective of jobs creation, namely, nationalization. But unless the nationalizations lead to an effective reorientation of the productive apparatus, there is no hope of success. One fear is that the nationalizations may, initially at least, merely further fragment the job market, with the nationalized firms providing the only centers of stability but at the price of a decline in their economic efficiency. The many steps taken to aid small and medium firms and to promote investment and protect jobs show that the government is striving to avoid any further deterioration in the employment picture. Despite the great influence of large firms on the general level of business activity and hence on employment, together with the decisive role played by the banking sector, it is clear that the nationalizations cannot produce positive results if there is a move toward protectionism and economic isolation. Preventing this is one of the government's major aims, as is evident from its devaluations of the franc.

Regarding the organization of industrial relations, there has been a certain redistribution of power within the system. To begin with, the role of the state has been greatly expanded. This is a common characteristic of all left-wing governments, but the way in which the expansion takes place varies so much from one case to another as to preclude comparison of, say, what is happening in France now with what happened in Sweden in the 1970s. This is not due solely to differences in economic circumstances, though the international economic crisis obviously plays a part. It is useful to distinguish two aspects of the social functions that the French state has now taken upon itself.

Fundamentally the state's role is one of making structural choices. It must redistribute income and not merely provide welfare to the underprivileged. What distinguishes the current situation from the period 1950–79, however, is that now the problem is not one of sharing wealth but rather of sharing austerity. The state must also enforce the law obliging labor and management to negotiate. Finally, the nationalizations have increased the already influential role of the state as employer in the social realm. The state showed that it could set an example for other employers in the way it dealt with the question of reducing the length of the workweek. This, and more generally the whole question of sharing available work, are probably the only remaining areas of negotiation possible.

The 35-hour week is a longstanding union demand, about which negotiations began as long ago as May 1978! On 23 December 1981 a Bill was passed reducing the official workweek to 39 hours and increasing annual paid vacations from four to five weeks. The government then decided to allow the application of this law to be decided by negotiation in each sector. This is a way not only of taking account of differences between the sectors but also of promoting negotiations as a way of finding novel solutions to the problem of sharing the available work. Negotiations are to be linked to the issue of increasing total employment; in addition, new regulations have been sponsored to govern the use of temporary labor. The government had to force employers to accept the new machinery for negotiations. Business opposition was highlighted by the bitterness of the discussions leading up to the "new workers' bill of rights" that originated with the report issued by Labor Minister J. Auroux and the passage of related laws. These laws are crucial, owing not so much to their financial impact as to their impact on the distribution of power within the firm and to the fact that they point up differences between the unions concerning the way in which workers should participate in decision-making.

The elimination of wages as the key negotiating issue, which as we have seen began as early as 1974–5 and which was made manifest by the June 1982 wage and price freeze (imposed in an effort to halt inflation), has revealed differences among unions as to the kind of future society that each would like to see. These divergences have emerged in the course of attempts to substitute the issue of employment for that of wages as the central focus of discussions.

This brings us to the second aspect of the state's function alluded to above, an aspect that is emerging with ever-increasing clarity: beyond the state's role in making structural choices it is playing an ever-larger role as mediator between labor and management. It is also forcing both sides to accept, at the political level, choices that cannot be made at the grassroots. This is made possible in part by the fact that the parties—particularly the Socialist Party—enjoy broader support than the unions, especially among better-paid wage-earners and salaried employees. Then, too, the government has the means to exert pressure on business firms by selectively granting credit. There are obvious limits to such a strategy not only domestically, where the government must face opposition from certain social groups and also maintain its electoral support, but also internationally, given the impossibility of withdrawing France from the international economy.

Conclusion

MARK KESSELMAN

The crisis that engulfed the entire French economy beginning in the mid-1970s soon engulfed organized labor. The conservative bloc governing France sponsored a fundamental restructuring and expansion of the French economy in the 1960s and 1970s. During these years the CGT and CFDT displayed a radical stance. However, partly to avoid responsibility for capitalist decisions, partly because the expanding economy made it possible for workers to achieve material gains, organized labor put major priority on bread-and-butter demands. Employers in turn sought to compensate for wage increases by increasing productivity and replacing recalcitrant workers with compliant machines (O'Connor, 1979). Ironically working-class wage militancy during the expansionary period served to stimulate capital accumulation and economic rationalization.

This can be seen most dramatically in the aftermath of the May 1968 uprising. Despite the fact that an unprecedented amount of work was lost in strikes and workers obtained the single largest wage increase ever, French national output and profits rose substantially in 1968. The general lesson of this period (as several chapters above discuss) is that wage gains served as a general equivalent or tradeoff which compensated for employer unresponsiveness on other issues, notably the control and content of work.

French macroeconomic regulation in the 1960s and early 1970s was informed by the Keynesian approach prevalent throughout advanced capitalism. It involved state-sponsored countercyclical measures to stimulate rapid capital accumulation and rationalization, which generated material benefits to reward the state and labor for tacitly accepting capitalist domination of production.

However, as analyzed above, France differed from comparable nations. First, the largest unions espoused demands going beyond material gains which looked toward fundamental changes in control of the labor process and the entire political economy. While union practice frequently failed to reflect these radical demands, as Segrestin points out, militant working-class and union actions in the 1970s did go beyond distributional issues. Yet the second difference between France and most other advanced capitalist nations was that the French labor movement was exceptionally weak, as exemplified by its low density and bitter internal divisions. This gave employers and the state a relatively free hand.

Thirdly, the French state was highly interventionist, reflecting habits going back centuries. The tendency was given added impetus in the postwar period. And when de Gaulle returned to power, he sponsored a massive restructuring of the French economy in order to maintain and improve France's international position.

de Gaulle was successful in his political and economic project—but this very success helped undermine the prevailing mode of regulation. Modernization decimated traditional social forces on whom the right depended and rationalization accelerated social devastation (what the CFDT called *les dégâts du progrès*). There was thus an increasing number of social costs, which made it ever more difficult for wage gains to serve as a general equivalent. Further, a tendency toward structural unemployment developed in the 1970s, a result of economic rationalization and international and domestic economic stagnation. Investment lagged, capital began to seek profitable outlets outside France, and new domestic investment (in labor-saving technology) began to produce unemployment, not new employment.

The period of rapid growth overlapped with the first signs of crisis; and there is no simple identity between the onset of political crisis (which can be dated from May 1968) and that of economic crisis (beginning in the mid-1970s). Yet new forms of class struggle help provide a key to these apparently divergent developments. As noted, the form that working-class militancy took in the 1960s helped facilitate economic expansion, high employment, and prosperity. But capital eventually attempted to counter wage militancy and curtail the benefits granted industrial workers. As Boyer, Coriat, and Erbès-Seguin describe, employers hired vulnerable categories of workers, including women, youth, immigrants, and part-time and temporary workers. One thus encounters a return to earlier forms of sweatshop labor, for example, Paris garment factories employing undocumented workers. These practices are not exclusively the realm of small archaic capitalist entrepreneurs; large corporations often disguise their resort to severe exploitation through subcontracting, which proliferated in France in the 1970s. But wage pressure contributed to a profits squeeze as the resistance of the newly incorporated workers contributed to the outbreak of the crisis.

Working-class political pressure also helped provoke the crisis, for the state expanded welfare programs and employee benefits in the early 1970s in an attempt to maintain labor peace. Increased taxes and state expenditures eventually proved a drain on capital accumulation.

Both economic growth and stagnation combined in the 1970s to end the virtuous circle of economic expansion and wage gains. On the one hand, growth became problematic. On the other hand, as unemployment, as well as Taylorism, part-time and temporary work proliferated and stable full-time employment was no longer the norm, unions were pressured from the base to extend demands beyond bread-and-butter issues. The disarray and crisis of unionism, as well as the crisis of the organized political left (following the breakdown of the Union of the Left in 1977), forced unions to rethink their global stance. Unions were forced to adopt a new posture after 1978, since it no longer seemed possible to expect a leftist government to sponsor progressive measures to deal with the crisis. Unions adapted to the new situation in diverse ways. The CFDT's policy of resyndicalisation emphasized the need to return to the level of concrete workplace struggles in an attempt to prefigure future change. This development could be described as a radical attempt by the CFDT to intervene at the workplace level to seek broader responsibilities as well as the use of direct action to force employers to bargain collectively and grant material concessions. But in practice the CFDT's stance signified that it considered broad changes unlikely and specific benefits the most that could be achieved.

The CGT, as Ross describes, hesitated between opposite goals after 1978. Like the CFDT, the CGT sought a wider role for the labor movement to prevent a conservative state allied with capital from imposing austerity policies as the "solution" to the crisis. This stance suggested an autonomous role for organized labor, as reflected in the CGT's attempt to impose industrial counterproposals. But quite quickly the CGT interpreted the need for broad-gauged action in a quite different fashion. The CGT soon moved closer to the PCF, on the grounds that other forces on the left (notably the CFDT and PS) were participating with the dominant conservative bloc in dismantling French industry under the guise of restructuring the economy.

Despite severe divisions within the left political party and union movement, the right's inability to deal with the crisis finally enabled the left to achieve a political breakthrough in 1981. What has been the effect on the working class and union movement of the leftist governing coalition dominated by the Socialist Party and including representatives from the Communist Party, Left Radicals, and political independents?

Initially the left government appeared to seek a radical version of social democracy in France, in which there were continuities with the conservative form of Keynesianism prevalent in France during the preceding period. However, when the Socialist government failed to achieve this goal, it embarked on the quest for a very different mode of regulation which places primary emphasis on the need for *rigueur*. The new approach may represent a barely disguised form of austerity or it may foreshadow a genuinely solidary, socialist transition. At this point the former tendency is clearly predominant.

The election of a left government provides a critical test of the claim by organized labor and left political parties in France that they resisted the blandishments of power in the past the better to sponsor radical changes in the future. The left government's specific reforms will first be summarized, especially as they relate to workers and trade unions; the two major phases of the government's overall approach will then be described.

(1) New rights for workers, unions, and representative mechanisms. The Socialist government sponsored a fundamental reform of industrial relations legislation, the Auroux reforms, which provide increased

protection for unions, particularly at the plant level, and encourage labor unions and other representative mechanisms to articulate workers' grievances and manage industrial conflict. The Auroux reforms extend legal protection to union locals in all plants regardless of plant size, and compel employers to engage in annual collective bargaining at the plant level over wages, hours, and working conditions, and at industry-wide levels over minimum wages. Every five years industry-wide collective bargaining is required over skill classifications. (In all cases the compulsion to bargain does not include the obligation to reach agreement.)

The unions' newly gained right to compel management to bargain collectively at the local level ranks as the single greatest change in the entire Auroux reforms. Until 1982 a majority of workers in France were not protected by local collective bargaining agreements. According to unpublished Ministry of Labor figures, fewer than one-tenth of workers in firms with under fifty employees were covered by local-level collective bargaining agreements. The proportion increased to 16 percent of workers in firms with 50–199 workers, 30 percent in firms with 200–499; and 53 percent in firms with over 500.

Unions are strengthened in other ways as well: shop stewards receive additional release time to conduct union business, and they gain the right to receive subsidized economic training. Unions obtained the right to more extensive information about the firm's operations.

The Auroux laws also provide workers at least six hours a year of release time to discuss working conditions. Works committees also gain new powers: increased rights to information concerning the firm's operations and a consultative voice over changes in the firm's overall operations (for example, curtailment of production, technological innovations). Like union delegates, elected members of works committees obtain release time to receive economic training. An economic commission is created to assist the works committee in large plants and the works committees gain the right to hire their own experts to advise on economic and technological matters.

The CGT and CFDT argued that the Auroux reforms were inadequate. They both advocated granting the works committee the right to exercise a suspensive veto over economic layoffs, authorizing elected occupational health and safety committees to immediately halt production in the event of an imminent danger, and enabling workers to have release time to participate in union meetings. The CGT demanded that political parties be granted legal protection within the firm, similar to the protection accorded unions, and that workers be permitted release time to participate in political party meetings in the firm. The CFDT sought greater rights for worker expression in shopfloor and office councils.

(2)   Reunifying the working class. By a series of legislatively authorized decrees the government regulated the situation of part-time workers, temporary workers, and the other workers not enjoying the legal benefits of full-time, permanent status. These measures ostensibly seek to develop greater solidarity and equality within the working class and to align the rights and protections of part-time and full-time workers. In

some respects, however, the 1982 regulations have an opposite effect, since they codify employers' rights to hire those who do not enjoy the status and benefits of full-time permanent workers.

(3) Employer disciplinary authority. Henceforth each employer must develop a disciplinary code which specifies the conditions under which workers are subject to sanctions. Disciplinary regulations are to be limited to measures necessary for the firm's safe, efficient operations. Penalties must be proportionate to the offense and a sanctioned worker gains the right to request a meeting with his or her supervisor, accompanied by someone of his or her choosing. Sanctions can be appealed to the labor conciliation boards on the grounds that the punishment is disproportionate to the breach of discipline.

(4) Workers in the civil service and within nationalized industries have gained new rights, including the right to discuss working conditions, organize, bargain collectively, and strike. Civil servants in subnational governments have obtained career protections modeled on national civil service regulations. Workers in nationalized industries are granted the right to elect one-third of the firm's board of directors as well as release time to participate in shopfloor or office councils to discuss the organization of production.

These measures represent the greatest cumulative shift ever occurring within the position of French labor (one-third of the labor code is modified). The industrial relations reforms are a key part of the overall change in the mode of regulation that the government sought to sponsor. Before turning to this broader issue, the significance of the Auroux reforms will be assessed.

The government argued that, in the words of the Minister of Labor, the reforms were a "commonsense revolution" (Auroux, 1982), a key part of the government's "tranquil revolution," and the cornerstone of the "new citizenship" that the government seeks to achieve. Prime Minister Mauroy argued that workers will no longer lose their citizenship rights when they enter the factory gate or office. The reforms thus extend the arena in which liberal democratic citizenship rights hold sway, as opposed to the ostensibly private sphere in which property rights prevail (Bowles and Gintis, 1982).

Although they are unprecedented in France, most features of the Auroux reforms are standard practice in many advanced capitalist nations. Swedish workers not only enjoy nearly all the new rights achieved by French workers but additional benefits that French unions failed to achieve, including the possibility for safety stewards to halt dangerous production processes and workers committees to veto layoffs.

The major tendency underlying the reforms is to encourage the rationalization of social relations of productions, by increasing the power of mechanisms mediating employer authority and employer–worker confrontation. The reforms involve a shift from what Edwards (1979) terms simple or technical to bureaucratic control. Edelman (1978) describes a similar process, what he calls the "legalization of the working class." Klare (1982) analyzes the contradictory consequences of liberal labor law in parallel fashion. Burawoy (1981) describes the development of quasi-institutionalized "games" in the workplace.

These scholars all point to a double-edged process which parallels (or, more accurately, overlaps) the development of liberal democratic citizenship rights within the political sphere. Workers gain increased rights to consultation and representation within the workplace, protection from arbitrary employer authority, and the right to discuss working conditions. These representative and consultative mechanisms are designed to facilitate the peaceful articulation and processing of class conflict within the workplace.

Yet the fact that workers have gained increased rights of representation and consultation is not a pure victory: the *quid pro quo* is the obligation to renounce the right to direct action and self-organization (see Offe and Wiesenthal, 1980; and Panitch, 1981). By guaranteeing the right to strike under certain conditions strikes become illegal under all other conditions. (This has not yet occurred in France but such a tendency is likely.) Informally the regularization and regulation of conflict blurs the sharp edges of class confrontation. The bureaucratization of class conflict transforms managerial coercion into consent, an extension to the workplace of the process Gramsci described in the political sphere.

The French government has made clear that it hopes to foster just this process. Cabinet ministers have warned workers that gaining the right to self-expression does not mean workers should constitute a parallel hierarchy to management. Mauroy argued that workers should have a right to be heard within the firm—but not to decide directly. The government asserts that dialogue should replace open conflict in the workplace. It has stated its aim—that unions and works committees will develop a new understanding of employers' position—what it calls economic logic; and employers a new understanding of workers' situation, what the government calls social logic.

The development of this process would reduce the government's responsibility for regulating class conflict. The locus of conflict regulation would shift from the state to institutionalized processes at the plant and industry level.

For such a change to occur employers would need to accept the legitimacy of unions, and unions the legitimacy of employers. The Auroux reforms seek to encourage this development. On the one hand, employers are compelled to bargain collectively. On the other hand, an unavowed aim of the reforms is to encourage the CGT and CFDT to act "responsibly" and moderately. By unions gaining a greater stake in the firm the process may be strengthened, which first emerged in the economic crisis, by which workers and unions came to identify with the firm. In the 1970s, as employment levels eroded and jobs became jeopardized, labor mobility diminished and workers demonstrated an attachment (born of insecurity) to defend the existence of the firm. This became most evident when, because of bankruptcy or disinvestment, a firm planned to close. Factory occupations were a frequent result, a dramatic evidence of worker identification with the firm.

The Auroux reforms need to be situated within a wider context of government-sponsored structural reforms. Two are especially note-worthy: decentralization and nationalization. Together these reforms suggest the ambitious and complex scope of the government's new regulatory project. Decentralization is designed to ease the state's responsibility for regulating local conflicts within France. It seeks to rationalize administrative activity, fragment conflict, and encourage private groups and subnational governments to articulate and process conflicts, rather than concentrating and centralizing conflicts under the aegis of the state (Kesselman, 1982).

Both the Auroux reforms and decentralization disengage the state. Thus freed from regulating secondary matters, the state becomes more capable of tackling the largest challenges of political-economic regula-tion. By nationalizing a substantial portion of finance, banking, and industry the state gains a large direct role organizing and financing pro-duction. Nationalization also enables the state to organize class conflict in a quite direct fashion as well. The government stated that the public sector should serve as a social laboratory; if the experiments succeed, they may be extended to the private sector. (One example is that workers in nationalized industry were granted release time to participate in union meetings and discuss the organization of production.)

The Two Phases of Regulation

Within the overall continuity of government efforts to forge a new mode of regulation one can distinguish two very distinct phases. The govern-ment first sought to restore French economic growth by sponsoring moderate increases in social transfers, reducing the workweek by one hour to encourage job creation, and providing modest investment incen-tives. These represented traditional Keynesian countercyclical techniques to boost aggregate demand and pump-prime in order to restore the con-ditions for economic growth. Even in this first phase the government was careful to restrain expectations by limiting redistributive measures.

At the same time the government asserted that, given the economic crisis and the passivity of the Barre government, more vigorous state action was needed. The government assigned high priority to the re-conquest of French markets, an improvement in French international economic competitiveness, greater emphasis on technological research and innovation, and industrial policy. These were the rationale for the structural reforms reviewed above, all introduced on the government's first year in office (although several years will be required for full implementation).

The Socialist government's interventionist approach aimed at achiev-ing the traditional Keynesian goal of rapid economic growth promoted by the appropriate mix of state policies. The government's position was that, given the right combination of state measures, the French economic crisis could be rapidly overcome.

Not all members of the government agreed. In particular, Jacques Delors and Michel Rocard doubted that vigorous state intervention would suffice to assure renewed economic growth. Six months after the government took office, Delors publicly proposed a pause in reforms. Rocard was more circumspect in public; nearly an additional year went by before he warned about the illusion that state intervention could suffice to achieve perpetually increasing levels of consumption.

Despite quite bitter criticism of this position, the government soon was persuaded by Rocard's and Delors's arguments. In part because the international economy remained stagnant—despite the predictions of a revival in 1982—French expansionary measures proved a boon to foreign companies exporting to France. But French producers neither increased foreign exports nor benefited from the French domestic upturn. More than half the newly created demand in 1981–2 was absorbed by imports. The predictable result was that inflation remained at high levels, French currency reserves were drained, the franc was weakened, and France's foreign debt soared. These alarming tendencies led to a fundamental change in government policy.

The second phase of regulation began in early 1982 and was extended in the following months. In April 1982 Mauroy announced that further increases in social transfers would be halted and no new social insurance charges imposed on firms in 1982–3. Henceforth the government began to emphasize that French prosperity depended on the survival and prosperity of French enterprises. In the new view priority had to be given to industrial development, with private firms playing a key role alongside nationalized firms.

Political officials from Mitterrand down began to praise the value of entrepreneurial ability, innovation, and profits. The government sponsored a series of measures to reduce business taxes, it sought to break the sliding wage scale linking wage gains to price rises, and it postponed reform measures (for example, reduction of the workweek). The major shift in policy occurred in June 1982 with a wage and price freeze unprecedented since the postwar period. Social expenditures were severely curtailed in the austerity budget proposed in September 1982. The government now stressed the need for rigor and sacrifice, which in practice meant shifting resources from consumption to investment.

Laurent Fabius, Budget Minister and close associate of Mitterrand, argued that in the past the state set a social objective and then raised sufficient taxes to achieve its goal. Henceforth the government would establish a ceiling on social expenditures and then allocate spending on the basis of this total. "We must transfer better rather than more" (*Le Monde,* 11 December 1982). Fabius suggested that social transfers had produced an undue sense of security and stifled initiative.

In the new view the left had typically regarded the production of a social surplus as unproblematic and had focussed on distributing the surplus. Now, however, the left needed to focus on the difficulties of producing a surplus in the first place. In the Orientation document guiding preparation of the Ninth Plan Rocard called for a new type of development founded on individual autonomy and greater initiative. The privileges that certain categories of workers and professions acquired during the expansionary period must be reduced.

The government argued that the left is uniquely qualified to promote the new type of growth, which involves sacrifices in consumption for the sake of industrial development in a mixed economy. According to Chevènement,

> Among the trumps that we possess to assure industrial renewal, the most important is the promotion of genuine social dialogue ... Never since the Liberation have conditions been as propitious as now to reduce social conflicts within industry (*Le Monde*, 16 November 1982).

How can the two phases of the government's approach be characterized? Initially the government sought to sponsor a new version of Keynesianism and social democracy in France, a nation lacking key features of social democracy. In particular, as pointed out above, France has never had institutionalized mechanisms for stabilizing class conflict, nor has there been a powerful centralized labor movement closely allied with a ruling political party. The government probably designed its structural reforms to produce a modified form of social democracy in France. However daring a departure from past practice, the new model was quite traditional viewed in comparative perspective. The government identified its major priority as expanding aggregate demand in order to enable French producers to anticipate an international economic revival. Thus French firms would be favorably situated to increase their share of domestic markets (the reconquest of French markets) and improve their international competitive standing. Industrial policies were to stress the development of advanced technologies and industries. It was assumed that economic growth would create new jobs and thus the process would help resolve the pressing unemployment problem.

The first phase was not a complete failure. French consumption did rise slightly in 1981; major structural reforms were successfully legislated. However, a durable economic revival did not occur. As noted above, neither the French nor the international economy revived in 1981–2. To the problems discussed above one should add the poor performance of the newly nationalized industries (as well as their need for fresh financing and the high cost of compensating stockholders).

The sharp turn toward austerity in June 1982 signified the new phase of the government's regulatory project. There were several elements of continuity with the first phase. For example, the government did not repudiate the reforms legislated in the first phase and continued to try melding social democracy with a more direct role for the state.

However, the watchword was now *rigueur*. Despite the fact that the new policies signified an end to stimulating expansion through consumption, the government denied that its approach resembled the austerity policies of the Barre government. According to Mauroy (*Le Matin,* 12 October 1982), whereas austerity was an end in itself, "*rigueur* is a means to achieve a policy whose objective remains growth." The new approach relied on a partial disengagement of the state, which was described as more selective state intervention. (See Jean-Marie Colombani, "Le pouvoir et la crise: à la fois 'plus d'état et moins d'état'," *Le Monde,* 16 December 1982.)

The measures initially proposed to create employment were given new meaning, since the government began tacitly to accept the inevitability of long-term unemployment in France. Since for the foreseeable future there would be fewer full-time jobs than people seeking them, the government came to view part-time and temporary work as desirable, rather than a phenomenon to be phased out in favor of permanent jobs. In the new view public policies would need to be devised to share the dwindling amount of work, rather than accepting a chasm between the employed and the unemployed.

Furthermore, in the new view, France would be even more compelled to recognize international economic constraints. This meant less emphasis on social justice and greater emphasis on the value of entrepreneurial initiative. Chevènement suggested that industrial policy should be at the intersection of the plan and market (*Le Monde,* 16 November, 1982). He identified five strategic axes: reducing energy dependence, modernizing basic industry, increasing the competitiveness of industries of transformation, promoting agriculture, and promoting new technologies, especially the electronuclear, space, ocean, and information sectors.

In face of the drastic new turn organized labor's reaction was surprisingly mild. There was one major sector of industrial militancy: the automobile industry. Unions (especially the CGT) supported the "May of the immigrant workers" (the strikes were mainly spearheaded by immigrant workers protesting repressive management methods and Taylorized jobs). But unions did not take the initiative in instigating the strikes and they remained confined to the automobile industry. Elsewhere, even in the depressed steel industry where further layoffs were scheduled despite Mitterrand's promises, labor militancy was quite low. This quiescence, as well as the government's new approach, can be interpreted in two quite contrary ways.

First, the new approach may constitute *Barrisme de gauche,* an austerity program that differs little from what the Barre government promised (although in practice it tempered its draconian policies for electoral reasons; if the right had won the 1981 elections, it would probably have adopted far more severe austerity policies). In this view the leftist government demands much of the working class and offers little in return. Although far from progressive, the new approach differs from traditional conservative governments or "hyper-capitalist" regimes (Amott and Krieger, 1982). The French Socialist government does not rely on market forces to stimulate capitalist rationalization. Instead, through nationalization, a substantial increase in state subsidies for research and development, and a coherent industrial policy, it directly sponsors economic rationalization.

The policy is promoted in the name of French national interests and international economic realities. It can also be justified by reference to one variant of Marxism, which argues that socialism will emerge from the fullest development of capitalist forces of production; relations of production will be transformed following the achievement of a society of abundance.

However, the government's new project may point in a quite different direction. It might accept the probability that stable economic growth has become quite unattainable. Making a virtue of a necessity, it could begin from the fact that the French economy can produce an adequate amount of material values such that there is no need to seek further growth. It would stress the anti-productivist and anti-statist promise of socialism: capitalism has been forced to seek ever-greater growth because capital is privately owned and controlled. Thus accumulation necessarily becomes imperative. A further result is that capitalism has been forced to promote consumerist values to artificially inflate consumer needs and to seek to persuade citizens that fulfillment lies through privatized, individually based consumption. The new approach would stress the value of material sufficiency not growth or affluence. It would deemphasize privatized, individual consumption in favor of social, collective consumption. It would give priority to community control, solidarity, and decentralized production and community.

In this perspective structural unemployment, rather than a disaster, emerges as an unprecedented achievement, for it signifies such high productivity that adequate output can be produced without the need for all people to work full-time. By sharing work, promoting solidaristic labor policies, and reducing class inequalities, full employment could be achieved on a part-time basis.

The new approach could be truly revolutionary by severing the connection between economic performance, material reward, and citizenship. This approach might occupy the zone between the global change called for by radical rhetoric and the economistic defense of particular gains that the workers' movement often emphasized in practice. But as applied in practice the new approach does not fall within this zone.

The key issue is whether the new measures create cohesion and solidarity within the working class, as well as redistribute power to workers in return for a stationary level of material gains. In the year following the new policy of *rigueur* the more conservative interpretation was clearly warranted: little power was redistributed by the structural reforms and whatever power was redistributed did not trickle down to the base. Nor did the union movement actively pressure the government for a more far-reaching transformation. There were multiple reasons for the unions' caution: habits dating from the previous decade, in which left unions and parties fostered patterns of representation rather than direct action, the unions' desire to consolidate their own positions with the

Socialist government, and the fact that unions and workers did not want to endanger the first left government in a generation.

Nor should the government's new orientation be interpreted as a complete break with previous approaches. While stressing the gravity of the crisis, it remained committed to restoring economic growth. And the government has sponsored measures in quite traditional top—down statist fashion, a result of the Socialist Party's own patterns and habits combined with traditional French political cultural patterns. And the vacuum on the left, with unions and left parties echoing government positions and failing to articulate autonomous positions, means that there is no pressure from the base for redistributing power.

Where, then, is the union movement in the new conjuncture? Union rivalry continues to flourish. Edmond Maire has declared that the CFDT no longer considers the CGT a privileged ally (*Le Monde*, 25 December 1982). The CGT continues to attack the CFDT and other unions. The unions have not coalesced around a global project and interunion rivalry remains intense since 10 May 1981.

Yet the structural reforms provide new rules of the game for the union movement. Further, unless the government provides incentives for workers to support its restrictive measures, whether described as resulting from austerity or *rigueur,* there is bound to be resistance at the base. This may well be directed against unions if they are too closely identified with the government. Thus unions may be forced, in their own organizational self-interest, to demand a greater role in shaping policies. The future of the workers' movement remains quite open.

Bibliography

Adam, Gérard (1964), *La CFTC 1940–58* (Paris: Armand Colin/FNSP).

Adam, Gérard (1965), *La CGT-FO* (Paris: FNSP).

Adam, Gérard (1967), "L'unité d'action CGT–CFDT," *Revue française de science politique,* vol. 17, no. 3 (June), pp. 576–90.

Adam, Gérard (1981a), "Entretien," *Démocratie moderne,* 22 October.

Adam, Gérard (1981b), "Les stratégies sociales: permanence ou changement?" *Projet,* no. 159 (November), pp. 1043–55.

Adam, Gérard, and Reynaud, Jean-Daniel (1978), *Conflits du travail et changement social* (Paris: PUF).

Adam, Gérard, Bon, Frédéric, Capdevielle, Jacques, and Mouriaux, René (1970), *L'Ouvrier français en 1970* (Paris: Armand Colin).

ADEFI (Association pour le Développement des Etudes sur la Firme et l'Industrie) (1981), *Les Mutations technologiques. VI, Recontres nationales de Chantilly (September 1980)* (Paris: Economica).

Aglietta, Michel (1979), *A Theory of Capitalist Regulation: The US Experience* (London: Schocken Books).

Albistur, Maité, and Armogathe, Daniel (1977), *Histoire du féminisme français du Moyen Age à nos jours* (Paris: Des femmes).

Althabe, G. (1982), "La gauche et le 'compromis social'," *Non!,* no. 13 (May–June), pp. 55–62.

Amott, Teresa, and Krieger, Joel (1982), "Thatcher and Reagan: state theory and the hyper-capitalist regime," *New Political Science,* no. 8 (Spring), pp. 9–37.

André, C., and Delormé, R. (1982), *L'Etat et l'économie* (Paris: Seuil).

Andreani, Edgard (1968), *Grèves et fluctuations, la France de 1890 à 1914* (Paris: Cujas).

Andrews, William, and Hoffmann, Stanley (eds) (1981), *The Fifth Republic at Twenty* (Albany, NY: SUNY).

Andrieux, Andrée, and Lignon, Jean (1981), "La CFDT, un phénomène original," *Projet,* no. 159 (November), pp. 1065–79.

Armington, K., *et al.* (1981), *Les Syndicats européens et la crise* (Grenoble: Presses universitaires de Grenoble).

Arrighi, Giovanni (1978), "Towards a theory of capitalist crisis," *New Left Review,* no. 112, pp. 3–24.

Auffray, Danièle, Collin, M., Baudoin, T., and Guillerm, A. (1979), *La Grève et la ville* (Paris: Christian Bourgois).

Auroux, Jean (1981), *Les Droits des travailleurs* (Paris: Documentation française).

Auroux, Jean (1982), "La révolution du bon sens," *Droit social,* no. 4 (April), p. 258.

Badie, Bertrand (1976), *Stratégie de la grève* (Paris: FNSP).

Baran, Paul, and Sweezy, Paul (1966), *Monopoly Capital* (New York: Monthly Review).

Barbier, C. (1982), *L'Organisation du travail* (Paris: Sycomore).

Barjonet, André (1968), *La CGT* (Paris: Seuil).

Barre, Raymond (1978), "Mon libéralisme," *L'Expansion,* no. 121 (September), pp. 154–71.

Barreau, Henri (1976), *Histoire inachevée de la convention collective nationale de la métallurgie* (Paris: CGT).

Barrier, Christiane (1975), *Le Combat ouvrier dans une entreprise de pointe* (Paris: Editions ouvrières).

Batstone, Eric (1978), *The Social Organization of Strikes* (Oxford: Basil Blackwell).

Bauchard, Philippe (1972), *Les Syndicats en quête d'une révolution* (Paris: Buchet/Chastel).

Bauchard, Philippe, and Bruzek, Maurice (1968), *Le Syndicalisme à l'épreuve* (Paris: Robert Laffont).

Baudoin, Thierry, and Collin, Michel (1981), "Les conséquences sociales de l'hetérogeneisation des formes d'emploi: le cas du mouvement syndical," Laboratoire de Sociologie de la Connaissance, Paris, December.

Beaujolin, F. (1982), *Vouloir l'industrie: pratique syndicale et politique industrielle* (Paris: Editions ouvrières).

Bell, Daniel (1973), *The Coming of Post-Industrial Society* (New York: Basic Books).

Belleville, Pierre (1963), *Une Nouvelle classe ouvrière* (Paris: R. Julliard).

Benassy, Jean Pascal, Boyer, Robert, and Gelpi, Rosa Maria (1979), "Régulation des économies capitalistes et inflation," *Revue économique,* vol. 30, no. 3 (May), pp. 397–41.

Berger, Suzanne, and Piore, Michael (1980), *Dualism and Discontinuity in Industrial Society* (Cambridge: Cambridge University Press).

Bergeron, André (1971), *Confédération Force Ouvrière* (Paris: Epi).

Bergeron, André (1975), *Lettre ouverte à un syndiqué* (Paris: Albin Michel).

Bergeron, André (1976), *Ma Route et mes combats* (Paris: Jean-Paul Ramsay).

Bergounioux, Alain (1975), *Force Ouvrière* (Paris: Seuil).

Bergounioux, Alain (1981), "Le vocabulaire des confédérations ouvrières: une analyse des spécificités," *Mots,* no. 2 (March), pp. 139–51.

Bergounioux, Alain (1982). *Force ouvrière aujourd'hui* (Paris: PUF).

Bergounioux, Alain, M.-F. Tournier, Launay, M.-F., Mouriaux, René, Sueur, Jean-Pierre, and Tournier, Maurice (1982), *La Parole syndicale* (Paris: PUF).

Bertrand, Hughes (1983), "Accumulation, régulation, crise: un modèle sectionnel théorique et appliqué," *Revue économique,* vol. 34, no. 2 (March), pp. 305–44.

Bertrand, Hughes, Mazier, Jacques, Picaud, Yves, and Podeuin, Gérard (1982), "Les deux crises des années trente et des années soixante-dix: une analyse en sections productives dans le cas de l'économie française," *Revue économique,* vol. 33, no. 2 (March), pp. 234–73.

Bleitrach, Danielle, and Chenu, Alain (1979), *L'Usine et la vie: luttes régionales, Marseille et Fos* (Paris: Maspero).

Bleitrach, Danielle, Lojkine, Jean, Oary, Ernest, Delacroix, Roland, and Mathieu, Christian (1981), *Classe ouvrière et social-démocratie: Lille et Marseille* (Paris: Editions sociales).

Blum-Girardeau, C. (1981), *Les Tableaux de la solidarité* (Paris: Documentation française).

Boccara, Paul (1977), *Etudes sur le capitalisme monopoliste d'état: sa crise et son issue* (Paris: Editions sociales).

Boccara, Paul (1982), "Pour de nouveaux critères de gestion," *Issues,* no. 11 (February).

Bon, Fréderic, and Burnier, Michel-Antoine (1966), *Les Nouveaux Intellectuels* (Paris: Seuil).

Bowles, Samuel (1982), "The post-Keynesian capital–labor stalemate," *Socialist Review,* no. 65 (September–October), pp. 45–72.

Bowles, Samuel, and Gintis, Herbert (1982), "The crisis of liberal democratic capitalism: the case of the United States," *Politics and Society,* vol. 11, no. 1, pp. 51–93.

Boyer, Robert (1978), "Les salaires en longue période," *Economie et statistique,* no. 103 (September), pp. 27–58.

Boyer, Robert (1979), "La crise actuelle: une mise en perspective historique," *Critiques de l'économie politique,* no. 7–8.

Boyer, Robert (1980), "Rapport salarial et analyses en terme de régulation: une mise en correspondence avec les théories de la segmentation du marché du travail," *Economie appliquée,* vol. 33, no. 2, pp. 491–510.

Boyer, Robert (1981), "Les transformations du rapport salarial dans la crise: une interprétation de ses aspects sociaux et économiques," *Critiques de l'économique politique,* no. 15–16 (April–June).

Boyer, Robert (1982), "La crise actuelle est-il la répétition de celle de 1929?" in AEP, *La Crise et sa gestion* (Paris: Borel-Express).

Boyer, Robert, and Mistral, Jacques (1982a), *Accumulation, Inflation, Crises,* 2nd edn (Paris: PUF).

Boyer, Robert, and Mistral, Jacques (1982b), "Internationalisation, technologies, rapport salarial: quelle(s) issue(s)?" Note No. 8212, CEPREMAP (Centre d'études perspectives d'économie mathématique appliquée à la planification), Paris.

Branciard, Michel (1974), *Cent Cinquante Ans de luttes ouvrières* (Lyon: Chronique sociale).

Branciard, Michel (1977), *Société française et luttes de classes 1967–77* (Paris: Chroniques sociales de la France).

Branciard, Michel, and Gonin, Marcel (1978), *Le Mouvement ouvrier 1815–1977* (Paris: CFDT).

Brechon, Pierre (1979), "Syndicalisme et politique sur le terrain de l'entreprise: essai d'analyse de la situation française," Institut d'études politiques, Grenoble.

Briefs, U. (1980), "Les syndicats face à la puissance technologique," *Projet,* no. 149 (November), pp. 1089–98.

Brizay, Bernard (1975), *Le Patronat* (Paris: Seuil).

Bruhat, Jean, and Piolot, Marc (1966), *Esquisse d'une histoire de la CGT* (Paris: CGT).

Brunel, Jean, and Saglio, Jean (1979), *L'Action patronale* (Paris: PUF).

Buci-Glucksmann, Christine, and Therborn, Goran (1981), *Le Défi social-démocrate* (Paris: Maspero).

Burawoy, Michael (1981), "Terrains of contest: factory and state under capitalism and socialism," *Socialist Review,* no. 53 (July–August), pp. 83–124.

Butera, F. (1977), *La Divisione del lavoro in fabrica* (Padua: Marsilio Editori).

Caire, Guy (1973), *Les Nouveaux marchés d'hommes* (Paris: Editions ouvrières).

Caire, Guy (1978), *La Grève ouvrière* (Paris: Editions ouvrières).

Caire, Guy (1982), "Précarisation des emplois et régulation du marché du travail," *Sociologie du travail,* n.s. no. 2, pp. 135–58.

Capdevielle, Jacques, Dupoirier, Elisabeth, and Lorant, Guy (1975), *La Grève du Joint français* (Paris: FNSP/Armand Colin).

Caroux, Jacques (1980), "La CFDT et la crise du syndicalisme," *Esprit,* no. 4 (April), pp. 3–8.

Carré, Jean-Jacques, Dubois, Pierre, and Malinvaud, Paul (1972), *La Croissance française* (Paris: Seuil).

Casassus, Cécilia (1979), "L'action collective pour l'emploi," thesis, Groupe de Sociologie du Travail, Paris.

Casassus, Cécilia (1980), "Les syndicats et l'emploi," CREEST (Centre de Recherches en Sciences sociales du Travail, Université de Paris-Sud CNRS), Paris.

Casassus, Cécilia, and Erbès-Seguin, Sabine (1979), *L'Intervention judiciaire et l'emploi: le cas du textile* (Paris: Documentation française).

CEPREMAP (Centre d'Etudes Prospectives d'Economie Mathématique Appliquée à la Planification) (1977), "Changements structurels du capitalisme français: formes de la regulation et nature de l'inflation," in *Approches de l'inflation.*

CERM (Centre d'Etudes et de Recherches marxistes) (1978), *La Condition feminine* (Paris: Editions sociales).

Ceyrac, François (1975), "L'après-crise," *L'Expansion,* no. 90 (November), pp. 191–4.

CFDT (Confédération Française Démocratique du Travail) (1966), "Pour une civilisation de l'habitat," *Formation,* no. 67 (March–April), pp. 86–90.

CFDT (1967), "Les problèmes posés par le développement urbain," *Formation,* no. 73 (May–June).

CFDT (1968), *Positions et action de la CFDT au cours des événements de mai–juin 1968* (Paris: CFDT).

CFDT (1970), *35ième Congrès confédéral, compte-rendu* (Paris: CFDT).

CFDT (1971), *La CFDT: textes et entretiens* (Paris: Seuil).

CFDT (1972), *Les Conditions du travail* (Paris: CFDT).

CFDT (1973), *36ième Congrès confédéral, compte-rendu* (Paris: CFDT).

CFDT (1974a), "Strategie de la CFDT et union des forces populaires," CFDT, Paris; mimeo.

CFDT (1974b), *Textes de base,* Vol. 1 (Paris: CFDT).

CFDT (1976), *La Crise* (Paris: CFDT).

CFDT (1977), *Textes de base,* Vol. 2 (Paris: CFDT).

CFDT (1978a), *Platforme CFDT, plan et nationalisations* (Paris: CFDT).

CFDT (1978b), *Positions et orientations de la CFDT* (Paris: CFDT).

CFDT (1978c), *Les Conditions du travail* (Paris: CFDT).

CFDT (1978d), "Conference: travail des femmes et l'action syndicale (rapports et interventions)," Working Paper, CFDT, Paris.

CFDT (1979), *Travail des femmes et actions syndicales: rapport et interventions de la conférence* (Paris: CFDT).

CFDT (1980), *Relations CFDT–CGT: unité d'action ou sectarisme?* (Paris: CFDT).

CFDT (1982a), *39ième Congrès de la CFDT, compte-rendu* (Paris: CFDT).

CFDT (1982b), "La situation économique actuelle et la politique économique du gouvernement," *Nouvelles CFDT,* no. 15.

CFDT BRAEC (Bureau de Recherches, d'Analyses et d'Etudes Confédérales) (1980), "A propos du marxisme," *Notes et documents du BRAEC,* no. 11 (January–March).

CFDT BRAEC (1981a), "Les jeunes et le travail," *Notes et documents du BRAEC,* no. 18.

CFDT BRAEC (1981b), "Mouvement ouvrier et unité d'action," *Notes et documents du BRAEC,* no. 16.

CFDT Fédérations de la Banque, de la Construction, Hacuitex, PTT, *et al.*

(1976), "Contribution au débat: les questions qui se posent aujourd'hui à la CFDT," Paris; mimeo.

CFDT Fédération Démocratique des Travailleurs des PTT (1975), *Des Idiots par milliers* (Paris: Maspero).

CFDT Fédération Générale de la Métallurgie (1979), *Avenirs de la sidérurgie: propositions de la FGM–CFDT* (Paris: CFDT).

CFDT Fédération Générale des Services et du Livre (1980), "Les assurances changent, le syndicat aussi," CFDT note de réflexion, Paris.

CFDT Syndicat National des Personnels de l'Energie Atomique (1975), *L'Electronucléaire en France* (Paris: Seuil).

CFTC (1964), "Rapport sur l'évolution et perspectives de la CFTC," CFTC Extraordinary Congress, Paris, 6–7 November.

CGT (1970), *37ième Congrès, compte-rendu in extenso* (Paris: CGT).

CGT (1972), "Pour des conditions de travail plus humaines en rapport avec notre temps: positions et propositions," CGT Commission Executive Report, Paris.

CGT (1973), *Les Femmes salariées: travaux de la cinquième conférence nationale* (Paris: Editions sociales).

CGT (1977), "Il faut que vivre le programme commun," CGT, Paris, November.

CGT (1978a), *L'Industrie française depuis 1958, un bilan accusateur* (Paris: CGT).

CGT (1978b), *Les Questions qui font bouger* (Paris: CGT).

CGT (1981), *Informatique et conditions du travail dans l'assurance et la banque* (Paris: CGT Centre confédéral d'études économiques).

CGT Centre Confédéral d'éducation ouvrière (n.d.), *Les Classes sociales et l'exploitation capitaliste,* Brochure de formation, série A (Paris: CGT).

CGT Fédération des Travailleurs de la Métallurgie (1978), "Face à la crise de la sidérurgie," *Le Guide du militant,* no. 136.

Chenu, Alain (1982), "Industrialisation, urbanisation et pratique de classe: le cas des ouvrièrs de la région marseillaise," thesis, University of Toulouse.

Commissariat Général du Plan (1981), *Plan intérimaire* (Paris: Documentation française).

Cordeiro, A. (1981), *Pourquoi l'Immigration en France: critique des idées reçues en matière d'immigration* (Creteil: Organisation Météorologique Mondiale).

Coriat, Benjamin (1979a), *L'Atelier et le chronomètre* (Paris: Christian Bourgois).

Coriat, Benjamin (1979b), "Le Fordisme, l'ouvrier-masse et la 'revalorisation du travail manuel'," *Economie et humanisme,* no. 248 (July–August), pp. 63–72.

Coriat, Benjamin (1981a), "Robots et automates dans les industries de série: esquisse d'une économie de la robotique industrielle," in ADEFI, *Mutations technologiques* (Paris: Economica), pp. 237–52.

Coriat, Benjamin (1981b), "L'atelier fordien automatisé, micro-électronique et travail ouvrier dans les industries de chaîne," *Non!,* no. 10 (November–December).

Coriat, Benjamin (1981c), "Relations industrielles, rapport salarial et régulation: l'inflexion libérale," May.

Coriat, Benjamin (1982), "Relations industrielles, rapport salarial et régulation," *Consommation,* no. 3.

Couffignal, Georges (1979), *Les Syndicats italiens et la politique* (Grenoble: Presses universitaires de Grenoble).

Critiques de le'économie politique (1981), "Segmentation du travail ou division du salariat?" *Critiques de l'économie politique,* no. 15–16.

Crouch, Colin, and Pizzorno, Alessandro (eds)(1978), *The Resurgence of Class Conflict in Western Europe since 1968,* 2 vols (London: Macmillan).

Dahrendorf, Ralf (1959), *Class and Class Conflict in Industrial Society* (Stanford, Calif.: Stanford University Press).

Damette, Felix, and Scheibling, Jacques (1979), *Pour une Stratégie autogestionnaire* (Paris: Editions sociales).

Dassa, Sami (1978), "Les Grèves de 1976: étude quantitative," Laboratoire de sociologie du travail et des relations professionnelles, Report, CNAM, Paris.

Declercq, Gilbert (1974), *Syndicaliste en liberté* (Paris: Seuil).

Delors, Jacques (1970), "La nouvelle société," *Preuves,* no. 2, pp. 95–107.

Descamps, Eugène (1971), *Militer* (Paris: Fayard).

Desrosières, Alain (1972), "Un découpage de l'industrie en trois secteurs," *Economie et statistique,* no. 40, pp. 25–40.

Didier, Michel (1982), "Crise et concentration du secteur productif," *Economie et statistique,* no. 144 (May), pp. 3–12.

Docre, Bernard, and Mars, Patrick (1979), *Dossier M comme militaire* (Paris: Alain Moreau).

Donnadieu, Gérard (1970), *Demain les Cadres* (Paris: Centurion).

Dourdan Conference (1982), *L'Emploi, enjeux économiques et sociaux* (Paris: Maspero).

Drugman, B. (1979), "Etat, capital et salariat," thesis, University of Grenoble.

Dubar, Claude (1980), *Formation permanente et contradictions sociales* (Paris: Editions sociales).

Dubois, Pierre (1974), *Mort de l'état-patron* (Paris: Editions ouvrières).

Dubois, Pierre (1976), *Le Sabotage dans l'industrie* (Paris: Calmann-Levy).

Dubois, Pierre (1978), "Travail et conflit dans l'industrie," dissertation, Groupe de sociologie du travail, Paris.

Dubois, Pierre (1981), *Les Ouvriers divisés* (Paris: FNSP).

Dubois, Pierre, Durand, Claude, and Bosc, S. (1975), *Décentralisations industrielles et relations du travail* (Paris: Documentation française).

Dubois, Pierre, Dulong, Renaud, Durand, Claude, Erbès-Seguin, Sabine, and Vidal, Daniel (1971), *Grèves revendicatives ou grèves politiques? Acteurs, pratiques et sens du mouvement de mai* (Paris: Antropos).

Dubois, Pierre, *et al.* (1976), *L'Autonomie ouvrière dans les industries de série. Vol. 2, Les réactions ouvrières* (Paris: Groupe de Sociologie du Travail).

Dubost, Nicolas (1979), *Flins sans fin* (Paris: Maspero).

Dull, Klaus (1982), "Employer strategies and new forms of work organization," paper presented to Division of Labor and Development of Industrial Relations Colloquium, Wissenschaftszentrum of Berlin, February.

Dunlop, John Thomas (1958), *Industrial Relations Systems* (New York: Holt).

Dunlop, John Thomas, and Galenson, Walter (1978), *Labor in the Twentieth Century* (New York: Academic Press).

Durand, Claude (1971), *Conscience ouvrière et action syndicale* (Paris: Mouton).

Durand, Claude (1981), *Chômage et violence* (Paris: Galilée).

Durand, Claude, and Dubois, Pierre (1975), *La Grève: enquête sociologique* (Paris: FNSP).

Durand, Michelle (1977), "Les conflits du travail: analyse structurelle," Centre de recherches en sciences sociales du travail, Université de Paris-Sud, Paris.

Durand, Michelle, and Harff, Yvette (1973), "Panorama statistique des grèves," *Sociologie du travail,* vol. 15, no. 4 (October–December), pp. 356–75.

Echevin, Pol (1970), "Les objectifs de la rentrée syndicale," *Projet,* no. 49 (November–December), pp. 1119–23.

Economie et politique (1982), "Forum sur l'intervention des travailleurs dans la gestion des entreprises," *Economie et politique* (June).

Edelman, Bernard (1978), *La Légalisation de la classe ouvrière* (Paris: Christian Bourgois).

Edwards, Richard (1979), *Contested Terrain: The Transformation of the Workplace in the Twentieth Century* (New York: Basic Books).

Ehrmann, Henry (1947), *French Labor from Popular Front to Liberation* (New York: Oxford University Press).

Eizner, Nicole, and Hervieu, Bertrand (1979), *Anciens Paysans, nouveaux ouvriers* (Paris: Harmattan).

Engels, Frederich (1961), *La Situation de la classe laborieuse en Angleterre* (Paris: Editions sociales).

Erbès-Seguin, Sabine (1971), "Les groupes sociaux dans l'inflation," *Sociologie du travail,* no. 4 (October–December), 371–85.

Erbès-Seguin, Sabine (1980), "Les relations collectives du travail," doctorat d'état, Université de Paris-VII, Paris.

Erbès-Seguin, Sabine, and Casassus, Cécilia (1977), "Les conditions du développement du conflit industriel," Groupe de sociologie du travail, Paris.

Esprit (1980), "La CFDT et la crise du syndicalisme," *Esprit,* no. 4 (April), pp. 1–86.

Faire (1979), *Crise et avenir de la classe ouvrière* (Paris: Seuil).

Feenberg, Andrew (1978), "From the May events to Eurocommunism," *Socialist Review,* no. 37 (January–February), pp. 73–107.

Fejtö, François (1966), *The French Communist Party and the Crisis of International Communism* (Cambridge, Mass.: MIT Press).

Fejtö, François (1980), *La Social-Démocratie quand même* (Paris: Laffont).

Fisher, Malcolm (1973), *Mesure des conflits du travail et leurs répercussions économiques* (Paris: OECD).

Fiszbin, Henri (1980), *Les Bouches s'ouvrent: une crise dans le Parti Communiste* (Paris: Grasset).

Force Ouvrière (FO) (1971), *Onzième Congrès confédéral, compte-rendu* (Paris: FO).

Force Ouvrière (1977), *Treizième Congrès confédéral, rapports* (Paris: FO).

Freyssenet, Michel (1975), *Les Conditions d'exploitation de la force de travail: données statistiques 1945–75* (Paris: Centre de sociologie urbaine).

Freyssenet, Michel (1977), *La Division capitaliste du travail* (Paris: Savelli).

Freyssinet, Jacques (1980), "Nouvelles tendances dans les politiques des entreprises en matières de gestion du personnel," note prepared for OECD expert meeting, 12–14 October.

Freyssinet, Jacques (1982), *Pratiques d'emploi des grands groupes français* (Grenoble: Presses universitaires de Grenoble).

Freyssinet, Jacques, *et al.* (1979), "La stratégie de structuration de l'emploi des grands groupes industriels," IREP, Grenoble.

Garicoix, Michel (1972), "De la CFTC à la Reconstruction: les groupes et les publications," Paris.

Gaudemar, Jean-Paul de (ed.)(1980), *Usines et ouvriers: figures du nouvel ordre productif* (Paris: Maspero).

Gault, François (1971), *Trois Grèves* (Paris: Calmann-Levy).

Geras, Norman (1981), "Classical Marxism and proletarian representation," *New Left Review,* no. 125 (January–February), pp. 75–89.

Germe, J. F., and Michon, François (1980), "Stratégies des entreprises et formes particulières d'emploi," paper presented to Séminaire d'Economie du Travail, Paris, June.

Germe, J. F., with Michon, François (1982), *Le Travail temporaire* (Paris: Sycomore).

Goetz-Girey, Robert (1965), *Le Mouvement de grèves en France* (Paris: Sirey).

Gonin, Marcel, *et al.* (roundtable)(1981), "Après l'élection présidentielle," *Projet,* no. 157 (July–August), pp. 783–98.

Gorz, André (1967), *Strategy for Labor,* trans. Martin Nicolaus and Victoria Ortiz (Boston, Mass: Beacon Press).

Gorz, André (1971), "Techniques, techniciens et luttes de classes," *Temps modernes,* no. 301–2 (August–September), pp. 140–80.

Gorz, André (1982), *Farewell to the Working Class,* trans. Mike Sonenscher (Boston: South End Press).

Gouldner, Alvin (1955), *Wildcat Strike* (London: Routledge & Kegan Paul).

Grando, J. M., Margirier, G., and Ruffieux, B. (1980), "Rapport salarial et compétitivité des économies nationales: analyse des économies britannique, italienne et ouest-allemande depuis 1950," thesis, Université de Grenoble-II, Grenoble.

Granger, Georges (1979), "Produire: pour qui? pourquoi?" *Dialectiques,* no. 28 (Autumn), pp. 99–108.

Granou, André (1982), "L'Hypothèque moderniste," *Temps modernes,* no. 430 (May), pp. 1931–57.

Granou, André, Baron, Yves, and Billaudot, Bernard (1979), *Croissance et crise* (Paris: Maspero).

Greffe, Xavier (1981), "Les modifications contemporaines de la politique sociale," in Institut d'études économiques de l'Université de Lyon, *Etat et régulation* (Lyon: Presses de l'Université de Lyon).

Greffe, Xavier, and Rosanvallon, Pierre (1978), "La recomposition de la classe ouvrière," *Projet,* no. 129, pp. 1066–74.

GRESP (1981a), "Accumulation et régulation en longue période: emploi, revenu salarial, prix et profit," Université de Rennes-I, Rennes.

GRESP (1981b), "La dynamique de la croissance en longue periode: éléments de comparisons internationales," Université de Rennes-I, Rennes.

Groux, Guy (1982), "Changement politique, droits des travailleurs, et négociations professionnelles en France," paper presented to Division of Labor and Development of Industrial Relations Colloquium, Wissenschaftszentrum of Berlin, February.

Groux, Guy, *et al.* (1981), *Les Communautés pertinentes de l'action collective: six études en perspective* (Paris: Laboratoire de sociologie du travail CNAM).

Guadilla, Naty Garcia (1981), *Libération des femmes: le MLF* (Paris: PUF).

Guerin-Henni, Anne (1980), *Les Pollueurs* (Paris: Seuil).

Guilbert, Madelaine (1974a), "De 1914 à nos jours," in E. Charles-Roux (ed.), *Les Femmes et le travail* (Paris: Courtille).

Guilbert, Madelaine (1974b), "Femmes et syndicats en France," *Sociologie et sociétés,* vol. 6, no. 1 (May), pp. 157–70.

Habert, Benoit (1977), "Etude de vocabulaire syndical: la résolution du 37ième congrès de la CFDT," thesis, University of Paris-X-Nanterre and ENS de Saint-Cloud.

Hamon, Hevré, and Rotman, Patrick (1982), *La Deuxième Gauche: histoire intellectuelle et politique de la CFDT* (Paris: Jean-Paul Ramsay).

Harff, Yvette (1981), *Les Attitudes des travailleurs à l'égard des produits* (Paris: Diffussion-Université-Culture).

Harff, Yvette, and Durand, Michelle (1977), *La Qualité de la vie: mouvement écologique, mouvement ouvrier* (Paris: Mouton).

Heritier, Pierre, Bonnevialle, Roger, Ion, Jacques, and Saint-Sernin, Christian (1979), *Cent Cinquante Ans de luttes ouvrières dans le Bassin Stéphanois* (St Etienne: Champ du possible).

Huiban, Jean-Pierre (1981), "Les contre-propositions industrielles comme élément de stratégie syndicale: analyse de la période 1973–80," thesis, Université de Paris-IX, Paris.

INSEE (Institut national des statistiques et des études économiques) (1974), *Fresque historique du système productif,* collection E, No. 27 (Paris: INSEE).

INSEE (1978), *Données sociales,* Collection des Ménages, M62–3 (Paris: INSEE).

INSEE (1979), *Tableaux de l'économie française* (Paris: INSEE).

INSEE (1981a), *Données sociales,* 4th edn, Collection des Ménages, M62–3 (Paris: INSEE).

INSEE (1981b), *L'Equipement des ménages en biens durables en 1981,* Collection des Ménages, M94 (Paris: INSEE).

INSEE (1981c), *Le Mouvement économique en France 1949–79* (Paris: INSEE).

INSEE (1982a), *Annuaire statistique de la France 1981* (Paris: INSEE).

INSEE (1982b), *Rapport sur les comptes de la nation, 1981,* Collection comptes et planification, C101–2 (Paris: INSEE).

INSEE (1982c), *Comptes de l'industrie,* Collection comptes et planification, C104 (Paris: INSEE).

INSEE (1982d), *La Crise du système productif* (Paris: INSEE).

Intersocial (1979), "Crise et avenir des relations professionnelles," *Intersocial,* no. 52 (September).

Intersocial (1980), "Le travail noir en Europe et aux USA," *Intersocial,* no. 61 (June).

Jaffré, Jerome (1982), "De Valéry Giscard d'Estaing à François Mitterrand: France de gauche, vote à gauche," *Pouvoirs,* no. 20, pp. 5–28.

Janco, M., and Furjot, D. (1972), *Informatique et capitalisme* (Paris: Maspero).

Javillier, Jean Claude (1976), *Les Conditions du travail* (Paris: PUF).

Jenson, Jane (1980), "The French Communist Party and feminism," *Socialist Register,* pp. 121–47.

Jenson, Jane (1982), "The modern women's movement in Italy, France and Great Britain: differences in life cycle," *Comparative Social Research,* vol. 5, pp. 341–75.

Jenson, Jane, and Ross, George (1979), "Strategies in conflict: the twenty-third congress of the French Communist Party," *Socialist Review,* no. 47 (September–October), pp. 71–99.

Jezequel, Claude (1981), "Aperçus statistiques sur la vie conventionnelle en France," *Droit social* (June).

Jobert, A., and Rozenblatt, P. (1983), "Signification et portée du contrat collectif de branche dans la structure des relations professionnelles en France," note prepared for meeting of International Labor Association, Kyoto, Japan, March.

Johnson, R. (1981), *The Long March of the French Left* (New York: St Martin's Press).

Julliard, Jacques (1977), *Contre la Politique professionnelle* (Paris: Seuil).

Kergoat, Danièle (1975), *Bulledor* (Paris: Seuil).

Kergoat, Danièle (1978), "Les pratiques ouvrières revendicatives: processus revendicatifs et dynamiques collectives," Centre de sociologie des organisations, Paris.

Kergoat, Jacques (1979–80), "Crise économique et combativité ouvrière," *Criti-*

ques de l'économie politique, nos 7–8 (April–September), pp. 197–220; and no. 10 (January–March), pp. 94–121.

Kergoat, Jacques (1981), "Le Parti Socialiste tel qu'en lui-même," *Critique communiste* (April).

Kergoat, Jacques (1982a), "Combativité, organisation et niveau de conscience dans la classe ouvrière," *Revue française des affairs sociales* (April–June).

Kergoat, Jacques (1982b), "La chute des effectifs syndiqués à la CGT," *Le Monde,* 8 June.

Kerr, Clark, and Siegel, Abraham (1952), "The interindustry propensity to strike: an international comparison," in Arthur Kornhauser (ed.), *Industrial Conflict* (Oxford: Blackwell), pp. 189–212.

Kerr, Clark, Dunlop, John, Harbison, Frederick, and Myers, Charles (1973), *Industrialisation and Industrial Man* (Harmondsworth: Penguin).

Kesselman, Mark (1982), "The tranquil revolution at Clochemerle: decentralization in France and the crisis of advanced capitalism," paper presented to Local Institutions in National Development: Strategies and Consequences of Local–National Linkages in the Industrial Democracies Conference, Bellagio, Italy.

Klare, Karl (1982), "Labor law and the liberal political imagination," *Socialist Review,* no. 61 (March–April), pp. 45–71.

Knowles, Kenneth (1952), *Strikes: A Study in Industrial Conflict* (Oxford: Blackwell).

Korpi, Walter, and Shalev, Michel (1980), "Strikes, power and politics in the Western nations 1900–76," in Maurice Zeitlin (ed.), *Political Power and Social Theory,* Vol. 1, pp. 301–34.

Korsakissok, C. (1980), "Informatique et libertés," *Options-Quinzaine,* no. 41.

Kourchid, Olivier (1976), "Crise économique et modes d'action ouvrière," CORDES Groupe de sociologie du travail, Paris.

Krasucki, Henri (1969), *Syndicats et lutte de classe* (Paris: Editions sociales).

Krasucki, Henri (1972), *Syndicats et socialisme* (Paris: Editions sociales)

Krasucki, Henri (1980), *Syndicats et unité* (Paris: Editions sociales).

Krumnow, Fredo (1974), *Croire* (Paris: Editions ouvrières).

Krumnow, Fredo (1976), *CFDT au coeur* (Paris: Syros).

Lagandré, François (1979), *Quels Cadres pour demain?* (Paris: Rivat).

Landier, Hubert (1981), *Demain, quels Syndicats?* (Paris: Libraire générale français).

Lange, Peter, Ross, George, and Vannicelli, Maurizio (1982), *Unions, Change and Crisis: French and Italian Union Strategy and the Political Economy 1945–80* (London: Allen & Unwin).

Laot, Jeanette (1981), *Strategie pour les femmes* (Paris: Stock).

Laot, Laurent (1977), *Les Organisations du mouvement ouvrier français aujourd'hui* (Paris: Editions ouvrières).

Lavau, Georges (1981), *A quoi sert le Parti Communiste Français?* (Paris: Fayard).

Lebrun, Pierre (1947), "Une tâche de notre mouvement syndical—le développement de la productivité du travail," *Travail et technique,* no. 10 (April).

Lefranc, Georges (1950), *Les Expériences syndicales en France de 1939 à 1950* (Paris: Editions Montaigne).

Lefranc, Georges (1969), *Le Mouvement syndical de la Libération aux événements de Mai–Juin 1968* (Paris: Payot).

Leger, Daniele (1982), *Le Féminisme en France* (Paris: Sycomore).

Lettieri, Antonio, and Santi, Paolo (1969), "Préhistoire de mai," *Politique aujourd'hui,* no. 5 (May), pp. 33–51.

Liaisons sociales (1980), "Syndicats II: organisations syndicales," *Liaisons sociales,* no. 8237 suppl. (April).

Ligue Communiste Révolutionnaire (LCR) (1979), *CFDT: le récentrage ou la gestion de l'austerité* (Paris: La Brèche).

Linhart, Danièle (1981), *L'Appel de la sirène* (Paris: Sycomore).

Linhart, Danièle, and Maruani, Margaret (1981), "Précarisation et déstabilisation des emplois ouvriers: approche exploratoire," final report submitted to Ministère du Travail, May.

Linhart, Danièle, and Rolle, Pierre (1982), "Droits du travail ou pouvoir des travailleurs," *Non!,* no. 13 (May–June), pp. 27–32.

Linhart, Robert (1978), *L'Etabli* (Paris: Minuit).

Lipietz, Alain (1979), *Crise et inflation: pourquoi?* (Paris: Maspero).

Lipietz, Alain (1980), "La double complexité de la crise," *Temps modernes,* no. 407 (June), pp. 2212–46.

Lipietz, Alain (1981), "Redéploiement industriel: le legs du libéralisme," *Le Débat,* no. 16 (November), pp. 39–49.

Lipietz, Alain (1982), "Croissance, crise et transformations du salariat industriel," CEPREMAP Note No. 8213.

Lobjeois, G. (1979), "L'action d'un comité d'entreprise pour le contrôle de l'informatique," *Cadres-CFDT,* no. 290 (September–October).

Lojkine, Jean (1972), "Pouvoir politique et lutte des classes à l'époque du capitalisme monopoliste d'état," *La Pensée,* no. 166 (December), pp. 142–68.

Lojkine, Jean (1982), "Crise et renouveau de la sociologie du travail: à propos du paradigme techniciste," *Sociologie du travail* (n.s.), no. 2 (February), pp. 192–206.

Lorant, Guy, Mandray, Noël, Anselme, Daniel, and CFDT Fédération Services (1972), *Quatre Grèves significatives* (Paris: Epi).

Lorwin, Val (1954), *The French Labor Movement* (Cambridge, Mass.: Harvard University Press).

Louis, Paul (1950), *La Condition ouvrière en France depuis cent ans* (Paris: PUF).

Louis Harris France (1977), *Structure des adhérents de la CGT et de la CFDT* (Paris: Louis Harris International).

Lozier, François (1980a), "La CFDT en chiffres," *Esprit,* no. 4 (April), pp. 15–26.

Lozier, François (1980b), "Une analyse des résultats des élections prud'homales dans le collège salariés," *Droit social,* no. 5 (May), pp. 16–34.

Madelin, Henri, Cayrol, Roland, Charlot, Jean, *et al.* (roundtable) (1978), "La France politique après les élections," *Projet,* no. 125 (May), pp. 530–49.

Magaud, Jacques (1974), "Vrais ou faux salariés," *Sociologie du travail,* no. 1 (January–March), pp. 1–18.

Maire, Edmond (1971), *CFDT: pour un socialisme démocratique, contribution de la CFDT* (Paris: Epi).

Maire, Edmond (1973), "Présentation du rapport général, 36ième congrès confédéral," CFDT, Nantes; mimeo.; reprinted in *Syndicalisme,* no. 1436, 15 March 1983.

Maire, Edmond (1980a), *Reconstruire l'espoir* (Paris: Seuil).

Maire, Edmond (1980b), "Quel socialisme autogestionnaire," *Esprit,* no. 4 (April), pp. 61–70.

Maire, Edmond (1982), "Donnez-nous du pouvoir," *L'Expansion,* no. 182 (May), pp. 77–81.

Maire, Edmond, and Julliard, Jacques (1975), *La CFDT d'aujourd'hui* (Paris: Seuil).

Maire, Edmond, and Perrignon, Claude (1976), *Demain l'Autogestion* (Paris: Seghers).

Maire, Edmond, Krumnow, Fredo, and Detraz, Albert (1973), *La CFDT et l'autogestion,* 2nd edn. (Paris: Cerf).

Mallet, Serge (1963), *La Nouvelle Classe ouvrière* (Paris: Seuil).

Mallet, Serge (1975), *Essays on the New Working Class,* trans. and ed. Dick Howard and Dean Savage (St Louis: Telos Press).

Malterre, André (1969), *Les Cadres et les réformes des entreprises* (Paris: France-Empire).

Malterre, André (1972), *La CGC, la révolte des mal aimés* (Paris: Epi).

Mandel, Ernest (1969), *Marxist Economic Theory* (New York: Monthly Review Press).

Martinet, Gilles (1979), *Sept Syndicalismes* (Paris: Seuil).

Maruani, Margaret (1978), "Les évolutions syndicales," *Critique socialiste,* no. 33 (December), pp. 69–96.

Maruani, Margaret (1979), *Les Syndicats à l'épreuve de féminisme* (Paris: Syros).

Maruani, Margaret (1980), "La CGT et la CFDT à l'épreuve des femmes," *Masses ouvrières,* vol. 2, no. 364 (November–December), pp. 43–51.

Meillassoux, Claude (1975), *Femmes, greniers, capitaux* (Paris: Maspero).

Mercier, Albert (1976), "Les conflits de longue durée," *CFDT aujourd'hui,* no. 22 (November–December), pp. 3–14.

Minc, Alain (1982), "France archaïque, France moderne?" *Le Débat,* no. 18 (January), pp. 26–32.

Ministère de l'Industrie (1981), *Chiffres Clés de l'énergie* (Paris: Ministère de l'Industrie).

Mistral, Jacques (1982), "La diffusion internationale inégale de l'accumulation intensive et ses crises," in J. L. Reiffers (ed.), *Economie et finance internationale* (Paris: Dunod).

Mitterrand, François (1980), *Ici et Maintenant* (Paris: Fayard).

Le Monde dossiers et documents (1981), "La CFDT," *Le Monde dossiers et documents,* no. 78 (February).

Montreuil, Jean (pseud.)(1946), *Histoire du mouvement ouvrier en France des origines à nos jours* (Paris: Aubier).

Morsel, H. (1979), "Conjoncture et structures économiques du monde jusqu'à la grand crise," in P. Leon (ed.), *Histoire économique et sociale du monde. Vol. 5, Guerres et crises 1914–47* (Paris: Armand Colin), pp. 145–88.

Moss, Bernard (1976), *The Origins of the French Labor Movement 1830–1914: The Socialism of Skilled Workers* (Berkeley, Calif.: University of California Press).

Mouriaux, René (1970), "La CGT depuis 1968," *Projet,* no. 49 November), pp. 1086–97.

Mouriaux, René (1972), "Livre I du *Capital* et sociologie de la classe ouvrière," *La Pensée,* no. 166 (December), pp. 69–81.

Mouriaux, René (1980), "La CGT de 1936 à 1948: structures syndicales et attitudes à l'égard des cadres," paper presented to Ingénieurs et société Colloquium Eco-Musée du Creusot, Loire.

Mouriaux, René (1981a), "Le syndicalisme français à l'épreuve de sept années de crise, 1974–81," in K. Armington *et al.* (eds), *Les Syndicats européens et la crise* (Grenoble: Presses universitaires de Grenoble).

Mouriaux, René (1981b), "La CGT face au nouveaux cours politique," *Projet,* no. 159 (November), pp. 1056–64.

Mouriaux, René (1982), *La CGT* (Paris: Seuil).

Moussy, Jean-Pierre, Begot, Georges, Delangre, Alain, *et al.* (1974), *Le "Mai" des banques* (Paris: Syros).

Moynot, Jean-Louis (1979a), "Base sociale et rôle révolutionnaire d'une démocratie de masse," *La Pensée,* no. 205 (June), pp. 88–109.

Moynot, Jean-Louis (1979b), "Le mouvement syndical en mouvement," *Dialectiques,* no. 28 (Autumn).

Moynot, Jean-Louis (1982a), *Au Milieu du gué* (Paris: PUF).

Moynot, Jean-Louis (1982b), "CGT: les raisons d'une crise," *Temps modernes,* no. 430 (May), pp. 1958–80.

Najmann, Maurice (1981), "Syndicats: la fin de 'l'homme de marble'," *Autrement* no. 29 (February), pp. 207–15.

Nassé, G., Moynot, J.-L., and Moreau, J. (1970), "Stratégies pour la rentrée," *Projet,* no. 49 (November–December), pp. 1051–5.

Noiriel, Gérard (1980), *Vivre et lutter à Longwy* (Paris: Maspero).

Nora, Simon, and Minc, Alain (1978), *L'Informatisation de la société,* multi vol. (Paris: Documentation française).

Noziére, André (1979), *Algérie, les chrétiens dans la guerre* (Paris: Cana).

Obadia, A. (1981), "Démocratie à l'entreprise: rapports sociaux," *Le Peuple,* no. 1121 (December).

O'Connor, James (1973), *Fiscal Crisis of the State* (New York: St Martin's Press).

O'Connor, James (1979), "Capital accumulation, economic crisis and the mass worker," *Social Praxis,* vol. 6, no. 1–2, pp. 5–18.

OECD (1975), *The Role of Women in the Economy* (Paris: OECD).

OECD (1978), *Le Chômage des jeunes,* 2 vols (Paris: OECD).

OECD (1980), *Etudes économiques de l'OCDE: France* (Paris: OECD).

Offe, Claude, and Wiesenthal, Helmut (1980), "Two logics of collective action: theoretical notes on social class and organizational form," in Maurice Zeitlin (ed.), *Political Power and Social Theory,* Vol. 1, pp. 67–115.

Oppenheim, Jean-Pierre (1973), *La CFDT et la planification* (Paris: Téma).

Panitch, Leo (1981), "Trade unions and the state," *New Left Review,* no. 125 (January–February), pp. 21–43.

Parti Communiste Français (PCF) (1957), *Femmes en France* (Paris: Editions sociales).

Parti Communiste Français (1965), *Femmes de vingtième siècle* (Paris: PUF).

Parti Communiste Français (1972), *Le Capitalisme monopoliste d'état* (Paris: Editions sociales).

Parti Communiste Français (1974), "Vingt-et-unième congrès du PCF," *Cahiers du communisme,* no. 10 (October–November).

Parti Communiste Français (1979), "Vingt-troisième congrès du PCF," *Cahiers du communisme,* no. 6–7 (July–August).

Parti Socialiste (1980), *Projet socialiste pour la France des années 80* (Paris: Club socialiste du Livre).

Perrot, Michelle (1974), *Les Ouvriers en grève: France 1871–90,* 2 vols (Paris: Mouton/De Gruyer).

Perrot, Michelle (1981), "L'évolution récente du pouvoir d'achat des salariés," *Economie et statistique,* no. 129 (January), pp. 37–48.

Pesquet, J. (1968), *Des Soviets à Saclay* (Paris: Maspero).

Pialoux, Michel (1981), "Force de travail et structure de classe: à propos de *Usines et ouvriers,"* *Critiques de l'économie politique,* no. 15–16 (April–June), pp. 119–20.

Piore, Michael (1978), "Dualism in the labor market: a response to uncertainty and flux, the case of France," *Revue économique,* vol. 19, no. 1 (January), pp. 26–48.

Piore, Michael (1982), "Convergence dans les systèmes nationaux de relations industrielles? Le cas de la France et des Etats-Unis," *Consommation,* no. 3.

Pius XI (1937), *Quadragesimo anno* (Paris: Editions Spes).

Pizzorno, Alessandro (1978), "Political exchange and collective identity in industrial conflict," in Colin Crouch and Alessandro Pizzorno (eds), *Resurgence of Class Conflict in Western Europe since 1968*, Vol. 2, pp. 277–98.

Poulain, Jean-Claude (1981), *CFDT, le rêve et la vie* (Paris: Editions sociales).

Poulat, Emile (1977), *Eglise contre bourgeoisie* (Tournai: Casterman).

Poulot, Denis (1980), *Le Sublime* (Paris: Maspero).

Prost, Antoine (1964), *La CGT à l'époque du front populaire (1934–39)* (Paris: FNSP/Armand Colin).

Que faire aujourd'hui? (1980), "Qu'est-ce que la CFDT?" *Que faire aujourd'hui,* nos 5 and 6.

Quiminal, Catherine (1982), "De l'Indigène à l'immigré: figures de politique étatique de l'immigration," in Christine Buci-Glucksmann (ed.), *La Gauche, le pouvoir, le socialisme* (Paris: PUF), pp. 167–71.

Rabaut, Jean (1978), *Histoire des féminismes francais* (Paris: Stock).

Ray, M. (1981), "Employés: les métamorphoses d'une communauté déracinée," in *Les Communautés pertinentes de l'action collectives* (Paris: Copédith-CNAM), pp. 79–100.

Renard, Georges, *et al.* (1937), *Anticipations corporatives* (Paris: Desclée de Brouwer).

Rerat, Françoise (1980), "Une forme de gestion de la main d'oeuvre: les techniques de précarisation de l'emploi," in Dourdan Conference, *L'Emploi: enjeux économiques et sociaux* (Paris: Maspero), pp. 44–59.

Rey, Henri (1981), "L'introduction du thème autogestionnaire dans 1a CFDT avant 1968," FNSP, Paris.

Reynaud, Jean-Daniel (1975), *Les Syndicats en France*, 2 vols (Paris: Seuil).

Reynaud, Jean-Daniel (1978), *Les Syndicats, les patrons et l'état* (Paris: Editions ouvrières).

Reynaud, Jean-Daniel (1980), "L'implantation cédétiste," *Que faire aujourd'hui*, no. 6, pp. 44–5.

Reynaud, Jean-Daniel (1982), *Sociologie des conflits du travail* (Paris: PUF).

Reynaud, Jean-Daniel, Bernoux, Philippe, and Lavorel, Lucien (1966), "Les syndicats ouvriers et leurs politiques des salaires," *Revue française du travail,* no. 3, pp. 1–28.

Rosanvallon, Pierre (1976), *L'Age de l'autogestion* (Paris: Seuil).

Rosanvallon, Pierre (1979), "Crise et décomposition de la classe ouvrière," in *Faire, Crise et avenir de la classe ouvrière* (Paris: Seuil).

Rosanvallon, Pierre (1980), "Le développement des économies souterraines et l'avenir des sociétés industrielles," *Le Débat* (June), pp. 15–27.

Rosanvallon, Pierre, and Viveret, Patrick (1977), *Pour une Nouvelle Culture politique* (Paris: Seuil).

Ross, Arthur, and Hartman, Paul (1960), *Changing Patterns of Industrial Conflict* (New York: Wiley).

Ross, George (1981), "Gaullism and organized labor: two decades of failure?" in William Andrews and Stanley Hoffmann (eds), *The Fifth Republic at Twenty* (Albany, NY: SUNY), pp. 330–47.

Ross, George (1982), *Workers and Communists in France* (Berkeley, Calif.: University of California Press).

Ross, George, and Jenson, Jane (1983), "The rise and fall of French Eurocommunism," in L. Graziano (ed.), *Eurocommunism Reconsidered* (London: Sage).

Roy, Joanine, "Les syndicats après le 10 mai," *Le Monde*, 31 December.

Rozenblat, P., Tabaton, F., and Tallard, M. (1980), "Analyse du conflit LIP et ses répercussions sur les pratiques ouvrières et les stratégies syndicales," thesis, Université de Paris-IX, Paris.

Sainsaulieu, Renaud (1970), "Fondements culturels de l'action syndicale dans l'entreprise," *Projet*, no. 49 (November–December), pp. 1065–76.

Salais, R. (1980), "Le chômage: un phénomène de fil d'attente," *Economie et statistique*, no. 123 (July), pp. 67–78.

Salon, Serge (1977), "Les rénumerations dans le Fonction Publique," *Après-Demain* (May–June), pp. 26–9.

Sardais, Claude (1982), "La CFDT, un syndicat venu d'ailleurs?" *Temps modernes*, no. 430 (May), pp. 1981–2000.

Sartre, Jean-Paul (1947), *Situations I* (Paris: Gallimard).

Sauvy, Alain (ed.)(1967–72), *Histoire économique de la France entre les deux guerres* (Paris: Fayard).

Scardigli, V. (1974), "Les grèves dans l'économie française," Centre de recherches et de documentation sur la consommation, Paris.

Schain, Martin A. (1980), "Corporatism and industrial relations in France," in Philip Cerny and Martin Schain (eds), *French Politics and Public Policy* (New York: St Martin's Press).

Schiffres, Michel (1972), *La CFDT des militants* (Paris: Stock).

Segrestin, Denis (1979), "L'identité professionnelle dans le syndicalisme français," *Economie et humanisme*, no. 245 (January–February), pp. 12–26.

Segrestin, Denis (1980), "Les communautés pertinentes de l'action collective: canevas pour l'analyse des fondements sociaux des conflits de travail en France," *Revue française de sociologie*, vol. 21, no. 2 (April–June), pp. 171–202.

Séguy, Georges (1972), *Le "Mai" de la CGT* (Paris: Julliard).

Séguy, Georges (1975), *Lutter* (Paris: Stock).

Sellier, François (1978), "France," in John Thomas Dunlop and Walter Galenson (eds), *Labor in the 20th Century* (New York: Academic Press).

Sellier, François (1979), *Les Salariés en France* (Paris: PUF).

Shorter, Edward, and Tilly, Charles (1971), "Le declin de la grève violente en France de 1890 à 1935," *Mouvement social*, no. 76 (July–September), pp. 95–118.

Shorter, Edward, and Tilly, Charles (1973), "Les vagues des grèves en France 1890–1968," *Les Annales*, no. 4 (July–August), pp. 857–87.

Shorter, Edward, and Tilly, Charles (1974), *Strikes in France 1830–1968* (London: Cambridge University Press).

Shryock, Richard (1983), "The CFDT: beyond really attainable French socialism?" *Telos*, no. 55 (Summer), pp. 75–94.

Silvestre, Jean-Jacques (1980), "Crise de l'emploi et formes de régulation du marché du travail en France 1978–80," report to French Economic Policy Conference, Washington, DC, May.

Simon, Catherine (1981), *Syndicalisme au féminin* (Paris: EDI).

Smith, W. Rand (1981), "Paradoxes of plural unionism: CGT–CFDT relations in France," *Western European Politics*, vol. 4, no. 1 (January), pp. 38–53.

Sociologie du travail (1970), "Le mouvement ouvrier en mai 1968," *Sociologie du travail*, vol. 12, no. 3 (July–September).

Sociologie du travail (1973), "Les grèves," *Sociologie du travail*, vol. 15, no. 4 (October–November).

Sociologie du travail (1974), "Mouvements sociaux d'aujourd'hui," *Sociologie du travail*, vol. 16, no. 3 (July–September).

Sociologie du travail (1977), "Action et négociation," *Sociologie du travail*, vol. 19, no. 4 (October–December).

Sorbets, Claude (1976), "Une praxis syndicale, la CFDT: analyse du fonctionnement des syndicats cédétistes girondais."

Soskice, D. (1978), "Wage inflation and strike activity," in Colin Crouch and Alessandro Pizzorno (eds), *Resurgence of Class Conflict in Western Europe since 1968*, Vol. 2,

Sudreau, Pierre (1975), *La Reforme de l'entreprise* (Paris: Union générale d'éditions).

Tarantelli, E., and Wilke, G. (1981), *The Management of Industrial Conflict in the Recession of the 1970s* (Florence: Badia Fiesolana).

Tavares, Jean (1980), "La 'synthèse' chrétienne, dépassement vers l'au-delà," *Actes de la recherche*, no. 4 (September), pp. 45–65.

Tavares, Jean (1981), "Le centre catholique des intellectuels français," *Actes de la recherche*, no. 38 (May), pp. 49–62.

Thibault, Marie Noëlle (1977), "La CFDT et son histoire," *Mouvement social*, no. 100 (July–September), pp. 93–8.

Thurow, Lester (1981), *The Zero-Sum Growth* (New York: Penguin).

Touraine, Alain (1977), *Un Désir d'histoire* (Paris: Stock).

Touraine, Alain (1978), *La Voix et le regard* (Paris: Seuil).

Treanton, J. R. (1964), "Les conflits du travail," in Georges Friedmann and Pierre Naville (eds), *Traité de sociologie du travail* (Paris: Armand Colin), Vol. 2, pp. 193–202.

Trempé, Rolande (1971), *Les Mineurs de Carmaux* (Paris: Editions ouvrières).

Trentin, Bruno (1979), "Les nouvelles figures du travailleur," *Dialectiques*, no. 28 (Autumn).

Tripier, Maryse (1970), "La revendication des 'conseils d'unité' au Commissariat à l'Energie Atomique en mai–juin 1968," *Revue française de sociologie*, vol. 11, no. 3 (July–September), pp. 351–67.

Tripier, Maryse (1980), "Syndicats ouvriers français, immigration et crises," *Pluriel*, no. 21, pp. 31–50.

Vacarie, Isabelle (1979), *L'Employeur* (Paris: Sirey).

Valet, Lucien, and Albert, Jean (1977), "Les défaillances d'entreprises: un tournant en 1974," *Economie et statistique*, no. 95 (December), pp. 33–42.

Vermeersch, Jeanette (1964), *Pour le Défense des droits sociaux de la femme et de l'enfant* (Paris: PCF).

Verret, Michel (1979), *L'Espace ouvrier* (Paris: Armand Colin).

Vidal, Daniel (1978), "*La Qualité de la vie*: compte-rendu," *Sociologie du travail*, vol. 20, no. 3 (July–September), pp. 334–8.

Vignaux, Paul (1973), "La CFDT: du syndicalisme chrétien au 'gauchissement'," *Contrepoint*, no. 9 (January), pp. 195–205.

Vignaux, Paul (1980), *De la CFTC à la CFDT: syndicalisme et socialisme* ("*Reconstruction*" *1946–72*) (Paris: Editions ouvrières).

Vincent. L. A. (1967–72), "Les comptes nationaux," in Alain Sauvy (ed.), *Histoire économique de la France entre les deux guerres* (Paris: Fayard).

Vincent, Madelaine (1976), *Femmes: quelle libération?* (Paris: Editions sociales).

World Federation of Trade Unions (1972), *Dossier sur l'environnement et les travailleurs* (Paris: World Federation of Trade Unions).

Zarifian, Philippe (1979a), "Tactique de lutte dans la sidérurgie," *La Nouvelle Critique* (April).

Zarifian, Philippe (1979b), "Restructurer or not?" *Dialectiques*, no. 28 (Autumn), pp. 109–18.

Zarifian, Phillipe (1981), "La gauche au pouvoir: l'économie, le politique et le social," *Dialectiques*, no 33 (Autumn).

List of Contributors

Georges Benguigui, maître de recherche, Centre National de la Recherche Scientifique (CNRS), Groupe de Sociologie du Travail, Paris-VII; he is coauthor of *Etre un Cadre en France?* and *La Fonction d'encadrement*.

Alain Bergounioux, maître-assistant in the Department of History, University of Franche-Comté, and maître de conférences at the Institut de'Etudes Politiques; he is author or coauthor of *La Social-Démocratie ou le compromis*, *Force Ouvrière aujourd'hui*, and *La Parole syndicale*.

Anni Borziex, chargé de recherche, CNRS, Laboratoire de Sociologie du Travail et des Relations Professionnelles, Conservatoire National des Arts et Métiers; she is author or coauthor of *Réorganisation du travail et dynamique des conflits*, *Syndicalisme et organisation du travail*, and *Le Temps des chemises*.

Robert Boyer, economist at the Centre d'Etudes Prospectives d'Economie Mathématique Appliquées à la Planification; he is coauthor of *Accumulation, Inflation, Crises*.

Benjamin Coriat, maître-assistant in economics, University of Paris-VII; he is author of *L'Atelier et le chronomètre*, *Science, technique, capitalisme*, and *La Robotique*.

Pierre Dubois, Professor of Sociology at University of Lille-III, and research associate, Groupe de Sociologie du Travail, CNRS; he is author of *Les Ouvriers divisés*, *Le Sabotage dans l'industrie*, *Mort de l'état-patron*, and *Le Recours ouvrier*.

Michelle Durand, maître de recherche (CNRS) at the Centre de Recherches en Sciences Sociales du Travail, University of Paris-XI; she is author or coauthor of *De l'OS à l'ingénieur* and *La Qualité de la vie: mouvement écologique, mouvement ouvrier*.

Sabine Erbès-Seguin, maître de recherche (CNRS), Groupe de Sociologie du Travail; she is author of *Démocratie dans les syndicats* and *Les Relations collectives du travail: pour une sociologie économique du conflit industrielle*.

Guy Groux, research associate (CNRS), Laboratoire de Sociologie du Travail et des Relations Professionnelles, Conservatoire National des Arts et Métiers; he is author of *Les Cadres* and numerous articles.

Yvette Harff, sociologist at the CNRS, Centre de Recherches en Sciences Sociales du Travail, University of Paris-XI; she is author or coauthor of *La Qualité de la vie: mouvement écologique, mouvement ouvrier* and *Les Attitudes des travailleurs à l'égard des produits*.

Jean-Pierre Huiban, economist at the Research Center Travail et Société, University of Paris-IX; he is author of a thesis on labor union counterproposals.

Jane Jenson, Associate Professor of Political Science at Carleton University; she is author or coauthor of *Crisis, Challenge, and Change: Party and Class in Canada* and *A View from the Inside: A French Communist Cell in Crisis*.

Jacques Kergoat, sociologist, chargé de mission in the Direction du Personnel et des Relations Sociales, Electricité de France; he is author or coauthor of *Profils de la social-démocratie européenne* and *Le Parti Socialiste*.

Mark Kesselman, Professor of Government at Columbia University; he is author or coauthor of *The Ambiguous Consensus*, *The Fifth Republic at Twenty*, *French Politics and Public Policy*, and *Socialism, the State, and Public Policy in France*.

Jean Lojkine, maître de recherche (CNRS) at the Centre d'Etude des Mouvements Sociaux, Ecole des Hautes Etudes en Sciences Sociales; he is author or coauthor of *Le Marxisme, l'état et la question urbaine* and *Classe ouvrière et social-démocratie: Lille et Marseille*.

Dominique Montjardet, chargé de recherche (CNRS), Groupe de Sociologie du Travail, Paris-VII; she is coauthor of *Etre un Cadre en France?* and *La Fonction d'encadrement*.

Bernard Moss, Professor of History at the University of New Zealand; he is author or coauthor of *The Origins of the French Labor Movement*, *Revolution and Reaction*, and *1830 in France*.

René Mouriaux, maître de recherche (CNRS), Centre d'Etudes de la Vie Politique Française, Fondation Nationale des Sciences Politiques; he is author or coauthor of *L'Ouvrier français en 1970*, *Les Syndicats ouvriers en France*, *Les Syndicats dans la société française*, and *La CGT*.

George Ross, Professor of Sociology, Brandeis University, and research associate, Center for European Studies, Harvard University; he is author or coauthor of *Workers and Communists in France*, *Unions, Change and Crisis: French and Italian Union Strategy and the Political Economy 1945–80*, and *A View from the Inside: A French Communist Cell in Crisis*.

Martin Schain, Associate Professor of Political Science, New York University; he is author or coauthor of *French Politics and Public Policy*, *French Communism and Local Power*, and *Socialism, the State, and Public Policy in France*.

Denis Segrestin, sociologist at the Laboratoire de Sociologie du Travail et des Relations Professionnelles, Conservatoire National des Arts et Métiers; he is author of numerous articles on the French labor movement and the process of collective action within the French working class.

Index

Figures in italics refer to tables

accords: territorial 240; national 241, 298; regional 241
accumulation *see* capital accumulation
ACO *see* Catholic Workers' Action
action, collective 199–209
Adam, Gérard: on neo-corporatism 172; on union rivalry 258, 260
Aglietta, Michel: on economic crisis 39
Amott, Teresa, and Krieger, Joel: on Socialist government 320
Andreani, Edgard: on strikes 212
anti-productivism 88–9
Antoinette: editorial board disciplined 9, 67, 169–70; magazine for women 162, 166
arbitration 83
Arrighi, Giovanni: on crisis of capitalism 4
Auroux, Jean, reforms 313–17; wage-labor relation redefined 32; increased union power 46, 309; favourable to CGT 68; FO opposition to 102; business community opposition to 142; and works councils 144
austerity: of Socialist government 5, 34, 313, 318; of Barre government 29, 81; of Giscard government 31: CFDT on 89; *rigueur* 319–20
autogestion: CGT opposition to 54; adopted by CGT 59, 239, 251–2; CFDT policy 78, 80, 88; and women 165; and *cadre de vie* 183–7; self-management 303
automation 42–3; and the working class 125–6, 128–30
autonomy: trade union 89, 93; union leadership 277

balance of payments 27, 34, 288
bankruptcy: and union counterproposals 230
Barre, Raymond 81; economic policies 4, 28, 30, 97, 113; 2nd Plan (1977) 283–4
Beaujolin, F.: on modernist strategy 37
Bergeron, André 96, 99, 103; on collective bargaining 94, 100; on non-wage issues 98; on Socialist government 102, 288; on industrial decision-making 229
Bertrand, Hughes: on accumulation 21, 25
Bilous, Alexandre 85
Boussac, Marcel 204
Bowles, Samuel, and Gintis, Herbert: on crisis of capitalism 4
Boyer, Robert: on wage-labor relation 18; on capital accumulation 26, 27, 39, 45; on wage policy 44
Buhl, René 58, 59; hounded out of CGT 67
Burawoy, Michael: on Auroux laws 316
Bureau Confédéral (BC): of CGT 58; of CFDT 78

cadre de vie 177; and CFDT 183, 184; and CGT 190-4
Caire, Guy: on temporary labor 44
capital accumulation 17, 18; and wage-labor relation 21-2, 45; boom in 24–6; based on mass consumption 25; export-based 25; crisis in 28–31, 39; and decline of working class 122
capitalism: instability of 40; crisis of 304
Casassus, Cecilia, *see* Erbès-Seguin, Sabine
Catholic Workers' Action (ACO) 84
Catholicism: and CFDT 86–7; social 179
CCF *see* Commission Confédérale Féminine Center for Socialist Education and Research (CERES) 80
Ceyrac, François: on recession 305
CFDT *see* Confédération Francaise Démocratique du Travail
CFTC *see* Confédération Francaise des Travailleurs Chrétiens
CGC *see* Confédération Générale des Cadres
CGT *see* Confédération Générale du Travail
Chaban-Delmas, Jacques: *contrats de progrès* 241–2
Chambre Syndical des VRP 105
Charpentié, Yves 114; on CGC strategy 111

Chérèque, Jacques 80, 246
Chevènement 319, 320
Chirac, Jacques 80, 114; reaction to economic crisis 26
Chotard, Yves: on destructuring 227
class collaborationism 52, 53, 54, 55; refused by unions 3; PS attacked for 62
class conflict: non-industrialized 2
CNPF *see* National Council of French Employers
collective bargaining: peak level 2, 22; Law on Collective Bargaining Agreements (1950) 22, 102; FO on 94, 96–7; territorial agreements *240*; and industrial counterproposals 234–5; local agreements 314
Colombani, Jean-Marie: on state intervention 320
co-management 137–8
comité d'entreprise see works councils
Commission Confédérale Féminine (CCF) 165
Common Program of the United Left: Mitterrand's dependency on 84; CGT on 162, 208, 239, 259; union reactions to 281–2; and nationalization 303
Communist Party *see* Parti Communiste Français
computerization 134–8, 140–1
concertation 108–9
Confédération Francaise des Travailleurs Chrétiens (CFTC): deconfessionalization 75–6; relations with CGC 112; and social issues 179
Confédération Francaise Démocratique du Travail (CFDT) 72, 75–92; and socialism 1, 79. political exchange 2; women 9, 163–6, 172–4; reaction to economic crisis 36; unity-in-action with CGT 53–4, 77, 79, 80–1, 260, 261, 268, 275–6; *autogestion* 55, 78, 80, 88, 183, 246; differences with CGT 55, 65, 78, 83–4; strikes 72; origins in CFTC 75–6; membership 76, 78, 87–8, 272, 285, 291, 294; 33rd Congress 77; 34th Congress 77; Bureau Confédéral 78; 35th Congress 79, 163–4, 183–4; 36th Congress 79; purges 81, 37th Congress 81–2, 173; National Council 82, 83, 173; 38th Congress 83, 171, 227–8; anti-Sovietism 83; and Socialist government 84, 288–93; 39th Congress 85–6, 174; religious connections 86–7; anti-productivism 88-9; and pay structure 106; and technology 132–4, 137; and work organization 148–50; and social issues 178–88; URP 181; and quality of life 181–8; anti-nuclear

struggle 185–7; and collective action 202–3, 208; ideology and industrial practice 245–51; and Common Program 246; and *contrats de progrès* 247; and *recentrage* 248; relations with CGT 257–76; and economic crisis 302–3; resyndicalization 313
Confédération Générale des Cadres (CGC) 7–8, 83, 104–15; and pay structure 105–6, 108; 1969 Congress 105; and industrial hierarchy 106–7; *concertation* 108–9; and employment 109–10; Estates General 111; relations with CGC 111–12; relations with FO 112, and Socialist government 113
Confédération Générale du Travail (CGT) 5, 51–74; socialism 1; political exchange 2; women 9, 161–3, 166–7, 168, 170–1; *Antoinette* 9, 67, 162, 166, 169–70; and economic crisis 36; origins of strategy 51–4; links with PCF 52, 54, 57, 63–6, 238; unity-in-action with CFDT 53–4, 63, 77, 80–1, 259–60, 261, 268, 275–6; differences with CFDT 55, 65, 83-4; politicization 56–7; Bureau Confédéral 58, 64, 67, 73–4; 40th Congress 58–60, 194, 227, 243, 264; proposition force unionism 60–2; steel industry policy 60–1, 83; National Confedaral Council 65; membership 66, 272, 274, 285, 291, 294; support for Socialist government 68–9, 288–9; pro-Sovietism 64, 69, 83; 41st Congress 69–70, 170, 252, 275; *oppositionnels* 73; and pay structure 106; relations with CGC 111–12; and technology 132–5; and co-management 137–8; and work organization 148–50; National Conference of Salaried Women 162, 170; and social environment 188–96; 33rd Congress 188; 34th Congress 189; 37th Congress 190; 38th Congress 191; and nuclear question 193–4, 195; and collective action 201; mobilization 208; ideology 238–43; *autogestion* 239, 251–2, 303; collective agreements 239–40; strikes 241, 242; relations with CFDT 257–76; *Courrier Confédéral* 272; eroding support 273; and economic crisis 302; and nationalization 303
Conference on Women's Work and Union Action 173
conflict, labor: wage-related 23; defense of jobs 27; decline in 30; regional 204; forms of action 219–21; regulation of 316; *see also* resistance, worker; strikes
Congresses: CFDT (33rd) 77; (34th) 77;

(35th) 79; (36th) 79; (37th) 81–2, 173; (38th) 83, 171, 227–8; (39th) 85–6, 174; CGC (1969) 105; CGT (33rd) 188; (34th) 189; (37th) 190, (38th) 191; (39th) 54; (40th) 58–60, 194, 227, 243, 264; (41st) 69–70, 170, 252, 275
Conseil National de la Résistance 19
conseils d'atelier see shopfloor councils
conseils des prud'hommes see labor conciliation boards
conservative government 3
consumerism 195
consumption 4, 24, 28; worker 18, 21, 23: domestic 288
contract negotiations 46–7; at firm level 298
contrats de progrès 3, 75, 79; CGT opposition to 55, 241–2; FO support for 96; signed by CFDT 247
Cordeiro, A.: on immigrant labor 44
Coriat, Benjamin: on automation 42, 125; on capital accumulation 45
corporationism 52
corporatism 36, 86, 100; Maire's critique of 85; neo-corporatism 89, 172; attacked by CFDT 202
counterproposals, economic 231
counterproposals, industrial 10, 61, 224–37; at firm level 230–1; at branch level 231–2
Courrier Confédéral: on CGT membership losses 272
Creuset, Le 107
Crisis and Future of the Working Class 119
crisis, economic 17, 29; USA 33; international 33–4, 39; effects on working class 226–7; worker reactions to 278–95; union response to 282–7; *see also* recession
crisis of unionism 271–6

Dassa, Sami: on strikes 216, 220
day of action *see journée d'action*
decentralization: of production 41, 43–4; of local collectives 130; of conflict 172; of planning 182; Auroux laws 317
decision-making: union exclusion from 297–8
Declerq, Gilbert 80, 84, and democratic planning180; on unity of action 268
defensive unionism 51–3, 61
Defferre, Gaston 77
de Gaulle, Charles: Gaullism 95; economic restructuring 312
Delors, Jacques 46; *Nouvelle Société* program 55, 79, 86, 299; *contrats de*

progrès 55, 241–2; on economic crisis 318
demand, stimulus of 31–3, 46, 288
demobilization 11
democracy: in the workplace 31, 59, 107; within the union 235
democratic planning 10, 180–3, 189
demonstrations: non-industrial 286; *see also journée d'action*
Depression, Great 18
Descamps, Eugène: 'The Evolution and Perspectives of the CFTC' 75–6; and unity-in-action 77, 260; appeal to Mendès-France 78
deskilling 140
Desrosières, Alain: on strikes 217
destructuring 227
Detraz, Albert 80
devaluation 24, 34, 288
disciplinary regulations 315
Dossier on the Environment and Workers 192
Dubar, Claude: on working-class qualification 127
Dubois, Pierre: on strikes 217, 219, 220
Dull, Klaus: on labor-management relations 142
Dunlop, John: on industrial relations 232
Durand, Claude: on strikes 219, 220
Durand, Michele: on strikes 220; *see also* Harff, Yvette

economic crisis 17, 29: USA 33; international 33–4, 39; and union strategy 226–7; worker reactions to 278–95; union policies towards 282–7; *see also* recession
economic policy, union 224–37; economic counterplan 231–4
Edelman, Bernard: on working class 23; on Auroux laws 315
Edwards, Richard: on Auroux laws 315
employers *see* National Council of French Employers
employment: defense of jobs 27, 46–7, 307, 309; female 29, 159; temporary 30, 44, 306, 320; promotion of 33, 320; National Pact on 283; *see also* jobs
energy 185–7
Engels, Friedrich: *Condition of the Working Class in England* 120, 121, 122
environment 3, 10, 192–6; social 184, 188–91; *Dossier on the Environment and Workers* 192; *see also cadre de vie*
Erbès-Seguin, Sabine, and Casassus, Cecilia: on strikes 220; on nationalization 302

Eurocommunism 106–7, 168
European Foundation for the
　Improvement of Living and Working
　Conditions 42
Evans, J.: on new technology 143
exports 24, 25

Fabius, Laurent: on social transfers 318
factionalism 289, 293, 294
Fédération de l'Education Nationale 108
Federation of the Democratic and
　Socialist Left (FGDS) 78
feminism 160, 170, 203
FGDS *see* Federation of the Democratic
　and Socialist Left
Fiterman, Charles 244
Force Ouvrière (FO) 4, 7, 82, 93–103;
　relations with CFDT 78, 82, 83;
　membership 93, 98, 291, 294;
　reformism 93; origins in CGT 93; 1971
　Convention 94; and Gaullism 95; and
　economic crisis 96–100; collective
　bargaining 94, 96–7, 243; strikes 97;
　National Confederal Committee 99;
　and Socialists 100–2, 288–9; political
　leanings 101; relations with CGC 112;
　ideology and industrial practice 243–5
Fordism 4, 18, 29, 40, 303
Frachon, Benoît 77
free market economy 27
French Confederation of Christian
　Workers *see* Confédération Francaise
　des Travailleurs Chrétiens
'French miracle' 17
Freyssenet, Michel: on working class de-
　qualification 127

Gaudemar, Jean-Paul: on mass worker
　127
Gilles, Christiane 58; resignation from
　CGT 67; on women and CGT 163;
　critical of PCF 169
Gintis, Herbert, *see* Bowles, Samuel
Giscard d'Estaing, Valéry 82; as Minister
　of Finance 24; electoral defeat 31
Goetz-Girey, Robert: on strike cycle 212,
　213, 220
Grandval, Gilbert 76
Greffe, Xavier: on social benefits 45
Grenelle accords 24, 32
grievance councils 286
Groupes Initiative et Responsabilité (GIR)
　114
Guilbert, Madelaine: on unions and
　women 161

Hacuitex: and CFDT socialism 80, 247
Harff, Yvette: on nationalization 138

Harff, Yvette, and Durand, Michel: on
　social issues 178
Hartman, Paul *see* Ross, Arthur
Héritier, Pierre 80
housing 181-2, 191

ideology: and industrial strategy 238–53;
　CGT 238–43; FO 243–5; CFDT
　245–51
immigrant worker 40, 44, 47, 283; lack of
　representation 3; militancy 279, 320;
　and strikes 202–3
imports 4, 33
incomes policy: FO opposition to 103;
　CGC opposition to 110
INDECOSA 195
industrial policy, union 224–37; CGT
　61–2; at firm level 229–31; at branch
　level 231–2; industrial counterproposals
　231–4
industrial relations *see* labor relations
inflation 24, 27, 28, 34, 300, 304
Institut National des Statistiques et des
　Etudes Economiques (INSEE) 43
institutions: institutionalization 225, 274;
　of the working class 277
investment 24, 28, 35, 288
Italy: decentralization of production 43

Jacquier, Jean-Paul 246
Jaffré, Jerome: on 1981 election 31, 287
Jeanneney, Jean-Marcel 77
Jeanson, André 183; 'Perspectives and
　Strategy' 79; on Communists 261
Jezequel, Claude: on collective bargaining
　97
jobs: defense of 27, 46–7, 307, 309;
　creation of 33; redesign of 41–2; *see
　also* employment
JOC *see* Young Christian Workers
Jouhaux, Léon 93
journée d'action 53, 56, 77; CFDT dislike
　of 54; CGT strategy 53, 56, 77, 243
Joxe, Pierre: on economic crisis 70
Julliard, Jacques 80

Kergoat, Danièle: on strikes 218
Kergoat, Jacques: on CGT membership
　66, 275; on working class consciousness
　278; on Socialist government 287
Kerr, Clark, and Siegel, Abraham: on
　strikes 217, 304
Keynesianism 31, 46, 225, 311, 319; of
　CGT 52, 70, 71; and CFDT 89
Klare, Karl: on Auroux laws 316
Knowles, Kenneth: on strikes 215
Korpi, Walter, and Shalev, Michael: on
　strikes 1

Korsakissok, C.: on computers 138
Krasucki, Henry 64, 65, 288; on trades
  unionism and socialism 55; and PCF
  58; secretary-general of CGT 68, 69; on
  reduced workweek 83; on hierarchical
  pay structure 106; on unity-in-action
  266–7; on Socialist government 288
Krieger, Joel, *see* Amott, Teresa
Krumnow, Fredo 247; *Croire* 88

Labi, Maurice 245
labor conciliation boards (*conseils des
  prud'hommes*): 1982 elections to *8*,
  104; reform of 83; FO success in
  elections to 99
labor force: changes to 274
labor-management relations 47, 300; crisis
  in 17, 297; and technology 141, 142;
  negotiations 297–8
labor relations: political exchange 1–2; as
  compromise 17; government
  intervention 28; legislative reform 313
Lambert, Jacqueline 58; hounded out of
  CGT 67
Lange, Peter: on journées 57
Laroze, Jean-Claude 65
Lavau, Georges: on union autonomy 89
Law on Collective Bargaining Agreements
  (1950) 22
layoffs 36; resistance to 41; of supervisory
  staff 109; legal constraints 301, 305
Legislation: collective bargaining 22;
  layoffs 301, 305; industrial relations 313
Le Guen report 133
Levard, Georges: on Communists 260
LIP 41, 79, 230
Lobjeois, G.: on technology 141
Lojkine, Jean: on semi-skilled worker 129
Luxemburg, Rosa: on unions 224

Maire, Edmond 79, 82, 188, 246; on 40th
  CGT Congress 60; on CGT and PCF
  links 65, 283; anti-marxist 81; view of
  Mitterrand 84; attacks on CGT 85-6,
  266, 322; denounces neo-corporatism
  89; on working class 120; on neo-
  Taylorism 134; on nuclear program
  187; on union model 228; on
  nationalization 236-7; critical of
  Common Program 246; on inflation
  248; on unity-in-action 262, 266, 275;
  on negotiation 265
Mallet, Serge: on technicians 125; on
  strikes 217
Malterre, André 114; on hierarchical pay
  structure 106; on industrial hierarchy
  107; on market economy 110; on
  industrial reform 111

management: labor-management relations
  17, 47, 297; worker management 41;
  co-management 137–8; scientific 146;
  social policy 152
Mansholt, Sicco 192
Marchais, Georges 283; CGT support 66
Marchelli, P. 114
Marx, Karl 132; *Capital* 121
Marxism 81, 89, 122; and CGT policy
  238
Matignon/Grenelle model 53
Mauroy, Pierre: fight against
  unemployment 308; on Auroux laws
  315; on worker committees 316; on
  austerity 320
May 1968 24; CFDT support for 78
Meillassoux, Claude: on wage labor 20
Menu, Jean 8, 83, 111
Mercier, Albert 246; on reduced
  workweek 84; on industrial
  counterproposals 230
Messmer, Pierre 79
militancy 1, 278–80, 289–90, 293; female
  279; immigrant 279; declining 284–5,
  287, 320
militants: gap between workforce and
  155–6
Minc, Alain, *see* Nora, Simon
minimum wage 23, 24, 31, 299
Ministry of National Solidarity 103
Mitterrand, Francois 84; 1974 election 80;
  FO support 100; CFDT support 283;
  1981 election victory 287
mobilization 3, 206, 267–71; of working
  class 199–209; regional 204
modernization, post-war 19; *see also*
  restructuring
Monmousseau, Gaston 19
Monory, René: on economic crisis 284
'moonlighting' 44
Moreau, Jacques 246; report 82, 264,
  270, 274; on mobilization 269
Mouriaux, René: on CGT 19; on
  CFDT/CGT rupture 65; on working
  class 121, 143
Moynot, Jean-Louis 58; on union strategy
  37, 52, 59–60, 61, 66; resignation from
  CGT 67; on Union de la Gauche 228;
  on capitalism 302

Nassé, G.: resigns from CGC 113
National Conference of Salaried Women
  162, 167
National Conference on Residential
  Living and Urban Planning 181
National Council of French Employers
  (CNPF) 32, 83, 304, 305
National Pact on Employment 283

nationalization: under Socialist
  government 12, 32, 130, 308, 317; FO
  attitude 102; CGT attitude 138; union
  reactions to 302, 303
negotiations, labor-management 297–8,
  309; and industrial policy 236; *see also*
  collective bargaining
neo-liberalism 45
New Left 245
non-wage issues 25, 40
Nora, Simon, and Minc, Alain: on
  technology 135
Nouvel Economiste 284
Nouvelle Société program 55, 79, 86, 299
nuclear program 139; CFDT on 133,
  185–7; CGT on 193–4

Obadia, A.: on technology 134
O'Connor, James: on state welfare
  politics 4
Offe, Claude, and Wiesenthal, Helmut:
  on political exchange 2
organization of production 3, 146–58;
  and technology 133–5; union reaction
  to innovation 148–50

Papon, Maurice: on economic crisis 281
Parti Communiste Française (PCF): and
  United Front 52; links with CGT 52,
  54, 57, 238, 259; disunity amongst
  leadership 58; 23rd Congress 62;
  rupture with socialists 62, 282–3; pro-
  Sovietism 63, 64, 69; in government 68;
  and women 162, 166–7, 168;
  Eurocommunism 166–7, 168;
  Programme Commun 281; membership
  291; electoral losses 291; Polish
  question 292
Parti Socialiste (PS): post-1981
  government 3, 31–5, 46–7, 71–2,
  287–92, 313–22; and CFDT 80; and
  FO 100; in local elections 280; and
  Communists 281–2; *Programme
  Commun* 281–2; Metz Congress 286;
  membership 291; and labor-
  management relations 297–310
party membership: increase 280; decline
  285
party-union relations 232–4, 283, 288–9;
  CGT 238; FO 244; CFDT 248
pay structure, hierarchical: CGC on
  105–6
PCF *see* Parti Communiste Francais
Perrot, Michelle: on strikes 212, 219; on
  standard of living 227
Peuple, Le 59, 132
Pialoux, Michel: on working class 121;
  on mass worker 127

Piore, Michael: on dual economy 44
Pizzorno, Alessandro: on political
  exchange 1
planning: democratic 10, 180, 189;
  Commissariat Général du Plan 34;
  economic 299, 301
pluralism, trades union 7, 53; and
  mobilization 201–2; CGT opposition to
  275
Poher, Alain 75; CFDT support for 78
political exchange 1–2
political mobilization: CGT 56, 63–6
political strategy 224–37, 258–67
politicization 287
Popular Republican Movement (MRP) 89
Poulat, Emile: *The Church against the
  Bourgeoisie* 88–9
Prévost, Hubert 84
price freeze 34
production: decentralization of 43–4;
  organization of 3, 133–5, 146–58
productivity 18, 24, 31; vs. wages 19–21;
  declining 27
profit 24, 26
Programme Commun see Common
  Program of the United Left
proposition force unionism: CGT 57–62,
  169
PS *see* Parti Socialiste
PSU *see* United Socialist Party
public sector employees 315
Pugo, M.: on SMIC 284

quality of life 181, 194
Questions qui font bouger, Les 167
Quiminal, Catherine: on immigrant labor
  44, 47

Rabaté, Lucien: on organization of
  production 146
radicalism 1, 4; rhetorical nature of 2–3
rank and file action 199–209
Ray, M.: on strikes 138
recentrage (recentering) 75, 89, 246, 264;
  CGT opposition to 65, 251; ratified by
  CFDT National Council 82, 83; and
  women 171–2, 175; and strikes 221;
  resistance to 248, 286
recession 26; and union policy 226–7
reformism: of labor movement 2, 3;
  union 93
regions: regional development 180, 191;
  regional action 204–6
resistance, worker 40–1
restructuring: union complacency 3;
  industrial 28, 41, 283, 298–9; economic
  312
resyndicalisation (reunionization) 83

retirement 110
Reynaud, Jean-Daniel: on CFDT 86–7
rivalry, interunion 257–76, 322
robotics 42–3, 136
Rocard, Michel 80, 84, 100, 283; CFDT
  support for 289; on economic crisis
  318; and 9th Plan 319
Rolant, Michel 246
Rosanvallon, Pierre 36; on decomposition
  of working class 119, 120, 227; on
  austerity 293
Ross, Arthur, and Hartman, Paul: on
  strikes 215
Ross, George: on CGT/PCF links 52
Roy, Joanine: on Mitterrand victory 266
Rozenblat, P.: on LIP 230

Sainjou, André 64
Sainsaulieu, Renaud: on unionization 267
Salais, R.: on unemployment 226
Sartre, Jean-Paul: on consciousness 179
Sauvy, Alain: on reduced workweek 35
Scardigli, V.: on strikes 213, 216
sections d'enterprise 24
Segrestin, Denis: on CFDT 260
Séguy, Georges: CGT Secretary General
  58; address to 40th CGT Congress 59;
  on split with CFDT 65; fired by CGT
  67; on women 162, 167, on unity-in-
  action 263-4, 266
self-management *see autogestion*
semi-skilled workers: and automation 129;
  strikes 147, 203
SGEN 87
Shalev, Michael, *see* Korpi, Walter
shopfloor councils (*conseils d'atelier*) 59,
  70, 81, 147, 158; FO opposition to 99
shop stewards 314
Shorter, Edward, and Tilly, Charles: on
  strikes 212, 216, 217, 218, 300
Siegel, Abraham, *see* Kerr, Clark
small businesses 43
Smith, W. Rand: on unity-of-action 271
social benefits 23, 31, 44–5
social democracy 3; FO 243, 313, 319
social environment: CFDT on 178–88;
  CGT on 188–96
social insurance 7, 103; retirement 110
social transfers 318
socialism 1, 79; worker-managed 246
solidarity contracts 33, 46
Solidarnosč: CGT attitude to 69; working
  class attitudes to 292
Soskice, D.: on strikes 213
state monopoly capitalism 54, 131
steel industry; crisis and CGT policy
  60–1; support for PCF 64; and CFDT
  83; *metallo* 200–1

Stoffaes, Christian 30
strikes 1, 210–23; defensive 1, 27, 30;
  rate of *26*, 290; LIP 41, 79; FO view
  of 97; in technological firms 138–9;
  semi-skilled workers 147, 203; decline
  in 178, 221, 284; women 203; statistics
  211, 221, 222; economic factors
  212–14; sociopolitical factors 214–16;
  and size of plant 216–17; and
  occupational groups 217–18; and
  unionization 218–19, 220; forms of
  action 219–21; coordination of 268;
  and economic crisis 279; politicization
  of 305
substitutionism 6
Sudreau, Pierre: and plant reform 152;
  on union rivalry 257
supervisory personnel: and CGC 104–15
  and technology 143–4; and strikes 205
support, union: declining 273–4
syndicalisme 77, 80, 313; neo-syndicalism
  62, 239, 246

Taylorism 4, 9, 40, 125, 134, 146, 303;
  resistance to 41
technology 3, 8–9, 42–3; postwar 20; and
  the working class 125–6, 128–30; and
  trade unions 132–45; and organization
  of work 133–5; and working conditions
  135–6; and strikes, 138
Thorez, Maurice: attack on CGT
  leadership 259
Thurow, Lester: on recession 227
Tilly, Charles, *see* Shorter, Edward
Touraine, Alain: on working class 120
Toutain, Roger 79
Toutée-Grégoire procedures 3, 213
transfer payments 46
transmission-beltism 57; CGT 62–7
transportation 181
Travail et Technique 133
Trentin, Bruno: on industrial
  counterproposals 233

UCC 137, 143
UCT *see* Union des Cadres et Techniciens
UFF *see* Union des Femmes Françaises
UGICT 143; UGICT-CGT 2nd Congress
  106; negotiations with CGC 112; on
  automation 135; and *cadre de vie* 194
UIMM *see* Union of Metal and Mining
  Industries
unemployment: under Barre government
  4, 24, 27, 28,284; benefits 26; under
  Socialist government 29, 226;
  compensation 83; women 175, 284;
  youth 279; layoffs 301, 305; structural
  321

Union de la Gauche 3, 52, 80, 161; CGT
    support 56; end of 57
Union des Cadres et Techniciens (UCT)
    113–14
Union des Femmes Françaises (UFF) 162
union membership: decline 3, 272, 274;
    CGT 66, 272, 274, 285, 291; CFDT 76,
    78, 87–8, 285, 272, 291; FO 93, 98,
    291; working class 201; and economic
    crisis 280; women 280
Union of Metal and Mining Industries
    (UIMM) 248; on *concertation* 109
Union of the Left *see* Union de la
    Gauche
unionization: low density 1, 5, 257, 267;
    defensive 51–4; and strikes 218–19;
    eroding union support 273
United Socialist Party (PSU) 79
United States of America: economic crisis
    33
unskilled workers: opposition to
    Taylorism 41
urban development 181–2, 189

Vallin, Camille 195
Ventejol, G.: 'The place of trade
    unionism in society' 94
Vie Ouvrière, La 59, 65
Vincent, Madeleine: *Femmes: Quelle
    libération?* 162

wage-labor relation 18, 20, 39; and
    accumulation 21–2; instability of 25–6;
    crisis 29–30; Auroux laws 32;
    redefinition of 38 wages: gains 4, 281,
    283; postwar compromise 18; vs.
    productivity 19–21; indirect 20;
    minimum 23, 24, 31, 299; and labor
    conflict 23; decline in 28, 290; freeze
    34, 44; SMIC 84, 240, 284; and CGC
    105–6, 108; maximalism 239–42; CGT
    targets 240–1; FO targets 244;
    negotiations 298–9; militancy 311
Wiesenthal, Helmut, *see* Offe, Claude
Women; lack of representation 3; issues

9; employment 29, 159; problem of
    159–76; women's movement 160, 203;
    CGT on 161–3, 168–70; Union des
    Femmes Françaises 162; National
    Conference of Salaried Women 162,
    167; CFDT on 163–5, 171–4; and
    autogestion 165; 'Sur les revendications
    des femmes salariées' 166; and
    Eurocommunism 166–7; unemployment
    175; strikes 203–4, 279; union
    membership 280; militancy 279
work organization *see* production,
    organization of
worker control *see autogestion*
worker management 41, 107
workerism, theoretical 126–8
working class 119–31; radicalism 4;
    decomposition 119–26, 227;
    recomposition 128–9; working
    conditions 135, 147, 151–4, 307;
    organized labor's view of 156–7; and
    union membership 200–2; institutions
    277–8; consciousness 280–2, 286–7,
    291–2; politicization 287; reunification
    314–15
working conditions 307; and technology
    135–6; fight for improvement 147;
    union research on 151–4
workplace relations; revision of 41
works committees/councils 158, 218, 314;
    elections to 5, 286; and new technology
    9; FO opposition to 99
workweek, reduced 29–30, 33, 34,
    249–50, 284, 290, 307, 309; CFDT on
    83, 84, 85–6; FO agreement 102
World Federation of Trade Unions: 1978
    Congress 263–4

Young Christian Workers (JOC) 238
youth: social benefits 45; unionization
    273; unemployment 279

Zarifian, P. 36; on *autogestion* 62; on
    union democracy 235